CHANGING WINDS

CHANGING WINDS

A NOVEL

BY
ST. JOHN G. ERVINE

WILDSIDE PRESS

TO

THE MEMORY OF RUPERT BROOKE

The translations from the Gaelic on pages 77 and 78 were made by the late P. H. Pearse, who was executed in Dublin for his part in the Easter Rebellion. The translations appeared in *New Ireland,* and I am indebted to the Editor of that review for permission to reprint them here.

THE FIRST BOOK
OF
CHANGING WINDS

There are waters blown by changing winds to laughter,
And lit by the rich skies, all day. And after,
  Frost, with a gesture, stays the winds that dance
And wandering loveliness. He leaves a white,
  Unbroken glory, a gathered radiance,
A width, a shining peace, under the night.

RUPERT BROOKE.

CHANGING WINDS

1

It would be absurd to say of Mr. Quinn that he was an ill-tempered man, but it would also be absurd to say that he was of a mild disposition. William Henry Matier, a talker by profession and a gardener in his leisure moments, summarised Mr. Quinn's character thus: "He'd ate the head off you, thon lad would, an' beg your pardon the minute after!" That, on the whole, was a just and adequate description of Mr. Quinn, and certainly no one had better qualifications for forming an estimate of his employer's character than William Henry Matier; for he had spent many years of his life in Mr. Quinn's service and had, on an average, been discharged from it about ten times per annum.

Mr. Quinn, the younger son of a poor landowner in the north of Ireland, had practised at the Bar without success. His failure to maintain himself at the law was not due to ignorance of the statutes of the land or to any inability on his part to distort their meaning: it was due solely to the fact that he was a Unionist and a gentleman. His Unionism, in a land where politics take the place of religion, prevented him from receiving briefs from Nationalists, and his gentlemanliness made it impossible for him to accept briefs from the Unionists; for if an Irish lawyer be a Unionist, he must play the lickspittle and tomtoady to the lords and ladies of the Ascendency and be ready at all times and on

3

all occasions to deride Ireland and befoul his countrymen in
the presence of the English people.

"I'd rather eat dirt," Mr. Quinn used to say, "than earn
my livin' that way!"

He contrived, however, to win prosperity by his marriage
to Miss Catherine Clotworthy, the only daughter of a Belfast mill-owner: a lady of watery spirit who irked her husband terribly because she affected an English manner and
an English accent. He was very proud of his Irish blood
and he took great pride in using Ulster turns of speech.
Mrs. Quinn, whose education had been "finished" at
Brighton, frequently urged him to abandon his "broad"
way of talking, but the principal effect she had on him was
to intensify the broadness of his accent.

"I do wish you wouldn't say *Aye*," she would plead,
"when you mean *Yes!*"

And then he would roar at her. "What! Bleat like a
damned Englishman! Where's your wit, woman?"

Soon after the birth of her son, she died, and her concern,
therefore, with this story is slight. It is sufficient to say of
her that she inherited a substantial fortune from her father
and that she passed it on, almost unimpaired, to her husband, thus enabling him to live in comfortable disregard of
the law as a means of livelihood. He had a small estate in
County Antrim, which included part of the village of
Ballymartin, and there he passed his days in agricultural
pursuits.

2

. Mr. Quinn, as has been stated, was a Unionist, and, in
spite of his Catholic name, a Protestant; but he had a poor
opinion of his Unionist neighbours who, so he said, were far
more loyal to England than England quite liked. He hated
the English accent . . . "finicky bleatin'," he called it
. . . and declared, though he really knew better, that all
Englishmen spoke with a Cockney intonation. "A lot of
h-droppers," he called them, adding, "God gave them a

decent language, but they haven't the gumption to talk it!"
The Oxford voice, in his opinion, was educated Cockney,
uglier, if possible, than the uneducated brand.

An Englishman, hearing Mr. Quinn talk in this fashion,
might pardonably have imagined that he was listening to a
fanatical Nationalist, a dynamiting Fenian, but if, being a
Liberal, he had ventured to advocate Home Rule for Ireland
in Mr. Quinn's presence, he would speedily have found that
he was in error. "Damn the fear!" Mr. Quinn would say
when people charged him with being a Home Ruler. The
motive of his Unionism, however, was neither loyalty to
England nor terror of Rome: it was wholly and unasham-
edly a matter of commerce. "The English bled us for
centuries," he would say, "an' it's only fair we should
bleed them. We've got our teeth in their skins, an' they're
shellin' out their money gran'! That's what the Union's
for—to make them keep on shellin' out their money. An'
instead of tellin' the people to bite deeper an' get more
money out of them, the fools o' Nationalists is tellin' them
to take their teeth out! Never," he would exclaim passionately, "never, while there's a shillin' in an Englishman's pocket!"

Mr. Quinn, of course, treated every Englishman he met
with courtesy, for he was an Irish gentleman, and he had
sometimes been heard to speak affectionately of some person of English birth. The chief result of this civility,
conjoined with the ferocity of his political statements, was
that his English friends invariably spoke of him as "a
typical Irishman." They looked upon him as so much
comic relief to the more serious things of their own lives,
and seemed constantly to expect him to perform some
amusing antic, some innately Celtic act of comic folly. At
such times, Mr. Quinn felt as if he could annihilate an
Englishman.

"Ah, well," he would say, restraining himself, "we all
know what the English are like, God help them!"

It was because of his strong feeling for Ireland and Irish

things that he decided to have his son, Henry, educated in Ireland. "Anyway," he said to the lad, "you'll have an Irish tongue, whatever else you have!" He sent the boy to a school in the County Armagh and left him there until he discovered that he was not being educated at all. He had questioned Henry on the history and geography of Ireland one day, and had found to his horror that while Henry could tell him exactly where Popocatepetl was to be found, and knew that Mount Everest was 29,002 feet high, and could name the kings of England and the dates of their accession as easily as he could recite the Lord's Prayer, he had no knowledge of the whereabouts or character of Lurigedan, a hill in the County Antrim, and could tell him nothing of the Red Earls and the beautiful queens of Ireland. He knew something that was true, and much that was not, of Queen Elizabeth and King Alfred, but nothing, true or false, of Deirdre and Red Hugh O'Neill.

"What the hell's the good of knowin' about Popocatepetl," Mr. Quinn shouted at him, "when you don't know the name of a hill on your own doorstep!"

Lurigedan was hardly "on his own doorstep," and Mr. Quinn himself only knew of it because he had once, very breathlessly, climbed to its summit, but an Irish hill was of more consequence to him than the highest mountain in the world; and so he descended upon the master of the school, a dreepy individual with a tendency to lament the errors of Rome, and damned him from tip to toe so effectually that the alarmed pedagogue gladly consented to the immediate termination of Henry's career at his establishment. Thereafter, Henry was educated in England, for Mr. Quinn did not propose to sacrifice efficiency to patriotism.

"An' if you come back talkin' like a damned Cockney," he said to his son as he bade good-bye to him, "I'll cut the legs off you!"

When Henry came home in the holidays, Mr. Quinn would spend hours in testing his tongue.

"Sound your *rs*," he would say repeatedly, because he regarded one's ability to say the letter *r* as a test of a man's control of the English language. "If you were to listen to an Englishman talkin' on the telephone, you'd hear him yelpin' *'Ah yoh thah?'* just like a big buck nigger, 'til you'd be sick o' listenin' to him! Say, *'Are you there?'*, Henry son!"

And Henry would say *"Are you there, father?"* very gravely.

"That's right," the old man would exclaim, listening with delight to the rolling *rs*. "Always sound your *rs* whatever you do. I'll not own you if you come home sayin *'Ah yoh thah?'* when you mean *'Are you there?'* Do you mind me, now?"

"Yes, father."

"Well, be heedin' me, then! Now, how are you on the *hs*. Are you as steady on them as you were when you were home before?"

Then Henry would protest. "But, father," he would say, "they don't all drop their *hs*. It's only the common ones that drop them! . . .

"They're all common, Henry . . . the whole lot, common as dirt!" Mr. Quinn retorted once to that, and then began to tell his son how the English people had lost the habits and instincts of gentlemen in the eighteenth century . . . "where Ireland still is, my son!" . . . and had become money-grubbers. "The English," he said, lying back in his chair and delivering his sentences as if he were a monarch pronouncing decrees, "ceased to be gentlemen on the day that Hargreaves invented the spinnin'-jenny, and landlords gave way to mill-owners." He stopped for a second or two and then continued as if an idea had only just come into his head. "An' it was proper punishment for Hargreaves," he said, "that the English let him die in the workhouse. Proper punishment. What the hell did he want to invent the thing for? . . ."

Henry looked up, startled by the sudden anger that

swept over his father, replacing the oracular banter with which he had begun his discourse on the decadence of manners in England.

"But, father," he said, "you aren't against machinery, are you?"

"Yes, I am," Mr. Quinn replied, banging the arm of his chair with his fist. "I'd smash every machine in the world, if I were in authority."

"That's absurd, father. I mean, what would become of progress?"

Mr. Quinn leaped out of his chair and strode up and down the room. "Progress! Progress!" he exclaimed. "D'ye think machines are progress? D'ye think a factory is progress? Some of you young chaps think you're makin' progress when you're only makin' changes. I tell you, Henry, the only thing that is capable of progression is the human soul, and machines can't develop *that!*" He came back to his seat as he said this and sat down, but he did not lie back as he had done before. He sat forward, gazing intently at his son, and spoke with a curious passion such as Henry had never heard him use before. "Look here, Henry!" he said, "there was a girl in the village once called Lizzie McCamley . . . a fine bit of a girl, too, big and strong, an' full of fun, an' she got tired of the village. Her father was a labourer, an' all she could see in front of her was the life of a labourer's wife. Well, it isn't much of a life, that, an' Lizzie's mother had a poor life even for a labourer's wife because McCamley boozed. I don't blame Lizzie for wantin' somethin' better than that. I'd have despised her if she hadn't wanted somethin' better. But what did she do? She had an uncle in Belfast workin' in your grandfather's mill, an' she came to me an' she asked me to use my influence with your grandfather to get her a job in the mill. An' I did. An' by God, I'm sorry for it! I'll rue it 'til my dyin' day, I can tell you!"

"But why, father?"

"Your grandfather gave her a job in the weavin' room of his mill. Do you know what that's like, Henry?" Henry shook his head. He had never been inside a linen-mill. "The linen has to be woven in a moist atmosphere, or else it'd become brittle an' so it wouldn't be fine," Mr. Quinn went on; "an' the atmosphere is kept moist by lettin' steam escape from pipes into the room where the linen is bein' woven—a damp, muggy, steamy atmosphere, Henry . . . an' Lizzie McCamley left this village . . . left work in the fields there to go up to Belfast an' work in that for ten shillin's a week! An' that's what people calls progress! I wish you could see her now—half rotten with disease, her that was the healthiest girl in the place before she went away. She's always sick, that girl, an' she can't eat anythin' unless her appetite is stimulated with stuff like pickles. She's anæmic an' debilitated, an' the last time I saw her, she'd got English cholera. . . . She married a fellow that was as sick as herself, an' she had a child that wasn't fit to be born . . . it died, thank God! . . . an' then she went back to her work an' became sicker. An' she'll go on like that 'til she dies, a rotten, worn-out woman, the mother of rotten children when she ought to have had fine healthy brats, an' could have had them too, if it hadn't been for this damned progress we're all makin'!"

Henry did not reply to his father. He did not know what to reply. His mind was still in the pliable state, and he found that he was being infected by his father's passion. But he had been taught at Rumpell's to believe in Invention, in Progress by the Development of Machinery, and so his mind reeled a little under this sudden onslaught on his beliefs.

"Well," said Mr. Quinn. "Is that your notion of progress, Henry? Makin' fine linen out of healthy girls?"

"No, father, of course not. Only! . . ."

Mr. Quinn stood up, and caught hold of his son's shoulder. "Come over to the window, Henry!" he said, and

they walked across the room together. "Look out there,"
he said, pointing towards the fields that stretched to the
foot of the hills. "That's fine, isn't it?" he exclaimed.

"It's very beautiful, father," Henry replied, looking
across the fields of corn and clover and the pastures where
the silken-sided cattle browsed and flocks of sheep cropped
the short grass.

"It's *land*, Henry!" said Mr. Quinn, proudly. "You
can do without machines in the long run, but you can't do
without *that!*"

3

"An' what do you think a mill-owner'd make of it,
Henry?" Mr. Quinn said as they stood there gazing
on the richness of the earth. Near at hand, they could
hear the sound of a lawn-mower, leisurely worked by William Henry Matier, and while they waited for him to come
into view, a great fat thrush flew down from a tree and
seized a snail and beat it against a stone until its shell was
broken. . . .

"I suppose he'd spoil it, father!" Henry answered.

"Spoil it!" Mr. Quinn exclaimed. "Damn it, Henry,
he'd desecrate it! He'd tear up my cornfields and
meadows and put factories and mills in their place!
That's what he'd do!" He turned sideways and leant
against the lintel of the window so that he was looking at
his son. "There was a fellow came to see me once," he
said, "from London. A speculatin' chap, an' he wanted
me to put capital into a scheme he had on. Do you know
what sort of a scheme it was, Henry?"

"No, father!"

"He wanted to develop the mineral resources of the
County Wicklow, an' he wanted me to lend him money to
do it. He said that some Germans had surveyed the whole
district, an' there was an immense fortune just waitin'
to be torn out of the earth. . . . I could hardly keep
my feet off his backside! 'Do you want to turn Glenda-

lough into a place like Wigan?' I said to him. 'It's all in
the interests of progress,' says he. . . . No, I didn't give
him any of my money. I was as civil to him as I could
be, an' he never knew how near he was to his death that
day. . . .''

Mr. Quinn's anger evaporated, and he began to laugh
to himself as he thought of the difficulty he had had in
restraining his rage against the speculator and how frightened that person would have been had he known how angry
he had made him.

"He was a little smooth chap," he said, "with smooth
hair an' smooth clothes an' a smooth voice. You could
hardly tell it was hair, it was that smooth. You'd nearly
think somebody had painted it on his skull. He couldn't
make me out when I said I'd rather starve than let a half-
penny of my money be used to make a mess of Glendalough, an' he talked about the necessity of havin' a broad
outlook on the world. I suppose he went away an' told
everybody that I was a reactionary an' a bad landlord.
Oh, I can hear him spoutin' away about me . . . he
got into parliament soon after that, an' used to denounce
landlords an' blether away about progress. An' I daresay
everybody that listens to him thinks I'm a stupid fellow,
standin' in the way of everything. I'm a landlord, an' so,
of course, I'm obsolete and tyrannical an' thick-headed,
an' all that, but I wouldn't treat one of my labourers the
way your grandfather treated his for the wide world.
Mind you, he was a religious man . . . I don't mean
that he pretended to be religious . . . he really was religious, after a fashion . . . wouldn't have missed goin'
to church or sayin' his prayers night *an'* mornin' for a
mint of money . . . an' yet there didn't seem to him to
be anything wrong in lettin' men an' women make money
for him in that . . . that disgustin' way. I can't understand that. I'm damned if I can!''

Something stirred uneasily in Henry's mind. He became acutely conscious of the principal source of his

father's income, and he remembered things that had been said to him by Gilbert Farlow at Rumpell's. Gilbert Farlow was his chief friend at Rumpell's, the English school to which he had been sent after his experience at Armagh, and Gilbert called himself an hereditary socialist because his father had been a socialist before him. ("He was one of the first members of the Fabian Society," Gilbert used to say proudly.) Gilbert had strong, almost violent, views on Personal Responsibility for General Wrongs. He always referred to rich people as "oligarchs," or "the rotters who live on rent and interest" and declared that it was impossible for them to escape from the responsibility for the social chaos by asserting that they, individually, had kind hearts and had never been known to underpay or overwork any one. Remembering Gilbert's views, Henry could not help thinking that it was all very well for his father to denounce the mill in that fashion, but after all he was living on the money that was made in it. . . .

"But, father," he said, hesitatingly, "haven't we got grandfather's money now . . . and the mill! . . ."

"No, not the mill, Henry. Your grandfather turned that into a limited company, an' your mother sold her shares in it. I told her to sell them!"

Henry's conscience still pricked him. It seemed to him that selling the shares was very like running away from the responsibility.

"But all the same," he said, "we've got money that was made out of the mill by grandfather . . ."

"So we have, Henry," Mr. Quinn replied good-temperedly, "an' we're makin' a better use of it than he did. Some one's got to use it, an' I'm doin' the best I can with it. You've only got to look at my land to see how well I've used the money. It's better land than it was when I got it, isn't it?" Henry nodded his head. Even he knew that much. "I've enriched it an' drained it an' improved it in ways that'll benefit them that come after me . . . not me, but you an' your children, Henry . . . an' that's a good use to make of it. I've planted trees that I'll never reap a ha'penny from, an' I've spent money on experiments that did me no good but helped to increase knowledge about land. Look at the labourers' cottages I've built, an' the plots of land I've given them. Aren't they good? Didn't I put up the best part of the money to build the new school because the old one was lettin' in the wind an' rain?''

Henry's knowledge of sociology was not sufficient to enable him to cope with these arguments . . . there was no Gilbert Farlow at his elbow to prompt him . . . and so he collapsed.

"I suppose you're right, father," he said.

"*Suppose* I'm right," Mr. Quinn replied. "*Of course* I'm right!"

"I know well," he continued after he had fumed for a few moments, "there's people . . . socialists an' radicals an' people like that . . . makes out that landlords are the curse of the world. They think we're nothin' in comparison with mill-owners an' that sort, but I tell you, Henry, whatever we are an' whatever we were, we're better than the people that have taken our place. *We* didn't tear up the earth an' cover it with slag-heaps or turn good rivers into stinkin' sewers. We didn't pollute the rivers with filth an' poison the fish!'' He turned suddenly to Henry and said in a quieter tone, "You've never seen Wigan, have you, Henry?''

"No, father.''

"Well, you'd think by the look of it, it was made on the seventh day . . . when God rested. Landlords didn't do that, Henry, or anything as bad as that. It was mill-owners that did it. Oh, I know well enough that landlords were not all they ought to have been, but I'm certain of this, that labourers on the land were healthier under landlords than they are under mill-owners, and even if we weren't as good to the labourers as we might have been, at least we had respect for God's world, an' I never met a mill-owner yet that had respect for anything but a bank-book. I've been in Lancashire an' I've listened to these mill-owners . . . I've listened to them talkin', an' I've listened to them eatin' an' drinkin' . . . an' they talked 'brass' an' they thought 'brass,' an' I'm damned if they didn't drink 'brass.' That's characteristic of them. They call money 'brass.' Brass! Do you think they care for the fine look of things or an old house or a picture or books or anything that's decent? No, Henry . . . all they care for is 'brass,' an' that's what's the matter with the English . . . they think too much about money . . . easy money . . . an' they think so much about gettin' it that none of them have any time to think of how they'll spend it when they do get it. An' they just fool it away! Eat it away, drink it away! An' then they have to go to Buxton an' Matlock an' Harrogate to sweat the muck out of their blood!"

Henry reminded his father of the bloods and bucks and macaronis of the eighteenth century . . . the last of the English gentlemen.

"After all, father, they weren't so very much better than the lot you're denouncing!"

"Yes, they were. They had the tradition of gentlemen behind them. They were drunkards and gamblers and women-hunters an' Lord knows what not, but behind it all, Henry, they had the tradition of gentlemen, an' that saved them from things that a mill-owner does as a matter of course. An' anyway, their theory was right. They thought more of spendin' money than of makin' it, an' that was right. It isn't makin' money that matters . . . any fool can do that . . . it's spendin' money that matters. You're less likely to make a mess of the world when you're spendin', than when you're makin', money, an' the English'll find that out yet. God'll not forget in a hurry the way they tore up their good land an' made dirty, stinkin' towns out of it, an' by the Holy O, He'll make them suffer for it. If I was an Englishman, I wouldn't want any one to see places like Wigan an' the towns where they dig coal an' make pottery . . . I'd . . . I'd be ashamed to look God in the face when I had mind of them. . . ."

4.

Late that night, long after Henry had gone to bed, Mr. Quinn came to his room and wakened him.

"What is it, father?" Henry said, starting up in alarm.

"It's all right, son," Mr. Quinn replied. "I'm sorry I startled you. I've been thinkin' over what I said to you this afternoon . . . about machinery. You're not to take me too seriously."

Henry, his eyes still full of sleep, blinked uncomprehendingly at his father.

"I mean, son," Mr. Quinn went on, "that it'd be silly to break up every machine in the world. Of course, it would! You must have thought I was daft talkin' like that. What I mean is, I'd smash up all the machines that make a mess of men an' women. That's all. I'm sorry I disturbed you, Henry, but I couldn't bear to think of you lyin' here mebbe thinkin' I was talkin' out of the back of my neck. I'm not very clever, son . . . I've a moidhered sort of a mind . . . an' I say things sometimes that aren't what I mean at all. You must be tired out, Henry. Good-night to you!"

"Good-night, father!"

Mr. Quinn walked towards the door of the room, shading the light of the candle from the draught, but before he had reached it, Henry called to him.

"Father," he said.

"Yes, Henry," Mr. Quinn replied, turning to look at his son.

"You're a Socialist!"

"No, I'm not. I'm a Conservative," said Mr. Quinn, and then he went out of the room, closing the door quietly behind him.

5

Many things troubled Mr. Quinn, but the thing that troubled him most was his son's nervousness. Henry, when he was a child, would cry with fright during a thunderstorm, and he never in after life quite lost the sense of apprehension when the clouds blackened. He loved horses, but he could not sit on a horse's back without being haunted by the fear that the animal would run away or that he would be thrown from his seat. He could swim fairly well, but he was afraid to dive, and he never swam far out of his depth without a sensation of alarm that he would not be able to return in safety.

"Your mother was like that," Mr. Quinn said to him once. "She never was in a theatre in her life, 'til I married her. Her father was too religious to let her go to such a place, an' I had the great job to persuade her to go with me. I took her to see Henry Irving in Belfast once, an' all the time she kept whisperin' to me, 'Suppose I was to die now, where'd I wake up?' That's a fact, Henry! Your mother was terribly frightened of hell. An' even when she got over that, she was always wonderin' if it was safe to go to a theatre. She'd imagine the place was sure to go on fire, an' then she'd be burned alive or get crushed to death or somethin' like that. I nearly felt scared myself, the way she went on! I wish you weren't so nervous, Henry!"

They were at Cushendall when Mr. Quinn said this. They had ridden over on bicycles intent on a day's picnic by the sea, and soon after they had arrived, Mr. Quinn itched to be in the water. They had stripped on the beach, and clambered over the rocks to a place where a deep, broad pool was separated from the Irish Sea by a thick wedge of rock, covered by long, yellow sea-weed. There was a swell on the sea, and so Mr. Quinn decided to swim in the pool. "This is a good place for a dive," he said, standing on the edge of the flat rock and looking down into the deep pool, and then he put his hands above his head and, bending forward, dived down into the water so finely that there was hardly any splash. He came up, puffing and blowing, shaking the water from his eyes and hair, and swam up and down the pool, now on his back, now on his side, and then suddenly with a shout he would curl himself up and dive and swim beneath the water, and again come up, red and shiny and puffing and blowing and shouting, "Aw, that's grand! Aw, that's grand!" He could stand on his hands in the water and turn somersaults and find pennies on the sandy bottom. He loved all sport, but the sport that he loved best was swimming. He liked to sit on a rock and let great waves come and hit him hearty thumps in the back. He liked to bury his face in the water. He liked the feel of the water on his body. He liked to stand up in the sunshine and watch the drops of water glistening on his body. He liked to lie on the sea-weed or the sand after his swim and let the sun dry him. "It's great health, this!" he would say, kicking and splashing in the sea.

"Come on," he shouted to Henry, after he had dived.

Henry was sitting on the sea-weed, with his arms clutched tightly round his shins, shivering a little in the wind.

"You'll catch your death of cold if you sit there instead of jumpin' in," his father called to him. "Dive, man! That's a grand place!"

Henry stood up . . . and then turned away from the rock. He caught hold of the sea-weed and slowly lowered himself into the water.

"That wasn't much of a dive," his father said, swimming up to him.

Henry did not answer. He swam across the pool and clambered out on the other side and waited for his father, who followed after him.

"I wish you weren't so nervous," Mr. Quinn said a second time, as he sat down on the sea-weed beside his son.

"So do I, father," Henry replied, "but I can't help it. I try to make myself not feel afraid, but I just can't. If I could only not think about it! . . ."

"Aye, that's it, Henry. You think too much. Do you mind that bit in Shakespeare about people that think bein' dangerous. Begod, that's true! Thin men think, that's what Shakespeare says, an' he's right, though I've known fat men to think, too, but anyway thin men aren't near the swimmers that fat men are. Well, I suppose it's no use complainin'. You can't help thinkin' if you have that kind of a mind . . . only I wish it didn't make a coward of you!"

A twist of pain passed over the boy's face when his father said "Coward," and instantly Mr. Quinn was sorry.

"I didn't mean that exactly," he said very quickly, putting out his hand and touching Henry's bare back. "I didn't mean *coward*, Henry. I know you're not that sort at all. It's just nervousness, that's what it is!"

He scrambled to his feet as he spoke, and stood for a moment or two, slipping about on the wet sea-weed. He slapped his big, hairy chest with his hands, and then he swung his arms over his head in order to send the blood circulating more rapidly through his veins.

"I wish I were as big and strong as you are, father!" said Henry, gazing at his father's muscular frame.

"You're a greedy young rascal," his father answered. "Sure, haven't you more brains in your wee finger than I have in my whole body, an' what more do you want? It would be a poor thing if your father hadn't got something you haven't. Come on, now, an' I'll swim you a race to the end of the pool an' back, an' then we must go home."

He plunged into the water and swam about, making a great noise and splash, and deliberately looking away from his son. He was giving him an opportunity to slip into the water without being seen to shrink from the dive.

"Are you comin', Henry?" he asked, without looking back.

"Yes, father," the boy replied, standing up and looking fearfully into the water. He lifted his hands above his head and drew in his breath. He moved forward, half shutting his eyes, and poised himself on the edge of the rock, ready for the plunge. Then he put his hands down again and lowering himself on to the sea-weed, slipped slowly into the water and struck out. "I'm coming, father!" he said.

"That's right, my son, that's right!" Mr. Quinn replied, looking round.

6

He did not speak of Henry's nervousness again, but it troubled him none the less. He himself was so fearless, so careless of danger, so eager for adventure that he could not understand his son's shrinking from peril.

"I used to think," he said to himself one day, "that boys took their physique from their mothers an' their brains from their fathers, but it doesn't seem to have worked out like that with Henry. He doesn't seem to have got anything from me. . . . It's a rum business, whatever way you look at it."

THE SECOND CHAPTER

1

MR. QUINN'S horror of the English people was neither consistent nor rigid. When the Armagh schoolmaster was found wanting, Mr. Quinn instantly decided to send Henry to Rumpell's, a famous English school, and here Henry soon made friends of Ninian Graham and Roger Carey and Gilbert Farlow. Gilbert Farlow was the friend for whom he cared most, but his affection for Ninian Graham and Roger Carey was very strong. Henry's soft nature was naturally affectionate, but there had been little opportunity in his life for a display of affection. His mother was not even a memory to him, for she had died while he was still a baby. Old Cassie Arnott had nursed him, but Cassie, at an age when it seemed impossible for her to feel any emotion for men, had suddenly married and had gone off to Belfast. His memory of her speedily faded. Cassie was succeeded by Matilda Turnbull, who drank, and was dismissed by Mr. Quinn at the end of a fortnight; and then came Bridget Fallon. . . . Bridget had the longest hold on his memory, but she, too, disappeared and was seen no more; for Mr. Quinn came on her suddenly one day and found her teaching "Master Henry" to say prayers to the Virgin Mary! She had put a scapular about his neck and had taught him to make the sign of the cross. . . .

"Take that damned rag off my child's neck," Mr. Quinn had roared at her, "an' take yourself off as soon as you can pack your box!"

And Bridget, poor, kindly, devout, gentle Bridget, was sent weeping away.

Long afterwards, Henry had talked to his father about Bridget, and Mr. Quinn had expressed regret for what he had said about the scapular. "I had no call to say it was a damned rag," he said, "though that's all it was. It meant a lot to her, of course, an' I suppose she was right to try an' make a Catholic of you. But I'd hate to have a son of mine a Catholic, Henry. It's an unmanly religion, only fit for women an' . . . an' actors! It's not religion at all . . . it's funk, Henry, that's what it is! I read 'The Garden of the Soul' one time, an' I'd be ashamed to pray the way that book goes on, with their 'Jesus, Mercy!' 'Mother of God, pity me!' 'Holy Saints, intercede for me!' Catholics don't pray, Henry; they whine; and I've no use for whinin'. If I can't go to heaven like a man, I'll go to hell like one. Anyway, if I commit a sin, I'll not whine about it, an' if God says to me on the last day, 'Did you commit this sin or that sin?' I'll answer Him to His face an' say, 'Yes, God, I did, an' if You'd been a man, You'd have done the same Yourself!' "

So it was that, in his childhood, no woman made a lasting impression on Henry's affectionate nature. No one, indeed, filled his affections except his father. Henry's love for his father was unfathomable. Their natures were so dissimilar that they never clashed. There were things about Henry, his nervousness, his sudden accessions of fright, which puzzled Mr. Quinn, and might, had he been a smaller man than he was, have made him angry with the boy, contemptuous of him; but when Mr. Quinn came across some part of Henry's nature which was incomprehensible to him, he tried first, to understand and then, failing that, to be tolerant. "We all have our natures," he used to say to himself, "an' it's no use complainin' because people are different. Sure, that's what makes them interestin' anyway!"

2

But Henry's affection for Gilbert Farlow and Ninian Graham and Roger Carey was a new affection, a thing that came spontaneously to him. There were other boys at Rumpell's whom he liked and others for whom he felt neither like nor dislike, but just the ordinary tolerance of temporary encounters and passing life; and there were a few for whom he felt a hatred so venomous that it sometimes frightened him. There was Cobain, a brutal, thick-jawed fellow who thumped small boys whenever they came near him, and there was Mullally! . . . He could not describe his feeling for Mullally! It was so strong that he could not sit still in the same room with him, could not speak civilly to him. And yet Mullally was civil enough to him, was anxious even to be friendly with him. There was something of a flabby sort in Mullally's nature that made Henry instinctively angry with him: his vague features, his weak, wandering eyes, peering from behind large glasses, his tow-coloured hair that seemed to have "washed-out," and above all, his squeaky voice that piped on one jerky note. . . .

It was Gilbert Farlow who gave Mullally his nick-name. (It was the time of the Boer War, and the nick-name came easily enough.) "He isn't a man," said Gilbert; "he's a regrettable incident!"

Gilbert Farlow, though he was the youngest and the slightest of the four boys, was the leader of them. He had the gift of vivid language. He could cut a man with a name as sharply as if it were a knife. He invented new oaths for the delight of Ninian Graham, who had a taste for strong language but no genius in developing it. It was he who appointed Roger to the office of Purse-Bearer because Roger was careful. It was he who decided that their pocket-money, with small exceptions, should be spent conjointly, and that no money should be spent unless three out of four consented to the expenditure. ("Damn it, is it my money or is it not?" said Ninian when the rule was proposed, and "Fined sixpence for cheek!" Gilbert replied, ordering Roger to collect the sixpence which was then divided between the three who had not murmured.) It was he who declared that "Henry" was too long and "Quinn," too short (though Roger said the words were exactly the same length) and insisted on calling Henry "Quinny" (which Roger said was actually longer than either of the displaced words. "Well, it sounds shorter," said Gilbert decisively).

Gilbert planned their lives for them. "We'll all go to Cambridge," he said, "and then we'll become Great!"

"Righto!" said Ninian.

"If any of our people propose to send us to Oxford, there's to be a row! Sloppy asses go to Oxford . . . fellows like Mullally!" Henry made a terrible grimace at the mention of Mullally's name and Gilbert, swift to notice the grimace, pointed the moral, "Well, Quinny, if your guv'nor tries to send you to Oxford, don't let him. Remember Mullally, the . . . the boiled worm!" he continued, "an' say you won't go!"

"But my father was at Oxford," said Roger quietly.

"Your father was a parson and didn't know any better," Gilbert replied. "And that reminds me, if one of us becomes a parson, the rest of us give him the chuck. Is that agreed?"

Ninian held up both his hands. "Carried unanimous!" he said.

"I don't know!" Henry objected. "I used to think it'd be rather nice to be a parson . . . standing in the pulpit in a surplice and talking like that to people!"

Gilbert got up from the grass where they were sitting. "He'll have to be scragged," he said.

"Righto!" said Ninian, and the three of them seized Henry and flung him to the ground and sat on him until he swore by the blood of his forefathers that he would never, never consent to be a clergyman. "Or give pi-jaws of any sort!" said Gilbert.

"Lemme go!" Henry squeaked, struggling to throw them off his back.

"When you've promised! . . ."

"Oh, all right, then!"

They released him and he stood up and straightened his clothes and searched his mind for something of a devastating character to say. "Funny ass!" he said at last, and then they scragged him again for being cheeky.

But he would have submitted to any amount of scragging from them because they were his friends and because he loved Gilbert and because they, too, in their turn submitted to being scragged.

3

When Henry had been at Rumpell's for a year, Ninian Graham asked him to spend the Easter holidays at his home in Devonshire. "I'll get my mater to write and ask you," he said. Henry hesitated. He had never spent a holiday away from home, and he knew that his father liked him to return to Ireland whenever he had the chance to do so. He himself enjoyed going home, but suddenly, when Henry had finished speaking, he felt a strong desire to accept this invitation. "I'll have to ask my father," he replied, and added, "I'd like to, Ninian. Thanks aw-f'lly!"

He had heard his father speak so contemptuously of English people that he was almost afraid to ask him for permission to accept Ninian's invitation. He wondered how he would explain his father's refusal to Ninian who was so kind. . . . But his fears were not warranted, for Mr. Quinn replied to his letter, urging him to accept the invitation.

"*Enjoy yourself,*" he wrote. "*The English are very hos-*

pitable when you get to know them, and the only way you can get to know them is to go and live in their homes! But I'll expect you to come here in the summer. You can bring your friends with you, the whole lot. William Henry says there'll be a grand lot of strawberries and goosegogs this year and you can all make yourselves as sick as you like on them.'' He signed himself, *''Your affectionate Father, Henry Quinn.''*

And so Henry had gone that Easter to Boveyhayne, where Mrs. Graham and her daughter Mary lived. Ninian and he had travelled by train to Whitcombe where they were met by old Widger and driven over hilly country to Boveyhayne. There was a long climb out of Whitcombe and then a long descent into Boveyhayne, after which the road ran on the level to the end of Hayne lane which led to the Manor. Before they reached the end of the lane, Old Widger turned to them and, pointing with his whip in front of him, said, laughingly, "Here be Miss Mary waitin' for 'ee, Mas'er Ninyan!"

Ninian stood up in the carriage and looked ahead. "Hilloa, Mary!" he shouted, waving his hand, and then, before Old Widger had time to pull up, he jumped into the road and ran on ahead. "Come on, Quinny!" he shouted, and Henry, suddenly shy, got out of the carriage and followed after him.

"You needn't wait for us, Widger!" Ninian shouted again. "We'll walk home!"

And Widger, smiling largely, drove on.

4

Mary Graham was younger than Ninian, nearly two years younger, and very different from him. He was big in body and bone, and fair and very hearty in his manner. When Ninian approved of you he did not pat your back: he punched it so that your bones rattled and your flesh tingled. All his movements were large, splashy, as Gilbert said, and his voice was incapable of whispers. But Mary was slight and small and dark and her laugh was like the sound of a little silver bell. She was standing on an earth mound at the entrance to the lane when Henry came up to Ninian and her, and he wondered to himself how her small, shapely head could bear the weight of the long dark hair which fell about her shoulders in a thick, flowing pile. Ninian was chattering to her so loudly and so rapidly that Henry could hardly hear her replies. . . .

"Oh, this is Quinny!" Ninian said, jerking his thumb in Henry's direction. "His real name is Quinn, Henry Quinn, but we call him 'Quinny.' At least, Gilbert does, so, of course we do too. And he's Irish, but he isn't a Catholic, and he says Irish people don't keep pigs in their houses, and they eat other things besides potatoes and . . . come on, Quinny, buck up and be civil!"

Mary stepped down from the mound, and held out her hand to Henry. "How do you do!" she said, smiling at him, and he took her hand and said he was very well and asked her how she did, and she said she was very well, and then she smiled again, and so Henry smiled too.

Ninian had moved on up the lane. "Buck up, you two!" he said. "I'm hungry!" He started to run, thinking of tea, and then he suddenly checked himself and came back. "I say, Mary," he said, "Quinny's fearfully gone on wildflowers and birds and . . . and Nature . . . and that sort of stuff. Show him the primroses and things, will you? I've got an awful hunger and I want to see the mater. Oh, Quinny, these are primroses, these yellow things, and Mary'll show you anything else you want to see. There's a jolly lot of honeysuckle and hazelnuts in these hedges later on. So long!" He went off again, running in a heavy, lumbering fashion because of the ascent and the broken, stony ground.

Henry stood still, waiting for Mary to make a decision. He could not think of anything to say and so he just smiled. He began to feel hot and uncomfortable, and it seemed to him suddenly that Mary must think he was a frightful fool, maundering about primroses and wild violets and bluebells, and yet not able to say a word for himself in her presence . . . standing there, grinning like . . . like anything, and . . . and not saying a word.

She was standing sideways, with her head turned to look at her brother, now disappearing round a bend in the lane, and Henry was able to observe her more closely. He saw that she was wearing a short frock, reaching to her knees, and he plucked up heart. "She's only a kid," he said to himself, and then said aloud to her, "It's awf'lly nice here!"

She turned towards him as he spoke and he saw that her face was still smiling. "Yes, isn't it?" she answered. "Shall we go on now, or would you like to gather some primroses. There are lots in this lane, or if you like to walk up to the copse, there are more there, and we can mix them with bluebells. I think primroses and bluebells are lovely together, don't you?"

He thought it would be nicer to go to the copse, and so they moved on up the lane.

"I like these high hedges," he said. "We don't have high hedges in Ireland. In lots of places we don't have hedges at all—only stone walls!"

Mary made a grimace. "I shouldn't like that," she exclaimed. "I love hedges . . . best in the spring because then they're new. There's always something living in them. I never go by the hedges without hearing something moving inside . . . birds and mice and things. Of course, it's very stuffy in the lanes in summer because the hedges are so high and the leaves are so thick and the air can't get through! . . . Look! Look!" She climbed on to the bars of a gate, and pointed, and he climbed on to the bars beside her, and saw the English Channel, shining like a sheet of silver in the setting sun.

"Can you see the trawlers coming home?" she said. "Out there! Do you see? Those are our boats . . . the

Boveyhayne boats. That one with the brown sails is Tom
Yeo's boat. He's awf'lly nice and his wife's going to have
a baby. He told me so, and they hope it'll be a boy because Jim Rattenbury—that's Tom Yeo's mate in the boat
. . . his wife had a daughter last month, and they all think
it would be awf'lly nice if Tom's son were to grow up and
marry Jim's daughter, and I think it would, and of course
it would, wouldn't it?''

"Would it?" said Henry.

"Of course it would. It would be so nice for everybody,
and then the boat could be left to Tom's son and it would
belong to Jim's daughter, too. I think that would be *very*
nice! I do hope they've caught a lot of fish!" She
jumped down from the gate and clapped her hands together. "I know," she said. "We won't pluck primroses
now. We'll go home and simply swallow our tea like lightning, and then we'll tear down to the beach and see them
landing the fish. Come on, let's run!" She started off
and then suddenly checked herself and said, "Oh, I think
I'd better call you 'Quinny,' like Ninian. It'll save a lot
of trouble, won't it? Mother won't call you that. She'll
probably call you 'Henry' or 'Harry.' If we hurry up,
we'll be just in time to see the boats beached!"

She ran off, laughing pleasantly, and he followed after
her.

"That's the copse," she shouted, pointing to the trees
on her left. "We'll soon be there!"

They reached the top of the lane and crossed a narrow
public road, and then were in a broad avenue, almost
arched by trees, at the end of which was the Manor. It
was a squarely-built sixteenth century house, made of stone,
taken from the Roman quarry a mile or two away on the
road to Franscombe. The first Graham to own it received
it and the lands adjacent to it from Henry the Second,
and ever since that time a Graham had been lord of the
manor of Boveyhayne. Ninian was the last of his line. If
he were to die, there would be no more Grahams at Bovey-

hayne. That was the fear that haunted Mrs. Graham. . . .

Mary ran swiftly across the grass in the centre of the avenue and pushed open the gate that led through a fine stone arch. She held the gate open for Henry, and then they both passed up the flagged path into the house.

"Mother, mother!" Mary shouted, quickly entering the drawing-room, "here's Quinny, and please can we have tea at once because the trawlers are just coming home and we want to see them being beached and . . . oh, I say, my hands are messy, aren't they. Still, it doesn't matter! I can wash them afterwards."

"My dear!" said Mrs. Graham reproachfully, and then she turned to greet Henry who had become awkward again. "How do you do, Mr. Quinn," she said, holding her hand out to him.

Henry flushed deeply. It was the first time any one had ever called him Mister, and he was very glad that Ninian was not present to hear. He was quite well, he said. No, he was not a bit tired. Yes, he would rather like to go to his room. . . . A maid had followed him into the room, and Mrs. Graham asked her to show Mr. Quinn to his room, and, flushing deeper still, he turned to go with her. As he left the room, he heard Mary saying to Mrs. Graham, "Oh, mother, you mustn't call him *Mr.* Quinn. He blushed frightfully when you said that. His name is 'Quinny,' or you can call him 'Henry' if you like!"

"I think I'll call him 'Henry,' my dear!" said Mrs. Graham.

5.

It seemed to Henry that Mrs. Graham was the most beautiful woman in the world, and he had a great longing that she would draw him to her, as she drew Ninian, and put her arms about him and kiss him. Sometimes he had faint memories of the way in which poor Bridget Fallon had hugged him, and how she had cried over him once when she told him that his soul would be damned forever because he was a "black Protestant." . . . He remembered that episode more vividly than any other because he had howled with fear when she narrated the pains and torments of hell to him. There had been a Mission at the chapel the previous week, and a preaching friar had frightened the wits out of her with his description of "the bad place." He had told the congregation of scared servants and frightened labourers that they would be laid on red-hot bars in hell and that the devil would send demons to nip their flesh with burning pincers. . . . Henry could not be comforted until she had promised to rescue him from the Evil One, and when she bade him wear the scapular, he hurriedly hung it round his neck as if he were afraid that before he could get it on, the Devil would have him. . . . Well, Bridget had loved him very tenderly, and of all the women he had ever known, she seemed to him to be the most beautiful. But Mrs. Graham was more beautiful than Bridget, more beautiful than Bridget could ever be. There was something so exquisite in her movements, her smile (Mary had her smile) and her soft sweet voice with its slight Devonshire burr, that Henry felt he wished to sit beside her and walk with her and always be by her. His sudden, growing love for her made him feel bold, and he lost the shy, nervous sensation he had had when he first came into her presence and heard her call him "Mr. Quinn," and so, when Ninian and Mary talked about the trawlers, he turned to Mrs. Graham quite naturally, and said, "Won't you come to the beach, too, Mrs. Graham?" Instantly Ninian and Mary were clamorous that she should go with them, and so she consented. . . .

"We'll have to hurry," said Mary, "because the boats come in awf'lly quick."

"My dear, I can't run," Mrs. Graham said.

It was Ninian who suggested that Widger should harness the pony and that they should drive down to the beach in the buggy. . . .

"Yes, yes," said Mary.

And Ninian went off to tell Widger to hurry harder than he had ever hurried before in his life.

"I'll do that for 'ee, Mas'er Ninyan, sure 'nough!" said Widger.

But Ninian and Mary were too impatient to wait for the buggy, and so they set off together, leaving Henry to follow with Mrs. Graham.

"Quinny'll drive you down, mater," Ninian said.

Mrs. Graham turned to Henry. "You won't let Peggy run away with me, will you?" she said, pretending to be alarmed, and Mary and Ninian burst into laughter at the thought of Peggy . . . which was short for Pegasus . . . running away with any one.

"He's fat and lazy," said Ninian.

"He goes to sleep in the shafts," Mary added, running out of the drawing-room on Ninian's heels.

6

Boveyhayne Bay is a little bay within the very large bay that is guarded at one end by Portland Bill and at the other end by Start Point. It lies in the shelter of two white cliffs which keep its water quiet even when the sea outside is rough, and so it is a fine home for fishermen though there is no harbour and the trawlers have to be hauled up the shingly beach every night. Nowhere else on that coast are chalk cliffs to be found, and the sudden whiteness of Boveyhayne Head and the White Cliff shining out of the red clay of the adjoining cliffs is a sign to sailors, passing down the Channel on their homeward beat, that they are off the coast of Devonshire. Mrs. Graham talked to Henry about the fishermen as they drove down Bovey Lane towards the village.

"I love Boveyhayne," she said, "because the people are so fine. They rely on themselves far more than any other people I know. That's because they're fishermen, I sup-

pose, and have no employers. They work for themselves
. . . and it's frightfully hard work too. People come to
Boveyhayne in the summer, but they can't spoil it because
the villagers don't depend on visitors for a living: they
depend on themselves . . . and the sea. There isn't a man
in Boveyhayne who is pretending to be a fisherman and is
really a cadger on summer visitors. Some of them won't
be bothered to take people out in rowing-boats—they feel
that that is work for the old. I used to wonder," she went
on, "why it was that I didn't really like the villagers in
other places, but I never found out why until I came to
Boveyhayne, and it was simply because I felt instinctively
that they were spongers . . . those other people . . . that
they hadn't any real work to do, and that they were living
on us like . . . like ticks on a sheep. The Boveyhayne
men are splendid men. It wouldn't make any difference
. . . much difference, anyhow . . . to them if another visitor never came to the place. And that is how it ought to
be in every village in England!"

Henry was not quite certain that he understood all that
she was saying, but he liked to listen to her, and so he did
not interrupt her, except to say "Yes" and "I suppose so"
when it seemed that she was waiting for him to say something.

"Do you like being in England?" she asked him suddenly.

"Oh, yes," he answered.

"Would you rather be in England than in Ireland?"

He did not know. He liked being at home with his
father, but he also liked being at Rumpell's with Gilbert
and Roger and Ninian, and now he felt that he would like
to be at Boveyhayne with Mrs. Graham and Mary.

"Perhaps you like people better than you like places,"
Mrs. Graham said.

"I don't know," he replied. "I hadn't thought about
that."

"You must come again to Boveyhayne. Perhaps, in the summer, Gilbert and Roger will come, too!"

Henry thought that that would be awf'lly jolly. . . .

They turned down the village street and left Peggy at the foot of it while they went down the slope leading on to the beach where the trawlers were now being hauled up by the aid of hand winches. Henry could see Mary and Ninian in the group of fishermen who were working the nearest winch. They had hold of one of the wooden bars and were helping to push it round.

"We'll go down to the boats," said Mrs. Graham, "and see the fish!"

She put her hand on his shoulder, and he helped to steady her as they walked across the shingle to where the boats were slowly climbing out of the sea over wooden runners on to the high stones.

One of the boats had already been hauled up, and the fishermen, having thrown out their gear, were now getting ready to sell their fish. They threw out a heap of skate and dun-cows,[1] and auctioned them to the dealers standing by.

"They're still alive," Henry whispered to Mrs. Graham as he watched the dun-cows curling their bodies and the skate gasping in the air. He looked over the side of the trawler and saw baskets of dabs and plaice and some soles and turbot and a couple of crabs. A plaice flapped helplessly and fell off the heap in the basket on to the bottom of the boat, and one of the fishermen trod on it. . . .

"They're _all_ alive," Henry said, turning again to Mrs. Graham.

"Yes," she answered.

"But . . . isn't it cruel? Oughtn't they to kill them?"

"It would take a long time to kill all those fish," she said. "Most of them are dead already, and the others will be dead soon. . . ."

---

1 Dog-fish.

But he could not rid himself of the feeling that the fish were suffering agonies, and he began to feel sick with pity.

"I think I'll go and see Mary and Ninian," he said to Mrs. Graham, edging away from the boat.

"All right," she replied.

But Ninian and Mary were on their way down to the boats, and so he did not get far.

"Come and see them cutting up the skate and dun-cows!" said Ninian, catching hold of Henry's arm and pulling him back.

"Yes, let's," Mary added.

The sick feeling was growing stronger in Henry. He hated the sight of blood. Once he had been ill in the street because William Henry Matier had shown a dead rabbit to him, the blood dribbling from its mouth . . . and the sight of a butcher's shop always filled him with nausea. He did not wish to see the skate cut up, but he felt that Mary would despise him if he did not go with Ninian and her, so he followed after them.

The fishermen were sharpening their knives on the stones when they came up to them, and then one of them seized a dun-cow and struck its head on the shingle and cut it open, while another fisherman inserted his knife into the quivering body of a skate and cut out the entrails and the head in circular pieces.

"But they're alive," said Henry.

"Of course, they're alive," said Ninian, seizing a dun-cow and smacking its head against the beach. "Here you are, Jim," he added, passing the dun-cow to a fisherman. "Here's another one!"

Henry could not stay any longer. He turned away quickly and almost ran up the beach. "Hilloa," Ninian shouted after him, "where are you going?"

He stopped for a moment and looked back, wondering what excuse he should make for his running away. "I . . . I'm just going to see if . . . if Peggy's all right!"

"*She's* all right," Ninian replied.

"I think I'll just go all the same," said Henry.

"But you'll miss it all," Mary called to him.

"I'll . . . I'll come back presently," he answered.

7

He had finished a game of cards with Mary and then Mary had gone off to bed. She had kissed her mother and Ninian, and then she held out her hand to him and said "Good-night, Quinny!" and he said "Good-night, Mary!" and held the door open for her so that she might pass out.

"Let's go out in a boat to-morrow," she said. "We'll go to the Smugglers' Cave. . . ."

"Yes, let's," he answered.

When she had gone, Mrs. Graham called him to her. "Come and sit here," she said, pointing to a footstool at her feet. Ninian was trying to solve a chess problem and was deaf to the whole world. . . .

"I suppose you didn't like to see the fish being gutted, Henry?" Mrs. Graham said.

He glanced up at her quickly. He had not spoken of his feeling to any of them because he was ashamed of it. "It's namby-pamby of me," he had said to himself. He flushed as he looked up, fearing that she must despise him for his weakness, and he almost denied that he had had any feeling at all about it; but he did not deny it. "I couldn't bear it, Mrs. Graham," he said quickly in a low voice. "I felt I should be ill if I stayed there any longer!"

"I used to feel like that," she said, patting his shoulder, "but you soon get used to it. The fishermen aren't really cruel. They are the kindest men I know!"

Ninian, having failed to solve his chess problem, got up from the table and stretched himself and yawned.

"I'm going to bed, Quinny," he said. "Are you coming?"

Henry rose and shook hands with Mrs. Graham. "Good-night," he said.

"Good-night, Henry!" she replied. "I hope you'll sleep well." And then she turned to kiss Ninian, who pushed a sleepy face against hers.

8

In the morning, there were fried plaice for breakfast, and Henry ate two of them.

"These are some of the fish you saw on the beach last night," said Mrs. Graham.

"Oh, yes," said Henry, reaching for the toast, and swallowing a mouthful of the fish. "And jolly nice, too!"

THE THIRD CHAPTER

1

HE stayed at Boveyhayne until the time came to return to Rumpell's, and the holiday passed so quickly that he could not believe that it was really over. They had picnicked in the Smugglers' Cave and on Boveyhayne Common where the gorse was in bloom, and Henry had plucked whinblossoms to dye Easter eggs when he found that the Grahams did not know that whinblossoms could be used in this way. "You boil the blossoms and the eggs together, and the eggs come out a lovely browny-yellow colour. We always dye our eggs like that in the north of Ireland!" And on the day they picnicked on Boveyhayne Common, Mrs. Graham took them down the side of the hill to the big farm at Franscombe and treated them to a Devonshire tea: bread and butter and raspberry jam and cream, cream piled thick on the jam, and cake. (But they ate so much of the bread and butter and jam and cream that they could not eat the cake.) And they swam every day. . . . Mary was like a sea-bird: she seemed to swim on the crest of every wave as lightly as a feather, and was only submerged when she chose to thrust her head into the body of some wave swelling higher and higher until its curled top could stay no longer and it pitched forward and fell in a white, spumy pile on the shore. She would climb over the stern of a rowing-boat and then plunge from it into the sea again, and come up laughing with the water streaming from her face and hair, or dive beneath Ninian and pull his feet until he kicked out. . . .

And then the last evening of his visit came. The vicar of Boveyhayne and his wife were to dine at the Manor that night, and so they were bidden to put on their company manners and their evening clothes. Ninian grumbled lustily when he heard the news, for he had made arrangements with a fisherman to "clean" a skate that evening when the trawlers came home. "I bet him thruppence I could do it as good as he could, and now I'll have to pay up. Beastly swizz, that's what it is!" he said to Henry in the stable where he was busy rubbing down Peggy, although Peggy did not need or wish to be rubbed down. "I think Mother ought to give me the thruppence anyhow! . . ."

After dinner, Ninian and Henry and Mary had contrived to miss the drawing-room, whither Mrs. Graham led the Vicar and his wife, and they went to the room which had been the nursery and was now a work-room, and lit the fire and sat round it, talking and telling tales and reading until the time came for Mary to go to bed.

"We're going soon, too!" said Ninian. "We've got to get up jolly early to-morrow, blow it! I hate getting up early!"

Henry yawned and stretched out his hands to the fire. "I wish I weren't going to-morrow," he said, half reflectively.

"So do I," Mary exclaimed.

She was sitting on the floor beside him and he turned to look at her, a little startled by the suddenness of her speech.

"I wish you weren't going," she said, sitting up and leaning against him as she was accustomed to lean against Ninian. "It's been great fun this Easter!"

Ninian caught hold of her hair and pulled it. "He isn't a bad chap, old Quinny," he said. "Soft-hearted, a bit!"

"Shut up, Ninian!" Henry shouted, punching him in the ribs.

But Ninian would not shut up. "Blubs like anything if you kill a rabbit or anything. He eats them all the same!"

Mary put her hands over Ninian's mouth. "Leave Quinny alone, Ninian," she said. "He's much nicer than you, and I do think it's horrid of you to go gutting fish just for fun. The fishermen have to do it, else we wouldn't get any breakfast, and of course plaice are very nice for breakfast. . . ."

"Yahhh!" yelled Ninian.

"Well, anyhow," she continued, "Quinny's much nicer than you are. Aren't you, Quinny?"

"No, he isn't," Ninian asserted stoutly. "I'm ten times nicer than he is!"

"No, you're not. . . ."

Henry, embarrassed at first by Mary's admiration, plucked up his spirits and joined in.

"Of course, I'm nicer than you are, Ninian," he said. "Anybody could see that with half an eye in his head!"

"All right, then, I'll fight you for it," Ninian replied, squaring up at him in mock rage.

"I'll box your ears for you, Ninian Graham!" said Mary, "and I won't let Quinny fight you, and Quinny, if you dare to fight him, I shan't like you any more. . . ."

"Then I won't fight him, Mary. She's saved your life, Ninian," he said, turning to his friend.

"Yahhh!" Ninian shouted.

"I'll get up very early to-morrow morning," said Mary, as she prepared to leave them, "and perhaps mother'll let me drive to Whitcombe with you to see you off!"

"No," Ninian objected, "we don't want you blubbing all over the platform! . . ."

"I shan't blub, Ninian. I never blub! . . ."

"Yes, you do. You always blub. You blubbed the last time and made me feel an awful ass!" he persisted.

"Well, I shan't blub this time, or if I do, it won't be about you. . . . Anyhow, I shall get up early and see Quinny off. I *like* Quinny! . . ."

Ninian pointed at Henry, and burst out laughing. "Oh! Oh, he's blushing! Look at him! Oh! Oh!!"

"Shut up, Ninian, you ass!" said Henry, turning away.

Mary went over to him and took hold of his arm. "Never mind, Quinny," she said, "I *do* like you. Good-night!"

Then she went out and left him alone with Ninian.

"I suppose," said Ninian when she had gone, "we ought to go down and say something to the Vicar!"

2

That night, Henry went to bed in the knowledge that he loved Mary Graham. "I'll marry her," he said, as he stripped his clothes off. "That's what I'll do. I'll jolly well marry her!"

In the excitement of his love, he forgot to wash his hands and face and clean his teeth, and he climbed into bed and lay there thinking about Mary. "I suppose," he said, "I ought to tell her about it. That ass, Ninian'll be sure to laugh if I tell him!" He sat up suddenly in bed. "Lord," he exclaimed, "I forgot to wash!" He got out of bed and washed himself. "Beastly fag, cleaning your teeth," he murmured, and then went back to bed.

"I know," he said, as he blew out the candle and hauled the clothes well about his neck. "I'll make Ninian look after the luggage and stuff, and then I'll tell her. On the platform! I hope she won't be cross about it!" And then he fell asleep.

3

In the morning, they went off, Mary with them, and they stood up in the carriage and waved their hands to Mrs. Graham until the dip in the road hid her from their view. Ninian, who had been so disdainful of "blubbers" the night before, sat down in a corner of the carriage and looked miserable, but neither Mary nor Henry said anything to him. They drove slowly down the Lane because it was difficult to do otherwise, but when they had come into the road that leads to Franscombe, Widger whipped up the horse, and the carriage moved quickly through the village, past the schools, until they came to the long hill out of the village . . . and there Jim Rattenbury was waiting for them.

"I brought 'ee a li'l bit o' fish, Mas'er Ninyan," he said, putting a basket into the carriage.

"I say, Jim!" Ninian exclaimed, forgetting his misery for a while. They thanked him for the gift and enquired about the baby Rattenbury and wished him good-luck in the mackerel fishing, and were about to go on when Ninian recollected his failure to keep his appointment with Tom Yeo on the previous evening. "Oh, Jim," he said, "I bet Tom Yeo thruppence I'd 'clean' a skate as good as he can, but I couldn't come . . . so here's the thruppence. You might give it to Tom for me, will you!"

Jim Rattenbury waved the money away. "Ah, that be all right, Mas'er Ninyan," he exclaimed. "You can try your 'and at it nex' time you comes 'ome. I'll tell Tom. 'Er'll be glad to 'ave longer to get ready for it, 'er will!" He laughed at his own joke, and they laughed, too. "Good luck to 'ee, Mas'er Ninyan," Jim went on, "an' to 'ee too, sir!" he added, turning to Henry.

"And me, Jim, *and* me!" Mary said impetuously.

"Why, o' course, Miss Mary, an' to 'ee, too!"

They drove on up the hill, from which they could look down on the village, tucked snugly in the hollow of the rising lands, and along the top of the ridge, gaining glimpses of the blue Channel, dotted far out with the sails of trawlers, and down the hair-pin road where the pine trees stand like black sentinels, through Whitcombe to the station. . . .

"I wish we weren't going! . . ." one or other of them said as they drove on.

"I'd love to have another swim," said Ninian.

"Or go out in a boat," said Henry.

The carriage entered the station-yard and they got out and walked towards the platform. There were very few people travelling by that early train, and Henry was glad because, if he could dispose of Ninian for a few moments, he thought he could settle his affairs with Mary.

"Ninian," he said, trying to speak very casually, "you and Widger can look after the luggage and tickets, can't you?"

Ninian, who had already induced one of the porters to describe a thrilling fox-hunt in which the fox took to the river and was killed, after a hard struggle, in the water, nodded his head and said "Righto!"

"Let's walk up and down," Henry said to Mary, and they walked towards the end of the platform. "It's been awf'lly nice here!" he added.

"Yes, hasn't it?" she replied. "You'll come again, won't you?"

"*Ra*-ther!" he exclaimed.

"How long will it be before you can come again?"

"I don't know. You see, my father'll expect me to go home in the summer. . . ."

"Oh!"

"But I might come for part of the hols. I'd like to!"

"Yes," she said, sliding one of her feet in front of her and regarding the tip of her shoe intently.

They did not speak for a few moments until he remembered that time was fleeting. "It's an awf'lly nice day," he said, and licked his lips.

"Yes, isn't it? . . ."

"Awf'lly nice," he continued and broke off lamely.

They could see the train coming into Coly station, and a sense of despair seized Henry when he thought that it would soon come into Whitcombe station and then go back again to the junction, carrying Ninian and him with it. He could feel his nervousness mounting up his legs until it began to gallop through his body. . . . He felt frightfully dry, and when he tried to speak, he could not do anything but cough. The train had started now from Coly station. He could see the white smoke rising from the engine's funnel almost in a straight line, so little wind was there in the valley. . . . "Oh, Lord!" he said to himself. . . .

"What age are you?" he suddenly demanded of her.

"Fourteen," she replied.

"I'm sixteen . . . nearly!" he continued.

"Ninian's over sixteen," Mary said, and added, "I wish I were sixteen!"

"Why?"

"Oh, I don't know. I just wish I were. When I'm sixteen, you'll be eighteen . . . nearly!"

"So I shall. I say, Mary! . . ."

"Yes, Quinny?"

He could hear the rattle of the train on the railway lines, and, turning towards the other end of the platform, he saw that Ninian, having settled about the luggage and finished listening to the story of the fox hunt, was approaching them. "Come on," he said, catching hold of Mary's arm and drawing her to the other end of the platform.

"But that's the wrong end," she protested.

"I say, Mary! . . ."

"Yes, Quinny?"

"Oh, I say, Mary! . . ."

"Yes? . . ."

"I'd like to marry you awf'lly, if you don't mind!"

It was out . . . oh, Lord, it was out! . . .

"Oh, I should love it, Quinny," said Mary, looking up at him and smiling.

"Would you really?"

"Yes. Of course, I would. Let's tell Ninian and Widger! . . .

Her suggestion alarmed him. Ninian would be sure to chaff him about it. . . . "Oh, not yet! . . ." he began, but he was too late. Ninian had come up to them, grumbling, "I thought you two'd started to leg it to Rumpell's. . . ."

Mary seized his arm and pressed it tightly. "Quinny and me are going to get married," she said.

"Silly asses," said Ninian. "Come on, here's the train in!"

4

They climbed into their carriage a few seconds before the train steamed out of the station again, and jammed themselves in the window to look out. Ninian was full of instructions to Widger about his terrier and his ferrets and a blind mouse that was supposed to recognise him with miraculous ease. There was also some point about the fox-hunt which required explanation. . . .

"Good-bye, Mary!" Henry said, taking hold of her hand and pressing it. "I suppose," he whispered, "I ought to give you a ring or something. Chaps always do that! . . ."

Mary shook her head. "I don't think mother would like that," she replied.

"Well, anyhow, we're engaged, aren't we?"

"Oh, of course, Quinny!"

"It's most awf'lly nice of you to have me, Mary!"

"But I like you!"

"Do you really?"

The guard blew his whistle and waved his flag and the train began to move out of the station. He stood at the window looking back at Mary standing on the platform, waving her hands to him, until he could see her no longer.

"What are you looking at?" Ninian asked, taking down the basket of fish which Jim Rattenbury had given him and preparing to open it.

"I'm looking at Mary," he answered.

"Sloppy ass!" said Ninian, and then he added excitedly, "Oh, I say, plaice and dabs and a lobster . . . a whopping big lobster! It's berried, too!" He pointed to the red seeds · in the lobster's body. "My Heavenly Father, Quinny!" he exclaimed, "what a tuck-in we'll have to-night!"

"Eh?" Henry replied vaguely.

THE FOURTH CHAPTER

1

GILBERT summoned Roger and Henry and Ninian to a solemn council. "Look here," he said, "I've made up my mind about myself!"

"Oh!" they exclaimed.

"Yes. I'm going to be a dramatist and write plays!"

"Why?" Ninian asked.

"I dunno! I went to see a play in the hols, and I thought I'd like to write one, too. It seems easy enough. You just make up a lot of talk, and then you get some actors to say it. . . ."

"I see," said Ninian.

"And when I was a kid," Gilbert continued, "I used to make up plays for parties. Jolly good, they were . . . at least I thought so!"

Gilbert, having settled what his own career was to be, was eager that his friends should settle what their careers were to be. "Roger, of course," he said, "has made up his mind to be a barrister, so that's him, but what about you, Ninian, and what about Quinny?"

Ninian said that he did not know what he should do. Mrs. Graham was anxious that he should become a member of parliament and lead the life of a country gentleman who takes an intelligent interest in his estate and his country. His Uncle George, the Dean of Exebury, oscillated between two opinions: one that Ninian should become a parson. . . .

Gilbert suddenly proposed a resolution, sternly forbidding their young friend, Ninian Graham, to become a parson on any conditions whatever. The resolution was seconded by Henry Quinn, and passed unanimously.

46

. . . and the other that he should enter the Diplomatic Service. The Dean had talked largely to Ninian on the subject of his career. On the whole he had inclined towards the Diplomatic Service. He had stood in front of the fire, his hands thrust through the belt of his apron and talked magnificently of the glories of diplomacy. "How splendid it would be, Ninian," he said in that rich, flowing voice which caused ladies to admire his sermons so much, "if you were to become an ambassador!" Ninian, feeling that he ought to say something, had murmured that he supposed it would be rather jolly. "An ambassador!" the Dean continued. "His Britannic Majesty's Ambassador to the Imperial Court of . . . of Vienna!" He liked the sound of the title so much that he repeated it: "His Britannic Majesty's Ambassador! . . ."

But Ninian had interrupted him. "I don't think I'd like that job very much, Uncle George!" he said. "You're supposed to have an awful lot of tact if you're an ambassador, and I'm rather an ass at tact!"

"Well, then, the Church!" the Dean suggested. "After all, the Church is still the profession of a gentleman! . . ."

But Ninian had as little desire to be a priest as he had to be an ambassador. He wished to be an engineer!

"A what?" the Dean had exclaimed in horror.

"An engineer, uncle!"

The Dean could not rid himself of the notion that Ninian was a small boy, and so he imagined that when Ninian said an "engineer," he meant a man who drives a railway engine. . . . The Dean was not insensible to the value of engineers to the community . . . in fact, whenever he travelled by train, he invariably handed any newspapers he might have with him to the engine-driver at the end of the journey, "because," he said, "I wish to show my appreciation of the fact that without his care and skill I might —er—have been—well involved in a collision or something of the sort!" But, while the occupation of an engine-driver was a very admirable one . . . very admirable one,

indeed . . . for a member of the working-class, it could
hardly be described as a suitable occupation for a gentleman. "I think," he said, "that engine-drivers get thirty-
eight shillings per week, or some such amount!" He ad-
justed his glasses and beamed pleasantly at Ninian. "My
dear boy," he said, "thirty-eight shillings per week is
hardly . . . hardly an adequate income for a Graham!"

Ninian did not like to ask his uncle George to "chuck it,"
nor did he care to tell him that he was making a frightful
ass of himself, and so he did not answer, and the beaming
old gentleman felt that he had impressed the lad. . . . It
was Mrs. Graham who reminded him of the larger functions
of an engineer.

"I think," she said, "that Ninian wishes to build bridges
and railways and . . . and things like that!"

"Oh!" said the Dean, and his countenance altered
swiftly. "Oh, yes, yes, yes! I was forgetting about
bridges. Dear me, yes! I remember meeting Sir John
Aird once. Remarkable man! Very remarkable man!
He built the Assouan Dam, of course. Well, that would
be a very nice occupation, Ninian. Rather different, of
course, from the Diplomatic Service . . . or the Church
. . . but still, very nice, *very* nice! And profitable, I'm
told! . . ."

2

"Anyhow," said Ninian, when he had related the story
of his uncle's views, "I'm going to be an engineer, no
matter what Uncle George says, and I'm not going to be
a parson and I'm not going to be a blooming ambassador,
and I'm not going into parliament to make an ass of
myself! . . ."

Ninian's chief horror was of "making an ass" of himself. It seemed that there was less likelihood of him doing
this at engineering than at anything else.

"And a very good engineer you'll be," Gilbert said

encouragingly. "You're always messing about with the insides of things, and I can't see what good that habit would be to an ambassador, or a parson, and anyhow you can't speak French for toffee, and that's the principal thing an ambassador has to do! Well, Quinny," he continued, turning to Henry, "what about you?"

"I used to think I'd like to be a clergyman," Henry answered.

"Oh, did you? . . ."

"And then," he went on 'rapidly, "I thought I'd like to be an actor! . . ."

They rose at him simultaneously. "A what?" they shouted.

"An actor," he repeated.

They gaped at him for a few moments without speaking. Then Ninian expressed their views. "You're balmy!" he said.

"Clean off your chump!" Gilbert added.

"It seems an odd choice," Roger said, quietly.

Henry blushed. "Of course," he hurried to say, "I've given up the idea. It was just a notion that came into my head!"

He went on to say that as Gilbert had resolved to be a writer, he did not see any reason why he should not become one too. "I've read an awful lot of books," he said, "so I daresay I could write one. I used to write things when I was a youngster, just like you, Gilbert!"

They gazed dubiously at Henry. A fellow who could make such choices of profession . . . a parson or an actor . . . was a rum bird, in their opinion, and they told him so. Gilbert said that the conjunction of *actor* with *parson* showed that all Henry cared about was the chance to show off. "All you want is to get yourself up," he said. "If you were a parson, you could get yourself up in a surplice! . . ."

"He'd turn High Churchman," Roger interrupted, "and trot about in chasubles and copes! . . ."

"And if he were an actor, he could get himself up in terrific style! . . ." Gilbert continued.

Henry got up and walked away from them. "It isn't fair," he said, as he went, "to chip me like that. I'm not going to be a parson and I'm not going to be an actor! . . ."

Gilbert followed him and brought him back to the council.

"All right, Quinny," he said, "we won't chip you any more. Only, don't talk like a soppy ass again, will you? Sit down and listen to me! . . ."

He forced Henry to sit beside him and then he proceeded to plan their lives for them.

"We'll all go to Cambridge," he said. "That's settled. I arranged that before, didn't I? Well, we all go to the same college, and we all promise to swot hard. We've got to Do Well, d'ye hear?" He said "do well" as if each word had a capital letter. "We've got to be the Pride of our College, d'ye hear, and work so that the dons will shed tears of joy when they hear our names mentioned. I draw the particular attention of Ninian Graham to what I am saying, and I warn him that if he goes on whittling a stick while I'm talking, I shall clout his fat head for him. I also trust that our young friend, Quinny, will make up his mind to work hard. He's Irish, of course, and we must make allowances for him! . . ."

There was almost a row when Gilbert said that, and it was not completely averted until Gilbert had admitted that the English had their faults.

"I need not say anything on the subject of hard work to our young friend, Roger," Gilbert continued, when the peace was restored, "beyond warning him of the danger of getting brain-fever. That's all I have to say about that. We're friends, we four, and we've got to do each other credit. Now, when we come down from Cambridge, my proposal is that we all live together in London. We can take a house and get some old girl to look after us. I know one who'll do. She lives in Cornwall, and she can cook . . . like anything. Is that agreed?''

''Carried unanimous,'' said Ninian.

''Good egg!'' Gilbert said.

3

But the plan was not carried out as Gilbert had made it. He and Ninian and Roger Carey went to Cambridge, but Henry did not go with them. It was Mr. Quinn who upset the plan. He suddenly gave notice to Rumpell's that Henry would not return to the school.

You're getting to be too English in your ways, Henry, he wrote to his son, *and I want you at home for a while. There's a young fellow called Marsh who can tutor you until you go to the University. I met him in Dublin a while since, and I like him. He's a bit cranky, but he's clever and he'll teach you a lot about Ireland. He's up to his neck in Irish things, and speaks Gaelic and wears an Irish kilt. At least he used to wear one, but he's left it off now, partly because he gets cold in his knees and partly because he's not sure now that the ancient Irish ever wore kilts. I think you'll like him! . . .*

''My God,'' said Gilbert when Henry read this letter to him, ''fancy being tutored by a chap who wears petticoats!''

''You ought to talk pretty plainly to your guv'nor, Quinny!'' Ninian said. ''I don't think you ought to let him do that sort of thing. Here we've settled that we're all going to Cambridge together, and your guv'nor simply lumps in and upsets everything!''

Henry declared that he would talk to his father and compel him to be sensible, but his attempt at compulsion was ineffective. Mr. Quinn had made up his mind that Henry was to spend several months at home, under the tutelage of John Marsh, and then proceed to Trinity College, Dublin.

"Trinity College, Dublin!" Henry exclaimed. "But I want to go to Cambridge! . . ."

"Well, you can't go then. You'll go to T.C.D. or you'll go nowhere. I'm a T.C.D. man, an' your gran'da was a T.C.D. man, an' so was his da before him, an' a damned good college it is, too!" Mr. Quinn had always called his father his "da" when Mrs. Quinn was alive because she disliked the word and tried to insist on "papa"; and now he used the word as a matter of habit. "What do you want to go to an English college for?" he demanded. "You might as well want to go to that Presbyterian hole in Belfast!"

"I want to go to Cambridge," Henry replied a little angrily and therefore a little precisely, "because all my friends are going there. They're going up next year, and I want to go with them. They're my best friends! . . ."

"Make friends in Ireland, then!" Mr. Quinn interrupted. "You don't make friends with Englishmen . . . you make money out of them. That's all they're fit for!"

He began to laugh when he said that, but Henry still scowled. "I hate to hear you talking like that, father!" he said. "I know you don't mean it. . . ."

"Don't I, begod? . . ."

"No, you don't, but even in fun, I hate to hear you saying it. I like English people. I'm very fond of Gilbert Farlow! . . ."

"A nice fellow!" Mr. Quinn murmured, remembering how he had liked Gilbert when he had visited Rumpell's once to see Henry.

"And Ninian Graham and Roger Carey, I like them, too, and so do you. You liked them, didn't you?"

"Very nice fellows, both of them, very nice . . . for all they're English!"

Henry wanted to go on . . . to talk of Mrs. Graham and of Mary . . . but shyness held his tongue for him.

"It's a habit I've got into," Mr. Quinn said, talking of his denunciation of the English, "but don't mind me, Henry. Sure, I'm like all the Ulstermen: my tongue's

more bitter nor my behaviour. All the same, my son,
you're goin' to T.C.D., an' that's an end of it. T.C.D.'ll
make a man of you, but Oxford 'ud only make a snivellin'
High Church curate of you . . . crawlin' on your belly to
an imitation altar an' lettin' on to be a Catholic! . . ."

"But I don't want to go to Oxford, father. I want to
go to Cambridge!"

"It's all the same, Henry. Oxford'll make a snivellin'
parson out of you, an' Cambridge'll turn you into a snivellin' atheist. I know them places well, Henry. I'm acquainted with people from both of them. All the Belfast
mill-owners send their sons there, so's they can be made
into imitation Englishmen. An' I tell you there's no
differs between Cambridge an' Oxford. You crawl on your
belly to the reredos at Oxford, an' you crawl on your belly
to Darwin an' John Stuart Mill at Cambridge. They can't
do without a priest of some sort at them places, an' I'm a
Protestant, Henry, an' I want no priest at all. Now, at
Trinity you'll crawl on your belly to no one but your God,
an' you'll do damn little of that if you're any sort of man
at all!"

Henry had reminded his father of the history and tradition of T.C.D., an ungracious institution which had taught
men to despise Ireland.

"Well, you needn't pay any heed to the Provost, need
you," Mr. Quinn retorted. "Is a man to run away from
his country because a fool of a schoolmaster hasn't the guts
to be proud of it? Talk sense, son! We want education
in Ireland, don't we, far more nor any other people want
it, an' how are we goin' to get it if all the young lads go
off to Englan' an' let the schoolmasters starve in Ireland!"

Henry still maintained his position. "But, father," he
said, "you yourself have often told me that Dr. Daniell
is an imitation Englishman. . . ." Dr. Daniell was the
Provost of Trinity.

"He is, and so is his whole family. I know them well
. . . lick-spittles, the lot of them, an' the lad that's comin'

after him, oul' Beattie, is no better . . . a half-baked snob
. . . I'll tell you a story about him in a minute . . . but all
the same, it's not them that matter . . . it's the place and
the tradition an' the feel of it all . . . do you make me
out?"

"Yes, father, I know what you mean!"

"You'd be like a foreigner at Cambridge . . . like one of
them fellows that come from India or Germany or places
like that . . . but at Trinity you'd be at home, in your own
country, Henry, where people with brains are badly
needed!"

He went on like that until he wore down Henry's desire
to go to Cambridge. "I'd rather you didn't go to a
university at all," he said, "than not have you go to
T.C.D."

"Very well, father!" said Henry, consenting.

"That's right, my son," the old man said, patting his
son on the back. "An' now I'll tell you that yarn about
Beattie. It'll make you split your sides!"

It appeared that Mr. Quinn had dined at a house in
Dublin where Dr. Beattie was also a guest, and the don
was telling tales as was his custom, of his acquaintances in
high places. The poor old clergyman had a weakness for
the company of kings and queens, and liked to tell people
of what he had said to an emperor or of what a prince had
said to him.

"I was talking to my friend, the Queen of Spain, a
short time ago," Dr. Beattie had said, "and I made a joke
which pleased her majesty. It was about my friend, the
Kaiser, who was present at the time. The Kaiser heard
us laughing, her majesty and me, and he came over to ask
us why we were laughing so heartily, the Queen and me.
The Queen was very embarrassed because, of course, I had
been making fun of the Kaiser, but I did not lose my self-
possession. I turned to the Emperor and said, 'Sir, the
Queen and I have known each other for a few moments
only, but already we have a secret between us!'" The

Kaiser was very tickled by my retort . . . very tickled
. . . and the Queen told me afterwards that it was very
adroit of me to get out of it like that. She said it was my
Irish wit! . . .''

It was at this point that Mr. Quinn had interrupted.
"An' what did your friend God say?" he had demanded
innocently.

Mr. Quinn sat back in his chair, when he had finished
telling the story, and roared loudly with laughter. "You
ought to have seen the oul' snob turnin' red, white an'
blue with rage," he shouted at Henry. "Such a take-
down! My God, what a take-down! There he was, the
oul' wind-bag, betherin' about his friend, the Queen of
Spain, an' his friend, the Emperor of Germany, an' there
was me, just waitin' for him, just waitin', Henry, an' the
minute he shut his gob, I jumped in, an' says I to him,
'An' what did your friend God say?' By the Holy O,
that was a good one! I never enjoyed myself so much as
I did that night, an' everybody else that was there was
nearin' burstin' with tryin' not to laugh. Do you mind
Lady Galduff?''

"Yes, father!"

"You mind her rightly, don't you? Well, when you go
up to Dublin, you're to call on her, do you hear? Never
mind about her manners. Ask her to tell you about me
an' Dr. Beattie . . . the way I asked him about his friend
God. Oh, Holy O! . . .''

He could proceed no further, for his sides were shaking
with laughter and the tears were streaming down his
cheeks and his cheeks were the colour of beetroot.

"You'll hurt yourself, father," said Henry, "if you
laugh like that!"

4

"Of course," said Mr. Quinn, after a while, "the man's
a great scholar, an' I mebbe did wrong to take him down

like that. But I couldn't help it, Henry. You see, he's
always makin' little of Irish things, an' I have no use for
a man like that. Not but what some people think too much
of Ireland an' too little of other places. Many's a time I
get ragin' mad when I hear some of the Nationalists
bleatin' about Ireland as if a bit of bog in the Atlantic
were worth the rest of the world put together. Do you
know what, I'm goin' to say somethin' that'll surprise
you. I don't believe Irishmen'll think properly about
Ireland 'til they stop thinkin' about it altogether. We're
too self-conscious. We haven't enough pride an' we've
too much conceit. That's the truth. You daren't say a
word of criticism about Ireland for fear you'd have the
people jumpin' down your throat—an' that's a sign of
weakness, Henry. Do you know why the English are as
strong as they are? It's because they'll let you criticise
them as much as you like, an' never lose their temper with
you. The only time I ever knew them to be flabby and
spineless was when the Boer War was on . . . an' they'd
scream in your face if you didn't say they were actin'
like angels. They were only like that *then,* but we're like
it *all* the time. The fools don't know that the best patriot
is the man that has the courage to own up when his country's in the wrong! . . .''

Mr. Quinn suddenly sat up stiffly in his seat and gaped
at his son for a few moments.

"Begod, Henry," he said, "I'm preachin' to you!"

"Yes, father, you are," Henry replied. "But I don't
mind. It's rather interesting!"

But the force had gone out of Mr. Quinn. The thought
that he had been preaching a sermon, delivering a speech,
filled him with self-reproach.

"I never meant to start off like that," he said. "I only
meant to tell you what was in my mind. You see, Henry,
I love Ireland an' I want to see her as fine as ever she
was . . . but she'll never be fine again 'til she gets back

her pride an' her self-respect. The English people have stolen that from us . . . yes, they have, Henry! I knew Arthur Balfour when he was a young man . . . I liked him too . . . but I'll never forget that it was him that turned us into a nation of cadgers. I'm not much of a thinker, Henry, but the bit of brain I have'll be used for Ireland, whatever happens. You've got more brains than I have, an' I'd like you to use them for Ireland, too.''

5

"This is the way I look at things," Mr. Quinn said later on. "The British people are the best people in the world, an' the Irish people are the best people in the British Empire, an' the Ulster people are the best people in Ireland!" He glanced about him for a few moments as if he were cogitating, and then he gave a chuckle and winked at his son. "An' begod," he said, "I sometimes think I'm the best man in Ulster!" He burst out laughing when he had finished. "Ah," he said, half to himself, as he stroked his fine beard, "I'm the quare oul' cod, so I am!"

"All the same," he went on, speaking soberly, "I'm not coddin' entirely. The Irish have plenty of brains, but they haven't any discipline, an' brains are no good unless you can control them. We need knowledge and experience, Henry, more nor anything else, an' the more knowledge we bring into the country, the better it'll be for us all. Too much imagination an' not enough knowledge . . . that's what's the matter with us. The English have knowledge, but they've small imagination! . . . I declare to my goodness, the best thing that could happen to the two of us, the English and the Irish, would be for some one to pass a law compellin' every Irishwoman to marry an Englishman, an' every Englishwoman to marry an Irishman. We'd get some stability into Ireland then . . . an' mebbe we'd get some intelligence into England.''

6

Henry acquiesced in his father's wishes, but he did so reluctantly. Gilbert's plan for their future had attracted him greatly. He saw himself passing pleasant years at Cambridge in learning and in argument. There was to be scholarship and company and curiosity and enquiry. They were to furnish their minds with knowledge and then they were to seek adventures in the world: a new order of Musketeers: Athos, Porthos, Aramis and D'Artagnan. . . . He let the names of the Musketeers slide through his mind in order, wondering which of them was his prototype . . . but he could not find a resemblance to himself in any of them. He felt that he would shrink from the deeds which they sought. . . . His mind went back again to thoughts of Cambridge. At all events, in the tourneys of the mind his part would be valiant. He would never shrink from combat with an intellect. . . . He supposed it would be possible to do at T.C.D. some of what he had proposed to do at Cambridge, but somehow T.C.D. did not interest him. It mattered as little to him as a Welsh University. It had no hold whatever on his mind. He knew that it was on the level of Oxford and Cambridge, but that knowledge did not console him. "It doesn't matter in the way that they do," he said to himself, and then he remembered something that Gilbert Farlow had said. "T.C.D. isn't Irish in the way that Oxford and Cambridge are English. It's *in* Ireland, but it isn't *of* Ireland!" Gilbert could always get at the centre of a thing. "Oxford and Cambridge have lots of faults," Gilbert had said, "but they're English faults. T.C.D. has lots of faults, but they're not Irish faults. Do you see what I mean, Quinny? It's . . . it's like a garrison in an unfriendly country . . . like . . . what d'ye call it? . . . that thing in Irish history . . . the Pale! That's it! It's the Pale still going on being a Pale long after the need for it had ceased. I don't think that kind of place is much good to Irishmen. You'd better come to Cambridge! . . ."

"I can't, Gilbert. My father's set his heart on my going to Trinity, and I must go. I'd give the world to go with you and Ninian and Roger, but I'll have to do what he wants. Anyhow, I can join you in London when you come down, and we can spend our holidays together. I'll get my father to ask you all to Ireland the first vac. after you've gone up, and perhaps Mrs. Graham'll ask us all to Boveyhayne. . . ."

7

Remembering what he had said to Gilbert about Boveyhayne, he remembered Mary Graham. He had not seen her since he had been to Boveyhayne at Easter, but he had written several times to her, lengthy letters, and had received short, shy replies from her; and sometimes he had tried to induce Ninian to talk about her. But "She isn't a bad little flapper!" was all that Ninian would say of his sister, and there was little comfort to be derived from that speech. Now, standing here in this window-corner, looking over the fields that stretched away to the Antrim mountains, Henry felt that Mary was slipping swiftly out of his life. It might be a very long time before he saw her again. . . . How beautiful she had looked that day when she stood on Whitcombe platform and waved her hand to him as the train steamed out of the station! He *must* marry her. Mrs. Graham *must* ask him to spend the next summer at Boveyhayne so that he could meet Mary again. Anyhow he would write to her. He would tell her all he was doing. He would describe his life at Trinity to her. He would remind her continually of himself, and perhaps she would not forget him. Girls, of course, were very odd and they changed their minds an awful lot. Ninian might invite some chap from Cambridge to Boveyhayne. . . . That would be like Ninian, to go and spoil everything without thinking for a moment of what he was doing. . . . If only Mary and he were a few years older, they could become formally engaged, and then everything would be all right, but Mary was so young . . .

THE FIFTH CHAPTER

1

SOON after Henry had returned to Ballymartin, John Marsh came to Mr. Quinn's house to prepare him for Trinity. "He'll put you in the way of knowin' more about Ireland nor I can tell you, Henry," Mr. Quinn said to his son on the evening before Marsh arrived, "an' a lot more nor you'll learn at Rumpell's, or, for that matter, at Trinity."

"Then why do you want me to go to Trinity?" Henry asked, still unable to conceal his disappointment at not being sent to Cambridge with his friends.

"I've told you that already," Mr. Quinn replied firmly, closing his lips down tightly. "I want you to have Irish friends as well as English friends, and I've learned this much from livin', that a man seldom makes friends . . . *friends,* mind you . . . after he's twenty-five. You only make acquaintances after that age. I'd like well to think there were people in Ireland that had as tight a hold on your friendship, Henry, as Gilbert Farlow and them other lads have. . . . An' there's another thing," he went on, leaning forward as he spoke and wagging his forefinger at Henry. "If you go to Trinity with a kindly feelin' for Ireland, it'll be something to think there's one man in the place that has a decent thought for his country an' isn't an imitation Englishman. Who knows what good you might do there?" He let his speculations consume him. "You might change the character of the whole college. You . . . you might make it Irish. You . . . you might be the means of turnin' the Provost into an Irishman an' start him takin' an interest in his country. The oul' lad might turn Fenian an' get transported or hung! . . ."

When he had ceased to speculate on what might happen

if Henry began an Irish crusade in Trinity, he spoke again of Marsh.

"You'll like him," he said. "I know you will. He's a bit off his head, of course, but that's neither here nor there. The man's a scholar an' I think he writes bits of poetry. I've never seen any of his pieces, but somebody told me he wrote things. I'd like well to have a poet in the house!"

"Is he a Catholic?" Henry asked.

His father nodded his head. "An' very religious, too, I believe," he said. "Still, that's neither here nor there. I met him up in Dublin. Ernest Harper told me about him!"

Ernest Harper was the painter-poet who had influenced so many young men in Ireland, and Mr. Quinn had come into the circle of his friends through the Irish co-operative movement. He had made a special visit to Dublin to consult Harper about the education of his son, telling him of his desire that Henry should have a strong national sense . . . "but none of your damned theosophy, mind! . . ." and Harper had recommended John Marsh to him. Marsh had lately taken his B.A. degree and he was anxious to earn money in circumstances that would enable him to proceed to his M.A.

"That lad'll do rightly," said Mr. Quinn, and he arranged to meet Marsh in the queer, untidy room in Merrion Square where Harper edited his weekly paper. "He has the walls of the place covered with pictures of big women with breasts like balloons," Mr. Quinn said afterwards when he tried to describe Ernest Harper's office, "an' he talks to you about fairies 'til you'd near believe a leprechaun 'ud hop out of the coalscuttle if you lifted the lid!"

Soon afterwards, they met, and Mr. Quinn explained his purpose to Marsh. "I'm not a Nationalist, thank God, nor a Catholic, thank God again, but I'm Irish an' I want my son to know about Ireland an' to feel as Irish as I do myself!"

Marsh talked about Nationalism and Freedom and English Misrule, but Mr. Quinn waved his hands before his face and made a wry expression at him. "All your talk about the freedom of Ireland is twaddle, John Marsh . . . if you don't mind, I'll begin callin' you John Marsh this minute . . . an' I may as well tell you I don't believe in the tyranny of England. The English aren't cruel—they're stupid. That's what they are—Thick! As thick as they can be, an' that's as thick as God thinks it's decent to let any man be! But they're not cruel. They do cruel things sometimes because they don't know any better, an' they think they're doin' the right things when they're only doin' the stupid thing. That's where we come in! Our job is to teach the English how to do the right thing." They smiled at him. "An' I'm not coddin,'" he went on. "I mean every word I say. It's not Home Rule for Ireland that's needed—it's Irish Rule for England; an' I'll maintain that 'til my dyin' day. . . . But that's neither here nor there. I think you're a fool, John Marsh, to go about dreamin' of an Irish Republic . . . you don't mind me callin' you a fool, do you? . . . but you love Ireland, and I'd forgive a man a great deal for that, so if you'll come an' be tutor to my son, I'll be obliged to you!"

And John Marsh, smiling at Mr. Quinn, had consented.

"That's right," Mr. Quinn said, gripping the young man's hand and wringing it heartily. "I like him," he added, turning to Ernest Harper, "an' he'll be good for Henry, an' I daresay I'll be good for him. You've an awful lot of slummage in your skull," he continued, addressing Marsh again, "but begod I'll clear that out!"

"Slummage?" Marsh asked questioningly.

"Aye. Do you not know what slummage is?"

He described it as a heap of steamy, flabby grain that is rejected by distillers after the spirit has been extracted from it. "An' it's only fit to feed pigs with, "he said, ending his description. "An' the kind of stuff you're lettin' out of you now is only fit for pub-patriots. How soon can you come to Ballymartin. The sooner the better!''

He tried to drop the discussion of politics, but was so fond of it himself that before he had settled the date of Marsh's appearance at Ballymartin, he was in the middle of another discussion. His head was full of theories about Ireland and about the world, and he loved to let his theories out of his head for an airing. He very earnestly desired to keep Ireland different from England. ''Ireland's the 'country' of this kingdom, an' England's the 'town,' '' he sometimes said, or when his mood was bitter, he would say that he wished to preserve Ireland as a place in which gentlemen could live in comfort, leaving England to be the natural home of manufacturers and mill-owners.

''But it's no good talkin' of separatin' the two countries,'' he said to Marsh, ''an' it's no good talkin' of drivin' the English out of Ireland because you can't tell these times who is English an' who is Irish. We've mingled our blood too closely for any one to be able to tell who's what. If you started clearin' out the English, you'd mebbe clear me out, for my family was planted here by William of Orange . . . an' the damnedest set of scoundrels they were, too, by all accounts! . . . an' mebbe, Marsh, you yourself 'ud be cleared out! . . . Aye, an' you, too, Ernest Harper, for all you're waggin' your oul' red beard at me. You're Scotch, man, Scotch, to the backbone! . . .''

Harper rose at him, wagging his red beard, and filling the air with terrible prophecies! . . .

''Ah, quit, man!'' said Mr. Quinn, and he turned and winked at Marsh. ''Do you know what religion he is?'' he said, pointing his finger at Harper. ''He's a Nonconformin' Theosophist!'' And he roared at his own joke.

''You can no more separate the destinies of England an' Ireland in the world,'' he went on, ''nor you can separate the waters of the Liffey an' the Mersey in the Irish Sea. Bedam, if you can!''

Mr. Quinn liked to throw out these aphorisms, and he

spent a great deal of time in inventing them. Once he flung a company of Dublin gossips into a rage because he declared that Dublin was called "the whispering gallery" and "the city of dreadful whispers" because it was populated by the descendants of informers and spies. That, he declared, was why Dublin people were so fond of tittle-tattle and tale-bearing and scandal-mongering. "The English hanged or transported every decent-minded man in the town, an' left only the spies an' informers, an' the whole of you are descended from that breed. That's why you can't keep anything to yourselves, but have to run abut the town tellin' everybody all the secrets you know!" And he charged them with constantly giving each other away. He repeated this generalisation about the Dublin people to John Marsh. "An' I tell you what'll happen to you, young fellow, one of these days. You'll be hanged or shot or transported or somethin,' an' half the people of this place'll be runnin' like lightnin' to swear an information against you, as sure as Fate. If ever you think of startin' a rebellion, John Marsh, go up to Belfast an' start it. People'll be loyal to you there, but in this place they'd sell you for a pint of Guinness!"

He was half serious in his warning to Marsh, but . . . "I should be glad to die for Ireland," Marsh replied, and it was said so simply that there was no priggishness in it. "I can think of no finer fate for an Irishman."

Mr. Quinn made a gesture of impatience. "It 'ud be a damn sight better to live for Ireland," he exclaimed angrily.

2

Henry was in the garden when John Marsh arrived, accompanied by Mr. Quinn. Two letters had come to him that morning from England—one from Gilbert Farlow and the other from Mary Graham, and he was reading them again for the seventh or eighth time when the dogcart drove up to the house.

My dear old ass, Gilbert wrote, *why grizzle and grouse
at the Bally Awful! That's my name now for things
which can't be helped. I've taught it to Ninian, but he
persists in calling it the Bloody Awful, which is low. He
says that doesn't matter because he is low. Roger and I
have had to clout his head rather severely lately . . . it
took two of us to do it . . . Roger held his arms while I
clouted him . . . because he has become fearfully demo-
cratic, meaning by that, that anybody who knows more
than his alphabet is an enemy of the poor. Roger and I
are dead nuts on aristocracy at present. We go about saying, "My God, I'm a superman!" and try to look like
Bernard Shaw. Roger only succeeds in looking like Little
Lord Fauntleroy. But all this is away from the point,
which is, why grizzle and grouse at the Bally Awful. If
your papa will send you to T.C.D., you must just grin
and bear it, my lad. I've never met anybody from Trinity . . . I suppose people do come out of it after they get
into it . . . but if you're careful and remember the example of your little friends, Gilbert and Ninian and Roger,
you'll come to no harm. And when you do come to London, we'll try to improve what's left of your poor mind.
It would be splendid to go to Ballymartin for the summer.
Tell your papa that Ninian and Roger and I solemnly
cursed him three times for preventing you from coming to
Cambridge, and then gave him three cheers for asking us
to Ireland. The top of the morning to you, my broth of
a boy, and the heavens be your bed, bedad and bejabers, as
you say in your country, according to Punch. Yours ever,
Gilbert.*
    P.S. What about that two bob you owe me?
Mary's letter was shorter than Gilbert's.

*I think it's awfully horrid of your father not to let you
go to Cambridge with Ninian and the others. I was so
looking forward to going up in May Week and so was
Mother. Of course, we shall go anyhow, but it would*

have been much nicer if you had been there. You would love Boveyhayne if you were here now. The hedges are full of wild roses and hazelnuts and there is a lovely lot of valaria on our wall. Old Widger says there will be a lovely lot of blackberries in September if everything goes well. I went out in a boat yesterday with Tom Yeo and I caught six dozen mackerel. You would have blubbed if you'd seen them flopping about in the bottom of the boat and looking so nice, and they were nice to eat. I love mackerel, don't you? Mother sends her love. Do write soon. I love getting letters and you write such nice ones. Your affectionate friend, Mary Graham. P.S. Love.

Mary always signed herself his affectionate friend. He had tried to make her sign herself his loving sweetheart, but she said she did not like to do that.

3

He hurriedly put the letters away, and rose to greet John Marsh who came across the lawn to him, talking to Mr. Quinn.

"This is John Marsh, Henry," Mr. Quinn said when he came up to him, and Henry and Marsh shook hands and murmured greetings to each other. "I'll leave you both here to get acquainted with each other," Mr. Quinn continued. "I've a few things to do about the house!" He went off at once, leaving them together, but before he had gone far he turned and shouted to Henry, "You can show him through the grounds! He'll want to stretch his legs after bein' so long in the train!"

"Very well, father!" Henry answered, and turned to Marsh.

His first impression of his tutor was one of insignificance. Marsh's clothes were cheap and ready-made, and they seemed to be a size too large for him. That, indeed, was characteristic of him, that he should always seem to be wearing things which were too big for him. His tie, too, was rising over the top of his collar. . . . But the sense of insignificance disappeared from Henry's mind almost immediately after Marsh had offered his hand to him and had smiled; and following the sense of insignificance came a feeling of personal shame that was incomprehensible to him until he discovered that his shame was caused because he had thought slightingly of Marsh, even though he had done so only for a few moments, and had allowed his mind to be concerned about the trivialities of clothes when it should have been concerned with the nature of the man who wore them. Henry's mind was oddly perverse; he had been as fierce in his denunciation of convention as ever Gilbert Farlow had been, but nevertheless he clung to conventional things with something like desperation. It was characteristic of him that he should palliate his submission to the conventional thing by inventing a sensible excuse for it. He would say that such things were too trivial to be worth the trouble of a fight or a revolt, and declare that one should save one's energies for bigger battles; but the truth was that he had not the moral courage to flout a convention, and he had a queer, instinctive dislike of people who had the courage to do so. . . . He knew that this habit of his was likely to distort his judgments and make him shrink from ordeals of faith, and very often in his mind he tried to subdue his cowardly fear of conventional disapproval . . . without success. But John Marsh had the power to conquer people. The gentleness of him, the kindly smile and the look of high intent, made men of meaner motive feel unaccountably ashamed.

He was a man of middle height and slender build. His high, broad brow was covered by heavy, rough, tufty hair that was brushed cleanly from his forehead and cut tidily about the neck so that he did not look unkempt. His long, straight nose was as large as the nose of a successful business man, but it was not bulbous nor were the nostrils wide and distended. It was a delicately-shaped and pointed

nose, with narrow nostrils that were as sensitive as the
nostrils of a racehorse: an adventurous, pointing nose
that would lead its owner to valiant lengths, but would
never lead him into low enterprises. He had grey eyes
that were quick to perceive, so that he understood things
speedily, and the kindly, forbearing look in them promised
that his understanding would not be stiffened by harsh-
ness, that it would be accompanied by sympathy so keen
that, were it not for the hint of humour which they also held,
he might almost have been mawkish, a sentimentalist too
easily dissolved in tears. His thick eyebrows clung closely
to his eyes, and gave him a look of introspection that mitigated the shrewdness of his pointing nose. There was some
weakness, but not much, in the full, projecting lower lip
and the slightly receding chin that caused his short, tightened upper lip to look indrawn and strained; and the big,
ungainly, jutting ears consorted oddly with the serious
look of high purpose that marked his face in repose. It
was as though Puck had turned poet and then had turned
preacher. One looked at the fleshy lower lip and the jutting ears, and thought of a careless, impish creature; one
looked at the shapely, pointing nose and the kindly, un-
flinching eyes, and thought of a man reckless of himself in
the pursuit of some fine purpose. One saw immediately
that he was a man who could be moved easily when his
sympathies were touched . . . but that he could hardly be
dissuaded from the fulfilment of his good intent. His Nationalism was like a cleansing fire; it consumed every im-
pure thing that might penetrate his life. It was so potent
that he did ridiculous things in asserting it. . . . It was
typical of him that he should gaelicise his name, and
equally typical of him that he should be undecided about
the correct spelling of "John" in the ancient Irish tongue.
He had called himself "Sean" Marsh, and then had called
himself "Shane" and "Shaun" and "Shawn." Once, for
a while, he transformed "John" into "Eoin" and then,
tiring of it, had reverted to "Sean." But this restlessness

over his name was not a sign of general instability of purpose. He might vary in the expression of his belief, but the belief itself was as immovable as the mountains.

4

It was said of him that on one occasion he had taken a cheque to a bank in Dublin to be cashed. An English editor had printed one of his poems and had paid for it . . . and he was not accustomed to receiving money for his poems, which were printed mostly in little Irish propaganda journals! He had endorsed the cheque in Gaelic, and the puzzled bank manager had demanded that it should be endorsed in English. . . . Marsh had given him a lecture on Irish history that lasted for the better part of half-an-hour . . . and then, because the manager looked so frightened, he had consented to sign his name in English.

5

They left the garden and walked slowly to the top of an ascending field where an old farm-horse, quit now of work, grazed in peace. It raised its head as they walked towards it, and gazed at them with blurred eyes, and then ambled to them. They stood beside it for a few moments while Marsh patted its neck with one hand and allowed it to nuzzle in the palm of the other. "I love beasts," he said, "Dogs and cats and birds and horses and cows . . . I think I love cows best because they've got such big, soft eyes and look so stupid and reproachful . . . except that dogs are very nice and companionable and faithful . . . but so are cats. . . ."

"Faithful? Cats?" Henry asked.

"Oh, yes . . . quite faithful if they like you. Why should they be faithful if they don't? Poor, old chap! Poor, old chap!" he murmured, thrusting his fingers through the horse's worn mane. "Of course, horses are

very nice, too,'' he went on. "And birds! . . . I suppose
one loves all animals. One has to be very brutal to hurt
an animal, hasn't one?''

Henry laughed. "The Irish are cruel to animals,'' he
said, "but the English aren't!''

Marsh flushed. "I've never been in England,'' he replied, looking away.

"Never?'' Henry exclaimed.

"No, and I shall never go there!''

There was a sudden ferocity in his voice that startled
Henry. "But why?'' he asked.

"Why? . . .'' Marsh's voice changed its note and be-
came quiet again. "I'm Irish,'' he said. "That's why!
I don't think that any Irishman ought to put his foot in
England until Ireland is free!''

Henry snapped at him impatiently. "I hate all that
kind of talk,'' he said.

Marsh looked at him in astonishment. "You hate all
. . . what talk?'' he asked.

"All that talk about Ireland being free!''

"But don't you want Ireland to be free?'' Marsh asked.

They had walked on across the field until they came to a
barred gate, and Marsh climbed on to the top bar and
perched himself there while Henry stood with his back
against the gate and fondled the muzzle of the horse which
had followed after them.

"I don't know what you mean when you say you want
Ireland to be free!'' Henry exclaimed.

"Don't know what I mean! . . .'' Marsh's voice became very tense again, and he slipped down from the gate
and turned quickly to explain his meaning to Henry, but
Henry did not wait for the explanation. "No,'' he interrupted quickly. "Of course, I don't know much about
these things, but I've read some books that father gave me,
and I've talked to my friends . . . one of them, Gilbert
Farlow, is rather clever and he knows a lot about politics
. . . he argues with his father about them . . . and I can't

see that there's much difference between England and Ireland. People here don't seem to me to be any worse off than people over there!''

"It isn't a question of being worse off or better off,'' Marsh replied. ''It's a question of being *free*. The English are governed by the English. The Irish aren't governed by the Irish. That's the difference between us. What does it matter what your condition is so long as you know that you are governed by a man of your own breed and blood, and that at any minute you may be in his place and he in yours, and yet you'll be men of the same breed and blood? I'd rather be governed badly by men of my own breed than be governed well by another breed. . . .''

Henry remembered Ulster and his father and all his kinsmen scattered about the North who had sworn to die in the last ditch rather than be governed by Nationalists. ''That's all very well,'' he said, ''but there are plenty of people in Ireland who don't want to be governed by your breed, well or bad!''

''They'd consent if they thought we had the ability to govern well,'' Marsh went on. ''Anyhow, we couldn't govern Ireland worse than the English have governed it!''

''Some people think you could! . . .''

But Marsh was in no mood to listen to objections. ''You can't be free until you are equal with other people, and we aren't equal with the English. We aren't equal with anybody but subject people. And they look down on us, the English do. We're lazy and dirty and ignorant and superstitious and priest-ridden and impractical and . . . and comic! . . . My God, *comic!* Whenever I see an Englishman in Ireland, running round and feeling superior, I want to wring his damned neck . . . and I should hate to wring any one's neck.''

Henry tried to interject a remark, but Marsh hurried on, disregarding his attempt to speak.

''How would they like it if we went over to their country and made remarks about them?'' he exclaimed. ''My

brother went to London once and he saw people making
love in public . . . fellows and girls hugging each other
in the street and sprawling about in the parks . . . all
over each other . . . and no one took any notice. It
wasn't decent. . . . How would they like it if we went
over there and made remarks about *that?* . . ."

Henry insisted on speaking. "But why should you hate
the English?" he demanded, and added, "I don't hate
them. I like them!"

"I didn't say I hated the English," Marsh replied. "I
don't. I don't hate any race. That would be ridiculous.
But I hate the belief that the English are fit to govern us,
when they're not, and that we're not fit to govern ourselves, when we are. I'd rather be governed by Germans
than be governed by the English! . . ." Henry moved
away impatiently. "Yes, I would," Marsh continued.
"At all events, the Germans would govern us well. . . ."

"You'd hate to be governed by Germans!"

"I'd hate to be governed by any but Irishmen; but the
Germans wouldn't make the muddles and messes that the
English make! . . ."

"You don't know that," Henry said.

But Marsh would not take up the point. He swung off
on a generalisation. "There won't be any peace or happiness in Ireland," he said, "until the English are driven out
of it. Even the Orangemen don't like them. They're
always making fun of them! . . ."

Henry repeated his assertion that he liked the English,
conscious that there was something feeble in merely repeating it. He wished that he could say something as
forceful as Marsh's statement of his dislike of England,
but he was unable to think of anything adequate to say.
"I like the English," he said again, and when he thought
over that talk, there seemed to be nothing else to say. How
could he feel about the English as John Marsh, who had
never lived in England, felt? How could he dislike them
when he remembered Gilbert Farlow and Roger Carey and

Ninian Graham and Mrs. Graham and Old Widger and
Tom Yeo and Jim Rattenbury . . . and Mary Graham.
His father had always spoken contemptuously of Englishmen, but he had never been moved by this violent antipathy
to them which moved Marsh . . . and most of his talk
against England was only talk, intended to sting the English out of their complacency . . . and he was eager to
preserve the Union between the two countries. But Marsh
wished to be totally separate from England. He was
vague, very vague, about points of defence, and he boggled
badly when Henry, trying to think like a statesman, talked
of an Army and a Navy . . . his mind wandered into the
mists of Tolstoyianism and then he ended by suggesting that
England would attend to these matters in self-defence. He
could not satisfy Henry's superficial enquiries about the
possibilities of trade conducted in Gaelic . . . but he was
positive about the need for separation, complete and ir-
remediable separation, from England.

"We're separated from them physically," he said, "and
I want us to be separated from them politically and spirit-
ually. They're a debased people! . . ." Henry muttered
angrily at that, for his mind was still full of Mary Graham.
"They're a debased people . . . that's why I want to get
free of them . . . and all the debasing things in Ireland
are part of the English taint. We've nothing in common
with them. They're a race of factory-hands and manufacturers; we're a race of farmers and poets; and you can
never reconcile us. All you can do is to make us like
them . . . or worse!"

Henry remembered how his father had fulminated
against the smooth Englishman who had proposed to turn
Glendalough into a place like the Potteries or Wigan.

"But isn't there some middle course?" he said weakly.
"Isn't there some way of getting at the minerals of Wicklow without making Glendalough a place like Wigan?"

"Not if the English have anything to do with it," Marsh
answered. "I don't know what Wigan is like . . . I sup-

pose it's horrible . . . but it's natural to Englishmen.
They trail that sort of place behind them wherever they go.
Slums and sickness and fat, rich men! If they had anything to do with developing Wicklow they'd make it
stink! . . ."

"Well, I don't know," Henry said wearily, for he soon
grew tired of arguments in which he was an unequal par-
ticipator. "I like the English and I can't see any good
in just hating them!"

"They found a decent, generous race in Ireland," Marsh
exclaimed, "and they've turned it into a race of cadgers.
Your father admits that. Ask him what he thinks of Arthur Balfour and his Congested Districts Board! . . ."

They went back to the house, and as they went, they
talked of books, and as they talked of books, Marsh's mind
became assuaged. He had lately published a little volume
of poems and he spoke of it to Henry in a shy fashion,
though his eyes brightened and gleamed as he repeated
something that Ernest Harper had said of them . . . but
then Ernest Harper always spoke kindly of the work of
young, sincere men.

"I'll give you a copy if you like," Marsh said to Henry.

"Oh, thank you!" Henry exclaimed. "I should love to
have it. I suppose," he went on, "it's very exciting to
have a book published."

"I cried when I first saw my book," Marsh answered
very simply. "I suppose women do that when they first
see their babies! . . ."

But Henry did not know what women do when they first
see their babies.

THE SIXTH CHAPTER

1

ALL through the summer, Henry and John Marsh worked together, making Irishry, as Marsh called it. They studied the conventional subjects in preparation for T.C.D. but their chief studies were of the Irish tongue and Irish history. Marsh was a Gaelic scholar, and he had made many translations of Gaelic poems and stories, some of which seemed to Henry to be of extraordinary beauty, but most of which seemed to him to be so thoughtless that they were merely lengths of words. There appeared to be no connexion between these poems and tales and the life he himself led—and Marsh's point was that the connexion was vital. One evening, Henry, who had been reading "The Trojan Women" of Euripides, turned to Marsh and said that the Greek tragedy seemed nearer to him than any of the Gaelic stories and poems. He expressed his meaning badly, but what it came to was this, that the continuity of life was not broken in the Euripidean plays: the life of which Henry was part flowed directly from the life of which Euripides was part; he had not got the sensation that he was a stranger looking on at alien things when he had read "The Trojan Women." "I can imagine all that happening now," he said, "but I can't imagine any of that Gaelic life recurring. I don't feel any life in it. It's like something . . . something odd suddenly butting into things . . . and then suddenly butting out again . . . and leaving no explanation behind it!"

He tried again, with greater success, to explain what he meant. "It's like reading topical references in old books," he said. "They mean nothing to us even when there are footnotes to explain them!"

Marsh had listened patiently to him, though there was anger in his heart. "You think that all that life is over?" he said, and Henry nodded his head.

"Listen," said Marsh, taking a letter from his pocket, "here is a poem, translated from Irish, that was sent to me by a friend of mine in Dublin. His name is Galway, and I'd like you to know him. Listen! It's called 'A Song for Mary Magdalene.'"

He read the poem in a slow, crooning voice that seemed always on the point of becoming ridiculous, but never did become so.

> O woman of the gleaming hair
> (Wild hair that won men's gaze to thee),
> Weary thou turnest from the common stare,
> For the Shuiler [1] Christ is calling thee.
>
> O woman with the wild thing's heart,
> Old sin hath set a snare for thee:
> In the forest ways forespent thou art,
> But the hunter Christ shall pity thee.
>
> O woman spendthrift of thyself,
> Spendthrift of all the love in thee,
> Sold unto sin for little pelf,
> The captain Christ shall ransom thee.
>
> O woman that no lover's kiss
> (Tho' many a kiss was given thee)
> Could slake thy love, is it not for this
> The hero Christ shall die for thee?

They were quiet for a while, and then Marsh turned to Henry and said, "Is that alien to you?"

"No," he answered, "but I did not say that it was all alien! . . ."

"Or this?" Marsh interrupted, taking up the manuscript

1 Shuiler: a tramp or beggar.

again. "Galway sent these translations to me so that I
might be the first to see them. He always does that. This
one is called 'Lullaby of a Woman of the Mountain.'"

> Little gold head, my house's candle,
> You will guide all wayfarers that walk this country.
>
> Little soft mouth that my breast has known,
> Mary will kiss you as she passes.
>
> Little round cheek, O smoother than satin,
> Iosa will lay His hand upon you.
>
> Mary's kiss on my baby's mouth,
> Christ's little hand on my darling's cheek!
>
> House, be still, and ye little grey mice,
> Lie close to-night in your hidden lairs.
>
> Moths on the window, fold your wings,
> Little black chafers, silence your humming.
>
> Plover and curlew fly not over my house,
> Do not speak, wild barnacle, passing over this mountain.
>
> Things of the mountain that wake in the night time,
> Do not stir to-night till the daylight whitens.

"That's alive, isn't it?" Marsh, now openly angry, demanded. "Do you think that song doesn't kindle the
hearts of mothers all over the world? . . . I can imagine
Eve crooning it to little Cain and Abel, and I can imagine
a woman in the Combe crooning it to her child! . . ."
The Combe was a tract of slum in Dublin. "It's universal
and everlasting. You can't kill that!"

"Then why has it got lost?"

"It isn't lost—it's only covered up. Our task is to dig
it out. It's worth digging out, isn't it? The people in
the West still sing songs like that. Isn't it worth while to
try and get all our people to sing them instead of singing
English music-hall stuff? . . ."

2

It was in that spirit that Marsh started the Gaelic class in Ballymartin. "And the Gaelic games," he said to Henry, "we'll revive them too!" Twice a week, he taught the rudiments of the Irish language to a mixed class of boys and girls, and every Saturday he led the Ballymartin hurley team into one of Mr. Quinn's fields. . . .

There had been difficulty in establishing the mixed classes. The farmers and the villagers, having first declared that Gaelic was useless to them—"they'd be a lot better learnin' shorthand!" said John McCracken—then declared that they did not care to have their daughters "trapesin' about the loanies, lettin' on to be learnin' Irish, an' them only up to devilment with the lads!" But Marsh overcame that difficulty, as he overcame most of his difficulties, by persistent attack; and in the end, the Gaelic class was established, and the Ballymartin boys and girls were set to the study of O'Growney's primer. Henry was employed as Marsh's monitor. His duty was to supervise the elementary pupils, leaving the more advanced ones to the care of Marsh. It was while he was teaching the Gaelic alphabet to his class, that Henry first met Sheila Morgan.

She came into the schoolroom one night out of a drift of rain, and as she stood in the doorway, laughing because the wind had caught her umbrella and almost torn it out of her hands, he could see the rain-drops glistening on her cheeks. She put the umbrella in a corner of the room, leaving it open so that it might dry more quickly, and then she shook her long dark hair back and wiped the rain from her face. He waited until she had taken off her mackintosh and hung it up in the cloakroom, and then he went forward to her.

"Have you come to join the class?" he asked, and she smiled and nodded her head. "It's a coarse sort of a night," she added, coming into the classroom.

He did not know her name, and he wondered where her

home was. He knew everybody in Ballymartin, and many of the people in the country outside it, but he had never seen Sheila Morgan before.

"I thought I might as well come," she said, "but I'm only here for a while!"

Then she did not belong to the village. "Yes? . . ." he said.

"It's quaren dull in the country," she continued, "an' the classes'll help to pass the time. I wish it was dancin', but!"

Dancing! They had not made any arrangements for dancing, though the Gaels were very nimble on their feet. He glanced at Marsh reproachfully. Why had Marsh omitted to revive the Gaelic dances?

"Perhaps," he said to Sheila, "we can have dancing classes later on. . . ."

"I'll mebbe be gone before you have them," she answered.

"How long are you staying for?" he asked.

"I don't know. I'm stopping with my uncle Matthew . . . it's him has Hamilton's farm . . . an' I'm stoppin' 'til he knows how his health'll be. He's bad. . . ."

He remembered Matthew Hamilton. "Is he ill?" he said.

"Aye. He's been sick this while past, an' now he's worse, an' my aunt Kate asked me to come an' stop with them to help them in the house. He's not near himself at all. You'd think a pity of him if you seen the way he's failed next to nothin'. . . . Is it hard to learn Irish?"

"You'd better come an' try for yourself," he replied, and then he led her up to Marsh and told him that a new pupil had come to join the class. There was some awkwardness about names. . . . "Och, I never told you my name," she said, laughing as she spoke. "Sheila Morgan!" she continued. "I live in County Down, but I'm stayin' with my uncle Matthew," she explained to Marsh.

"Do you know any Gaelic at all?" Marsh asked.

"No," she replied. "I never learned it. Are you goin' to have any dancin' classes?"

Henry insisted that they ought to have had dancing classes as well as a hurley team. "The hurley's all right for the boys," he said, "but we've nothing for the girls. . . ."

"But you'd want boys at the dancin' as well," Sheila interrupted. "I can't bear dancin' with girls!"

"No, of course not," said Henry.

Marsh considered. "Who's to teach the dancing?" he asked, adding, "I can't!"

"I'd be willin' to do that," Sheila said. "Mebbe you'd join the class yourself, Mr. Marsh?"

Marsh laughed, but did not answer.

"It'll be great value," she went on. "There's nothin' to do in the evenin's . . . nothin' at all . . . an' it's despert dull at night with nothin' to do! . . ."

"I'll think about it," said Marsh. "You can begin your Gaelic study now," he added. "Mr. Quinn'll give you a lesson! . . ."

3

It was Jamesey McKeown who caused the decision to hold the dancing classes to be made as quickly as it was. Jamesey was one of the pupils in the advanced section of the Gaelic class . . . a bright-witted boy of thirteen, with a quick, sharp way. One day, Marsh and Henry had climbed a steep hill outside the village, and when they reached the top of it, they found Jamesey lying there, looking down on the fields beneath. His chin was resting in the cup of his upturned palms.

"God save you, Jamesey!" said Marsh, and "God save you kindly!" Jamesey answered.

The greeting and the reply are not native to Ulster, but Marsh had made them part of the Gaelic studies, and whenever he encountered friends he always saluted them so.

His pupils, falling in with his whim, replied to his salute
as he wished them to reply, but the older people merely
nodded their heads or said "It's a soft day!" or "It's a
brave day!" or, more abruptly, "Morra, Mr. Marsh!"
The Protestants among them suspected that the Gaelic sal-
utation was a form of furtive Popery. . . .

They sat down beside the boy. "I suppose you'll be
leaving school soon, Jamesey?" Marsh asked.

"Aye, I will in a while," Jamesey answered.

"What class are you in?"

"I'm a monitor, Mr. Marsh. I'm in my first year! . . ."

Henry sat up and joined in the conversation. "Then
you're going to be a teacher?" he said.

"No, I'm not," Jamesey replied. "My ma put me in
for the monitor to get the bit of extra education. That's
all!"

"What are you going to be, Jamesey? A farmer?" said
Marsh.

"No. I wouldn't be a farmer for the world! . . ."

"But why?"

The boy changed his position and faced round to them.
"Sure, there's nothin' to do but work from the dawn till
the dark," he said, "an' you never get no diversion at all.
I'm quaren tired of this place, I can tell you, an' my ma's
tired of it too. She wudden be here if she could help it,
but sure she can't. It's terrible in the winter, an' the win'
fit to blow the head off you, an' you with nothin' to do
on'y look after a lot of oul' cows an' pigs an' things. I'm
goin' to a town as soon as I'm oul' enough! . . ."

They talked to him of the beauty of the country. . . .

"Och, it's all right for a holiday in the summer," he
said.

. . . and they talked to him of the fineness of a farmer's
life, but he would not agree with them. A farmer's life
was too hard and too dull. He was set on joining his
brother in Glasgow. . . .

"What does your brother do, Jamesey?" Marsh asked.

"He's a barman."

"A barman!" they repeated, a little blankly.

"Aye. That's what I'm goin' to be . . . in the same place as him!"

They did not speak for a while. It seemed to both of them to be incredible that any one could wish to exchange the loveliness of the Antrim country for a Glasgow bar. . . .

"What hours does your brother work?" Marsh asked drily.

"He works from eight in the mornin' till eight at night, an' it's later on Saturdays, but he has a half-day a week til himself, an' he has all day Sunday. They don't drink on Sunday in Glasgow!"

Marsh smiled. "Don't they?" he said.

"It's long hours," Jamesey admitted, "but he has great diversion. D'ye know this, Mr. Marsh!" he continued, rolling over on his side and speaking more quickly, "he can go to a music-hall twice on the one night an' hear all the latest songs for tuppence. That's all it costs him. He goes to the gallery an' he hears gran', an' he can go to two music-halls in the one night . . . *in the one night,* mind you . . . for fourpence! Where would you bate that? You never get no diversion of that sort in this place . . . only an oul' magic-lantern an odd time, or the Band of Hope singin' songs about teetotallers! . . ."

That was the principal burden of Jamesey's complaint, that there was no diversion in Ballymartin. "If you were to go up the street now," he said, "you'd see the fellas stan'in' at the corner, houl'in' up the wall, an' wonderin' what the hell to do with themselves, an' never gettin' no answer! . . ."

"You never hear noan of the latest songs here," he complained again. "I got a quare cut from my brother once, me singin' a song that I thought was new, an' he toul' me it was as oul' as the hills. It was more nor a year oul', anyway! . . ."

4

They came away from the hill in a mood of depression. It seemed to Henry that the Gaelic Movement could never take root in that soil. What was the good of asking Jamesey McKeown to sing Gaelic songs and till the land when his heart was hungering for the tuppeny excitements of a Glasgow music-hall? What would Jamesey McKeown make of Galway's translations? Would

> O woman of the gleaming hair
> (Wild hair that won men's gaze to thee),
> Weary thou turnest from the common stare,
> For the Shuiler Christ is calling thee.

bind him to the nurture of the earth when

> What ho! she bumps

called him to Glasgow?

"We must think of something!" Marsh was saying, but Henry was busy with his own thoughts and paid no heed to him.

What, after all, had a farm to offer a quick-witted man or woman? That girl, Lizzie McCamley of whom his father had spoken once, she had preferred to go to Belfast and work in a linen mill and live in a slum rather than continue in the country; and Jamesey McKeown, who was so quick and eager and anxious to succeed, had weighed farms and fields and hills and valleys in the balance and found them of less weight and value than a Glasgow bar and a Glasgow music-hall. Henry remembered that his father was more interested in the land than most men—and he resolved to ask for his opinion. What was the good of all this co-operation, this struggle to discover the best way of making the earth yield up the means of life, this effort to increase and multiply, when nothing they could do seemed to make the work attractive to those who did it? . . .

Marsh was still murmuring to him. "I see," he was saying, "that something must be done. That girl . . . what's her name? . . . Sheila something? . . ."

"Sheila Morgan!" Henry said.

"Yes. Sheila Morgan . . . she said something about dancing classes, didn't she? We'll start a dancing class . . . we'll teach them the Gaelic dances! . . ."

It suddenly seemed funny to Henry that Marsh should propose to solve the Land Problem . . . the real Land Problem . . . by means of dancing classes.

"They'll want more than that," he said. "They can't always be dancing!"

"No," Marsh answered, "but we can begin with that!"

Marsh's depression swiftly left him. He began to speculate on the future of the countryside when the Gaelic revival was complete. There would be Gaelic games, Gaelic songs, Gaelic dances and a Gaelic literature. "I don't see why we shouldn't have a theatre in every village, with village actors and village plays. . . . There must be a great deal of talent hidden away in these houses that never comes out because there is no one to bring it out. . . . I wish you were older, Henry, and were quit of Trinity. You and I . . . and Galway . . . of course, we must have Galway . . . might start the Movement on a swifter course than it has now! . . ." He broke off and made a gesture of impatience. "Oh, my God, why can't a man do more!" he said.

5

Henry put the question to his father, and Mr. Quinn considered it for a while.

"I don't know," he answered, "what to say. You'd think people would find more to interest them in the land than in anything else . . . but they don't. There's so much to do, an' it's so varied, an' you have it all under your own eye . . . you begin it an' carry it on and you end it . . . an' yet somehow! . . . An' then the whole

family understands it and can take an interest in it.
You'd think that that would hold them. There isn't any
other trade in the world that'll take up a whole family an'
give them all somethin' to talk about an' think over an'
join in. But I've never known a bright boy or girl on a
farm that wasn't itchin' to get away from it to a town!"

"But something'll have to be done, father!" Henry
urged. "We must have farmers! . . ."

"Aye, something'll have to be done, but I'm damned if
I know what. I suppose when they've developed machinery
more an' can make transit easier . . . but sometimes I half
think we'll have to breed people for the land . . . thick
people, slow-witted people, clods . . . an' just let them
root an' dig and grub an' . . . an' breed!" He got up as
he spoke, and paced about the room. "No, Henry, I've
got no remedy for you! The Almighty God'll have to
think of a plan. *I* can't!"

6

Sheila Morgan did not know any of the ancient Gaelic
dances, nor did any one in Ballymartin. She knew how to
waltz and she could dance the polka and the schottishe.
"An' that's all you need!" she said. There were two old
women in the village who danced a double reel, and Paddy
Kane was a great lad at jigs. . . .

"Perhaps later on," Marsh said, "we can get some one
to teach them Gaelic dances!"

And so the classes began. Marsh had announced at the
Language class that the first of the Dancing Classes would
be held on the following Thursday . . . and on Thursday
every boy and girl and young man and woman in Ballymartin had crowded into the schoolroom where the class
was to be held.

"There are more here than come to the Language class,"
Marsh exclaimed in astonishment when he entered the room.

"Dancing seems to be more popular than Gaelic," Henry replied.

"I don't know how we shall teach them all," Marsh went on. "I can't dance . . . and she can't possibly teach them all!"

But there was no need to teach them to dance—they had all learned to dance "from their cradles," as some one said, and in a little while the room was full of dancing couples.

Sheila Morgan had gone smilingly to John Marsh as he entered the room. "We're all ready," she said, and waited.

"Oh, yes!" he replied, a little vaguely.

She looked at him for a few moments, and then went on. "If you were to lead off," she suggested.

"Me? But I can't dance! . . ."

"You can't dance!"

"No," he continued. "Somehow, I've never learnt to dance!" She looked disappointed. "I thought mebbe you an' me 'ud lead off," she said.

"I'm sorry," he replied. "Perhaps Mr. Quinn can dance! . . ."

Henry gave his arm to her and they walked off, to begin the slow procession round the room until all the couples were ready.

"I think Mr. Marsh is the only one in the place that can't dance," Sheila said, as she placed her hand on Henry's shoulder.

He put his arm round her waist and they moved off in the dance. "I suppose he is," he answered.

7

He danced with her several times. Her cheeks were glowing and the lustre of her eyes was like the sparkle of the stars. Her lips were slightly parted, and now and then her breath came quickly. As they swung round and round, she sometimes closed her eyes and then slowly opened them again. He became aware of some strange emotion that he had never known before.

"I love dancin'," she murmured, half to herself.

"Yes," he replied, scarcely knowing that he was speaking.

"I love dancin'," she said again, and again he said "Yes" and no more. . . .

He led her to a seat at the side of the room and sat down on the chair next to it. They did not speak, but sat there watching the swift movements of the other dancers. Marsh was somewhere at the other end of the room, looking on . . . a little puzzled, a little disturbed . . . but pleased, too, because the dancers were pleased. He was wondering why the interest in the Gaelic language was not so strong as the interest in the waltz. "A foreign dance, too . . . not Gaelic at all!"

But Henry had forgotten the Gaelic movement, and was conscious only of the girl beside him and her glowing cheeks and her bright eyes and the softness of her. . . . She was older than he was, a couple of years and he noticed that she had just "put up" her hair. It had been hanging loosely when he first saw her, and he wondered which he liked better, the loose, hanging hair, or the hair bound round her head. Her slender white neck was revealed now that her hair was up, and it was very beautiful, but he thought that after all, his first sight of her, as she stood in the doorway, the raindrops still on her face, and flung back the long, loose strands of dark hair that lay about her shoulders . . . he still thought that was the loveliest vision of her he had seen. . . .

Then he remembered Mary Graham. She, too, had long loose hair that lay in dark lengths about her shoulders, and her eyes, too, could shine . . . but she was a girl, and Sheila was a woman! . . . He was engaged to Mary, of course . . . well, was it an engagement? They had been sweethearts and he had told her he loved her and she had said that she would marry him . . . and all that . . . but they were kids when that happened. Ninian had called him a sloppy ass! . . . This was different. His feeling for Sheila Morgan was different from his feeling for Mary Graham. He had never felt for any one as he felt for Sheila. He seemed unaccountably to be more aware of Sheila than he was of Mary. He could not altogether understand this difference of sensation . . . but sometimes when he had been with Mary, he had forgotten that she was a girl . . . she was just some one with whom he was playing a game or going for a walk or taking a bathe in the sea. But he could not forget that Sheila was a woman. When he had danced with her and his arm was about her waist and her fingers were in his . . . he seemed to grow up. He felt as if something at which he had been gazing uncomprehendingly for a long time, had suddenly become known to him. He recognised something . . . understood something which had puzzled him.

"Let's dance again," he said, standing up before her.

"All right," she answered, rising and going to him.

"I love dancing," he said to her.

"Yes," she murmured in reply.

8

When the dance was over, he took her to her uncle's farm. Marsh, overcome by headache, had gone home before the dance was ended, and Henry felt glad of this. He waited in the porch of the schoolhouse while Sheila put on her coat and wrap, and wondered why his feeling for her was so different from his feeling for Mary Graham, and while he wondered, she came to him, gathering up her skirts.

"Isn't the sky lovely?" she said, glancing up at the stars, as they walked out of the school-yard into the road.

He glanced up too, but did not answer.

"Millions an' millions of them," she said. "You'd wonder the sky 'ud hold them all!"

"Yes," he said.

"Many's a time I wonder about the stars," she went on. "Do you ever wonder about them?"

"Sometimes."

"Do you think there's people in them, the same as there is on the earth?"

"I don't know," he answered.

"This is a star, too, isn't it?" she asked.

"Yes."

"An' shines just like them does?"

"Yes, I think so!"

"That's quare!" She walked on for a few yards without speaking, and her eyes were fixed steadily on the starry fields. "It's funny," she said, "to think mebbe there's people up there lookin' at us an' them mebbe thinkin' about this place what we're thinkin' of them. Wouldn't you love to be able to fly up to one of them an' just see if it's true? . . ."

He laughed at her and she laughed in response. "I'm talkin' blether," she said, stumbling over a stone in the road.

"Mind!" he warned her, putting out his hand to steady her.

"I was nearly down that time," she said. "These roads is awful in the dark . . . you can't see where you're goin' or what's in the way!"

"No," he replied.

Her arms were crooked because she was holding her skirts about her ankles, and as she stumbled against him a second time, he put out his hand and caught hold of her arm, and this time he did not withdraw it. He slipped his arm inside hers and drew her close to him, and so they walked on in the starlight up the rough road that led to Matthew Hamilton's farm.

"It's quaren late," she said, moving nearer to him.

"Yes," he answered.

There was a rustle in the trees as the night wind blew

through the branches, and they could hear the silken murmur of the corn as it bent before the breeze. Now and then there was a flutter of wings in a hedge as they passed by, and the low murmurs of cattle and sheep came from the fields.

"I wish it were next Thursday," he said.

"So do I," she replied.

"I wish we could have two dancing-classes in the week instead of one!"

"So do I," she said.

"But we can't manage that," he continued. "You see we have two nights for the Language class! . . ."

"You could have one night for the Language class," she said, "and two nights for dancing!"

"I don't think Marsh would like that," he answered.

They walked on for a while, thinking of what Marsh would say, and then she broke the silence.

"I don't see the good of them oul' language classes," she said.

"Don't you?"

"No. I'd rather be dancin' any day! . . ."

9

He left her at the gate that led into the farm-yard.

"Good-night," he said, holding out his hand to her.

"Good-night!" she replied.

But still he did not move away nor did she open the gate and pass into the yard.

"I shall look forward to Thursday," he said.

"So shall I!"

"Good-night!"

"Good-night!"

He still held her hand in his and as she made a movement to draw it away, he suddenly pulled her to him and put his arms about her and kissed her.

"Sheila!" he said.

"Let me go!" she whispered.

She drew away from him, and stood looking at him for a few moments. Then she pushed the gate open and walked into the yard.

"Good-night!" she said.

THE SEVENTH CHAPTER

1

His habit had been to work in the morning with Marsh, and then, after light luncheon, they walked through the country during the afternoon, climbing hills or tramping heavily through the fields or, going off on bicycles, to bathe at Cushendall. Sometimes, Mr. Quinn accompanied them on these expeditions, and then they had fierce arguments about Ireland, but more often Marsh and Henry went off together, leaving Mr. Quinn behind to ponder over some problem of agriculture or to wrangle with William Henry Matier on what was and what was not a fair day's work. But now, Henry began to scheme to be alone. On the day after he had taken Sheila Morgan to her uncle's farm, he had been so restless and inattentive during his morning's work that Marsh had asked him if he were ill.

"I'm rather headachy," he had answered, and had gladly accepted the offer to quit work for the day.

"Would you like to go out for a walk?" Marsh had asked. "The fresh air! . . ."

And Henry had replied, "No, thanks! I think I'll just go up to my room!"

He had gone to his room and then, listening until he had heard Marsh go out, he had descended the stairs and, almost on tiptoe, had gone out of the house by a side-door, and, slipping through the paddock as if he were anxious not to be seen, had run swiftly through the meadows and corn-fields until he reached the road that led to Hamilton's farm. He had not decided what he was going to do when he had reached the farm. Sheila would probably be busy about the house or she might have work to do in the farmyard. Now that her uncle was ill, some of his labour would have to be done by others. But he would be less in the way, he thought, in the morning than he would be in the evening when the cows were being milked . . . though he might offer to help her to strain the milk and churn it, if she did that, and he could scald the milk-pans and . . . do lots of things! The evening, however, was still a long way off, but the morning was . . . *now!* And he wished very much to be with Sheila . . . now . . . this moment!

He saw her before she saw him. She had her back to him, and she was bending over her uncle who was sitting at the door of the farmhouse, with a rug wrapped round his legs. Henry, suddenly shy, stood still in the "loanie," looking at her and trying to think of something to say to her which would make his appearance there at that hour natural; but before he had thought of something that was suitable, she turned and saw him, and so he went forward, tongue-tied and awkward.

"Here's Mr. Quinn!" she said to her uncle . . . she had never known him as Master Henry, and she had not yet learned to call him by his Christian name alone.

The farmer looked up. "You mane Mr. Henry," he said, and Henry, listening to him, felt that at last he was near manhood, for people were shedding the "Master."

"Good-morning, Hamilton!" he said, holding out his hand to the farmer. "How're you to-day?"

"Middlin', sir . . . only middlin'. This is the first I've been out of the house this long while, but the day's that warm, I just thought I'd like to get a heat of the sun, bad or no bad. It's a terrible thing to be helpless like this . . . not able to do a han's-turn for yourself! . . ."

"Ah, quit, Uncle Matt!" Sheila interjected. "Sure, you'll soon be all right an' runnin' about like a two-year oul'!" She turned to Henry. "He's an awful man for wantin' to be doin' things, an' it's sore work tryin' to get him to sit still the way the doctor says he's to sit. Always wantin' to be up an' doin' somethin'! Aren't you, Uncle Matt?"

"Ay, daughter, I am. I was always the lad for work! . . ."

"You're a terrible oul' provoker, so you are. You're just jealous, that's it, an' you're heart-feard we'll mebbe all learn how to look after the farm better nor you can!"

The old man smiled and took hold of her hand and fondled it. "You're the right wee girl," he said affectionately. "Always doin' your best to keep a man's heart up!"

"Indeed, then," she said briskly, "you gimme enough to do to keep your heart up. You're worse nor a cradleful of childher! . . . Here, let me wrap this shawl about your shoulders! Aren't you the oul' footer to be lettin' it slip down like that? . . . There now!"

He lay back in his chair while she folded the shawl about him, and smiled at her. "God content you, daughter!" he murmured.

2

"Well?" she said to Henry as they moved towards the byre.

He had sat with the farmer for a while, talking of the weather and the crops and the prospects of the harvest, and then, seeing Sheila going across the yard, he had followed her.

"Well?" she said, looking at him quizzically.

He did not know what to say, so he stood there smiling at her. Her arms were bare to the bend, and the neck of her blouse was open so that he saw her firm, brown throat.

"Well!" he replied, still smiling, and "Well?" she said again.

She went into the byre, and he followed her to the door, and stood peering into the dark interior where a sick cow lay lowing softly.

"Is that all you have to say for yourself?" Sheila called to him.

"I have a whole lot to say," he replied, "but I don't know how to say it!"

She laughed at that, and he liked the strong, quick sound of her laughter. "You're the quare wee fella," she exclaimed.

Wee fellow! He flushed and straightened himself.

"I was passing along the road," he said stiffly, "and I thought I'd come up and see your uncle! . . ."

"Oh!" she answered.

"Yes. My father was wondering yesterday how he was getting on, so I just thought I'd come over and see him. I suppose you're busy?"

"You suppose right!"

He moved a step or two away from the door of the byre. "Then I won't hinder you in your work," he said.

"You're not hinderin' me," she replied, coming out of the dark byre as she spoke. "It would take the quare man to hinder *me!* Where's Mr. Marsh this mornin'?"

"Oh, somewhere!"

"I thought you an' him was always thegether. You're always about anyway!"

He felt strangely boyish while she was talking. Last night, when he had drawn her to him and had kissed her soft, moist lips, he had felt suddenly adult. While his arms were about her, he was conscious of manhood, of something new in his life, something that he had been grow-ing to, but until that moment had not yet reached . . . and now, standing in the strong sunlight and looking into her firm, laughing eyes, his manhood seemed to have re-ceded from him, and once more he was . . . a wee fellow, a schoolboy, a bit of a lad. . . . His vexation must have been apparent in his expression, for she said "What ails you?" to him.

"Nothing," he replied, turning away.

It was she who was making him feel schoolboyish again.

She looked so capable and so assured, standing outside the byre-door, with a small crock in her hands, that he felt that she was many years older than he was, that she knew far more than he could hope to know for a long time. . . .

She put the crock down and came close to him and took hold of his arm. "What ails you?" she said again, peering up into his face and smiling at him.

He looked at her with sulky eyes. "You're making fun of me," he said.

She shook his arm and pushed him. "G'long with you!" she said. "A big lump of a fella like you, actin' the chile! . . ." She picked up the crock and handed it to him. "Here," she said, "carry that into the house, will you, an' ask me aunt Kate to give you the full of it with yella male, an' then hurry back. I'll be up in the hayloft," she added, moving off.

3

He laid the crock of yellow meal down on a wooden box in the barn, and then climbed up the ladder to the hayloft.

"Wheesht," she said, holding up her hand. "There's a hen sittin' here, an' I don't want her disturbed!" He climbed into the loft as quietly as he could. "They'll soon be out now," she went on, "the lovely wee things! . . . What did you come here for, the day?"

"To see you!" he answered.

"Then that was a lie about comin' to see my Uncle Matt?"

He nodded his head.

"I thought as much. Sit down here by the side of me!"

He sat down on the hay where she bade him. "Are you angry with me?" he asked, making a wisp of hay.

"What would I be angry for?"

He did not know. Last night, perhaps, when he had kissed her?

"Oh, that!" she said. "Sure, that's nothin'!"

"Nothing?"

Why, then, had she left him so suddenly? She must have known how much he had to say to her. . . .

"Look at the time it was!" she exclaimed. "An' me havin' to get up at five an' let the cows out. . . . *You* weren't up at no five, I'll bet!" He had risen at eight. "Eight!" she exclaimed. "That's no hour of the day to be risin'. If you were married to me, I'd make you skip long before that hour!"

Married to her! . . .

"Sheila," he whispered, taking hold of her arm.

"Well?" she said, thrusting a hay-stalk into his hair.

"I love you, Sheila!" he whispered, coming closer to her.

"Do you, indeed?" she answered.

"I do, Sheila, I do. . . ."

He raised himself so that he was kneeling in front of her. His shyness had left him now, and the words were pouring rapidly out of his mouth.

"The minute I saw you in the door of the schoolroom that night, I was in love with you. I was, indeed!"

"Were you?"

"Yes. I couldn't help it, Sheila, and the worst of it was I didn't know what to say to you. And then, last night . . . when we were walking up the 'loanie' together and I was holding your arm . . . you know! . . . like this. . . ." He took hold of her arm as he spoke and pressed it in his. . . . "I felt like . . . like. . . ."

"Like what?"

"I don't know. Like anything. You *will* marry me, Sheila? You *do* love me? . . ."

She withdrew her arm from his and struck him lightly with a wisp of hay. "You're in a terrible hurry all of a sudden!" she said. "One minute you hardly know me, an' the next minute you're gettin' ready to be married to me. You're a despert wee fella!"

Wee fellow again!

"I'm not so very young," he said.

"What age are you?" she asked.

"I'm nearly seventeen," he replied.

She jumped up and stood over him. "God save us," she said, "that's the powerful age. You'd nearly bate Methusaleh!"

He stood up beside her. "Now, you're laughing at me again," he complained.

"No, I'm not," she answered.

She laid her hand on his shoulder and gripped it firmly, and stood thus, looking at him intently. Then she drew him into her arms and kissed him. "I like you quaren well," she said, holding him to her.

"Do you, Sheila?"

"Aye, of course I do, or I wouldn't be huggin' you like this, would I? Did you bring the yella male?"

He nodded his head. "It's down below," he said.

"Dear, oh, dear," she sighed. "I've wasted a terrible lot of time on you, Mr. Quinn! . . ."

"Call me 'Henry,' " he said.

"I'll call you 'Harry,' " she answered.

"You can call me anything you like! . . ."

She pinched his cheek. "You're a dear wee fella," she said. He did not mind being called a "wee fella" now. "But you're keepin' me from my work," she went on.

He seized her hand impetuously. "Take a day off," he said, "and we'll go for a long walk together!"

She laughed at him. "You quality people is the great ones for talk," she replied. "An' how could I take a day off an' me with my work to do?"

"Well, this evening then," he urged.

"There'll be the cows to milk! . . ."

"I'll come and help you."

"But sure you can't milk!"

"No, I can't milk, of course, but I can do anything else you want done. I can hold things and . . . and run mes-

sages . . . and just help you. Can't I? And then, when
you've finished your work, we'll go and sit in the clover
field. . . ."

"An' get our death of cold sittin' on the damp ground.
Dear O, but men talks quare blether!"

He tried to persuade her that dew was not damping.
. . . "Ah, quit!" she exclaimed . . . and then he begged
for her company in a walk along the Ballymena Road.

"I suppose I'll have to give in to you," she said.
"You're a terrible fella for coaxin'!"

She moved towards the trap where the head of the ladder
showed, and prepared to descend from the loft.

"What time will I come for you?" he asked, following
her.

"Half-seven," she answered, going down the ladder.
"I'll be well done my work then!"

He stood above her, looking down through the trap.
"We generally have dinner at half-past seven," he said.

"You should have your dinner in the middle of the day,
like us," she answered, and added, decisively, "It's half-
seven or never!"

"All right," he exclaimed, stooping down carefully and
putting his feet on a rung of the ladder. "I'll come for
you then. I'll manage it somehow."

4

He told his father that he did not want any dinner.
John Marsh had enquired about his headache, and Henry
had said that it was better, but that he thought he would
like to be quiet that evening. He said, too, that he had
made up his mind to go for a long, lonely walk. "But
what about your dinner?" Mr. Quinn had said, and he had
answered that he did not want any. "If I'm hungry," he
added, "I can have something before I go to bed."

He felt vaguely irritated with John Marsh who first pes-
tered him . . . that was the word Henry used in his mind

. . . with sympathy and then lamented that his headache would prevent him from helping that evening at the Gaelic language class. "Still, I suppose we'll manage," he ended regretfully.

"I don't suppose there'll be many at the class," Henry replied almost sneeringly.

"Why?" said Marsh.

"Oh, well," Henry went on, "after last night! . . ."

"You mean that they think more of dancing than they do of the language?" Marsh interrupted, and there was so much of anxiety in the tone of his voice that Henry regretted that he had sneered at him.

"Well, that's natural," he said, trying to think of some phrase that would mitigate the unkindness of what he was saying, and failing to think of it. "After all, it *is* much more fun to dance than to learn grammar. . . ."

"But this is the *Irish* language," Marsh persisted, as if the Irishness of the tongue transcended the drudgery of learning grammar.

Mr. Quinn crumpled the *Northern Whig* and threw it at Marsh's head. "You an' your oul' language!" he exclaimed. "What good'll it do anybody but a lot of professors. Here's the world tryin' to get Latin an' Greek out of the universities, an' here's you tryin' to get another dead language into them!"

There followed an argument that developed into a wrangle, in the midst of which Henry, flinging a consolatory speech to Marsh, escaped from the house. "You'll get all the keen ones to-night," he said. "That'll be some consolation to you!"

It was too soon to go up to Hamilton's farm. The dairy work would hardly be done, and there would be the evening meal to prepare, and he knew that he would not be welcome in the middle of that activity. He did not wish to return to the room where his father and John Marsh were arguing about the Irish language, nor did he wish to go and sit in his own room until the time came to go and meet Sheila. If Hannah were to make some sandwiches for him, in case he should feel hungry, he would go to the bottom fields and lie in the long grass by the brook until it was time to meet Sheila. He went downstairs to the kitchen and found Hannah busy with the night's dinner.

"Well, Master Henry?" she said.

He told her of his headache and his desire for a solitary walk, and asked her to cut sandwiches for him.

"I will with a heart an' a half," she said, "when I've strained these potatoes. Sit down there a while an' content yourself till I've done. . . ."

He took the sandwiches from her and went off to the bottom fields. The sky was full of mingled colours and long torn clouds that looked like flights of angels, and hidden in the fold of one great white strip of cloud that stretched up into the heavens, the sickle moon shone faintly, waiting for the setting sun to disappear so that she should shine out with unchallenged refulgence. He stood a while to look at the glory of the sky, and munched his sandwiches while he looked. He had always had a sensuous love of fine shapes and looks; the big bare branches of an old tree showing darkly against a winter sky or the changing colour of clouds at sunset, transfused at one moment to the look of filmy gold as the sun sent his rays shining upwards, darkened at the next, when the sun had vanished, so that they had the colour of smoke and made a stain as if God had drawn a sooty thumb across the sky; but now his sensuousness had developed, and he found himself full of admiration for things which hitherto he had not observed. That evening, when the cart-horses were led home, he had suddenly perceived that their great limbs were beautiful. He had stood still in the lane to watch them going by, and had liked the heavy plunging sound of their hoofs on the rough road, and the faded look of the long hair that hung about their houghs; but more than these he had liked the great round limbs of them, so full of strength. He remembered that once at Boveyhayne, Mary

Graham and he had argued about the sea-gulls. She had
"just loved" them, but he had qualified his admiration.
He liked the long, motionless flight of the gulls as they
circled through the air, and the whiteness of their shapely
bodies and the grey feathers on their backs, but he disliked the small heads they had and the long yellow beaks
and the little black eyes and the harsh cry . . . and he had
almost sickened when he saw them feeding on the entrails
that were thrown to them by the fishermen. . . . But now,
since he had fallen in love with Sheila Morgan, it seemed
to him that everything in the world was beautiful; and
lying here in the long grass, he yielded himself to the loveliness of the earth. He lay back and closed his eyes and
listened to the sounds that filled the air, the noise of
pleased, tired things at peace and the subdued songs of
roosting birds. He could hear shouts from the labourers
in the distant hayfields and, now and then, the slow rattle
of a country cart as it moved clumsily along the uneven
roads that led from the fields to the farmyards. There was
a drowsy buzz of insects that mingled oddly with the bur-
ble of the stream and the lowing of the cattle. . . . He lay
there and listened to a lark as it flew up from the ground
with a queer, agitated flutter of wings, watching it as
it ascended high and higher until it became a tiny speck,
and then he sat up and watched it as it descended again,
still flying with that queer, agitated flutter of wings, until
it came near the earth, when its song suddenly ceased and
it changed its flight and fell swiftly to its nest.

He rose up from the grass and walked over to the stream
and dipped his hands into it, splashing the water on to the
grass beside him. The sunlight shone on his hand and
made the wet hairs shine like golden threads. . . .

5

He was kneeling there at the side of the stream, looking
at the wet glow of his hand when the fear of death came

to him, and instantly he was terrified when he thought that
he might die. The consciousness of life was in him and
the desire to continue and to experience and to know were
quickening and increasing. It seemed to him then that if
he were to die at that moment, he would have been cheated
of his inheritance, that he would have a grievance against
God for all eternity. . . . He moved away from the brook
and sank back into the grass, shaken and disconcerted.
Until that moment, he had never thought of death except
as a vague, inevitable thing that came to all creatures
some time . . . generally when they were old and had lost
the savour of life. He had never seen a dead man or
woman and he was unfamiliar with the rites of burial. He
knew, indeed, that people die before they grow old, that
children die, but until that moment, death had not become
a personal thing, a thing that might descend on *him*. . . .

He shut his eyes and tried to close the thought of death
out of his mind, but it would not go away. He began to
sing disconnected staves of songs in the hope that he would
forget that he was mortal. . . . There was a song that
Bridget Fallon had taught him when he was a child, and
now after many years, he was singing it again:

> There were three lords came out of Spain,
> They came to court my daughter Jane.
> My daughter Jane, she is too young,
> And cannot bear your flatt'ring tongue.
> So fare you well, make no delay,
> But come again another day. . . .

But the thought of death still lay heavy on his mind,
and so he got up and left the field and hurried along the
road that led to Hamilton's farm.

"Oh, my God," he cried to himself, "if I were to die
now, just when I'm beginning to know things! . . ."

He began to run, as if he would run away from his own
thoughts. The torn strips of clouds, that had looked like

molten gold, were now darkening, and their darkness seemed ominous to him. The steepness of the "loanie" made him pant and presently he slackened his pace and slowed down to walking. His eyes felt hot and stiff in their sockets and when he put his hand on his forehead, he felt that it was wet with sweat.

"I'm frightened," he said to himself. "Scared! . . ."

He wiped his forehead and then crumpled his handkerchief in his hot palms.

"I'm rattled," he went on to himself. "That's what I am. Oh, my God, I *am* scared! . . ."

He looked about him helplessly. He could see a man tossing hay in a field near by, and he watched the rhythmical movement of his fork as it rose and fell.

"I couldn't die now," he thought. "I *couldn't*. It wouldn't be fair. I wouldn't let myself die . . . I wouldn't!"

And as suddenly as the fear of death had fallen on him, it left him.

"Good Lord!" he said aloud, "what an ass I am!"

6

Sheila was sitting on a stool in front of the door. Her uncle had gone to bed, and her aunt, tired after her day's work and her attendance on the sick man, was lying on the sofa, dosing.

"I wondered were you comin'," Sheila said as he came up to her.

"You knew I'd come," he answered.

"I didn't know anything of the sort," she exclaimed, getting up from the stool. "Fellas has disappointed me before this."

"Have you had other sweethearts?" he asked, frowning.

She laughed at him. "I've had boys since I was that high," she replied, holding out her hand to indicate her height when she first had a sweetheart. "What are you lookin' so sore about? D'ye think no one never looked at me 'til you came along? For dear sake!"

She rallied him. Was she the first girl he had ever loved? Was she? Ah, he was afraid to answer. As if she did not know! Of course, she was not the first, and dear knows she might not be the last . . .

"I'll never love any one but you, Sheila! . . ."

"Wheesht will you, or my aunt'll hear you!"

"I don't care who hears me! . . ."

"Well, I do then. Come on down the loanie a piece, an' you can say what you like. I love the way you talk . . . you've got the quare nice English accent!"

He followed her across the farmyard and through the gate into the "loanie."

"My father wouldn't like to hear you saying that," he said.

"Why?" she asked. "Does he not like the English way of talkin'?"

"Indeed, he does not. He loves the way you talk, the way all the Ulster people talk! . . ."

"What! Broad an' coarse like me?" she interrupted.

Henry nodded his head. "He doesn't think it's coarse," he said. "He thinks it's fine!"

Sheila pondered on this for a few moments. "He must be a quare man, your da!" she said.

They walked to the foot of the "loanie" and then turned along the Ballymena road.

"Does he know you come out with me?" she said.

"Who?" he answered.

"Your da."

"No. You see! . . ." He did not know what to say. It had not occurred to him to talk about Sheila to his father, and he realised now that if it had, he probably would not have done so.

"But if you're goin' to marry me? . . ." Sheila was saying.

"Oh, of course," he replied. "Of course, I shall have to tell him about you, won't I? I just didn't think of it. . . . Then you're going to marry me, Sheila?" he demanded, turning to her quickly.

"Och, I don't know," she answered. "I'm too young to be married yet, an' you're younger nor me, an' mebbe we'd change our minds, an' anyway there's a quare differs atween us."

"What difference is there between us?" he said, indignantly.

"Aw, there's a quare deal of differs," she maintained. "A quare deal. You're a quality-man! . . ."

"As if that matters," he interrupted.

"It matters a quare lot," she said.

They sat down on a bank by the roadside and he took hold of her hand and pressed it, and then he put his arm about her and drew her head down on to his shoulder.

"Somebody'll see you," she whispered.

"There's no one in sight," he replied.

"Do you love me an awful lot?" she asked, looking up at him.

"You know I do."

"More nor anybody in the world?"

He bent over and kissed her. "More than anybody in the world," he answered.

"You're not just lettin' on?" she continued.

"Letting on!"

"Aye. Makin' out you love me, an' you on'y passin' the time, divertin' yourself?"

He was angry with her. How could she imagine that he would pretend to love her? . . .

"I do love you," he insisted, "and I'll always love you. I feel that . . . that! . . ."

He fumbled for words to express his love for her, but could not find any.

"Ah, well," she said, "it doesn't matter whether you're pretendin' or not. I'm quaren happy anyway!"

She struggled out of his embrace and put her arms round his neck and kissed him. She remained thus with her arms round him and her face close to his, gazing into his eyes as if she were searching for something. . . .

"What are you thinkin', Sheila?" he asked.

"Nothin'," she said, and she drew him to her and kissed him again.

"I wish I was older," he exclaimed presently.

"Why?"

"Because I could marry you, then, and we'd go away and see all the places in the world. . . ."

"I'd rather go to Portrush for my honeymoon," she said. "I went there for a trip once!"

"We'd go to Portrush too. We'd go to all the places. I'd take you to England and Scotland and Wales, and then we'd go to France and Spain and Italy and Africa and India and all the places."

"I'd be quaren tired goin' to all them places," she murmured.

"And then when we'd seen everything, we'd come back to Ireland and start a farm. . . ."

She sat up and smiled at him. "An' keep cows an' horses," she said.

"Yes, and pigs and sheep and hens and . . . all the things they have. Ducks and things!"

"I'd love that," she said, delighted.

"We'd go up to Belfast every now and then, and look at the shops and buy things! . . ."

"An' go to the theatre an' have our tea at an eatin'-house?"

"We'd go to an hotel for our tea," he said.

"Oh, no, I'd be near afeard of them places. I wasn't reared up to that sort of place, an' I wouldn't know what to do, an' all the people lookin' at me, an' the waiters watchin' every bite you put in your mouth, 'til you'd near think they'd grudged you your food!"

They made plans over which they laughed, and they

mocked each other, teasing and pretending to anger, and he pulled her hair and kissed her, and she slapped his cheeks and kissed him.

"I'd give the world," she said, "to have my photograph took in a low-neck dress. Abernethy does them grand! . . ." She stopped suddenly and turned her head slightly from him in a listening attitude.

"What's up?" he asked.

"Wheesht!" she replied, and then added, "D'ye hear anything?"

He listened for a moment or two, and then said, "Yes, it sounds like a horse gallopin'. . . ." They listened again, and then she proceeded. "You'd near think it was runnin' away," she said.

The sound of hooves rapidly beating the ground and the noise of quickly-revolving wheels came nearer.

"It *is* runnin' away," she said, getting up from the bank and moving into the middle of the road where she stood looking in the direction from which the sound came.

"Don't stand in the road," Henry shouted to her. "You might get hurt."

She did not move nor did she appear to hear what he was saying. He had a strange sensation of shrinking, a desire not to be there, but he subdued it and went to join her in the middle of the road.

"Here it is," she said, turning to him and pointing to where the road made a sudden swerve.

He looked and saw a galloping horse, head down, coming rapidly towards them. There was a light cart behind it, bumping and swaying so that it seemed likely to be overturned, but there was no driver. It was still some way off, and he had time to think that he ought to stop the frightened animal. If it were allowed to go on, it might kill some one in the village. There would be children playing about in the street. . . .

"I'll stop it," he said to himself, and half-consciously he buttoned his coat.

He tried to remember just what he ought to do. William Henry Matier had told him not to stand right in front of a runaway horse, but to move to the side so that he could run with it. He would do that, and then he would spring at its head and haul the reins so tightly that the bit would slip back into the horse's mouth. . . . He moved from the middle of the road, and was conscious that Sheila had moved, too. His breath was coming quickly, and he felt again that sense of shrinking, that curious desire to run away. He saw a wheel of the cart lurch up as it passed over a stone in the road, and instantly panic seized him. "My God," he thought, "if that had been me! . . . He saw himself flung to the ground by the maddened horse and the wheel passing over his body, crunching his flesh and bones. He had the sensation of blood gushing from his mouth, and for a moment or two he felt as if he had actually suffered the physical shock of being broken beneath the cart wheel. . . .

"I can't!" he muttered, and then he turned and ran swiftly to the side of the road and climbed on to the bank, struggling to break through the thorn hedge at the top of it. His hands were torn and bleeding and once he slipped and fell forward and his face was scratched by the thorns. . . .

7

He had thrown himself over the hedge and had lain there, with his eyes closed, trembling. He was crying now, not with fright, but with remorse. He had failed in courage, and perhaps the horse had dashed into the village and killed a child. . . . He wondered what Sheila would say, and then he started up, his eyes wide with horror, thinking that perhaps Sheila had been killed. He climbed up the bank, and jumped over the low hedge into the roadway. There were some men approaching him, coming from the direction in which the horse had come, but he did not pay any heed to them. He began to run towards the village. A little distance from the place where he and Sheila had stood to watch the oncoming animal, the road made another bend, and when he had reached this bend, he met Sheila.

"You needn't hurry *now*," she said.

He did not hear the emphasis she laid on the word "now." "Are you all right?" he asked anxiously.

She did not answer, but strode on past him.

"Are you all right?" he repeated, following after her.

"It's a bit late to ask that," she said, turning and facing him. "I might 'a' been killed for all you cared, so long as you were safe yourself!"

He shrank back from her, unable to answer, and the men came up, before she could say anything else to him.

"Did ye see the horse runnin' away?" one of them said to her.

"You'll find it down the road a piece," she replied. "It's leg's broke. It tum'led an' fell. Yous'll have to shoot it, I s'pose!"

They supposed they would. The driver had been drinking and in his drunkenness he had thrashed the poor beast. . . . "But he'll never thrash another horse, the same lad," said the man who told them of the circumstances. "He was pitched out on his head, an' he wasn't worth picking up when they lifted him. Killed dead, an' him as drunk as a fiddler! Begod, I wouldn't like to die that way! It 'ud be a quare thing to go afore your Maker an' you stinkin' wi' drink!"

The men went on, leaving Sheila and Henry together. She stood watching the men, oblivious seemingly of Henry's presence, until he put out his hand and touched hers.

"Sheila!" he said.

She snatched her hand away from him. "Lave me alone!" she exclaimed, and moved to the side of the road further from him.

"I meant to try and stop it," he said, "but somehow I couldn't. I . . . I did my best!"

He had followed her and was standing before her, pleading with her, but she would not look at him. He stood for a while, thinking of something to say, and then put out his hand again and touched hers. "Sheila," he said.

She swung round swiftly and struck him in the face with her clenched fist.

"How dare you touch me!" she cried and her eyes were full of fury.

"Sheila!"

"Don't lay a finger on me . . . you . . . you coward you! You were afeard to stop it, an' you run away, cryin' like a wee ba!" He tried to come to her again, but she shrunk away from him. "Don't come a-near me," she shouted at him. "I couldn't thole you near me. I'd be sick! . . ."

She stopped in her speech and walked away from him. He stared after her, unable to think or move. He could feel the smart of her blow tingling in his face, and he put his hand up mechanically to his cheek, and as he did so, he saw that his hand was still trembling. He could see her walking quickly on, her head erect and her hands clenched tightly by her side. He wanted to run after her, but he could not move. He tried to call to her, but his lips would not open. . . .

The light was fading out of the sky, and the night was covering up the hills and fields, but still he stood there, staring up the road along which she had passed out of his sight. People passed him in the dusk and greeted him, but he did not answer, nor was he aware when they turned to look at him. Once, he was conscious of a loud report and a clatter of feet, but he did not think of it or of what it meant. In his mind, smashing like the blows of a hammer, came ceaselessly the sound of Sheila's voice, calling him a coward. . . .

8

It was quite dark when he moved away. His mouth was very dry and his eyes were hot and sore, and his legs dragged as he walked. He was tired and miserable and he had a frightful sense of age. That morning he had wakened to manhood, full of pleasure in the beauty of living and growing things; now, he was like an old man, longing for death but afraid to lose his life. There were stars above him, but no moon, and the tall trunks of the trees stood up like black phantoms before him, moaning and crying in the wind. He could hear the screech-owls hooting in the dark, and the lonely yelp of a dog on a farm.

He began to hurry, walking quickly and then running, afraid to look back, almost afraid to look forward . . . and as he ran, suddenly he fell on something soft. His hands slipped on wetness that smelt. . . .

In the darkness he had fallen over the body of the horse which had been shot while he was standing where Sheila had left him. He gaped at it with distended eyes, and then, with a loud cry, he jumped up and fled home, with fear raging in his heart.

THE EIGHTH CHAPTER

1

He fell asleep, after a long, wakeful night, and did not hear the maid who called him. Mr. Quinn, when he was told of the heaviness of Henry's slumber, said "Let him lie on!" and so it was that he did not rise until noon. He came down heavy-eyed and irritable, and wandered about the garden in which he took no pleasure. Marsh came to him while he was there, full of enthusiasm because more pupils had attended the Language class than he had anticipated.

"That girl, Sheila Morgan, wasn't there!"

"Oh!" said Henry.

"I thought she'd be certain to come. She seemed so anxious to join the class. Perhaps she was prevented. I hope you'll be able to come to-night, Henry! . . ."

Henry turned away impatiently. "I don't think I shall go again," he said in a surly voice.

Marsh stared at him. "Not go again!" he exclaimed.

"No."

"But! . . ."

"Oh, I'm sick of the class. I'm sick of the whole thing. I'm sick of Irish! . . ."

Marsh walked away from him, walked so quickly that Henry knew that he was trying to subdue the sudden rage that rose in him when people spoke slightingly of Irish things, and for a few moments he felt sorry and ready to follow him and apologise for what he had said; but the sorrow passed as quickly as it came.

"It's absurd of him to behave like that," he said to himself, and went on his way about the garden.

114

Presently he saw Marsh approaching him, and he stood still and waited for him.

"I'm sorry, Henry," Marsh said when he had come up to him.

"It was my fault," Henry replied.

"I ought not to have walked off like that . . . but I can't bear to hear any one talking! . . ."

"I know you can't," Henry interrupted. "That's why I ought not to have said what I did!"

But Marsh insisted on bearing the blame. "I ought to have remembered that you're not feeling well," he said, reproaching himself. "I get so interested in Ireland that I forget about people's feelings. That's my chief fault. I know it is. I must try to remember. . . . I suppose you didn't really mean what you said?"

"Yes, I did," Henry replied quickly.

"But why?"

"I don't know. I just don't want to. What's the good of it anyhow? . . ."

Good of it! Henry ought to have known what a passion of patriotism his scorn for the Language would provoke.

"Oh, all right, John!" he said impatiently. "I've heard all that before, and I don't want to hear it again. You can argue as much as you like, but I can't see any sense in wasting time on what's over. And the Irish language is over and done with. Father's quite right!"

Marsh's anger became intensified. "That's the Belfast spirit in you," he exclaimed. "The pounds, shillings and pence mood! I know what you think of the language. You think, what is the commercial value of it? Will it enable a boy to earn thirty shillings a week in an office? Is it as useful as Pitman's Shorthand? That's what you're thinking! . . ."

"No, it's not, but if it were, it would be very sensible!"

"My God, Henry, can't you realise that a nation's language is the sound of a nation's soul? Don't you understand, man, that if we can't speak our own language then our souls are silent, dumb, inarticulate? . . . don't you see what I mean? . . . and all the time we're using English, we're like people who read translations. I don't care whether it is commercially valuable or not. That's not the point. The point is that it's *us*, that it's *our* tongue, *our* language, that it distinguishes us from the English, insists on our difference from them. Do you see what I mean, Henry? We *are* different, aren't we? You realise that, don't you? We *are* different from the English, and nothing will ever make us like them. My God, I'd hate to be like them! . . .''

Henry fled from him, and, scarcely knowing what he was doing, ran across the fields towards Hamilton's farm. As he went up the ''loanie,'' he remembered that Sheila had struck him in the face in her rage at his cowardice, and he stopped and wondered whether he should go on or not. And while he was waiting in the ''loanie,'' she came out of a field, driving a cow before her.

2

She did not speak, though he waited for her to say something. The cow ambled up the ''loanie,'' and Sheila, glancing at him as if she did not recognise him, passed on, following it.

''Sheila!'' he called after her, but she did not answer, nor did she turn round.

''I want to speak to you,'' he said, going after her.

''I don't want to speak to you,'' she replied, without looking at him.

''But you must! . . .'' He thrust himself in front of her, and tried to take hold of her hands, but she eluded him. She lifted the sally rod she had in her hand and threatened him with it. ''I'll lash your face with this if you handle me,'' she said.

"All right," he answered, dropping his hands and waiting for her to beat his face with the slender branch.

She looked at him for a few moments, and then she threw the sally rod into the hedge.

"What do you want?" she asked, and the tone of her voice was quieter.

The cow, finding that it was not being followed, cropped the grass in the hedge and as they stood there, facing each other, they could hear the soft munch-munch as it tore the grass from the ground.

"What do you want?" Sheila said again.

"I want to speak to you! . . ."

"Well, speak away!"

But he did not know what to say to her. He thought that perhaps if he were to explain, she would forgive, but now that the opportunity to explain was open to him, he did not know what to say.

"Are you turned dummy or what?" she asked, and the cruelty in her voice was deliberate.

"Sheila," he began, hesitatingly.

"Well?"

"I'm sorry about last night!"

"What's the good of bein' sorry? . . ."

"I meant to stop it! . . ."

"I daresay," she said, laughing at him.

"I did. I did, indeed. I can't help feeling nervous. I've always been like that. I want to do things . . . I try to do them . . . but something inside me runs away . . . that's what it is, Sheila . . . it isn't me that runs away . . . it's something inside me!"

"Bosh," she said.

"It's true, Sheila. My father could tell you that. I always funk things, not because I want to funk them, but because I can't help it. I'd give the world to be able to stop a horse, like that one last night, but I can't do it. I get paralysed somehow! . . ."

"I never heard of any one like that before," she exclaimed.

"No, I don't suppose you have. If you knew how ashamed I feel of myself, you'd feel sorry for me. I was awake the whole night!"

"Were you?"

"Yes. I kept on thinking you were angry with me and that I was a coward, and I could feel your fist in my face! . . ."

"I'm sorry I hit you, Henry!"

"It doesn't matter," he replied. "It served me right. And then when I did sleep, I kept on dreaming about it. Do you know, Sheila, I fell over the horse last night in the dark . . . they left it lying in the road after they shot it . . . and my hands slithered in the blood! . . ."

"Aw, the poor baste!" she said, and she began to cry. "The poor dumb baste!"

"And I kept on dreaming of that . . . my hands dribbling in blood. . . . och! . . ."

He could not go on because the recollection of his dreams horrified him. They had moved to the side of the "loanie" and he mechanically stopped and plucked a long grass and began to wind it round his fingers.

"I think and think about things," he murmured at last.

She put out her hand and touched his arm. "Poor Henry," she said.

He threw the grass away and seized her hand in his.

"Then you'll forgive me?" he said eagerly.

She nodded her head.

"And you'll still be my sweetheart, won't you, and go for walks with me? . . ."

She withdrew her hand from his. "No, Henry," she said, "you an' me can't go courtin' no more!"

"But why?"

"Because I couldn't marry a man was afeard of things. I'd never be happy with a man like that. I'd fall out with you if you were a collie, I know I would, an' I'd be miserable

if my man hadn't the pluck of any other man. I'm sorry
I bate you last night, but I'd do it again if it happened another time . . . an' there'd be no good in that!''

"But you said you'd marry me! . . .''

"Och, sure, Henry, you know well I couldn't marry you.
You wouldn't be let. I'm a poor girl, an' you're a high-up
lad. Whoever heard tell of the like of us marryin', except mebbe in books. I knew well we'd never marry, but
I liked goin' about with you, an' listenin' to your crack,
an' you kissin' me an' tellin' me the way you loved me.
You've a quare nice English voice on you, an' you know it
well, an' I just liked to hear it . . . but didn't I know
rightly, you'd never marry the like of me!''

"I will, Sheila, I will!''

"Ah, wheesht with you. What good 'ud a man like you
be to a girl like me. I'll have this farm when my Uncle
Matt dies, an' what use 'ud you be on it, will you tell me,
you that runs away cryin' from a frightened horse?''

"You could sell the farm! . . .''

"Sell the farm!'' she exclaimed. "Dear bless us, boy,
what are you sayin' at all? Sell this farm, an' it's been
in our family these generations past! There's been Hamiltons in this house for a hundred an' fifty years an' more.
I wouldn't sell it for the world!''

"But I must have you, Sheila. I must marry you!''

"Why must you?''

"I just must! . . .''

She turned to look at the grazing cow, and then turned
back to him. "That's chile's talk,'' she said. "You must
because you must. Away on home now, an' lave me to do
my work. Sure, you're not left school yet!'' She left
him abruptly, and walked up to the cow, slapping its flanks
and shouting "Kimmup, there! Kimmup!'' and the beast
tossed its head, and ran forward a few paces, and then
sauntered slowly up the "loanie'' towards the byre.

"Good-bye, Henry!'' Sheila called out when she had
gone a little way.

"Will you be at the class to-night!" he shouted after her.

"I will not," she answered. "I'm not goin' to the class no more!"

He watched her as she went on up the "loanie" after the cow, hoping that she would turn again and call to him, but she did not look round. He could hear her calling to the beast, "Gwon now! Gwon out of that now!" and then he saw the cow turn into the yard, and in a moment or two Sheila followed it. He thought that she must turn to look at him then, and he was ready to wave his hand to her, but she did not look round. "Gwon now! Gwon up out of that!" was all that he heard her saying.

3

His father was standing at the front door when he returned home. Mr. Quinn's face was set and grave looking, and he did not smile at his son.

"I want you, Henry," he said, beckoning to him.

"Yes, father?" Henry replied, looking at his father in a questioning fashion. "Is anything wrong?"

Mr. Quinn did not answer. He turned and led the way to the library.

"Sit down," he said, when Henry had entered the room and shut the door.

"What is it, father?"

"Henry, what's between you an' that niece of Matt Hamilton's?"

"Between us!"

"Aye, between you. You were out on the Ballymena road with her last night when I thought you were in bed with a sore head."

All the romance of his love for Sheila Morgan suddenly died out, and he was conscious of nothing but his father's stern look and the stiff set of his lips as he sat there at his writing-table, demanding what there was between Henry and Sheila.

"I'm in love with her, father!" he answered.

"Are you?"

"Yes, father, but she's not in love with me. She's just told me so."

"You've seen her this mornin' again?"

"Yes."

"Well, I'm glad she has more sense nor you seem to have. Damn it, Henry, are you a fool or what? The whole of Ballymartin's talkin' about the pair of you. Do you think that you can walk up the road with a farm-girl, huggin' her an' kissin' her an' doin' God knows what, an' the whole place not know about it?"

"I didn't think of that, father! . . ."

"Didn't think of it! . . . Look here, Henry, Sheila Mor-,ran's a respectable girl, do you hear? an' I'll not have you makin' a fool of her. I know there's some men thinks they have a right to their tenants' daughters, but by God if you harmed a girl on my land, Henry, I'd shoot you with my own hands. Do you hear me?"

Henry looked at his father uncomprehendingly. "Harm her, father!" he said.

"Aye, harm her! What do you think a girl like that, as good-lookin' as her, gets out of goin' up the road with a lad like you that's born above her? A bellyful of pain, that's all!"

"I don't know what you mean, father!"

"Well, it's time you learned. I'll talk to you plumb an' plain, Henry. I'll not let you seduce a girl on my land, do you hear? They can do that sort of thing in England, if they like . . . it's nothin' to me what the English do . . . but by God I'll not have a girl on my land ruined by you or by anybody else!"

Mr. Quinn's voice was more angry than Henry had ever heard it.

"Father," Henry said, "I want to marry Sheila! . . ."

"What?"

Mr. Quinn's fist had been raised as if he were about to bang his desk to emphasise his words, but he was so startled by Henry's speech that he forgot his intention, and he sat there, open-mouthed and wide-eyed, with his fist still suspended in the air, so that Henry almost laughed at his comical look.

"What's that you say?" he said, when he had recovered from his astonishment.

"I want to marry her, but she won't have me!"

Mr. Quinn's anger left him. He leant back in his revolving chair and laughed.

"By God, that's good!" he said. "By God, it is! Marry her! Oh, dear, oh, dear!"

"I don't know why you're laughing, father! . . ."

"An' I thought you up to no good. Oh, ho, ho!" He took out his handkerchief and rubbed his eyes. "Well, thank God, the girl's got more wit nor you have. In the name of God, lad, what would you marry her for?"

"Because I love her, father!"

"My backside to that for an answer!" Mr. Quinn snapped. "You know well you couldn't marry her, a girl like that!"

"I don't know it at all! . . ."

"Well, I'll tell you why then. Because you're a gentleman an' she isn't a lady, that's why. There's hundreds of years of breedin' in you, Henry, an' there's no breedin' at all in her, nothin' but good nature an' good looks! . . ."

"The Hamiltons have lived at their farm for more than a hundred and fifty years, father!"

"So they have, an' decent, good stock they are, but that doesn't put them on our level. Listen, Henry, the one thing that's most important in this world is blood an' breedin'. There's people goes about the world sayin' everybody's as good as everybody else, but you've only got to see people when there's bother on to find out who's good an' who isn't. It's at times like that that blood an' breedin' come out! . . .''

It was then that Henry told his father of his cowardice when the horse ran away. He told the whole story, and insisted on Sheila's scorn for him. Mr. Quinn did not speak while the story was being told. He sat at the desk with his chin buried in his fingers, listening patiently. Once or twice he looked up when Henry hesitated in his recital, and once he seemed as if he were about to put out his hand to his son, but he did not do so. He did not speak or move until the story was ended.

"I'm glad you told me, Henry," he said quietly when Henry had finished. "I'm sorry I thought you were meanin' the girl an injury. I beg your pardon for that, Henry. The girl's a decent girl, a well-meant girl . . . a well-meant girl! . . . I wish to God, you were at Trinity, my son! Come on, now, an' have somethin' to ate. Begod, I'm hungry. I could ate a horse. I could ate two horses! . . .'' He put his arm in Henry's and they left the library together. "You'll get over it, my son, you'll get over it. It does a lad good to break his heart now an' again. Teaches him the way the world works! Opens his mind for him, an' lets him get a notion of the feel of things! . . .''

They were just outside the dining-room when he said that. Mr. Quinn turned and looked at Henry for a second or two, and it seemed to Henry that he was about to say something intimate to him, but he did not do so: he turned away quickly and opened the door.

"I suppose John Marsh is eatin' all the food," he said with extraordinary heartiness. "Are you eatin' all the food, John Marsh? I'll wring your damned neck if you are! . . .''

4

That evening, after dinner, Mr. Quinn and John Marsh were sitting together. Henry had gone out of the room for a while, leaving Mr. Quinn to smoke a cigar while John Marsh corrected some exercises by the students of the Language class.

"Marsh!" Mr. Quinn said suddenly, after a long silence.

Marsh looked up quickly. "Yes, Mr. Quinn!" he replied.

"Henry's in love! . . ."

"Is he?"

"Yes. With that girl, Sheila Morgan, Matt Hamilton's niece!"

Marsh put his exercises aside. "Dear me!" he exclaimed.

There did not appear to be anything else to say.

"So I'm goin' to send him away," Mr. Quinn went on.

"Away?"

"Yes. I don't quite know where I shall send him. It's too soon yet to send him up to Trinity. I've a notion of sendin' you an' him on a walkin' tour in Connacht. The pair of you can talk that damned language 'til you're sick of it with the people that understands it!"

Marsh was delighted. He thought that Mr. Quinn's proposal was excellent, and he was certain that it would be very good for Henry to come into contact with people to whom the language was native.

"Wheesht a minute, Marsh!" Mr. Quinn interrupted. "I want to talk to you about Henry. It's a big thing for a lad of his age to fall in love!"

"I suppose it is."

"There's no supposin' about it. It is! He's just at the age when women begin to matter to a man, an' I don't want him to go an' get into any bother over the head of them!"

"Bother?"

"Aye. Do you never think about women, John Marsh?"

"Oh, yes. Sometimes. One can't help it now and then! . . .

"No, begod, one can't!" Mr. Quinn exclaimed. "Do you know this, John Marsh, I never can make out whether God did a good day's work the day He made women! They're the most unsettlin' things in the world. You'd think to look at me, I was a fairly quiet sort of a steady man, wouldn't you? Well, I'm not. There's whiles when a woman makes my head buzz . . . just the look of her, an' the way she turns her head or moves her legs. I'm a hefty fellow, John Marsh, for all I'm the age I am, an' I know what it is to feel damn near silly with desire. But all the same, I can keep control of myself, an' I've never wronged a woman in my life. That's a big thing for any man to be able to say, an' there's few that can say it, but I tell you it's been a hell of a fight! . . ."

He lay back in the chair and puffed smoke above his head for a while. "A hell of a fight," he murmured, and then did not speak for a while.

"Yes?" said John Marsh.

"I've been down the lanes of a summer night, an' seen young girls from the farms about, with fine long hair hangin' down their backs, an' them smilin' an' lovely . . . an' begod, I've had to hurry past them, hurry hard, damn near run! . . . Mind you, they were good girls, John Marsh! I don't want you to think they were out lookin' for men. They weren't. But they were young, an' they were just learnin' things, an' I daresay I could have had them if I'd tried . . . an' I don't think there's any real harm in men an' women goin' together . . . but we've settled, all of us, that, real or no real, there is *some* sort of harm in it, an' we've agreed to condemn that sort of thing, an' so I submit to the law. Do you follow me?"

"No, not quite. Those sort of things don't arise for me. I'm a Catholic and I obey the Church's laws! . . ."

"I know you do. But I'm a man, not a Catholic! . . .

Now, don't lose your temper. I couldn't help lettin' that slip out. . . . What I mean is this. There's a lot of waywardness in all of us, that's pleasant enough if it's checked when it gets near the limit of things, but there has to be a check!"

"Yes?" Marsh said. "And in my case the check is the Church, the expression on earth of God's will! . . ."

"Well, in my case it isn't. In my case it's my sense of responsibility as a gentleman. We've got ourselves into crowds that must be controlled somehow, and there isn't much room for wayward people in a crowd. That's why geniuses get such a rotten time. Now, my notion of a gentleman is a man who controls the crowd by controllin' himself. D'you follow me? He knows that the crowd'll bust up an' become a dirty riot if it's let out of control, an' he knows that he can influence it best an' keep the whip hand of it, if it knows that he isn't doin' anything that he tells it not to do. D'you see?"

"Yes," Marsh said. "That's the Catholic religion! . . ."

"I know as well as I'm livin'," Mr. Quinn went on, "that I have enough power over myself to know when to stop an' when to go on. That's been bred in me. That's why I'm a gentleman. But I know that if I let myself do things that I can control, I'll be givin' an example to hundreds of other people who aren't gentlemen an' can't control themselves . . . don't know when to stop an' when to go on . . . an' so I don't do them. An' that's a gentleman's job, John Marsh, an' when gentlemen stop that, then begod it's good-bye to a decent community. That's why England's goin' to blazes . . . because her gentlemen have forgotten the first job of the gentleman: to keep himself in strict control, to be reticent, to conceal his feelings!"

But John Marsh would not agree with him. "England is going to blazes," he said, "because England has lost her religion. If England were Catholic, England would be noble again! . . ."

"Just like France and Spain and Italy," Mr. Quinn

replied. "Bosh, John Marsh, bosh! I tell you, the test of a nation is this question of gentlemen! . . ."

"The test of a nation is its belief in God . . . its church," said John Marsh.

"Well, Ireland believes in God, doesn't it? The Catholic Church is fairly strong here, isn't it? An' what sort of a Church is it? A gentleman's church or a peasant's church? Look at the priests, John Marsh, look at them! My God, *what* bounders! Little greedy, grubbin' blighters, livin' for their Easter offerin's, an' doin' damn little for their money. What do you think takes them into the church? Love of God? Love of man? No, bedam if it is. Conceit an' snobbery an' the desire for a soft job takes about nine out of ten of them. . . . Well, well, I'm runnin' away from myself. What I want to say is this: the Catholic church'll never be worth a damn in Ireland or anywhere else, 'til its priests are gentlemen. No church is worth a damn unless its priests are gentlemen!"

"But what do you mean by gentlemen, Mr. Quinn?"

"I mean men who are keepin' a tight hold on themselves. Mortifyin' their flesh . . . all that sort of stuff . . . so that they won't give the mob an excuse for breakin' loose!"

Marsh wondered why Mr. Quinn was talking in this strain and tried to draw him back to the subject of Henry's love of Sheila.

"I'm comin' to that," said Mr. Quinn, pointing his cigar at him. "Listen, John, there were two men that might have done big things in Irelan' and Englan'—Parnell an' Lord Randolph Churchill, an' they didn't because they weren't gentlemen. They couldn't control themselves. There isn't a house in Ulster that hasn't got the photographs of those two men in some album. . . ."

"Parnell?" Marsh exclaimed.

"Aye, Parnell. Him an' Randy Churchill side by side in the one album! Lord bless me, John Marsh, the Ulster people took great pride in Parnell, even the bitterest Orangeman among them, because he was a man, an' not a gas-bag like Dan O'Connell. Of course, he was a Protestant! . . . But he couldn't keep from nuzzlin' over a woman . . . an' up went everything. An' Randy Churchill . . . I mind him well, a flushed-lookin' man. . . . I heard him talkin' in Belfast one time . . . he bust up everything because he would not control himself. If he'd been a gentleman . . . but he wasn't . . . the Churchills never were. . . . Nor was Parnell. Well, now, I don't want Henry to go to bits like that. Henry's got power of some sort, John . . . I don't know what sort . . . but there's power in him . . . and I want it to come out right. He's the sort that'll go soft on women if he's not careful. He'd be off after every young, nice-lookin' girl he meets if he were let . . . an' God knows what the end of that would be. There's this girl, Sheila Morgan . . . you've seen her? . . .''

Marsh nodded his head, and said, "She comes to the Language class.''

"Well, you know the sort she is: fine, healthy, good-lookin', lusty girl. That sort stirs the blood in a lad like Henry. I want him to get into the state in which he can look at her an' lave her alone! Do you follow me?''

"Yes.''

"He's not in that state now. He's soft, oh, he's damned soft. Look here, John Marsh, do you know what I think about young fellows? I think they're the finest things in the world. Youth, I mean. An' I figure it out this way, that Youth has the right to three things: love an' work an' fun; an' it ought to have them about equally. The only use of old people like me is to see that the young 'uns don't get the proportions all wrong, too much love an' not enough work, or the other way round. Henry's very likely to get them all wrong, an' I want to see that he doesn't. Now, you understand me, don't you? I'm a long-winded man, an' it's hard to make out what I'm drivin' at, but that can't be helped. Everybody has a nature, an' I have mine, an' bedam to it!''

"What do you want me to do?" Marsh asked, putting his exercises together.

"I want you to try an' put some big wish into his heart," Mr. Quinn replied. "Try an' make him as eager about Irelan' as you are. I want him to spend himself for something that's bigger than he is, instead of spendin' himself on something that's smaller than he is."

"But why not do that yourself, Mr. Quinn?"

Mr. Quinn got up from his chair and walked about the room. "It's very hard for a man to talk to his son in the way that a stranger can," he said. "An' besides I . . . I love Henry, John Marsh, an' my love for him upsets my balance!"

"Can't you control that, Mr. Quinn?" Marsh asked.

"Control it! Begod, John Marsh, if you were a father you wouldn't ask such a damn silly question. Here, have a cigar! Henry's comin' back!"

When Henry entered the room, his father was lying back in his chair, puffing smoke into the air, while John Marsh was cutting the end of his cigar.

"The post's come in," he said.

"Anything for me?" his father asked.

"No. There was only one letter. For me. It's from Ninian Graham!"

"Nice chap, Ninian Graham," Mr. Quinn murmured.

"He wants me to go over to Boveyhayne for a while."

"Does he?"

"Yes. Gilbert Farlow's staying with them. I should like to go."

"Well, we'll see about it in the morning," said Mr. Quinn. "I was thinking of sending you on a walking tour with John here. To Connacht!"

"You could talk to the people in Irish, Henry," John added.

Henry twirled Ninian's letter in his fingers. "I'd like to go to Boveyhayne," he said. "I want to see Ninian and Gilbert again! . . ."

"But the language, Henry! . . ."

"I hate the damned language!" Henry exclaimed passionately. "I'm sick of Ireland. I'm sick of! . . ."

Mr. Quinn got up and put his hand on Henry's shoulder.

"All right, Henry," he said. "You can go to Boveyhayne!"

5

Up in his bedroom, Henry re-read Ninian's letter, and then he replied to it. Ninian wrote:

Blighter:

Gilbert's here. He's been here for a week, and he says you ought to be here, too. So do I. Can't you come to Boveyhayne for a fortnight anyhow? If you can stay longer, do. Gilbert says it's awful to think that you're going to that hole in Dublin where there isn't even a Boat Race, and the least you can do is to come and have a good time here. I can't think why Irish people want to be Irish. It seems so damn silly. Gilbert's writing a play. He has done about a page and a half of it, and it's most awful bilge. He keeps on reading it out to me. He read some of it to me last night when I was brushing my teeth which is a damn dangerous thing to do, and I had to clout his head severely for him. He is a chap. He got poor Mary into a row on Sunday. We took him to church with us, and when the Vicar was reading the first lesson, all about King Solomon swanking before the Queen of Sheba and showing off his gold plate, Gilbert turned to Mary and said out loud, "Ostentatious chap, Solomon! Anybody could see he was a Jew!" and Mary burst out laughing. The Vicar was frightfully sick about it, and jawed Gilbert after the service, and the mater told Mary the truth about herself. I must say it was rather funny. I very nearly laughed myself. Do be a decent chap and come over soon. You'll just be in time for the mackerel fishing. Gilbert

*and Mary and I went out with Jim Rattenbury yesterday
and caught dozens.*

Your affectionate friend,

Ninian Graham.

Henry's reply was:

Dear Ninian:
 *Thanks awfully. I'll come as soon as I can get away.
I spoke to my father to-night, and he says I can go to
Boveyhayne. I'll send a telegram to you, telling you when
to expect me. I'm looking forward to reading Gilbert's
play. I hope he'll have more of it written by the time I
get to Boveyhayne. A page and a half isn't much, is it?
and I don't wonder you get sick of hearing it over and
over. I shall have to write something, too, but I don't
know what to write about. We can talk of that when we
meet. It is awfully kind of Mrs. Graham to have me again.
Please thank her for me, and give my love to Mary and
Gilbert, and tell him not to be an old ass, yapping like that
in church. No wonder the vicar was sick.*

Your affectionate friend,

Henry Quinn.

THE NINTH CHAPTER

1

THREE days later, Henry left Ballymartin and travelled to Belfast in the company of John Marsh. In Belfast they were to separate: Marsh was to return to Dublin and Henry was to cross by the night boat to Liverpool, and proceed from there to London, and then on from Waterloo to Boveyhayne. Marsh, a little sad because the Bally-martin classes must now collapse, but greatly glad to return to the middle of Irish activities in Dublin, had turned over in his mind what Mr. Quinn had said about Henry's future, and he was wondering exactly what he should say to Henry. They had several hours to spend in Belfast, and Marsh proposed that they should visit the shipyards and, if they had time, inspect a linen mill; and Henry, who had always felt great pride when he saw the stocks and gantries of the shipyards and reflected that out of the multitudinous activities of Ulster men the greatest ships in the world were created, eagerly assented to Marsh's proposal. Mr. Quinn had given them a letter of introduction to a member of the great firm of Harland and Wolff, and Mr. Arthurs, because of his friendship for Mr. Quinn, conducted them through the yard himself.

They stayed so long in the shipyard that there was no time left for the visit to the linen mill, and so, when they had had tea, they set off to the Great Northern Railway station where Marsh was to catch his train to Dublin.

Mr. Arthurs' immense energy and his devotion to his work and his extraordinary pride not only in the shipyard but in the men who worked in it had made a deep impression on Marsh and Henry. He seemed to know the most minute details of the vast complication of functions that operated throughout the works. While they were passing through one of the shops, a horn had blown, and instantly a great crowd of men and lads had poured out of the yard on their way to their dinner, and Mr. Arthurs, standing aside to watch them, and greeting here one and there another, turned to Marsh and said, "Those are my pals!" Thousands of men, grimy from their work, each of them possessed of some peculiar skill or great strength, thousands of them, "pals" of this one man whose active brain conceived ships of great magnitude and endurance! Mr. Arthurs had passed through the shipyard from apprenticeship to directorship: he had worked in this shop and in that, just as the men worked, and had learned more about shipbuilding than it seemed possible for any man to learn. "He knows how many rivets there are in the *Oceanic*," one of the foremen in the yard said to Marsh when they were being shown round. "He's the great boy for buildin' boats!"

Marsh, until then, had never met a man like Mr. Arthurs. His life had been passed in Dublin, among people who thought and talked and speculated, but seldom did; and he had been habituated to scoffing talk at Belfast men . . . "money-grubbers" . . . mitigated, now and then, by a grudging tribute to their grit and great energy and resource. Mr. Arthurs had none of the money-grubbing spirit in him; his devotion to his work of shipbuilding was as pure as the devotion of a Samurai to the honour of Japan; and Marsh, who was instantly sensitive to the presence of a noble man, felt strongly drawn to him.

"I wish we could get him on our side, Henry!" he said, as they sat in the station, waiting for the train to draw up to the platform. "I'd give all the lawyers we've got for that one man!"

"Father thinks Tom Arthurs is the greatest shipbuilder that's ever lived," Henry answered.

"He might be the greatest Irishman that's ever lived," Marsh rejoined, "if he'd only give a quarter of the devotion to Ireland that he gives to ships."

"I suppose he thinks he's giving all his devotion to Ireland now . . . and he is really. Isn't he, John? His firm is famous all over the world, and he's one of the men that have made it famous. It must be very fine for him to think that he's doing big things for his country!"

Marsh nodded his head. "We're rather foolish about Belfast in Dublin," he said. "After all, real work is done here, isn't it? And the chief industry of Dublin . . . what is it? Absolutely unproductive! Porter! Barrels and barrels of it, floating down the Liffey and nothing, *nothing real*, floating back! I like that man Arthurs. I wish to heaven we had him on our side!"

"He's a Unionist," Henry replied.

It occurred to Marsh, in the middle of his reflections on Tom Arthurs, that he should ask Henry what he proposed to do for Ireland.

"I'd like to do work as big and fine as Arthurs does," he said. "Wouldn't you, Henry?"

"Yes."

"What *do* you propose to do, Henry?"

"I don't know. I haven't thought definitely about that sort of thing yet. I've just imagined I'd like to do *something*. I'm afraid I can't build ships! . . ."

"There are other things besides ships, Henry!"

"I know that. John, I'm going to say something that'll make you angry, but I can't help that. When Tom Arthurs was showing us over the Island, I couldn't help thinking that all that Gaelic movement was a frightful waste of time!" Marsh made a gesture, but Henry would not let him speak. "No, don't interrupt me, John," he said. "I must say what I feel. Look at the Language class at Ballymartin. What's been the good of all the work you put into it?"

"We've given them a knowledge of a national separateness, haven't we?"

"Have we? They were keener on the dances, John. I don't believe we've done anything of the sort, and if we had, I think it would be a pity!"

"A pity! A pity to make the Irish people realise that they're Irish and different from the English!"

"Oh, you won't agree, I know, John, but I think Tom Arthurs is doing better work for Ireland than you are," Henry retorted.

"He's doing good work, very good work, but not better work than I am. He's establishing an Irish industry, but I'm helping to establish an Irish nation, an Irish soul! . . ."

"That's what you want to do, but I wonder whether it's what you are doing," said Henry.

They were silent for a while, and before they spoke again, the train backed into the station, and they passed through the barriers so that Marsh could secure his seat.

"Well, what do *you* propose to do for Ireland?" Marsh asked again, when he had entered his carriage.

"The best I can, I suppose. I don't know yet! . . ."

Marsh turned quickly to Henry and put his hand on his shoulder. "Henry," he said, "I hope you don't mind . . . I know about Sheila Morgan and you! . . ."

"You know? . . ."

"Yes. I'm sorry about that. I don't think you should let it upset you!"

Henry did not reply for a few moments, but sat still staring in front of him. In a sub-conscious way, he was wondering why it was that the carriages were not cleaner. . . .

"I'm frightfully miserable, John," he said at last.

"But why, Henry?"

"Oh, because of everything. I don't know. I'm a fool, I suppose!"

"You're not going to pieces just because you've fallen

in love with a girl and it's turned out wrong? My dear
Henry, that's a poor sort of a spirit!''

"I know it is, but I'm a sloppy fellow! . . .''

"This affair with Sheila Morgan is all the more reason
why you should think of something big to do. I wish you
were coming to Dublin with me now. Dublin's very beautiful in the summer, and we could go up into the mountains
and talk about things.''

"Oh, well, we shall meet in Dublin fairly soon,'' Henry
replied, smiling at Marsh. It had been settled that he was
to enter Trinity a little earlier than his father had previously planned.

"Yes, that's true!''

The hour at which the train was due to depart came,
and Henry got out of the carriage and stood on the platform while Marsh, his head thrust through the window,
talked to him.

"You might write to me,'' he said. "We ought not to
drift away from each other, Henry! . . .''

"We won't do that. We'll see each other in Dublin.''

"Yes, of course. You must meet Galway when you come
back. He's a schoolmaster and a barrister and a poet
and heaven knows what not. He's a splendid fellow. Perhaps he'll persuade you to take more interest in Irish
things!''

"Perhaps!''

The guard blew his whistle, and the train began to move
out of the station.

"Don't get too English, Henry!'' Marsh shouted, waving his hand in farewell.

Henry smiled at him, but did not answer.

"Good-bye!'' Marsh called to him.

"Good-bye!'' Henry answered.

The train swung round a bend and disappeared on its
way south, and Henry, strangely desolate, turned and
walked away from the station.

2

In the excitement of leaving Ballymartin and sight-seeing in the shipyard, he had almost forgotten Sheila Morgan, but now, his mind stimulated by his talk with Marsh and his spirit depressed by his loneliness, his thoughts returned to her, and it seemed to him that he detested her. She had insulted him, struck him, humiliated and shamed him. When he remembered that he had told her of his love for her and had asked her to marry him, and had been told in reply that she wanted a man, not a coward, he felt that he could not bear to return to Ireland again. His mood was mingled misery and gladness. At Boveyhayne, thank heaven, he would be free of Sheila and probably he would never think of her again. Gilbert and Ninian would fill his mind, and of course there would be Mrs. Graham and Mary. Mary! It was strange that he should have let Mary slip out of his thoughts and let Sheila slip into them. He had actually proposed to Mary and she had accepted him, and then he had left her and forgotten her because of Sheila. He remembered that he had not replied to the letter she had written to him before John Marsh came to Ballymartin. He had intended to write, but somehow he had not done so . . . and then Sheila came, and it was impossible to write to her. He wondered what he should say to her when they met. Would she come to Whitcombe station to meet him? What was he to say to her? . . .

He had treated her shabbily. Of course, she was only a kid, as Ninian himself would say, but then he had made love to her, and anyhow she would be less of a kid now than she was when he last saw her. . . . He got tired of walking about the streets, and he made his way to the quays and passed across the gangway on to the deck of the steamer. A cool air was blowing up the Lagan from the Lough, and when he leaned over the side of the ship he could see the dark skeleton shape of the shipyard. His thoughts were extraordinarily confused, rambling about his father and Sheila Morgan and John Marsh and Mary Graham and Tom Arthurs and Ireland and ships and England and Gilbert Farlow and Ninian and Roger. . . .

"I ought never to have thought of any one but Mary," he said to himself at last. "I *really* love her. I was only . . . only passing the time with Sheila!"

"Well, thank God I'll soon be in Devonshire," he went on, "and out of all this. If only my Trinity time were over, and I were settled in London with Gilbert and the others, I'd be happy again!" He thought of John Marsh, and as he leant over the side of the boat, looking down on the dark water flowing beneath him, he seemed to see Marsh's eager face, framed in the window of the railway carriage. He almost heard Marsh saying again, "Well, what do *you* propose to do for Ireland? . . ."

"Oh, damn Ireland," he said out loud.

He walked away from the place where he had imagined he had seen Marsh's face peering at him out of the water, and as he walked along the deck, he could hear the noise of hammering in the shipyard made by the men on the night-shift. Tom Arthurs's brain was still working, though Tom Arthurs was now at home.

"That's real work," Henry murmured to himself, "and a lot better than gabbling about Ireland's soul as if it were the only soul in the world! Poor old John! I disappoint him horribly. . . ." He was standing in the bows of the boat, looking towards the Lough. "I wonder," he said to himself, "whether Mary'll be at Whitcombe station!"

3

The peculiar sense of isolation which overwhelms an Irishman when he is in England, fell upon Henry the moment he climbed into the carriage at Lime Street station. None of the passengers in his compartment spoke to each other, whereas in Ireland, every member of the company would have been talking like familiars in a few minutes. About an hour after the train had left Liverpool, some one leant across to the passenger facing him and asked for a match, and a box of matches was passed to him without a word from the man who owned them. "Thanks!" said the passenger who had borrowed the box, as he returned it. No more was said by any one for half an hour, and then the man opposite to Henry stretched himself and said, "We're getting along!" and turned and laid his head against the window and went to sleep.

"We *are* different!" Henry thought to himself. "We're certainly different . . . only I wonder does the difference matter much!"

He tried to make conversation with his neighbour, but was unsuccessful, for his neighbour replied only in monosyllables, and sometimes did not even articulate at all, contenting himself with a grunt. . . .

"Well, why should he talk to me?" Henry thought to himself. "He isn't interested in me or my opinions, and perhaps he wants to read or think! . . ."

Marsh would have denied that the man wanted to think. He would have denied that the man had the capacity to think at all. Henry remembered how Marsh had generalised about the English. "They live on their instincts," he had said. "They never live on their minds!" and he had quoted from an article in an English newspaper in which the writer had lamented over the decline and fall of intellect among his countrymen. The writer declared that no one would pay to see a play that made a greater demand upon the mind than is made in a musical comedy, and that even this slight demand was proving to be more than many people could bear: the picture palace was destroying even the musical comedy.

"But are we any better than that?" Henry had asked innocently, and Marsh, indignant, had declared that the Irish were immeasurably better than *that*.

"But are we?" Henry asked himself as the train swiftly moved towards London.

And through his mind there raced a long procession of questions for which he could not find answers. His mind was an active, searching mind, but it was immature, and there were great gaps in it that could only be filled after a long time and much experience. He had not the knowledge which would enable him to combat the opinions of Marsh, but some instinct in him caused him to believe that Marsh's views of England and Ireland were largely prejudiced views. "I don't feel any less friendly to Gilbert and Ninian and Roger than I do to John Marsh or any other Irishman, and I don't feel that John understands me better than they do!" That was the pivot on which all his opinions turned. He could only argue from his experience, and his experience was that this fundamental antagonism between the Irish and the English, on which John Marsh insisted, did not exist. When Marsh declared passionately that he did not wish to see Ireland made into a place like Lancashire, he was only stating something that many Englishmen said with equal passion about the unindustrialised parts of England. Gilbert Farlow denounced mill-owners with greater fury than Mr. Quinn denounced them. . . . It seemed to Henry that he could name an English equivalent for every Irish friend he had.

"There are differences, of course," he said to himself, remembering the silent company of passengers who shared his compartment, "but they don't matter very much!"

"I wish," he went on, "John Marsh weren't so bitter against the English. Lots of them would like him if he'd only let them!"

He looked out of the window at the wide fields and herds of cattle and comfortable farmhouses, built by men whose lives were more or less secure, and . . . "Of course!" he exclaimed in his mind. "That's the secret of the whole thing! When our people have had security for life as long as these people have had it, their houses will be as good as these are, and their farms as rich and clean and comfortable!''

One had only to remember the history of Ireland to realise that many of the differences between the English and the Irish were no more than the differences between the hunter and the hunted, the persecutor and the persecuted. How could the Irish help having a lower standard of life than the English when their lives had been so disrupted and disturbed that it was difficult for them to have a standard of life at all? Now, when the disturbance was over and security of life had been obtained (after what misery and bitterness and cruel lack of common comprehension!) the Irish would soon set up a level of life that might ultimately be higher than that of the English.

"Of course," said Henry, remembering something that his father had said, "there'll be a Greedy Interval!"

The Greedy Interval, the first period of prosperity in Ireland when the peasants, coming suddenly from insecurity and poverty to safety and well-being, would claw at money like hungry beasts clawing at food, had been the subject of many arguments between Mr. Quinn and John Marsh, Mr. Quinn maintaining that greed was the principal characteristic of a peasant nation, inherent in it, inseparable from it.

"Look at the French," he had said on one occasion. "By God, they buried their food in their back-gardens rather than let their hungry soldiers have it in the Franco-German War! Would an aristocrat have done that, John Marsh? They saw their own countrymen who had been fighting for them, starving, and they let them starve! . . .''

It was the same everywhere. "I never pass a patch of allotments," he said, "without thinkin' that their mean, ugly, *little* look is just like a peasant's mind, an' begod I'm glad when I'm past them an' can see wide lands again!" Peasants were greedy, narrow, unimaginative, lacking in public spirit. In France, in Belgium, in Holland and Russia, in all of which countries Mr. Quinn had travelled much, there was a peasant spirit powerfully manifested, and almost invariably that manifestation was shown in a mean manner.

"That's what your wonderful Land Laws are going to do for Ireland!" Mr. Quinn had exclaimed scornfully. "*We're* to be thrown out of our land, an' louts like Tom McCrum are to be put in our place! . . ."

Henry had sympathised with his father then, but he felt that the best of the argument was with John Marsh who had replied that the Irish landlords would never have been dispossessed of their land, if they had been worthy of it. "If they'd thought as much about their responsibilities as they thought about their rights, they'd still have their rights!" he said.

"I suppose that's so," Henry said to himself, picking up a paper that he had bought in Liverpool and beginning to read. "I must talk to Gilbert about it!"

4

Ninian and Gilbert met him at Whitcombe station. As he stood on the little platform of the carriage, he could see that Mary was not with them, and he felt disappointed. She might have come, too! . . .

"Here he is," he heard Gilbert shout to Ninian as the train drew up. "Hilloa, Quinny!"

"Hilloa, Gilbert!"

"Hop out quickly, will you!"

He hopped out as quickly as he could and said "Hilloa!" to Ninian, who said "Hilloa!" and slapped his back and called him an old rotter.

"Widger'll take your luggage," Gilbert said, taking control of their movements as he always did. "Hang on to this, Widger," he added, taking a handbag from Henry and throwing it into Widger's arms. "Show him the rest of your stuff, Quinny, and let's hook off. We're going to walk to Boveyhayne. You'll need a stretch after sitting all that time, and Ninian's getting disgustingly obese, so we make him run up and down the road over the cliff three times so's to thin him down! ..."

"Funny ass!" said Ninian.

"Mrs. Graham wanted Mary to come with us, but we wouldn't let her. We're tired of females, Ninian and I, and Mary's very femaley at present. She's started to read poetry! ..."

"Out loud!" Ninian growled. "I'm sick of people who read out loud to me. When Mary's not spouting stuff about 'love' and 'dove' and 'heaven above' and that sort of rot, Gilbert's reading his damn play to me!"

"I'll read it to you, Quinny!" Gilbert said, linking his arm in Henry's.

They had left the station, and were now walking along the unfinished road above the shingle. There was a heat haze hanging over the smooth blue sea, so that sky and water merged into each other imperceptibly. In front of them, they could see the white cliffs of Boveyhayne shining in the descending sun. There were great stalks of charlock, standing out of the grass on the face of the cliffs, giving them a golden head.

"If Marley's on Whitcombe beach, we'll row over to Boveyhayne," said Ninian. "You'd like to get on to the sea, wouldn't you, Quinny?"

Henry nodded his head.

"No," said Gilbert, "we won't. We'll sit here for a while, and I'll read my play to Quinny. I carry it about with me, Quinny, so that I can read it to Ninian whenever his spirits are low!"

"I never saw such a chap!" Ninian mumbled.

"This great, hairy, beefy fellow," Gilbert went on, seizing hold of Ninian's arm with his disengaged hand, "does not love literature! ..."

Ninian broke free from Gilbert's grip. "Marley *is* on the beach," he said, and ran ahead to engage the boat.

"Well, Quinny!" said Gilbert, when Ninian had gone.

" Well, Gilbert!" Henry replied.

"How's Ireland? Still making an ass of itself?"

Henry made no answer to Gilbert's question because he knew that an answer was not expected. Had any one else spoken in that fashion to him, any other Englishman, he would probably have angered instantly, but Gilbert was different from all other people in Henry's eyes, and was privileged to say whatever he pleased.

"Gilbert," he said, "I want to have a long jaw with you about something! . . ."

The English way of speaking came naturally to him, and he said "a long jaw about something" as easily as if he had never been outside an English public school.

"What?" Gilbert said.

"Oh, everything. Ireland and things!"

"All right, my son!"

"You see! . . ."

"Wait though," said Gilbert, "until we catch up with Ninian. He ought to hear it, too. He has a wise old noddle, Ninian, although he's such a fat 'un. . . . My God, Quinny, isn't he getting big? If he piles up any more muscle, he'll have to go to Trinity Hall and join the beefy brutes and get drunk and all that kind of manly thing!" They came up with Ninian as he spoke. "Won't you, Ninian?"

"Won't I what?" Ninian replied.

"Have to go to Trinity Hall if you go on being a beefy Briton. Hilloa, Marley!"

"Good-evenin', sir!" said old Marley.

They got into the boat, and Ninian rowed them round the white cliff to Boveyhayne beach, where they left the boat and walked up the village street to the lane that led to Boveyhayne Manor.

"Henry wants to talk about the world, Ninian!" said Gilbert as they left the beach. "We'd better have a good old gabble after dinner to-night, hadn't we?"

"It doesn't matter what I say," said Ninian, "you'll

gabble anyhow. Anything to keep him from reading his blooming play to me!'' he added, turning to Henry.

5

He had a sense of disappointment when he met Mary. In his reaction from Sheila Morgan, he had imagined Mary coming to greet him with something of the alert youthfulness with which she had met him when he first visited Boveyhayne, but when she came into the hall, a book in her hand, he felt that there was some stiffness in her manner, a self-consciousness which had not been there before.

"How do you do?" she said, offering her hand to him like any well-bred girl.

She did not call him "Quinny" or show in her manner or speech that he was particularly welcome to her.

"I suppose," he thought to himself, "she's cross because I didn't answer her letter!"

He resolved that he would bring her back to her old friendliness. . . .

"I expect you're tired," she said. "We'll have tea in a minute or two. Mother's lying down. She's not very well!"

She would have said as much to a casual acquaintance, Henry thought.

"Not well!" he heard Ninian saying. "What's the matter with her?"

"She's tired. I think she's got a headache. There was a letter from Uncle Peter!" Mary answered, and her tone indicated that the letter from Uncle Peter accounted for everything.

"Oh!" said Ninian, scowling and turning away.

They went into the drawing-room to tea, and Henry had a sense of intruding on family affairs, mingled with his disappointment because Mary was not as he had expected her to be. It might be, of course, that the letter from Uncle Peter had affected Mary almost as much as it seemed to have affected Mrs. Graham, and that presently she would be as natural as she had been that other time . . . but then he remembered that Gilbert had said that she was "being very femaley at present." She poured out tea for them as if she were a new governess, and she reproved Ninian once for saying "Damn!" when he dropped his bread and butter. . . .

"Mary's turned pi!" said Ninian.

She frowned at him and told him not to be silly.

"She calls the Communion Service the Eucharist, and crosses herself and flops and bows! . . ."

"You're very absurd, Ninian!" she said.

Almost unconsciously, he began to compare her to Sheila Morgan. He remembered the free, natural ways of Sheila, and liked them better than these new, mannered ways of Mary. How could any one prefer this stiltedness to that ease, this self-consciousness to that state of being unaware of self? . . . In Belfast, when he had left John Marsh, and in his loneliness had thought of the way Sheila had humiliated him, he had had a sharp sense of revulsion from her, a loathing for her, a desire never to see her again; but now, sitting here looking at Mary and oppressed by her youngladyishness, his longing for Sheila came back to him with greater strength, and he resolved that he would write to her that night and beg her to forgive him for his cowardice and let him be her sweetheart again. . . .

"Will you have some more tea?" Mary was saying to him, and he started at the sound of her voice.

"Oh, thanks!" he said, passing his cup to her.

"Thinking, Quinny?" Gilbert exclaimed, reaching for a bun.

"Eh? Oh, yes! I was thinking!" he answered. "What time does the evening post go out?" he said to Ninian.

"Six-twenty-five," Ninian answered.

"Thanks. I just want to write to Ireland! . . ."

"It'll get there just as soon if you post it to-morrow," said Gilbert.

Mary left them. "I'm going up to mother," she said, as she got up from the tea table. "She's awfully sorry she couldn't be down to welcome you," she added to Henry who had moved to open the door for her.

"I hope she'll soon be better," he answered.

When she had gone, Ninian got up and cursed lustily. "Damn and blast him," he said.

They did not speak. They knew that Ninian's anger had some relation to Mrs. Graham's headache and the letter from Uncle Peter, and they felt that it was not their business to speak, even though Ninian had drawn them into the affair.

"I'm sorry," said Ninian, sitting down again. "I ought not to have broken out like that before you chaps, but I couldn't help it."

Henry coughed as if he were clearing his throat, but he did not speak, and Gilbert sat still and gazed at the toe of his shoe.

"He always upsets mother, damn him!" Ninian looked up at them. "My Uncle Peter married a girl in a confectioner's shop at Cambridge. He's that kind of ass! He never writes to mother except when he's in a mess, and he always expects her to get him out of it. I can't stand a man who does that sort of thing. She's an awful bitch, too . . . his wife! We had them here once! . . . My God!"

Ninian lay back in his seat and remained silent for a while as if he were contemplating in his mind the picture of Uncle Peter and his wife on that awful visit to Boveyhayne. They waited for him to continue.

"I used to feel ashamed to go into the village," he said at last. "The way she talked to the fishermen—one minute snubbing them, and the next, talking to them as if she were a servant-girl. They didn't like it. Jim Rattenbury hated it, I know. She wasn't one of us and she wasn't one of them. A damned in-between, that's what she was. And Uncle Peter used to get drunk! . . . I'm awfully sorry, you chaps, I oughtn't to be boring you like this!"

"That's all right," said Gilbert.

"I was jolly glad when they went," Ninian went on. "Jolly glad! Poor mother had a hell of a time while they were here!"

"I suppose so," Henry murmured, hardly knowing what to say.

"I can't understand a man marrying a woman like that," Ninian said. "I mean, I can understand a fellow ragging about with a girl, but I can't understand him marrying her and . . . and upsetting things!"

It was on the tip of Henry's tongue to say something about Ninian's belief in democracy, for he remembered that Gilbert, in one of his letters, had declared that Ninian had become a I'm-as-good-as-you-and-a-damn-sight-better-politician, but he did not say it.

"The girl isn't happy. Anybody can see she isn't happy, and Uncle Peter isn't happy, and between them they make us damn miserable. That kind of marriage is bound to fail, *I* think. People ought to marry in their own class! . . ."

"Unless they're big enough to climb out of it," said Gilbert.

"*She* isn't!"

It came to Henry suddenly that he was proposing to do what Ninian's Uncle Peter had done: marry a girl who was not of his class. He listened to Ninian and Gilbert as they talked of this intimate mingling of classes, and wondered what they would say if they knew of Sheila. Gilbert and Ninian were agreed that on the whole it was foolish for a man to marry that kind of girl. "It doesn't work," said Gilbert, and he told a story of a man whom his father had known, an officer in the Indian army who developed communist beliefs when he retired and had married his cook. "It's a ghastly failure," said Gilbert.

"I'm all for equality," Ninian said, "but it's silly to think that we're always equal now. We're not! . . ."

"And never will be," Gilbert interjected.

"I don't agree with you, Gilbert. I think that things like habits and manners can be fairly equalised! . . ."

"Minds can't!"

"No, of course not, but decent behaviour can, and it's silly to start mingling classes until you've done that. You rub each other the wrong way over little things that don't really matter, but that irritate like blazes. I've talked about it with mother. She used to think I was the sort of chap who'd do what Uncle Peter did. Uncle Peter frightened me off that kind of thing!"

It was absurd, Henry thought, to think that all women were like Uncle Peter's wife. Sheila was not that sort of girl at all. She would not make a man feel ashamed! . . .

He broke off in the middle of his thoughts to listen to Gilbert who was enunciating a doctrine that was new to Henry.

"There are aristocrats and there are plebs," said Gilbert, "and they won't mingle. That's all about it. I believe that the majority of the working people are different from us, not only in their habits . . . that's nothing . . . just the veneer . . . but in their nature. We've been achieved somehow . . . evolution and that sort of thing . . . because they needed people to look after them and direct them and control them. We're as different from working people as a race-horse is from a cart-horse. Things that are quite natural to us are simply finicky fussy things to them. I wish to God talking like this didn't make a fellow feel like a prig! . . ."

He broke off almost angrily.

"Let's go out," he said. "I want to smoke!"

"But it's true all the same," he went on when they got

outside, almost as if he had not broken his speech.
"Whether we tried for it or not, we've got people separated into groups, and we'll never get them out of them.
Some of us are servants and some of us are bosses, and
we've developed natures like that, and we can't get away
from them!" Henry reminded them of men who had
climbed from low positions to high positions. "They're
the accidents," Gilbert went on. "They prove nothing,
and I'm certain that if you could go back into their an-
cestry, you'd find they sprang from people like us, who
had somehow slithered down until the breed told and a
turn up was taken! . . ."

They argued round and round the subject, admitting
here, denying there. . . .

"Anyhow," Gilbert ended, "it is true that a man who
marries a village girl makes a mistake, isn't it?"

"Not always," Henry replied.

"Nearly always," said Gilbert.

"Uncle Peter made a mistake anyhow," Ninian said.

6

He went to his room, pleading that he was tired, to
write his letter to Sheila before dinner. As he was going
upstairs, Mary began to descend, and he saw that her look
was brighter.

"Go back," she called to him, waving her hand as if to
thrust him down the stairs again. "It's unlucky to pass
people on the stairs. Don't you know that?"

He descended again as she bade him, laughing as he did
so, and waited until she had come down.

"Mother's much better now," she said when she had
reached his side. "She's coming down to dinner."

"I'm awfully glad," he replied. He hesitated for a
second or two, standing with one foot on the last step of
the stairs. "I say, Mary," he said.

"Yes, Quinny!" she answered, turning to him.

So she had not forgotten that she had called him by his nick-name.

"I say, Mary," he said again, still undecided as to whether he should speak his mind or not.

"Yes?" she repeated.

He went up a step or two of the stairs. "Oh, I don't know," he exclaimed. "I only wanted to say how nice it is to be here again!"

"Oh, yes!" Mary said, and he imagined that her tone was one of disappointment.

"I'll be down presently," he went on, and then he ran up the stairs to his room.

"I don't know," he said to himself, as he closed his door. "I'm damned if I know!"

He sat down at the writing-table and spread a sheet of notepaper in front of him. "I wish I knew! . . ." he murmured, and he wrote down the date. "Mary is awfully nice, and I like her of course, but Sheila! . . ."

He put the pen down again and sat back in his chair and stared out of the window. Out in the farmyard, he could hear the men bedding the horses, and there was a clatter of cans from the dairy where the women were turning the milk into cream. He could hear a horse whinnying in its stall . . . and as he listened he seemed to see Sheila, as he had seen her on her uncle's farm before he had failed in courage, standing outside the byre with a crock in her hands and a queer, teasing look in her eyes. "You're the quare wee fella!" she was saying, and then, "I like you quaren well! . . ."

He seized the pen again and began to write.

7

He had almost finished the letter when Gilbert knocked on his door and shouted, "Can I come in, Quinny?"

He put the letter under the blotting paper, and called, "Yes, Gilbert!" in reply.

"Aren't you ready yet?" Gilbert asked.

"No, not yet, but I won't be long changing!"

"Righto!" said Gilbert, going to the other window and looking across the fields. "Rum go about Ninian's uncle, isn't it?" he said, playing with the tassle of the blind.

"Eh?" said Henry.

"There must be something low in a man who marries a woman like that, don't you think?"

"Oh, I don't know. Why should there be?"

"Obvious, isn't it? I mean, there can't be much in common otherwise, can there? Unless the man's a sentimental ass. It's as if you or I were to marry one of the girls out there in the yard, milking the cows. She'd be awfully useful for that job . . . milking cows . . . but you wouldn't want her to be doing it all the time. It depends, I suppose, on what you want to do. If you've got any ambition! . . ."

He did not finish the sentence, but Henry understood and nodded his head as if he agreed with him.

"I must trot off," Gilbert said suddenly, going towards the door. "I'm keeping you! . . ." He paused with his fingers on the handle of the door. "I say, Quinny," he said, "do you know anything about women?"

"No, not much," Henry answered. "Do you?"

"No. Funny, isn't it?" he replied, and then he went out of the room.

Henry sat still for a moment, staring at the closed door, and then turned back to the writing-table and took the letter to Sheila from beneath the blotting-paper. He read it through and sat staring at it until the writing became a dancing blur. . . . He got up, carrying the letter in his hand, and went to the door and opened it. He tried to call "Gilbert!" but the name came out in a whisper, and before he could call again, he heard the noise of laughter and then the sound of a young voice singing. Mary was downstairs, teasing Ninian. He could hear Ninian, half laughing, half growling, as he shouted, "Don't be an old ass, Mary!"

He shut the door and went back to the writing-table, still holding the letter in his hand, and while he stood there, a gong was sounded in the hall.

"Lord!" he said, "I shall have to hurry!" and he tore up the letter and put it in the waste-paper basket.

8

They passed their time in bathing and boating and walking, and sometimes Mary was with them, but mostly she was not. They went out in the mornings, soon after breakfast, taking food with them, and seldom returned until the evening. They took long tramps to Honiton and Lyme Regis and Sidmouth, and once they walked to Exeter and returned home by train. Mary liked boating and bathing, but she did not care for walking, and the distances they travelled were beyond her strength; and so it came about that gradually, during Henry's stay at Boveyhayne, she ceased to take part in their outings. It seemed odd to him that she did not make any reference to their love-making. She called him "Quinny" and was friendly enough, but she called Gilbert by his Christian name and was as friendly with him as she was with Henry. He felt hurt when he thought of her indifference to him. "You'd think she'd forgotten about it!" he said to himself one evening when he was sitting alone with her in the garden, and he oscillated between the desire to ignore her and the desire to have it out with her; but he dallied so long between one desire and the other that Gilbert and Ninian and Mrs. Graham had joined them before he had made a decision. He could not understand Mary. She seemed to have grown shy and quiet and much less demonstrative than she had been when he first knew her.

"Mary's growing up," Mrs. Graham said to him one

evening, irrelevantly; and of course she was, but she had
not grown up so much that there should be all this difference between Mary now and Mary then.

"Oh, well!" he generally concluded when his thoughts
turned to her, "she's only a kid!"

And sometimes that explanation seemed to satisfy him.
There were other times when it failed to satisfy him, and
he told himself that Mary was justly cold to him because
he had not been loyal to their compact. He had not answered her letters and he had made love to Sheila Morgan.
"I suppose," he said to himself, "I'd be at Ballymartin
now, making love to Sheila, if it hadn't been for that
horse!"

He tried on several occasions to talk to Mary about
her unanswered letter, to invent some explanation of his
neglect, but always he failed to say anything, too nervous
to begin, too afraid of being snubbed, too eager to leave the
explanation over until the next day; and so he never "had
it out" with her.

"I am a fool!" he would say to himself in angry rebuke,
but even while he was reproaching himself, his mind was
devising an excuse for his behaviour. "We're really too
young," he would add. "It's silly of me to think of this
sort of thing at all, and Mary's still a schoolgirl! . . ."

"I'll just say something to her before I go away," he
thought. "Something that will . . . explain everything!"

Then Mr. Quinn wrote to him to say that he was in London on business. He was anxious that Henry should come
to town so that they could return to Ireland together.
"We'll go to Dublin," he wrote, "and I'll leave you there.
You needn't come to Ballymartin until the end of the first
term."

He felt strangely chilled by his father's letter. This
jolly holiday at Boveyhayne was to be the end of one life,
and the journey to Dublin was to be the beginning of another; and he did not wish to end the one life or begin the

other. He could feel growing within him, an extraordinary hatred of Trinity College, and he almost wrote to his father to say that he would rather not go to a University at all than go to T.C.D. It was cruel, he told himself, to separate him from his friends and compel him to go to a college that meant nothing on earth to him.

"I shan't know any one there," he said to Gilbert and Ninian, "and I probably won't want to know any one. It's a hole, that's what it is, a rotten hole. If the dons were any good, they'd be at Oxford or Cambridge! . . ."

"You're not much of a patriot," Ninian said.

"I don't want to be a damned patriot. I want to be with people I like. I don't see why I should be compelled to go and live with a lot of people I don't know and don't care about, just because I'm Irish and they're Irish, when I really want to be with you and Gilbert and Roger. . . . I haven't seen Roger since I left Rumpell's and I don't suppose I shall see him for a long time!"

Gilbert tried to mock him out of his anger. "This emotion does you credit, young Quinny!" he said, "and we are touched, Ninian and I. Aren't we, Ninian? But you must be a man, Quinny! Four years hence, we shall all meet in London, *Deo volente*, and we'll be able to compare the education of Ireland with the education of England. Oh, Lordy God, I sometimes wish we hadn't got minds at all. I think it must be lovely to be a cow . . . nothing to do but chew the damned cud all day. No soul to consider, no mind to improve, no anything! . . ."

Gilbert and he left Boveyhayne together, but Gilbert was only going as far as Templecombe with him, where he was to change on his way to Cheltenham. Ninian and Mary saw them off at Whitcombe, and when he remembered the circumstances in which she had seen him off before, Henry had a longing to take hold of her arm and lead her to the end of the platform, as he had done then, and tell her that he was sorry for everything and beg her to start again

where they had left off that day . . . but Gilbert was there
and Ninian was there, and there was no opportunity, and
the train went off, leaving the explanation unmade.

9

"Good-bye, Quinny!" Gilbert said at Templecombe.

"Good-bye, Gilbert!" Henry answered in a low tone.

"I suppose you'll write to me some day?"

"I suppose so. Yes, of course! . . ."

"Ripping day, isn't it? Shame to be wasting it in a
blooming train!"

"Yes!"

He wished that the train would break down so that he
need not part from Gilbert yet, but while he was wishing,
it began to move. Gilbert stood back from the carriage and
waved his hand to him, and Henry leant with his head
through the window of his carriage, smiling. . . .

"Damn Trinity," he said, sitting back in his seat, and
letting depression envelop him. "Damn and blast Trinity! . . ."

THE SECOND BOOK
OF
CHANGING WINDS

I write of Youth, of Love, and have Accesse
By these, to sing of cleanly-Wantonnesse.

HERRICK.

THE FIRST CHAPTER

1

HENRY QUINN climbed into a carriage at Amiens Street station and sat back in his seat and puffed with pleasure, blowing out his breath with a long "poo-ing" sound. He was quit of Trinity College at last! Thank God, he was quit of it at last! The hatred with which he had entered Trinity had, in his four years of graduation, been mitigated . . . there were even times when he had kindly thoughts of Trinity . . . but every letter he received from Gilbert Farlow or Ninian Graham or Roger Carey stirred the resentment he felt at his separation from his friends who had gone to Cambridge, and so, in spite of the kindlier feeling he now had for the College, he was happy to think that he was quitting it for the last time. "But it isn't Irish," he insisted when his father complained of his lack of love for Trinity. "It's . . . it's a hermaphrodite of a college, neither one thing nor another, English nor Irish. I always feel, when I step out of College Green into Trinity, that I've stepped right out of Ireland and landed on the point of a rock in the middle of the Irish Sea . . . and the point pricks and is damned uncomfortable!"

"You've got the English habit of damning everything, Henry!" his father replied at a tangent.

But Henry would not be drawn away from his argument.

"The atmosphere of the place is all wrong," he went on. "The Provost looks down the side of his nose at you if he thinks you take an interest in Ireland!"

Mr. Quinn, in his eagerness to defend his College from reproaches which he knew to be deserved, reminded Henry that the Provost had a considerable reputation as a Greek scholar, but his effort only delivered him more completely into Henry's hands.

"But, father," Henry said, "you yourself used to say what's the good of knowing all about Greece when you don't know anything about Ireland. I don't care about Greece and all those rotten little holes in the Ægean . . . that's dead and done with . . . but I do care about Ireland which isn't dead and done with!"

It was then that Mr. Quinn found consolation. "Well, anyway, you've learned to love Ireland," he said. "Trinity's done that much for you!"

"Trinity hasn't done it for me," Henry answered, "I did it for myself."

Lying back in his seat, waiting for the train to steam out of the station on its journey to Belfast, Henry remembered that conversation with his father, and his mind speculated freely on his attitude towards Trinity. "I don't care," he said, "if I never put my foot inside the gates again!"

Something that Patrick Galway said to him once, when he and John Marsh were talking of Trinity, came back to his memory. "The College is living on Oliver Goldsmith and Edmund Burke," Galway said, and added, "It's like a maiden lady in a suburb giving herself airs because her great-grandfather knew somebody who was great. It hasn't produced a man who's done anything for Ireland, except harm, not in the last hundred years anyhow. Lawyers and parsons and officials, that's the best Trinity can do! If you think of the Irishmen who've done anything fine for Ireland, you'll find that, when they came from universities at all, they came from Oxford or Cambridge, anywhere on God's earth but Trinity. Horace Plunkett was at Oxford. . . ."

"Eton, too!" Marsh had interjected.

"Yes, Eton!" Galway went on. "Think of it! An Irish patriot coming from Eton where you'd think only Irish oppressors would come from! If Plunkett had been

educated in an Irish school and sent to Trinity, do you
think he'd have done anything decent for Ireland?''

"Yes," Henry had replied promptly. "He's that kind
of man!''

"No, he wouldn't," Galway retorted. "They'd have
educated the decency out of him, and he'd have been a . . .
a sort of Lord Ashtown!''

But Henry would have none of that. He would not believe that a man's nature can be altered by pedagogues.

"Horace Plunkett would have been a good Irishman if
he'd been born and reared and educated in an Orange
Lodge," he said.

"I'm not talking about natures," Galway replied. "I'm
talking about beliefs. They'd have told him it was no
good trying to build up an Irish nation. . . .''

"He wouldn't have believed them," Henry retorted.
"Damn it, Galway, do you think a man like Plunkett would
let a lot of fiddling schoolmasters knock him off his balance?''

"I'm a schoolmaster," Galway answered, "and I know
what schoolmasters can do!'' His voice changed, deepen-
ing, as he spoke. "I know what the young teachers in
Ireland mean to do!''

"What do they mean to do?'' Henry had asked jokingly.

"Make Irishmen," Galway answered.

"If only Trinity would make Irishmen," he went on,
"we'd all be saved a deal of trouble. But it won't, and
when a man of family, like Plunkett, is born with good will
for Ireland, he has to go to England to be educated. And
he ought to be educated in Ireland, and he would be if
Trinity were worth a damn. I wish I were Provost, I'd
teach Irishmen to be proud of their birth!''

"Well, when we've made Ireland a nation," said Henry,
chaffing him, "we'll make you Provost of Trinity!'' and
Galway, though he knew that Henry was jesting, smiled
with pleasure.

"When Ireland is a nation!'' Marsh murmured dreamily.

2

It was extraordinary, Henry thought, how little at home
he had felt in Dublin. He had the feel of Ballymartin
in his bones. He had kinship with the people in Belfast.
At Rumpell's and at Boveyhayne he had had no sensation
of alien origin. He had stepped into the life of the school
as naturally as Gilbert Farlow had done, and at Boveyhayne, even when he still had difficulty in catching the
dialect of the fishermen, he had felt at home. But in Dublin, he had an uneasy feeling that after all, he was a
stranger. In his first year at Trinity, he had been brutally contemptuous of the city and its inhabitants. "They
can't even put up the names of the streets so that people
can read them," he said to John Marsh soon after he arrived in Dublin. "They're so *damned* incompetent!"
And Marsh had told him to control his Ulster blood.
"You're right to be proud of Ulster," he had said, "but you
oughtn't to go about talking as if the rest of Ireland were
inhabited by fools!"

"I know I oughtn't," Henry replied, "but I can't help
it when I see the way these asses are letting Dublin down!"

That was how he felt about Dublin and the Dublin people, that Dublin was being "let down" by her citizens.
His first impression of the city was that it was noble, even
beautiful, in spite of its untidiness, its distress. He would
wander about the streets, gazing at the fine old Georgian
houses, tumbling into decay, and feel so much anger against
the indifferent citizens that sometimes he felt like hitting
the first Dublin man he met . . . hitting him hard so that
he should bleed! . . ."

"I feel as if Dublin were like an old mansion left by
a drunken lord in the charge of a drunken caretaker," he
said to Marsh. "It's horrible to see those beautiful houses
decaying, but it's more horrible to think that nobody
cares!"

Marsh had taken him one Sunday to a house where there

were ceilings that were notable even in Dublin which is
full of houses with beautiful ceilings.

"If we had houses like that in Belfast," Henry had said,
as they came away, "we wouldn't let them become slums!"

"No," retorted Marsh, unable to restrain himself from
sneering, "you'd make peep-shows out of them and charge
for admission!"

"Well, that would be better than turning them into
slums," Henry answered good-humouredly.

"Would it?" Marsh replied.

"Would it?" Henry wondered. The train was now on
its way to Belfast, and, looking idly out of the window, he
could see the waves of the Irish Sea breaking on the sands
at Malahide, heaving suddenly into a glassy-green heap,
and then tumbling over into a sprawl of white foam.
Would it? he wondered, thinking again of what Marsh had
said about the Georgian houses with their wide halls and
lovely Adams ceilings. There was no beauty of building
at all in Belfast, and no one there seemed anxious that
there should be: in all that city, so full of energy and purpose and grit and acuteness of mind, there did not appear
to be one man of power who cared for the fine shape or the
good look of things; but, after all, was that so very much
worse than the state of mind of the Dublin people who,
knowing what beauty is, carelessly let it decay? He began
to feel bitterly about Ireland and her indifference to cul-
ture and beauty. He told himself that Ireland was the
land of people who do not care. . . .

"They've got to be made to care!" he said aloud.

But how was it to be done? . . .

His sense of being an alien in Dublin had persisted all
the time that he had lived there. The Dublin people were
gregarious and garrulous, and he was solitary and reflec-
tive. Marsh and Galway had taken him to houses where
people met and talked without stopping, and much conversation with miscellaneous, casually-encountered people
bored Henry. He had no gift for ready talk and he dis-

liked crowds and he was unable to carry on a conversation with people whom he did not know, of whose very names he was ignorant. Sometimes, he had envied Marsh and Galway because of the ease with which they could converse with strangers. Marsh would talk about himself and his poems and his work with an innocent vanity that made people like him; but Henry, self-conscious and shy, could not talk of himself or his intentions to any but his intimates. Sitting here, in this carriage, from which, even now, he could see in the distance, veiled in clouds, the high peaks of the Mourne mountains, he tried to explain this difference between Marsh and himself. Why was it that these Dublin men were so lacking in reticence, so eager to communicate, while he and Ulstermen were reserved and eager to keep silent? He set his problem in those terms. He identified himself as a type of the Ulsterman, and began to develop a theory, flattering to himself, to account for the difference between Dublin people and Ulstermen . . . until he remembered that Ernest Harper was an Ulsterman. Mr. Quinn had taken Henry to see Harper on the first Sunday evening after they had arrived in Dublin from England, and Harper had received him very charmingly and had talked to him about nationality and co-operation and the Irish drama and the strange inability of Lady Gregory to understand that it was *not* she who had founded the Abbey Theatre, until Henry, who had never heard of Lady Gregory, began to feel tired. He had waited patiently for a chance to interpolate something into the monologue until hope began to leave him, and then, with a great effort he had interrupted the flow of Harper's vivid talk and had made a reference to a picture hanging on the wall beside him. It showed a flaming fairy in the middle of a dark wood. . . .

"Oh, yes," Harper said, "that's the one I saw!"

"You saw?" Henry had exclaimed in astonishment.

And then he remembered that Harper spoke of fairies as intimately as other men speak of their friends. . . .

"Good God!" he thought, "*where am I?*" and wondered what Ninian Graham would make of Ernest Harper.

Harper was an Ulsterman, and so was George Russell, whom people called "A.E." Marsh and Galway, now almost inseparable, had taken Henry to hear George Russell speaking on some mystical subject at the Hermetic Club, and Henry, bewildered by the subject, had felt himself irresistibly attracted to the fiery-eyed man who spoke with so little consciousness of his audience. After the meeting was ended, he had walked part of the way home with Russell and had listened to him as he said the whole of his lecture over again . . . and he left him with a feeling that Russell was unaware of human presences, that the company of human beings was not necessary to him, that his speech was addressed, not to the visible audience or the visible companion, but to an audience or a companion that no one but himself could see. Was there any one on earth less like the typical Ulsterman than George Russell, who preached mysticism and better business, or Ernest Harper who took penny tramrides to pay visits to the fairies?

No, this theory of some inherent difference between Ulstermen and other Irishmen would not work. There must be some other explanation of Henry's dislike of crowds, his silence in large companies, his inability to assert himself in the presence of strangers. Why was it that he was unable to talk about himself and the things he had done and the things he meant to do as Marsh talked? It was not because he was more modest, had more humility, than Marsh; for in his heart, Henry was vain. . . . And while he was asking himself this question, suddenly he found the answer. It was because he was afraid to talk about himself, it was because he had not got the courage to be vain and self-assertive in crowds. His inability to talk among strangers, to make people cease their own conversation in order to listen to him, was part of that cowardice that had prevented him from diving into the sea when he went with his father to swim at Cushendall and had sent him shiver·

ing into the shelter of the hedge when the runaway horse
came galloping down the Ballymena road. . . .

This swift, lightning revelation made him stand up in
the carriage and gape at the photographs of Irish scenery
in front of him.

"Oh, my God!" he said to himself, "am I always to be
tortured like this?"

4

He sat back in his seat and lay against the cushions
without moving. He saw himself now very clearly, for
he had the power to see himself with the closest fidelity.
He knew now that all his explanations were excuses, that
the bitter things he had sometimes said of those who had
qualities which he had not, were invented to prevent him
from admitting that he was without courage. Any fight,
mental or physical, unnerved him when it brought him into
personal contact with his opponents. He could *write*
wounding things to a man, but he could not *say* them to
him without losing possession of himself and his tongue;
and so he passed from the temper of a cool antagonist to
that of an enraged shrew. He had tried to explain the
garrulity of the Dublin people by saying that they were
obliged to talk and to persist in talking because "otherwise
they'd start to think!" but he knew now that that was not
an accurate explanation, that it was an ill-natured attempt
to cover up his own lack of force.

"And that's worse than cowardice," he said to himself, "to excuse my own funkiness by pretending that courage isn't courage!"

He remembered that he had invented a bitter phrase
about Yeats one night when he had seen the poet in a house
in Dublin. "Yeats is behaving as if he were the arch-
angel Gabriel making the Annunciation!" he had said, and
the man to whom he had said it had laughed and asked
what Henry thought Yeats was announcing.

"A fresh revision of one of his lyrics," he had replied. . . .

"And I'd give the world," he said now, "to be able to put on his pontifical air!"

He had a shrinking will; his instinct in an emergency was to back away from things. He had not got the capacity to compel men to do his bidding by the simple force of his personality. If he succeeded in persuading people to do things which he suggested to them he was only able to do so after prolonged discussion, sometimes only after everything else had failed. At Rumpell's, Gilbert had made suggestions as if they were commands that must instantly be obeyed . . . and they had been instantly obeyed; but when Henry made suggestions, either people did not listen to them or, having listened to them, they acted on some other suggestion, until at last, Henry, disheartened, seldom proposed anything until the last moment, and then he made his proposal in a way which seemed to indicate that he thought little of it; and when some of his suggestions were accepted and had proved, in practice, to be good, his attitude had been, not that of the man who is absolutely sure of himself, but rather of the man who gasps with relief because something that he thought was very likely to be a failure, had proved to be a success.

Depression settled on him so heavily that he began to believe that he was bound to fail in everything that he undertook to do, and when he thought of the bundle of manuscript in his portmanteau, he had a sudden inclination to take it out and fling it through the window of the carriage. He had not spoken of his writing to any one except John Marsh, and to him, he had only said that he intended to write a novel some day. Once, indeed, he had said, "I've written quite a lot of that novel I told you about!" but Marsh, intent on something else, had answered vaguely, "Oh, yes!" and had changed the conversation, leaving Henry to imagine that he had little faith in his power to write. He had been so despondent after that,

that he had gone back to College and, having re-read what he had written, had torn the manuscript in pieces and thrown it into the grate because it seemed so dull and tasteless. He had not written a word after that for more than a month, and he might not have written anything for a longer period had he not heard from Gilbert Farlow that he had finished a comedy in three acts and had sent it to Mr. Alexander. The news stimulated him, and in a little while he was itching to write again. In the evening, he began to re-write the story and thereafter it went on, sometimes quickly, sometimes slowly, until it was finished. His feelings about it changed with remarkable rapidity. He read it over, in its unfinished state, many times, feeling at one time it was excellent, and at another time that it was poor, flatulent stuff, without colour or vivacity.

Writing did not give pleasure to him: it gave him pain. He felt none of that exultation in creating characters which he had been told was part of the pleasures of an author. There were times, indeed, when he felt a mitigated joy in writing because his ideas were fluent and words fell easily off his pen, but even on those occasions, the labour of writing hurt him and exhausted him. The times of pleasurable writing were short interludes between the long stretches of painful writing, little oases that made the journey across the desert just possible. And then there were those periods of appalling misery when, having ended a chapter, he wondered what he should make his people do next. He would leave them, landed neatly at the end of some adventure or emotional crisis, feeling that the story was going on splendidly and that his power to write was full and strong, and then, having written the number of the next chapter, he would reach forward to write the first word . . . and suddenly there was devastation in his mind, and "My God! I don't know what to make them do now!" he would say.

He had read in a literary journal that some authors planned their stories before they began to write them. They prepared a summary of the tale, and then enlarged the summary. They knew exactly what was to happen in each chapter. A character could not move or rise or sit down or turn pale or look pleased without the author having known about it long before the act was performed. It was as if the author could count the very hairs on the heads of his people. "Just like God!" Henry had said to himself when he had finished reading the article. . . . He had tried to make a plan, and, after much labour, had completed one; but it was useless to him, for when he came to write out the story, his characters kicked it aside and insisted on behaving in some other way than he had planned that they should behave. It was as if they had taken their destinies into their own hands and insisted on living their lives in accordance with their own wishes instead of living them in accordance with his. . . . It was fortunate then that he began to read "Tristram Shandy," for when he saw how Sterne's pen, refusing to obey him, had filled some of his pages with curly lines and dots and confusions, had even declined to fill a chapter at all, impudently skipping it, he realised that authors are but creatures in the hands of some force that wills them to create things which they cannot control and sometimes cannot understand.

Writing his book had given him one pleasure. On the day on which he wrote the last word of it, he felt joy. Before he began to write, he had read in Forster's "Life of Dickens" that the great novelist had parted from his characters with pain. Henry parted from his characters with pleasure. "Thank God," he said, as he put down his pen, "I've finished with the brutes!"

He had enjoyed reading the story in its finished state, and when he had packed the manuscript into his portmanteau, he had felt that the story was good, and had sat in a chair dreaming of the success it would make and the praise he would receive for it. He tried to calculate the number of copies that would be sold, basing his calculations on the total population of the British Isles. "There are over forty millions of people in England and Wales alone," he said to himself, "and another ten millions, say, in Scotland and Ireland . . . about fifty millions in all. I ought to sell a good many copies . . . and then there's America!" He thought that ten per cent. of the population might buy the story, and believed that his estimate was modest until he remembered that ten per cent. of fifty millions is five millions! . . .

And that made him laugh. Even he, in his wildest imaginings, did not dream of selling five million copies of his novel.

5

He wished now that he had asked John Marsh and Patrick Galway to read the story and tell him what they thought of it. They were honest men, and would criticise his work frankly. At that moment, he had an insatiable longing to know the truth, mingled with a strange fear of knowing it. What he wished to know was whether or not he had the potentialities of a great author in him. He knew that his story was not commonplace stuff, but he was afraid that it might only be middling writing, and he did not wish to be a middling writer. If he could not be a great writer, he did not wish to be a writer at all. There were thousands and thousands of novels in the world which did no more for men than enable them to put their minds to sleep. Henry did not wish to add a book to their number. There were other books, fewer in number than those, which showed that their authors had some feeling for life, but not enough, and these authors went on, year after year, producing one or more novels, each of which "showed promise," but never showed achievement. The life these men pursued always eluded them. It was impossible for Henry to join the crowd of people who produced books which perished with the generation that they pleased. That much he knew. But he was eager that he should not fall into the ranks of the semi-great, the half-clever; and his fear was that his place was in their midst.

While he was ruminating in this manner, he remembered that Gilbert Farlow had written to him a few days before he left Dublin, and he ceased to think of his career as a writer and began to search his pockets for Gilbert's letter. "I'll show the manuscript to Gilbert," he said to himself. "Old Gilbert loves telling people the truth!"

He found the letter and began to read it. *"Quinny,"* it began, for Gilbert had abandoned "dears" because, he said, he sometimes had to write to people who were detestable:

"Quinny: How soon can you get quit of that barrack in Dublin where your misguided father thinks you are being taught to be Irish? Cast your eyes on the address at the head of this notepaper. It is a noble house that Roger and I have discovered. Ninian has seen it and he approves of it. I said I'd break his blighted neck for him if he disapproved of it, which may have had something to do with his decision, though not much, for Ninian has become a very muscular young fellow and I shouldn't have liked the job of breaking his neck very much. Roger and I have been here for a week now, and Ninian joins us at the end of the month. He's down at Boveyhayne at present, catching lobsters and sniffing the air, all of which he says is very good for him and would be better for me. And you. And Roger. There is a tablet on the front wall of the house, fixed by the London County Council, which says that Lord Thingamabob used to live here sometime in the eighteenth century. The landlord tried to raise the rent on that account, but we said we were Socialists and would expect the rent to be decreased because of the injury to our principles caused by residence in a house that had been inhabited by a member of the cursed, bloated and effete aristocracy. He begged our pardon and said that in the circumstances, he wouldn't charge anything extra, but he had us in the end, the mouldy worm, for he said that it was the custom to make Socialists pay a quarter's rent in advance.

The result was that Roger had to stump up . . . I couldn't for I was broke . . . which made dear little Roger awfully unpleasant to live with for a whole day. I offered to go back and tell the man that we weren't Socialists at all, but Improved Tories, but he said I'd done enough harm. It's a pity that old Roger hasn't got a better sense of humour.

We have chosen two rooms for you, one to work in, and the other to sleep in. We're each to have two rooms, so that we can go and be morose in comfort if we want to; but I daresay in the evenings we'll want to be together. I've thought out a scheme of decoration for your room— all pink rosebuds and stuff like that. Roger asked me not to be an ass when I told him of it. His notion is a nice quiet distemper. Perhaps you'd better see to the decoration yourself although I must say I always thought your taste was perfectly damnable.

By-the-way, there's a ghost in this house. It's supposed to be the ghost of Lord Thingamabob, and I believe it is. I saw it myself three nights ago, and it was as drunk as a fiddler. My God, Quinny, it's a terrible thing to see an intoxicated spook. Roger wouldn't believe me when I told him about it afterwards. He said I was drunk myself and that he heard me tumbling up the stairs to bed. Which is a lie. I did see it, and it was drunk. I heard it hiccough! I wouldn't say it was drunk if it wasn't. De mortuis nil nisi bonum, Quinny, and it would be a very dirty trick to slander a poor bogey that can't defend itself. It looked very like its descendant, Lord Middleweight, and it had the same soppy grin that he has when he thinks he's said something clever. Damned ass, that chap!

Alexander sent my comedy back. He sent a note along with it and told me what a clever lad I am and more or less hinted that when I've grown up, I can send him another play. I suppose he thinks I'm a kid in knickerbockers. The result of this business is that I'm going to try and get a job as a dramatic critic. If I do, God help the next play he produces. I'm a hurt man, and I shall let the world know about it. I'm half-way through another piece which will take some place by storm, I hope. It's a very bright play, much better than the muck Oscar Wilde wrote, not so melodramatic, and tons better than anything Bernard Shaw has written. It's all about me.

We've got an old woman called Clutters to housekeep for us. I chose her on account of her name, and it is a piece of good luck that she cooks extraordinarily well. There is also a maid, but we don't know her name, so we call her Magnolia. I'm really writing all this rot to get myself into the "twitter-twitter" mood. One of the characters in my new comedy talks like a character in a book by E. F. Benson, and I have to work myself up into a state of babbling fatuity before I can write her lines for her.

Come to London as soon as you can.

Gilbert.

6

The prospect of settling in London in the society of his schoolfriends pleased him. Marsh and Galway had tried to persuade him to make his home in Dublin, pleading that it was the duty of every educated Irishman to live in Ireland. "We haven't got many educated men on our side," Marsh said, "not a hundred in the whole of Ireland, and we need people like you!" They talked of political schemes that must be prepared for the parliament that would some day be re-established in College Green. "And they can only be prepared by educated men," Marsh said.

Henry would not listen to them. His longing was to be with Gilbert and Roger and Ninian in London. Dublin made very little appeal to him, and the job of regenerating Ireland was so immense that it frightened him. "I haven't got a common ground with you people," he said to Marsh and Galway. "You're Catholic to start off with, and I'm like my father, I think the Catholic religion is a contemptible religion. And you're not interested in anything but Ireland and the Gaelic movement. I'm interested in everything!"

"Don't you want to do *anything* for Ireland then?" John Marsh had asked.

"Oh, yes! I'll vote for Home Rule when I get a vote," he had replied.

"I know what your end will be," Patrick Galway added in a sullen voice. "You'll become a Chelsea Nationalist . . . willing to do anything for Ireland but live in it!"

Well, who would want to live in Ireland with its pennyfarthing politics! London for him! London and a sense of bigness, of wide ideas and the constant interplay of many minds!

He would talk to his father about Gilbert's proposal. There would be all sorts of subjects to discuss with him, that and the question of an allowance and the question of a career. . . .

The train ran swiftly through the suburbs of Belfast and presently pulled up at the terminus. He descended from his carriage and called a jarvey who drove him across the city to the Northern Counties station where he took train again. It was late that night when he arrived at Ballymartin.

THE SECOND CHAPTER

1

Mr. Quinn had become more absorbed in the Irish Agricultural Co-Operative Movement, and he used the home farm for experiments in scientific cultivation. His talk, when Henry returned home, was mainly about a theory of tillage which he called "continuous cropping," and it was with difficulty that Henry could persuade him to talk about Gilbert's proposal that he should join the household in Bloomsbury.

"I'm glad you've come home, Henry," he said after breakfast on the morning following Henry's return. "This system of continuous cropping is splendid, but it wants careful attention. You've got to adjust it continually to circumstances . . . you can't follow any rules about it . . . and if you'll just stay here and help me with it, we'll be able to do wonders with the home farm!"

Henry did not wish to settle in Ballymartin, at all events not for a long time.

"I want to go to London, father!" he said.

"London! What for?" Mr. Quinn exclaimed, and then before Henry could say why he wished to go to London, he added, "You'll have to settle on something, Henry. I always meant you to take over the estate fairly soon, to work things out with me. Don't you want to do that?"

"Not particularly, father!"

"Well, what's to become of you, then? Do you want to go into the Army? It's a bit late! . . ."

"No, father!"

"Or the Navy? But you should have gone to Osborne long ago if you wanted to do that!"

Henry shook his head.

"Well, what do you want to do. Are you thinkin' of the law?"

"I don't care about the law, father! . . ."

"I don't care about it myself, Henry. I was no good at it, an' mebbe that's the reason I think so little of it. But we have to have lawyers all the same. It would be a good plan now to sentence criminals to be lawyers, wouldn't it? 'The sentence of the Court is that you be taken from this place an' made to practise at the Bar for the rest of your natural life, an' may the Lord have mercy on your soul!' Begod, Henry, that's a great notion!"

Henry interrupted his father's fancy. "I want to write," he said.

"Write!" Mr. Quinn exclaimed. "Write what?"

"Books. Novels, I think! . . ."

Mr. Quinn put down his paper and gaped at his son. "Good God," he said, "an author!"

"Yes, father."

"You're daft, Henry!"

Henry got up from his chair, and went across to his father and took hold of his shoulder affectionately. "No, father, I'm not," he answered.

"Yes, you are, I tell you. You're clean cracked! . . ."

"I've written one novel already."

Mr. Quinn threw out his hands in a despairing gesture. "Oh, well," he said, "if you've committed yourself. . . . Where is it?"

"It's upstairs in my room. The manuscript, I mean. Of course, it hasn't been published yet."

A servant came into the room to clear away the remains of the breakfast, and Mr. Quinn got up from his chair and walked through the open window on to the terrace.

"What's it about?" he said to Henry who had followed him.

"Oh, love!" Henry answered, seating himself beside his father.

Mr. Quinn grunted. "Huh!" he said, gazing intently at the gravel. "Is it sloppy?"

"I don't think so, father. At least, I hope it isn't!"

"Or dirty?"

"No, it isn't dirty. I *know* it isn't dirty," Henry said very emphatically.

Mr. Quinn did not answer for a while. He got up from his seat and walked to the end of the terrace where he busied himself for a few moments in tending to a rosebush. Then he returned to the seat where Henry had remained, and said, "Will you let me read it, Henry?"

"Why, yes, father. Of course, I will," Henry answered, rising and moving towards the house. "I'd like you to read it," he added. "Perhaps you'll tell me what you think of it?"

"I will," Mr. Quinn replied, closing his lips down tightly.

"I'll just go and get it," Henry said, and he went into the house.

Mr. Quinn remained seated on the terrace, looking rigidly in front of him, until Henry returned, carrying a pile of manuscript. He took the paper from him without speaking, and glanced at the first sheet on which Henry had written in a large, clear hand:

DRUSILLA: A NOVEL

BY

HENRY QUINN.

and then he turned the page and read what was written on the second sheet:

TO

MY FATHER

He looked at the dedication for a longer time than he had looked at the title-page, and his hand trembled a little as he held the paper.

"I thought you wouldn't mind, father!" Henry said.

"Mind!" Mr. Quinn replied. "No, I don't, Henry. I . . . I like it, my son. Thanks, Henry. I . . ." He got up and moved quickly towards the window. "I'll just go in an' start readin' it now," he said.

2

He returned the manuscript to Henry on the following afternoon. "I've read worse," he said.

He walked to the end of the terrace and then walked back again. Then he shouted for William Henry Matier, who came running to him. He pointed to a daisy on the lawn and asked the gardener what the hell he meant by not keeping the weeds down.

"Ah, sure, sir! . . ."

"Root the damn thing up," Mr. Quinn shouted at him, "an' don't let me see another about the place or I'll shoot the boots off you! I don't know under God what I keep you for!"

"Now, you don't mean the half you say, sir! . . ."

"You're not worth ninepence a week!"

"Aw, now," said Matier, who knew his master, "I'm worth more'n that, sir!"

"How much are you worth? Tell me that, William Henry Matier!"

William Henry rooted up the daisy, and then said that he wouldn't like to put too high a price on himself. . . .

"You'd be a fool if you did," Mr. Quinn interrupted.

". . . but I'd mebbe be worth about double what you named yourself, sir!"

"Eighteenpence!" Mr. Quinn exclaimed.

"Aye, that or a bit more. Were you wantin' anything else, sir!" He winked heavily at Henry as he turned away.

"You're not worth the food you eat," Mr. Quinn said.

"Aw, now, sir, you never know what anybody's worth 'til you have need of them," Matier replied. "A man

mightn't be worth a damn to you one day, an' he'd mebbe
be worth millions to you the next!''

"There's little fear of you bein' worth millions to any
one. Run on now an' do your work if you've any work to
do!'' Mr. Quinn turned to Henry as the gardener went off.
"I suppose you'll be wantin' to live in London for the rest
of your life?''

"I should like to go there for a while anyway, father!''

"Huh! All you writin' people seem to think there's no
life to be seen anywhere but in London. As if people
hadn't got bowels here as well as in town!''

"I don't think that, father! . . .''

"Oh, well, it doesn't matter whether you think it or not,
you'll not be happy 'til you get to London, I suppose.
You'll stay here a wee while anyway, won't you? You've
only just come home, an' it's a long time since I saw you
last!''

"I'll stay as long as you like, father.''

"Very well, then. I'll tell you when I've had enough of
your company an' then you can go off to your friends.
How much money do you think you'll need in London?
Don't ask for too much. I need every ha'penny I have for
the work. You've no notion what a lot it costs to experi-
ment wi' land, an' I'm not as rich as you might imagine!''

Henry hesitated. He had never talked about money
with his father, and he had a curious shyness about doing
so now. "I don't know,'' he replied. "Would two hundred a year be too much? . . .''

"I'll spare you two hundred an' fifty!''

"Thank you, father. It's awfully good of you!''

"Ah, wheesht with you! Sure, why wouldn't a man be
good to his own son. I suppose now you want to hear
what I think of your book?''

Henry smiled self-consciously. "Yes, I should like to
know your opinion of it. I thought at first you didn't
think much of it. You didn't say anything! . . .''

"I'll give you a couple of years to improve it,'' Mr.

Quinn answered. "If you can't make it better in that time, you're no good!"

"I suppose not."

"An' don't hurry over it. Go out an' look about you a bit. There's a lot of stuff in your story that wouldn't be there if you had any gumption. Get gumption, Henry!"

"I'll try, father. Of course, I know I'm very inexperienced. . . ."

"You are, my son, an' what's more you're tellin' everybody how little you know in that book of yours. Man, dear, women aren't like that! . . . Well, never mind! You'll find out for yourself soon enough. Mind, I don't mean to say that there aren't some good things in the book. There are . . . plenty! If there weren't, I wouldn't waste my breath talkin' to you about it. But there are things in it that are just guff, Henry, just guff. The kind of romantic slush that a young fellow throws off when he first realises that women are . . . well, women, damn it! . . . I wish to God, you would write a book about continuous croppin'! Now, there's a subject for a good book! There's none of your damned love about that! . . ."

3

He had not seen Sheila Morgan since the morning after he had failed to stop the runaway horse. Many times, indeed, she had been in his mind, and often at Trinity, in the long sleepless nights that afflict a young man who is newly conscious of his manhood, he had turned from side to side of his bed in an impotent effort to thrust her from his thoughts. He made fanciful pictures of her in his imagination, making her very beautiful and gracious. He saw her, then, with long dark hair that had the lustre of a moonless night of stars, and he imagined her, sitting close to him, so that her hair fell about his head and shoulder and he could feel the slow movement of her breasts against his side. He would close his eyes and think of her lips on his, and her heart beating quickly while his thumped so loudly that it seemed that every one must hear it . . . and thinking thus, he would clench his fists with futile force and swear to himself that he would go to her and make her marry him. Once, when he had spent an afternoon at the Zoo in the Phœnix Park, he had lingered for a long while in the house where the tigers are caged because, suddenly, it seemed to him that the graceful beast with the bright eyes resembled Sheila. It moved so easily, and as it moved, its fine skin rippled over its muscles like running water. . . .

"I don't suppose she'd like to be called a tigress," he had thought to himself, laughing as he did so, "but that's what she's like. She's beautiful. . . ."

And later in that afternoon, he thought he saw a resemblance between Mary Graham and a brown squirrel that sat on a branch and cracked nuts, throwing the shells away carelessly . . . the Mary he had known when he first went to Boveyhayne, not the Mary he had seen on his last visit.

He wondered whether Sheila had altered much, and then he wondered what change four years had made in Mary Graham. Sheila, who had been dominant in his mind in his first year at Trinity, had receded a little into the background by the time he had quitted Dublin, but Mary, never very prominent, had retained her place, neither gaining nor losing position. It was odd, he thought to himself, that he had not been to Boveyhayne in the four years he had been at T.C.D. Mrs. Graham had invited him there several times, but he had not been able to accept the invitations: once his father had been ill, and he had had to hurry to Portrush, where he was staying, and remain with him until he was well again; and another time he had been with Gilbert Farlow at his home in Kent; and another time had agreed to go tramping in Connacht with Marsh and Galway. Ninian and Gilbert and Roger had spent a holiday at Ballymartin. . . . Ninian took a whole week to realise that

he was in Ulster and not in Scotland, and Gilbert begged
hard for the production of a typical Irishman who would
say "God bless your honour!" and "Bedad!" and "Bè-
jabers!" and pretended not to believe that there were not
any "typical Irishmen". . . and went away, vowing that
they would compel Mr. Quinn to invite them to stay with
him in the next vac. It was then that Ninian decided that
he would like to be a shipbuilder. Mr. Quinn had taken
them to Belfast to see the launch of a new liner, and Tom
Arthurs had invited them all to join the luncheon party
when the launch was over. The Vicereine had come from
Dublin to cut the ribbon which would release the great ship
and send it moving like a swan down the greasy slips into
the river; and Tom Arthurs had conducted her through
the Yard, telling her of the purpose of this machine and
that engine until the poor lady began to be dubious of her
capacity to launch the liner. There were other guides, explaining, as Tom Arthurs explained, the functions of the
Yard to the visitors, but Ninian had contrived to attach
himself to Tom Arthurs and he listened to him as he talked,
as simply as was possible, of the way in which great ships
are built. Thereafter, Ninian had tongue for none but
Tom Arthurs, and he told him, when the party was over
and the guests were leaving the Yard, that he would like
to work in the Island. Tom had doubted whether Cambridge was the proper preparation for shipbuilding. . . .
"I was out of my apprenticeship when I was your age," he
said . . . but he said that Ninian could think about it more
seriously and then come to him when his time at Cambridge was up.

"I'm thinking seriously of it now," said Ninian.

"All right, my boy!" Tom Arthurs answered, laughing,
and slapped him on the back. "We'll see what we can do
for you!"

And Ninian, flushing like a girl, went away full of happiness, and soon afterwards began to imitate Tom Arthurs'
Ulster speech in the hope that people would think he was

related to the shipbuilder or, at all events, a countryman of his.

It was odd, indeed, that Henry had not seen Mary in that time, but it was still more odd that he had not seen Sheila. Matt Hamilton had died soon after Henry had entered Trinity, but Mrs. Hamilton still had the farm which, people understood, was to be left to Sheila when her aunt died. He had not cared to go to the farm . . . a mixture of pride and shyness prevented him from doing so . . . but he had hoped to meet her on the roads about Ballymartin. "Perhaps by this time," he said to himself, "she will have forgotten my funk!" But although he frequently loitered in the roads about the "loanie," he never met her, and it was not until he said some casual things to William Henry Matier that he discovered that she was not at the farm. "I heerd tell she was visitin' friends in Bilfast!" Matier said, and with that he had to be content. Ninian and Gilbert and Roger were at Ballymartin then, and he had little opportunity to mourn over her absence; indeed, when he remembered that they were with him, he was glad that she was not at the farm: their presence would have made difficulties in the way of his intercourse with her. He would try to be alone at Ballymartin, in the next vacation, and then he would be able to bring her to his will again. But he did not spend the next vacation at home, and so, with this and other absences from Ballymartin, he was unable to see her for the whole of his time at Trinity. Neither he nor his father had spoken of her since the day when Mr. Quinn had solemnly led him to the library to rebuke him for his sweethearting. Mr. Quinn, indeed, had almost forgotten about Henry's lovemaking with Sheila, and when he met the girl and remembered that there had been lovemaking between his son and her, he thought to himself that Henry had probably completely forgotten her. . . .

He wished to see her again, and his desire became so strong that he started to walk across the fields to the

"loanie" that led to Hamilton's farm before he was aware
of what he was about. His mind filled again with the
visions he had had of her at Trinity, and he imagined that
he saw her every now and then hiding behind a tree, ready
to spring out on him and startle him with a loud whoop, or
running from him and laughing as she ran. . . .

4

He met her in the "loanie," and for a few moments he
did not recognise her. She was sitting on the grass, in
the shade of a hedge, huddling a baby close to her breast,
and he saw that she was suckling it.

"Oh, Henry, is that you?" she said, starting up hurriedly so that the baby could not suck. She drew her
blouse clumsily together, but the fretful child would not be
pacified until she had started to feed it again, and so she
resumed her seat on the grass.

"I didn't know you were back," she said, holding the
baby up to her. "Are you here for long?"

He did not answer immediately. He had not yet completely realised that this was Sheila whom he had been
eager to marry, and then when he understood at last that
this indeed was she, something inside him kept exclaiming,
"But she's got a baby!" and he wondered why she was
feeding it.

"Are you married, Sheila?" he said.

She laughed at him, and answered, "That's a quare question to be askin', an' me with this in my arms!" She
looked at the baby as she spoke.

"I didn't know you were married," he replied. "I
was coming up to the farm to see you!"

"I've been married this year past," she said.

"I didn't know," he murmured. "No one told
me! . . ."

And suddenly he saw that her face was coarser than it
had been when he loved her. Her hair was tied untidily

about her head, and he could see that her hands, as she held the child, were rough and red, and that her nails were broken and misshapen. Her boots were loosely laced, and she seemed to be sprawling. . . .

"I'm all throughother," she said, as if she realised what was in his mind and was anxious to excuse herself to him. "This wee tory hardly gives me a minute's peace, an' my aunt's not so well as she was!"

He nodded his head, but did not speak.

"Is it a boy or a girl?" he asked after a while.

"It's a boy," she said, "an' the very image of his da. He's a lovely child, Henry. Just look at him!"

He came nearer to her and looked at the baby who had his little fingers at her breast as if he would prevent her from taking it from him. The child, still sucking, looked up at him with greedy-sleepy eyes.

"Isn't he a gran' wee fella?" she went on, eyeing her son proudly.

"Whom did you marry?" he asked.

"You know him well," she answered. "Peter Logan that used to keep the forge . . . that's who I married. D'ye mind the way he could bend a bar of iron with his two hands? . . ."

Henry remembered. "Doesn't he keep the forge now?" he asked.

"No, he sold it to Dan McKittrick when he married me. We needed a man on the farm, an' he's gran' at it. There isn't a one in the place can bate him at the reapin', an' you should see the long, straight furrows he can plough. The child's the image of him, an' I declare by the way he's tuggin' at me . . . be quit, will you, you wee tory, an' not be hurtin' me with your greed! . . . he'll be as strong as his da, an' mebbe stronger!"

"Are you stayin' long?" she said again.

"No," he answered. "I'm going to London! . . ."

"London! Lord bless us, that's a long way!"

"I'm going soon . . . in a day or two," he went on,

making his resolution as he spoke. The sight of her bare
breast embarrassed him, and he wanted to go away
quickly.

"You're a one for roamin' the world, I must say!" she
said. "You're no sooner here nor you're away again.
Mebbe you'll come up an' see my aunt . . . she was talkin'
about you only last week . . . an' Peter'd be right an'
glad to welcome you!"

"No, thanks, not to-day," he answered. "I've something to do at home . . . I'm sorry! . . ."

"But you said you were comin' to see me! . . ."

"I know, but I've just remembered something . . . I'm
sorry!" He was speaking in a jerky, agitated manner and
he began to move away as if he were afraid that she would
detain him. "I'll come another time," he added.

"Well, you're the quare man," she said. "Anybody'd
think you were afeard of me, the hurry you're in to run
away!"

He laughed nervously. "Of course, I'm not afraid of
you," he exclaimed. "Why should I be?"

"I don't know!" She looked at him for a few seconds,
and then the whimsical look that he remembered so well
came into her eyes. "D'ye mind the way you wanted to
marry me, Henry?" she said.

"Yes . . . yes! Ha, ha!"

"An' now I've this! It's a quaren funny, isn't it?"

"Funny?"

"Aye, the way things go. I wonder what sort of a child
I'd a' had if I'd married you!"

"I really don't know! . . . I'm afraid I must go now!"

"Well, good-bye, Henry! I'll mebbe see you again some
time!"

She held out her hand to him and he took it, and then
dropped it quickly.

"Yes, perhaps," he answered, and added, "Good-bye!"

He went off quickly, not looking back until he had
reached the foot of the "loanie," and then he stood for a

second or two to watch her. She was busy with her baby
again. He could see her white breast shining in the sunlight, and her head bent over the sucking child.

"Well, I'm damned," he said to himself, as he hurried
off.

And as he hurried home, his mind set on quitting Ballymartin as speedily as possible, he remembered the casual
way in which she had spoken of their possibly meeting
again. "I'll mebbe see you some time!" she had said.
So indifferent to him as that, she was, so happy in her love
for her husband whom he remembered as a great big, hairy,
tanned man who beat hot iron with heavy hammers and
bent it into wheels and shoes for horses.

"She takes more interest in that putty-faced brat of
hers than she does in me," he said to himself, angrily, and
then, so swift were his changes of mood, he began to laugh.
"Of course, she does," he said aloud. "Why shouldn't
she? It's hers, isn't it?"

He remembered her young beauty and contrasted it with
her appearance when he saw her in the "loanie" with her
child. In a few years, he thought, she would be like any
village woman, worn out, misshapen, tired, with gnarled
knuckles and thickened hands. Already she had begun to
neglect her hair. . . .

"It's a damned shame," he murmured. "If she'd married me she'd have kept her looks! . . ."

"But she wouldn't marry me," he went on. "I wasn't
man enough for her. . . . My God, I wish I was out of
this!"

5

"Father," he said when he got home, "I'd like to go to
London at once!"

"You can't go this minute, my son. There's no train
the night!"

"I mean, I want to go as soon as possible!"

Mr. Quinn glanced sharply at him. "You're in a desperate hurry all of a sudden," he said. "What's up?"

"Nothing, father, only I want to get to work, and I can't work here! . . ."

"Restless, are you? I was hopin' you'd give me a bit of your company a while longer! . . ."

"I'm sorry, father! . . ."

"That's all right, my boy, that's all right. When do you want to go?"

"To-morrow!"

"You've only been home a short time. . . . Never mind! I'll come up to Belfast an' see you off. There's a Co-operative Conference there the day after the morra, an' I may as well go up with you as go up alone!"

Henry knew that his father was hurt by his sudden decision to leave Ballymartin, and he felt sorry for the old man's disappointment, but he felt, too, that he could not bear to stay near Hamilton's farm at present, knowing that Sheila, whom he had loved and idealised, was likely to meet him in the roads at any moment, a baby in her arms, perhaps at her breast, and a husband somewhere near at hand.

"I must go," he told himself. "I must get over this. . . ."

6

Mr. Quinn and he travelled to Belfast together on the following morning, and they spent the hour before the steamer sailed for Liverpool in pacing up and down the deck.

"You can write to me when you get to London," Mr. Quinn said, and Henry nodded his head.

He was very conscious now of his father's disappointment, and although he was determined to go to London, he was moved by the affectionate way in which the old man tried to provide for his needs on the journey.

"Hap yourself well," he had said when they crossed the gangway on to the boat. "These steamers never give you enough clothes on your bunk. I'd put my overcoat on top of the quilt if I were you! . . ."

They stood for a time looking across the Lagan at the shipyard, and talked about the possibility of Ninian Graham entering the shipbuilding firm, and then they moved to the side of the boat that was against the quay-wall. The hour at which the steamer was to depart was drawing near and the number of passengers had increased. They could hear the noise of the machinery as the cargo was lowered from the quay into the hold, and now and then, the squealing of pigs as the drovers pushed them up the gangways. A herd of cattle came through the sheds and stumbled in a startled, stupid fashion on to the lower decks, while the drovers thwacked them and shouted at them. There was a small crowd of people, friends of passengers and casual onlookers, standing on the quay waiting to see the ship go out, and some of them were shouting messages to their friends. Henry had always liked to watch crowds at times such as this, and often in Dublin, he had spent a while in Westland Row Station, looking at the people who were going to England. He was so interested in the crowd on the quay that he did not hear his father speaking to him.

"I want to speak to you, Henry," the old man said, and then receiving no answer, he said again, "I want to speak to you, Henry!"

"Yes, father?" Henry answered, without looking up.

"Turn round a minute, Henry! . . ." He hesitated, and Henry turning round, saw that his father was embarrassed.

"What is it, father?" he said.

"I just wanted to say something to you, Henry. You see, you're beginnin' another life . . . out of my control, if you follow me . . . not that I ever tried to boss you. . . ."

"No, father, you've never done that. You've been awfully decent to me!"

"Ah, now, no more of that! I just wanted to say somethin' to you, only I don't rightly know how to begin. . . ." He fumbled for words and then, as if making a reckless plunge, he blurted out, "Do you know much, Henry?"

"Know much?" Henry answered vaguely.

"Aye. About women an' things? Did you know any women in Dublin?"

"Oh, yes, a few!" Henry answered.

"Did . . . did you have anything to do with them?"

"Anything to do with them!"

"Aye!"

Henry began to comprehend his father's questions. "Oh, I . . . I kissed one or two of them!" he said.

"Was that all?" Mr. Quinn's voice was so low that Henry had difficulty in hearing him.

"Yes, father," he answered.

"You know, don't you, that there's other things than kisses? Or do you not know it?"

Henry nodded his head.

"I'm . . . I'm not interferin' with you, Henry. I'm not just askin' for the sake of askin' . . . but . . . well, do you know anything about those . . . things?"

He moved slightly as he spoke, as if, by moving, he could take the edge off his question.

"I know about them, father. Something!" Henry said huskily, for his father's questions embarrassed him strangely.

"You've never . . . you've never! . . ."

"No, father!"

Mr. Quinn turned away and looked over the side of the boat. He seemed to be watching a piece of orange peel which floated between the wall and the side of the boat. The first bell of warning to friends of passengers was sounded, and he turned sharply and looked at his son. "I'll have to be goin' soon," he said.

"That's only the first bell, father," Henry replied. "There's plenty of time yet!"

"Aye!" Mr. Quinn glanced about the deck which was now covered by passengers. "You'll have plenty of company goin' over," he said.

"Yes!"

They were making conversation with difficulty. Mr. Quinn felt nervous and a little unhappy because Henry was leaving him so soon, and Henry felt disturbed because of the strange conversation he had just had with his father. He had a shamed sense of intrusion into privacies.

"It's very interestin' to see a boat goin' out to sea," Mr. Quinn was saying. "I used to come down here many's a time when I was a young fellow just to watch the steamers goin' out. Did you ever stan' on top of a hill an' watch a boat sailin' out to sea?"

"No, I don't remember doing that!"

"It's a fine sight, that! You see her lights shinin' in the dark a long way off, but you can't see her, except mebbe the foam she makes, an' begod you near want to cry. That's the way it affects me anyway. . . . Henry, if you ever get into any bother over the head of a woman, you'll tell me, won't you, an' I'll stan' by you!" He said this so suddenly, coming close to Henry as he said it, that Henry was startled. "You'll not forget," he went on.

"No, father, I won't forget!"

"I've been wantin' to say that to you for a good while, but it's a hard thing for a man to say to his own son. I could say it easier to somebody else's son nor I can to you. London's a quare place for a young fella, Henry, but it's no good preachin' to men about women . . . no good at all. The only thing you can do is to stan' by a man when he gets into bother. That's all, except to hope to God he'll not disgrace his name if he's your son. You know where to write to, Henry, if you need any help! . . . Hilloa, there's the second bell!"

They could hear the sailors calling out "Any more for the shore!" and the sound of hurried farewells and the shuffle of awkward feet along the gangways.

"Good-bye, Henry!"

"Good-bye, father!"

"You'll not forget to write now an' awhile?"

"I'll write to you the minute I get to London!"

"Ah, don't hurry yourself! You'll mebbe be tired out when you arrive. Just wait 'til the mornin', an' write at your leisure. . . ."

"Hurry up, sir!" an impatient sailor said.

"Ah, sure, there's plenty of time, man! Good-bye, Henry! I believe I'm the last one to go ashore. Well, so long!"

They shook hands, and then the old man went down the gangway.

"Any more for the shore?" the sailor shouted, unloosing the rope that held the gangway fast to the ship. Then the gangway was cast off. A bell rang, and in an instant the sound of the screws beating in the water was heard. A shudder ran through the boat as the engines began to move, and slowly the gap between the ship and the quay widened. Henry smiled at his father, and the old man blinked and smiled back. The passengers leant against the side of the boat and shouted farewells and messages to their friends on shore. "Mind an' write!" "Remember me to every one, will you!" "Tell Maggie I was askin' for her!" Then hats were waved and handkerchiefs were floated like flags. . . . A woman stood near to Henry and cried miserably to herself. . . . The ship swung into the middle of the Lagan and began to move down towards the sea. Henry could still see his father, standing under the yellow glare of a large lamp hanging from the shed. He had taken off his hat, and was waving it to his son. It seemed to Henry suddenly that the old man's hair was very grey and thin. . . . He took out his handkerchief and waved it vigorously in response. Somewhere in the steerage people were singing a hymn:

'Til we me . . ee . . eet, 'til we me . . eet,
'Til we meet at Je . e . su's feet . . . Jesu's feet,
'Til we me . . ee . . eet, 'til we me . . eet,
God be with you 'til we meet again!

The slurring, sentimental sounds became extraordinarily human and moving in the dusky glow, and he felt tempted to hum the words under his breath in harmony with the singers in the steerage; but two men were standing behind him, and he was afraid they would overhear him. He could hear one of them saying to his companion, "I always say, eat as much as you can stuff inside you, an' run the risk of bein' sick. Some people makes a point of eatin' nothin' at all when they're crossin' the Channel, but they're sick all the same, an' they damn near throw off their insides. A drop of whiskey is a good thing! . . ."

The boat was making way now, and the people on the quay were ceasing to have separate outlines: they were merging in a big, dark blur under the yellow light. Henry could not see his father at the spot where he had stood when the ship moved away, and he felt disappointed when he thought to himself that the old man had not waited until the last moment. Then he saw a figure hurrying along the quays, waving a large white handkerchief. . . . It was his father, trying to keep pace with the boat, and Henry shouted to him and waved his hands to him in a kind of delirium. Gradually the boat outstripped the old man, and at last he stood still and watched it disappearing into the darkness. He was still waving to Henry, but no sound came from him. He seemed to be terribly alone there on the dark quay. . . . Henry shuddered in the night air, and glancing about him saw that most of the passengers had gone down to the saloon or to their cabins. He, too, was almost alone. He turned to look again at his father, straining to catch the last glimpse of him, and while he was straining thus, he heard the old man's voice vibrating across the river to him. "Good-bye Henry!" he shouted. "God bless you, son!" and Henry felt that he must leap overboard and swim back to the shore. He waved his handkerchief towards the place where his father was standing and tried to shout "Good-bye, father!" to him, but his voice rattled weakly in his throat, and he felt tears starting in his eyes.

"It's silly of me to behave like this," he murmured to himself, rubbing his eyes with his hand.

The boat had passed between the Twin Islands and was now sailing swiftly down the Lough towards the Irish Sea. The lights on the quay faded into a faint yellow blur, like little lost stars, and presently, when the cold airs of the sea struck him sharply, he turned and went towards the saloon.

"I hope to goodness it'll be smooth all the way over," he said to himself.

THE THIRD CHAPTER

1

Roger Carey and Gilbert Farlow met him at Euston.

"Hilloa, Quinny!" Gilbert said, "I've been made a dramatic critic, and I'm to do my first play to-night!"

"Hurray!" he answered, and turned to greet Roger.

"We've bagged a taxi," Gilbert went on. "The driver looks cheeky . . . that's why we hired him. We'll give him a tuppenny tip and then we'll give him in charge! . . ."

"All taxi drivers are cheeky," Roger interrupted.

"But this is a very cheeky one! . . . Hi, porter!"

It was extraordinarily good to be with Gilbert and Roger again; extraordinarily good to hear Gilbert's exaggerated speech and see him ordering people about without hurting their feelings; extraordinarily good to listen to Roger's slow, unflickering voice as he stated the facts . . . for Roger had always stated the facts. In all their discussions, it was Roger who reminded them of the essential things, refusing persistently to be carried away by Gilbert's imagination or Ninian's impatience. People were sometimes irritated by Roger's slow, imperturbable way of speaking . . . they called him a prig . . . but as they knew him better, they lost their irritation and thought of him with respect. "But we're all prigs," Gilbert said once in reply to some one who sneered at Roger. "Ninian and Quinny and Roger and me, we're frightful prigs. That's because we're so much brainier than most people. Of course, Roger was Second Wrangler, and that affects a man, I suppose, but he's terribly clever, young Roger is! . . ."

As they drove home, Gilbert told their news to Henry.

195

"Ninian's coming up to-morrow . . . sooner than he
meant to. He's very keen on going to Harland and Wolff's,
but he's afraid he's too old to begin building ships. Tom
Arthurs says he ought to have gone straight to the Island
from Rumpell's instead of going to Cambridge, and poor
old Ninian was horribly blasphemous about it all. It's
funny to hear him trying to talk like an Orangeman . . .
he mixes it up with Devonshire dialect . . . and thinks he's
imitating Tom Arthurs. I suppose he'll have to content
himself with building railways and things like that. It's a
great pity!"

"I don't believe he really wants to be a shipbuilder,"
Roger said. "He likes Tom Arthurs, and he wants to be
what Arthurs is. That's all. If Arthurs were a comedian,
Ninian would want to be a comedian, too!"

"It must be splendid," Henry murmured, "to be able
to influence people like that!"

The taxi drew up to the door of a house in one of the
quieter Bloomsbury squares, and Henry, looking out of
the window, while Gilbert opened the door of the cab, saw
that the garden in the centre of the square was very green.
He could see figures in white flannels running and jumping,
and the sound of tennis balls, as they collided with the
racquets, pleased him.

"Your room overlooks the square," Gilbert said, as
Henry got out of the cab.

"Splendid!" he replied. "I shall imagine I'm in Dublin when I look out of the window. It's just like Merrion
Square! . . ."

"Well, pay the cabby, will you? I'm broke!" said Gilbert.

"You always are," Roger murmured.

2

Ninian joined them on the following day, very cheer-
less and irritable. It was impossible for him to enter the

shipbuilding firm owing to his age, and so he had decided to enter the offices of a firm of engineers in London. "Anybody can build a damned railway," he said, "but it takes a man to build a ship. I'd love to build a liner . . . one that could cross the Atlantic in four days!"

"Four days!" Gilbert scoffed. "My dear Ninian, boats don't crawl across the ocean! People want boats that will take them to New York in twenty-four hours! . . ."

"And now, young fellows!" he went on, "it's time that we thought seriously about our immortal souls!"

"Oh, is it?" said Ninian.

"Yes, it is," Gilbert replied.

They had dined, and were now sitting in Gilbert's room in the lax attitude of people who have eaten well and are content.

"Here we are," Gilbert went on, using his pipe as a modulator of his points, "four bright lads simply bursting with brains, and the question is, what is to become of us? The Boy: What Will He Become? Take Roger, for example, will he become Lord Chancellor of England, or a footling little Registrar of a footling County Court? . . ."

"I haven't had a brief yet," Roger interrupted, "so that question's somewhat premature, isn't it?"

"I'm not talking about *now* . . . I'm talking about the future," Gilbert replied. "We ought to have some notion of what we're going to do with our lives. . . . As a matter of fact," he continued, "your career's fairly certain, Roger. With all that brain oozing out of you, you're bound to become great. But what about little Ninian here? And Quinny? And me? Ninian's a discontented sort of bloke, and he's quite likely to make a mess of things unless we look after him. He may turn out to be a very great engineer or he may go back to Boveyhayne and play the turnip-headed squire! . . ."

"Always rotting a chap," Ninian mumbled.

"And Quinny . . . what about little Quinny? He's written a novel! . . ."

"Written a what?" Ninian demanded, sitting up sharply.

"Have you, Quinny?" said Roger.

Henry blushed and nodded his head. "It isn't good," he said. "I shall have to re-write it!"

"My Lord," said Ninian, "fancy one of us writing a book!"

Gilbert slapped him on the side of the head. "You forget, Ninian, that I've written a play! . . ."

"A play's not a book! . . ."

"*My* plays are books," Gilbert retorted. "Well, now," he went on, "what's to become of little Quinny: a tip-top novelist with a limited circulation or a third-rater who sells millions?"

"What about yourself?" Ninian said.

"I'm coming to myself. Will I become a great dramatist, like Shakespeare and Bernard Shaw and all those chaps, or merely turn out hack plays? . . ."

"And the answer is?"

"I don't know, but I'll tell you in ten years' time. We're a brainy lot of lads, and I'm the brainiest of the lot! . . ."

"Oh, no, you're not," said Ninian. "I've quite a respectable amount of brain myself, but the very best brain in the room belongs to Roger. Doesn't it, Roger?"

"I don't despise my brain, Ninian!" Roger answered.

"Observe the modest demeanour of the truly great man," Gilbert exclaimed. "You'll have to go into politics, Roger. It isn't any good being a barrister unless you do!"

"I've thought of that," Roger answered. "At the moment, I'm wondering which side I'm on. I might manage to get a seat as a Liberal, but I don't believe it would be of much use to me if I got it. I think I shall join the Tories! . . ."

"Are you a Tory?" Ninian said, "I thought you were a Liberal!"

"No, I'm a barrister. You see," he went on, as if he were arguing a case, "the Liberal majority is too big and

there are far too many clever young men in the party. I
should only be one of a crowd if I went into the House
now as a Liberal . . . and of course I'm not likely to be
given a chance of standing for a seat because they've a lot
of people on the list already. But the Tories have hardly
any clever chaps left. There's Balfour and there's Chamberlain . . . and then what is there?''

"Nothing!" said Gilbert.

"A clever man of my age has the chance of a lifetime
with the Tories now," Roger continued. "Look at F. E.
Robinson . . . and he's only a third-rater!"

Gilbert told a story of the early days of the Tory Party
after the General Election of 1900 when the Tories had been
completely routed by the Liberals. "The Tory remnant
was as thick-headed as it could be," he said, "and the
Liberals were bursting with brains. Balfour came into the
House one night . . . he'd just been re-elected . . . and
he sat down beside Chamberlain. They were frightfully
blue. Balfour had a look at the Liberals, and then he
turned to his own back-benches and had a look at the
Tories. Of course, it may not be true, but they say he
went pale with fright. He turned to Chamberlain and
said, "My God, Joseph!" and then Chamberlain turned
and looked at the Tories and said, "My God, Arthur!"
You see, Chamberlain never noticed things until Balfour
pointed them out to him, and then he noticed them too
much. They went out of the House immediately afterwards and shook hands with each other, and Chamberlain
said 'Arthur, we're the Opposition!' And so they were.
Poor Balfour was awfully lonely after Chamberlain crocked
up. Not a soul on his own side that was fit to talk to!
It was easy enough for F. E. Robinson to make a name in a
crowd like that. And they loathe him, too. He's such a
bounder! But they need a fellow to heave mud, so they
put up with him. Roger's got more brains in his little
finger than that fellow has in his whole body. Haven't
you, Roger?''

"People don't have brains in their little fingers," Roger answered.

"You should join the Tories, Roger," Ninian said. "There really isn't much difference between them. My father was a Conservative, but my Uncle Geoffrey was a Liberal. When father was in, uncle was out. It amounted to the same thing in the end! . . ."

"But Roger ought to be a different sort of Tory!" Gilbert exclaimed. "It's no good having all his brain if he's just going to peddle around with the same old stuff. . . ."

"I don't intend to do that," said Roger.

"Well, what do you intend to do?"

Ninian seized a cushion and put it behind his back. "Let's have a good old argle-bargle," he said. "What do you say, Quinny?"

Henry, who had not joined in the discussion, leant forward and smiled. "Oh, I like listening to you," he answered. "You're all so sure of yourselves! . . ."

Gilbert turned on him. "Well, aren't you sure of yourself?" he demanded.

"No, I'm not," Henry answered. "I never am!"

"That's queer," said Gilbert.

"Damned queer," said Ninian.

"Why are you so uncertain of yourself?" Roger asked.

"Don't you feel sure that you'll be a great novelist?" Gilbert added before Henry had time to reply to Roger's question.

"I know jolly well I shall be a clinking good engineer!" Ninian said.

Henry had a shy unwillingness to discuss himself in front of the others, although they were his closest friends. He felt that he could not sit still while they watched him as he told them of his ambitions and his fears.

"Oh, don't let's talk about me," he said. "Go on with your argle-bargle." He was speaking hurriedly, so that he had difficulty in articulating his words. "You were

saying something, Ninian, weren't you . . . no, it was you,
Roger, about politics! . . ."

"Oh, yes!" Roger answered.

"Rum chap, you are!" Gilbert said to Henry in a low
voice.

3

"You see," said Roger, "my notion is to restore the
prestige of the Tories. Somehow, they've let themselves
get the reputation of being consciously heartless. The
Liberals go about proclaiming that they are the friends
of the poor, and the inference is that the Tories are the
friends of the rich!"

"So they are," said Ninian.

"So are the Liberals!" said Roger.

"So's everybody!" said Gilbert.

"But the Tories aren't culpably the friends of the rich,"
Roger continued. "I mean, they don't go into parliament
with the intention of exploiting poor men for the benefit
of rich men. It isn't true that they are indifferent to the
fate of poor men; but they have allowed the Liberals to
give them that character. I've always said that the Tories
have the courage of the Liberals' convictions! . . ."

Gilbert lay back on the floor with his arms under his
head. "I remember the first time you said that. It was
in the Union!" he exclaimed.

"I shall say it again in the House some day," Roger
retorted. "I'm not trying to be funny when I say that. I
think the history of the Tory Party shows very plainly
that the Tories have done very admirable things for the
working-people: Factory Acts and Housing schemes and
Workmen's Compensation Acts. Well, I want the Tory
Party to remember that it is the custodian of the decency
of England. It isn't decent that there should be hungry
children and unemployed men and badly-housed families.
That kind of thing is intolerable to a gentleman, and a

Tory is a gentleman. It seems to me inconceivable that a Tory should be willing to make money by cheating a child out of a meal . . . but there are plenty of Liberals who do that. And I'm against all this legislation which makes some public authority do things for people which they ought to be doing for themselves. I mean, I hate the notion of the State feeding hungry school-children because the parents cannot afford to feed them, when the proper thing to do is to see that the parents are paid enough for their work to enable them to feed their children themselves. I suppose I'm sloppy . . . the Fabians used to say so at Cambridge . . . but I prefer the spectacle of a family round its own table to the spectacle of a crowd of assorted youngsters round a municipal school table! And I don't think we're getting the most out of our people! Just think of the millions of men and women in this country who really do not earn more than their keep! That isn't good enough. If you can only just keep yourself going, then you've no right to go . . . except to hell as quickly as possible. My idea is that we waste potentialities at present, not by squandering them, but by never using them. All those poor people, for example, how do we know that some of them, if given an opportunity, would not be amazingly worth while! There must be a great deal of brain-power simply chucked away or misused. I know that lots of people believe that men of genius work their way up to their level no matter how low down they begin, but I doubt that, and anyhow I'm not talking of geniuses . . . I'm talking of the average clever man . . . there must be men of good average quality lost in slums because none of us have taken the trouble to clear the ground for them. And the ground has to be cleared! You can't grow wheat on a sour soil. I often think when I see some hooligan brought into Court that, given a real chance, he might have been a better judge than the man who sends him to gaol. The Tory's job is to restore the balance of things. It isn't only to maintain the level, but to raise it and to keep on raising it. . . . I believe in the State of Poise, of equitable adjustment, in which every man will be able to move easily to his proper place. . . . There are so many obstacles now in the way of man finding his place that, even if he has the strength to get over them, he probably won't have the strength to fill it. . . ."

"My view, perhaps, is narrower than yours, Roger," Henry said, "but I see all these people chiefly as men and women who are shut out of things: books and pictures and plays and music and all the decent things. I don't believe that if they had the chance they would all read Meredith and admire Whistler and go to see Shaw's plays and want to listen to Wagner . . . that's not the point, and anyhow the middle and the upper classes are not all marvellously cultured. My point is that their lives are such that they don't even know of Meredith and Whistler and Shaw and Wagner. They don't even know of the second-rate people or the third rate. Magnolia, for instance . . . I suppose she reads novelettes, and when she grows out of novelettes, she won't read anything. And she can't afford to go to a West End theatre. . . . When I think of these people, millions of 'em, I think of them as people like Magnolia, completely shut out of things like that, not even aware of them. . . ."

They spent the remainder of the evening in argument, their talk ranging over the wide field of human activity. They established a system of continual criticism of existing institutions. "Challenge everything," said Gilbert; "make it justify its existence." They tried to discover the truth about things, to shed their prejudices and to see the facts of life exactly as they were. "The great thing is to get rid of Slop!" said Roger. "We've got to convince the judge as well as move the jury. It isn't enough to make the jury feel sloppy . . . any ass can do that. You've got to convince the old chap on the bench or you won't get a verdict. That's my belief, and I believe, too, that the jury is more likely to listen to reason than people imagine!''

They did not finish their argument that evening nor on any particular evening. They were spread over a long period, and were part of the process of clearing their minds of cobwebs.

Gilbert had dedicated his life to the renascence of the drama and had written a couple of plays which, he admitted to his friends, had not got the right stuff in them. ''I don't know enough yet,'' he said once to Henry, ''but I'm learning. . . .'' His dramatic criticism was very pointed, and he speedily acquired a reputation among people who are interested in the theatre, as an acute but harsh critic, and already attempts had been made by theatrical managers either to bribe him or get him dismissed from his paper. The bribing process was quite delicately operated. One manager wrote to him, charmingly plaintive about his criticism, and invited him to put himself in the manager's place. ''I assure you,'' he wrote, ''I would willingly produce good work if I could get it, but I can't. Come and see me, and I'll show you a pile of plays that have arrived within the last fortnight. I know quite well, without reading them, that not one of them will be of the slightest worth!'' And Gilbert had gone to see him, and had been received very charmingly and told how clever he was, and then the manager had offered to appoint him reader of plays at a pleasant fee! . . . Following that attempt at bribery came the anger of an actor-knight who declined to admit Gilbert to his theatre, a piece of petulance which delighted him.

''The great big balloon,'' he said to his editor when he was told of what the actor-knight had said over the telephone. ''My Lord, when I hear him spouting blank verse through his nose! . . .''

''That's all very fine,'' the editor retorted ruefully, ''but your criticism's doing us a lot of harm. Jefferson of the Torch Theatre cancelled his advertisement the day after your notice of his new play appeared!''

"Ridiculous ass!" said Gilbert.

"Well, if you say his play's the worst that's ever been put on any stage, what do you expect him to do? Fall on your neck and say, 'Bless you, brother!'? You might try to be kinder to them, Farlow, and do for the love of God remember the advertisement manager. If you could get the human note in your stuff! . . .''

"The what?"

"The human note. I'm a great believer in the human note.''

Gilbert left the office as quickly as he could and went home. He came into the dining-room where the others were already seated at their meal.

"You're late again, Gilbert," said Roger. "Hand over your sixpence!"

Roger, who was never late for anything, had instituted a system of fines for those who were late for meals. The fine for unpunctuality at dinner was sixpence.

"I haven't got a tanner, damn it," Gilbert snapped, "and I'm looking for the human note. That's why I'm late. My heavenly father, I'm hungry! What is there?"

"Sixpence for being late for dinner," said Roger quietly, "and tuppence for blasphemy!"

He entered the amounts in the "Ledger," and then returned to his seat. "You already owe six and three-pence," he said, as he sat down, "and this evening's fines bring it up to six and elevenpence. You ought to pay something on account, Gilbert! . . .''

"Pass the potatoes and don't bleat so much!" said Gilbert. "Look here, Quinny," he said as he helped himself to the potatoes, "what's the human note, and don't you think tuppence is too much for blasphemy?"

"Ask Ninian," Henry answered. "He knows all about humanity!"

"No, he doesn't. Bally mechanic! Aren't you, Ninian? Aren't you a damn little mechanic with a screw-driver for a soul! . . ."

"You'll get a punch on the jaw in a minute, young fellow me lad!" Ninian exclaimed, leaning over the table and slapping Gilbert on the cheek.

"Fined fourpence for threat of physical violence and ninepence for executing the same," Roger murmured. "I'll enter it presently."

"Somebody should slay Roger," Gilbert said. "Somebody should take hold of his neat little neck and wring it! . . ."

They finished their meal and sat back in their chairs, smoking and chattering.

"What's all this about the human note, Gilbert?" Henry asked, and Gilbert explained what had happened to him in the editor's room. "I stopped a bobby in the Strand and asked him about it," he said, "but he told me to move on. You ought to know what the human note is, Quinny. You're a novelist, and novelists are supposed to know everything nowadays!"

He did not wait for Henry to explain the meaning of the human note. "I know what Dilton means by it," he said. "When *he* talks of the human note he means the greasy touch!"

"Slop in fact!" said Roger.

"That's it. Slop! My God, these journalists do love to splash about in their emotions. They can't mention the North Pole without gulping in their throats. Dilton gave me an example of the human note. There was a bye-election in the East End the other day and one of the candidates put his unfortunate infants into 'pearlies' and hawked them about the constituency in a costermonger's barrow, carrying a notice with 'Vote for Our Daddy!' on it. Dilton damned near blubbed when he told me about it!"

"Rage?" said Henry.

"Rage!" Gilbert exclaimed. "Good Lord, no! The man was moved, touched! . . . He blew his nose hard, and then told me that one touch of nature makes the whole world kin! I'm damned if he didn't write a leading article about it . . . and they give him a couple of thousand a year for organising sniffs for the million. All over Enggland, I suppose there were people snivelling over those brats and telling each other that one touch of nature makes the whole world kin! . . . Oof! gimme the whisky, somebody, for the love of the Lordy God! I want to be sick when I think of the human note!"

"Well, of course," said Roger, "the slop is there, and it's no good getting angry about it. What I want is a Party that won't deal in it. I've always believed that the mob likes an honest man, even if it does call him a Prig, and I'm perfectly certain that when a Prig gets let down by the mob it's because in some subconscious way it knows he's only pretending to be honest . . . unless, of course, it's gone off its head with passion of some sort: Boer war jingoism and that kind of thing. And my notion of a member of parliament is a man who represents some degree of general feeling. If he doesn't represent that general feeling he can only do one of two things: try to convert the general opinion to his point of view or else, if he can't convert it, tell it he'll be damned if he'll represent it any longer. That's the attitude I shall adopt in the House! . . ."

But Gilbert thought that this was a dangerous attitude to maintain.

"If you maintain it too long, you'll never get an office," he said, "and so the only work you'll be able to do will be critical work: you'll never get a chance to do anything constructive; and if you let the Government nobble you, and give you an Under Secretaryship the moment they see you getting dangerous, then you're done for. And anyhow, I don't believe in independent members of parliament. A certain number of sheep are necessary in every organisation, in parliament as much as anywhere else. It would be absolutely impossible to carry on Government if the whole six hundred and seventy members of parliament were as clever and as independent as Lord Hugh Cecil. You must have sheep and lots of 'em! . . ."

"But they needn't be dead sheep," said Roger. "They needn't be mutton, need they?"

"No, they needn't be mutton, but they must be sheep," Gilbert replied.

"All the politicians I've ever met," said Ninian, "were like New Zealand lamb . . . frozen!"

Gilbert leaped on him and slapped his back, capsizing him on to the floor. "Ninian, my son," he said, "that's a good line. Do you mind if I put it in my comedy. It doesn't matter whether you do or not, but I'd like your consent."

"Don't be an old ass," said Ninian.

"Can I use that line about the New Zealand lamb? . . ."

"Yes, yes . . . any damn thing . . . only get off my chest! You're . . . you're squeezing the inside out of me. Get up, will you! . . ."

"I'm really quite comfortable, thanks, Ninian. If it weren't for this whacking big bone here! . . ."

He did not complete the sentence, for Ninian, with a heaving effort, threw him on to the floor, where they scrambled and punched each other. . . .

"There is a fine of eighteenpence," said Roger, "for disorderly conduct. I'll just enter it against you both!"

The combatants rose and routed Roger, and when they had disposed of him, Ninian agreed to let Gilbert use his line about the frozen meat. "I shall expect you to put a note in the programme that the epigram in the second act was supplied by Mr. Ninian Graham," he said.

"*The* epigram!" Gilbert exclaimed. "*The* epigram!"

"Why, will there be any more?" said Ninian innocently.

Hostilities thereupon broke out again.

4

They sat up late that night talking of themselves and
of England and public affairs. Roger was interested in
Trade Unions, and he lamented the fact that the Tories had
allowed an alliance to be formed between Labour and
Liberalism. "Ask any workman you meet in the street
whether he'd rather work for a Liberal or a Tory, and I
bet you what you like, the chances are that he'll plump for
the Tory. His experience is that the Tory's the better
employer, and the reason why that's so is that the Liberal
conducts his business on principles, whereas the Tory conducts his on instincts. In principle, the Liberal concedes
most things to the workman, but in practice he doesn't:
in principle, the Tory concedes nothing to the workman,
but in practice he treats him decently. The workman
knows that, but the fool goes and votes for the Liberal,
and the fool of a Tory lets him! . . . You know," he went
on, "this Trade Union movement has got on to wrong lines
altogether. Their chief function seems to be to protect
their members from . . . well, from being cheated. That's
what it comes to. I don't blame 'em. They've had to
behave like that. I don't think any one can read Webb's
'Industrial Democracy' and 'The History of Trade Unionism' without feeling that, on the whole, employers have
been rather caddish to workmen . . . so I don't blame the
Unions for making so much fuss about their rights. But
I'd like to see them making as much fuss about the quality
of the work done by their members. That's their real function. It isn't enough to keep up the standard of wages
and of conditions of employment—they ought also to keep
up the standard of work!"

This led them into a wrangle about the responsibility
for the blame for this indifference to quality of work.

"I suppose," said Roger, "employers and employed are
to blame. I think myself it's the result of a world tendency towards hustle . . . to get the thing done as quickly

as possible without regard to the quality of it. I suppose a modern contractor would break his heart if he were asked to spend his lifetime on *one* cathedral . . . but people were proud to do that in the Middle Ages. We'd build half a dozen cathedrals while a Middle Ages man was decorating a gargoyle!''

"Well, we have this comfort," said Ninian, "the modern builder's stuff won't last as long as Westminster Abbey!''

"I hate all this bleat about the Middle Ages," Gilbert exclaimed. "I'm surprised to hear you, Roger, talking like that fat papist, Belloc. One 'ud think to hear you talking that no one ever did shoddy work until the nineteenth century, but Christopher Wren let a lot of shoddy stuff into St. Paul's Cathedral. There were fraudulent contractors then, and jerry-builders, just as there are now, and there probably always will be people who give a bad return for their wages! . . .''

"That's why I want to see the Tory Party resuscitated," said Roger. "I want to limit the number of such people and to make every man feel that it's a gentlemanly thing to do your best, whatever your job is, and that payment has nothing whatever to do with the way you do your work!''

The whole industrial system would need re-shaping, the whole social system would need re-shaping, the Empire would need re-shaping.

"This craving for cheapness has cheapened nothing but life," said Roger, "and it brings incalculable trouble with it. I mean, a ha'penny saved now means pounds lost later. Oh, that's a platitude, I know, but we pay no heed to it. I've never been to America, but we know quite well that one of the most serious problems for the Americans is the negro problem. I heard a Rhodes scholar talking about it once. He simply foamed at the mouth. He hadn't any plan for it . . . didn't seem to realise that a plan could be made . . . and you know they've only got that problem through the greediness of their ancestors. Negroes aren't native to America. The planters wanted cheap labour and so they imported them . . . and the end of that business is the Negro Problem!''

"And lynchings and a Civil War in between," Henry murmured. "That's the most hateful part of it . . . the killing and the bitterness."

"Great Scott!" said Ninian, "think of all those Yankees killing each other so that niggers might wear spats and top hats and sing coon songs in the music halls! . . . Damn silly, I call it!"

"We've got to make people believe that it isn't what you get that matters, but what you do," Roger went on. "All this footling squabble between workmen and employers about a farthing an hour more or a farthing an hour less . . . isn't decent . . . it isn't gentlemanly. Oh, I know very well that the counter-jumper thinks it's very clever to trick a customer out of a ha'penny . . . but it doesn't last, that kind of profit. We lost America because we behaved like cads to the colonists, and we'll lose everything if we continue to play the counter-jumper trick. It isn't very popular now to talk about gentlemen . . . people sneer at the word . . . but I'd rather die like a gentleman than live like a cad . . . and that's the spirit I want to see restored to the Tory Party. It's awfully needed in England now!"

They began to lay plans for an Improved Tory Party that included an alliance with Labour and a closer confederation of the colonies, together with a definite understanding with America.

"And what about Ireland?" said Henry.

"Oh, of course, Ireland must have Home Rule and be treated like a colony. Nobody but a fool wants to treat it in any other way!" said Roger.

"There are an awful lot of fools in the world," Gilbert said.

"I know that," Roger retorted, "but need we trouble about them?"

"We've got to get a group of fellows together on much

the same principle as the Fabian Society . . . no one to
be admitted unless he has brains and is willing to work
without payment. *Look* at the work that Sidney Webb
and Bernard Shaw and all those people did for Socialism
for nothing, even paying for it out of their own pockets
when they weren't over-flush . . . my goodness, if we can
only get people with that kind of spirit into our group,
we'll mould the world! By the way, we ought to pinch
some ideas from the Fabians! We could meet somewhere
. . . here, to begin with. And when we've got a group of
fellows together with some notion of what we all want to
do, we can start inviting eminent ones to talk to us . . .
and heckle the stuffing out of them!"

Gilbert was able to tell them a great deal about the
origin of the Fabian Society . . . for his father was one
of the founders of it . . . and he told them how the Society
had invited Mr. Haldane to talk to them . . . and of the
way in which they had fallen on him in the discussion and
left all his arguments in shreds when the meeting
ended. . . . "If we can get Balfour or Asquith or some
other Eminent Pot here," he said, "and simply argue
hell's blazes out of him . . . my Lordy God, that 'ud be
great!"

"They're not likely to come," said Ninian.

"I don't know. Eminent Ones sometimes do the most
unusual things!"

Ninian yawned and stretched his arms. "I move that
this House be now adjourned!" he said.

But they ignored his sleepiness, and he would not move
away from their company.

"Well, we've settled what our future is to be," said Gilbert.

"What is it to be?" Ninian interrupted, stifling another
yawn.

"Weren't you listening? We're to be Improved Tories
. . . and we're to improve the Universe, so to speak.
We've just settled it. All the Old Birds are to be hoofed

out of office, and we're to take their places, and I thoroughly approve of that. In my opinion, any man who wants to occupy a place of authority after the age of sixty should be publicly and cruelly pole-axed. I can't stand old men . . . they're so cowardly and so obstinate and so conceited!''

"The great thing," said Roger, "is to keep ourselves from sloppiness. We mustn't make fools of ourselves!''

"The principal way in which a man makes a fool of himself," Gilbert added, "is in connexion with the female species. Is that what you mean, Roger?'' Roger nodded his head. "Pay attention to that, Ninian," Gilbert went on. "You have a weakness for females, I've noticed!''

Ninian, suddenly forgetting his fatigue, sat up in his seat. "I say, let's jaw about women," he said.

"No," Gilbert replied. "We won't . . . not at this hour of the morning!'' But, disregarding his decision, he went on, "My view of women is that we all make too much fuss about 'em! Either we damn them excessively or we praise them excessively. They're a cursed nuisance in literature. All the writers seem to think that man was made for woman or woman for man, and they write and write about sex and love as if there weren't other things in the world besides women!''

"I'd like to know what else we were made for?'' Henry said.

"We were made to do our jobs," Roger answered. "I believe in what I may call the modified anchorite . . . women are too emotional and get between a man and his work. Love is an excellent thing . . . excellent . . . but there are other things! . . .''

"What else is there?'' Henry demanded almost crossly. He felt vaguely stirred by what was being said, vaguely antagonistic to it.

"Oh, lots of things," Roger answered. "Fighting for your place, moving multitudes to do your will . . . oh, lots of things!''

Gilbert had read some of Henry's novel, and he now began to talk about it.

"You turn on the Slop-tap too often," he said. "Quinny, my son, you're a clever little chap, but you're frightfully sloppy. I've read a lot more of your novel. . . ."

"Yes?" said Henry, nervously anxious to hear his criticism.

"Slop!" Gilbert continued. "Just slop, Quinny! Women aren't like lumps of dough that a baker punches into any shape he likes, and they aren't sticks of barley sugar. . . ."

"No, they aren't," Roger interrupted. "Wait till you see my cousin Rachel. . . ."

"Have you got a cousin, Roger? How damned odd!" said Gilbert.

"Yes. I must bring her round here one evening. She's not a bad female . . . quite intelligent for her sex. Go on!"

"They're like us, Quinny!" Gilbert continued. "They're good in parts and bad in parts. That's the vital discovery of the twentieth century, and I've made it! . . ."

Henry had been eager to hear Gilbert's criticism of his novel, but this kind of talk irritated him, though he could not understand why it irritated him, and his irritation drove him to sneers.

"I suppose," he said, "you want to substitute Social Reform and Improved Toryism for Romance. Lordy God, man, do you want to put eugenics and blue-books in place of the love of woman?"

"You're getting cross, Quinny! . . ."

"No, I'm not!"

"Oh, yes, you are . . . very cross . . . and you know what the fine for it is. If you want my opinion, here it is. I *am* prepared to accept eugenics and blue-books as a substitute for the love of women . . . if they're interesting,

of course. That's all I ask of any one or anything . . .
that it shall interest me. I don't care what it is, so long
as it doesn't bore me. Women bore me . . . women in
books and plays, I mean . . . because they're all of a pattern: lovebirds. I've never seen a play in which the
women weren't used for sloppy emotional purposes. The
minute I see a woman walking on to the stage, I say to
myself, 'Here comes the Slop-tap!' and as sure as I'm
alive, the author immediately turns the tap on and the
woman is over ears and head in slop before we're two-
thirds through the first act. And they're not like that in
real life, any more than we are. We aren't continually
making goo-goo eyes, nor are they. I'm going to write a
play one of these days that will stagger the civilised world,
I tell you! It'll be bung full of women but it won't have
a word of slop from beginning to end! . . .''
"It'll be a failure," said Ninian.
"Oh, from the box-office point of view, no doubt! . . .''
"No, from the common sense point of view. I'm on the
side of Quinny in this matter, and I'm as much of an authority on women as you are, Gilbert. I've loved three
different barmaids and a young woman in a tobacconist's
shop, and I say, what the hell is the good of talking all this
rubbish about men and women trotting round as if male
and female He had not created them. When I see a woman,
if she's got any femininity about her at all, I want to hug
her and kiss her, and I do so, if I can, and so does any
man if he is a man. I belong to the masculine gender
and she belongs to the feminine . . . and that's all there's
to be said about it. If we were neuters, we'd be characters
in your play, Gilbert. . . .''
"I don't want to kiss every girl I meet," said Gilbert.
They howled at him in derision. "Oh, you liar!" said
Henry, forgetting his anger.
"You hug women all day long, you Mormon!" Ninian
roared, "or you would if they'd let you!"

"That's why you react so strongly from love in your plays," Roger said judicially. "You can't leave them alone in real life. . . ."

"I don't mean to say I haven't kissed a girl or two," Gilbert admitted.

"*A girl or two!* Listen to him!" Ninian went on. "Oh, listen to the innocent babe and suckling. A girl or two! Look here, let's make a census of 'em. What was the name of that girl whose brother got sent down? Lady Something? . . ."

"Lady Cecily! . . ."

"Shut up!" Gilbert shouted at them, and his voice was full of rage. He stood over them, glaring at them fiercely. . . .

"I say, Gilbert!" said Henry, "what's up?"

He recovered himself. "I'm sorry," he said. "I didn't mean to lose my temper!"

"That's all right, Gilbert," Ninian murmured. "It was my fault. I oughtn't to have rotted you like that!"

"It doesn't matter," Gilbert answered.

5

They were silent for a while, disconcerted by Gilbert's strange outburst of anger, and for a few moments it seemed as if their argument must end now. Ninian began to yawn again, and he was about to propose once more that they should go to bed, when Gilbert resumed the discussion.

"You make no allowance for reticence," he said to Henry. "That's what Roger really wants in politics . . . reticence!"

"In everything," Roger exclaimed

"I know," Gilbert went on. "When I first went in to the *Daily Echo* office, I saw a notice in the sub-editor's room which tickled me to death. Elsden, the night editor, had put it up, and it said that the word 'gutted' was not to be used in describing the state of a house after a

fire. I went to Elsden . . . I like him better than any one
else in the *Echo* office . . . and asked him what was the
matter with the word. 'Well, my dear chap,' he said,
'think of guts! I mean to say, *Guts!* Hang it all, we
must cover up something!' I thought he was being rather
old-maidish then, but I'm not sure now that Elsden's point
of view hasn't got something behind it. He just wanted
to be decently quiet about things that aren't pretty! I
don't think it's necessary to blurt out everything, and I'm
certain that if you keep on washing your dirty linen in
public, people will end up by thinking you've got nothing
else but dirty linen. Your characters," he added, turning
to Henry, "go about, splashing in their emotions as if they
were trick swimmers or . . . or damn little journalists. I
tell you, Quinny, love's a private, furtive thing, a secret
adventure, and open exposure of it is a sort of profan-
ity. . . ."

"No," said Henry emphatically. "Love's made nasty
by secrecy!" He began to spread himself. He had been
reading some of the authors of the Yellow Book period.
"It seems to me," he said, "that the marriage rite is
broken, incomplete. In a healthy state, the whole function
would be performed in public . . . in . . . in a cathedral,
say. There'd be a procession of priests in golden chasubles, and acolytes swinging carved censers, and boys with
banners, and hidden choirs chanting long litanies. . . ."

"I shall be sick in a minute!" said Gilbert. "You're
talking like an over-ripe Oscar Wilde, Quinny, and if you
were really that sort of animal I'd have you hoofed out of
this. Get out the whisky, Ninian, for the love of the Lordy
God! This æsthetic stuff makes my inside wobble!"

Ninian went to the sideboard and took hold of the
whisky bottle. "I don't much like that sort of talk myself," he said. "It's too clever-clever for my taste. I
shouldn't let it grow on me, Quinny, if I were you. You'll
get a reputation like bad eggs, and people'll think you've
strayed out of your period and got lost. As a matter of

fact, Gilbert, you don't really want whisky, and you're only
going to drink it for effect, so you shan't have any!''

He returned to his seat, as he spoke, and sat down.
Henry had a quick sense of shame. He had spoken insin-
cerely, for effect . . . in order to impress them with his
cleverness, and their answer to him filled him with a sense
of inferiority. He felt that they must despise him, and
feeling that, he began to despise himself.

"My own feeling about these things," said Ninian, "is
perfectly simple. I believe in lust. I'm a lustful man
myself, and so, I believe, is Roger! . . ."

"No, I'm not," Roger exclaimed.

"Well, I am," Ninian proceeded. "Lust is the motor
force of the world. . . ."

"No, it isn't," Gilbert interrupted. "The whole of civilisation depends upon the human stomach. If men would
live without eating . . . the whole of this society would
dissolve. Lust is subordinate to the stomach, Ninian.
You've never seen a starving man in a purple passion, have
you?''

Ninian leant forward and tapped the table with his
knuckles. "I say that lust is the motor force of the
world," he said, "and I think you might let me finish
my sentences, Gilbert. You are so eager to vent your own
views that you won't let any one else vent his. . . ."

"What's the good of venting your views if they're
wrong, damn it!" said Gilbert.

"Well, let me finish venting 'em anyhow. Assuming
that I'm right, I say you should treat lust exactly as you
treat the circulation of your blood: don't fuss about it.
It's a natural function, neither beautiful nor ugly. It's
just there, and that's all about it. The fellow who dithers
about it as if he'd invented a new philosophy on the day he
first slept with a woman, is a dirty, neurotic ass. So is the
fellow who pretends that there's no such thing as sex in
the world. Male and female created He them, and I can
tell you, He jolly well knew what He was up to!''

Roger flicked the ash from his cigarette and coughed slightly.

"I think," he said, "we talk too much about these things. They pass the time, of course, but not very profitably. Whatever the Universal Motive may be . . . I'm talking, of course, without prejudice . . . it'll express itself in complete disregard of our feelings and views. I have had no experience of women otherwise than in the capacity of a mother, several aunts, a nurse, a number of cousins, and also some waitresses in restaurants. . . ."

"Roger's never kissed a woman in a sexual sense in his life," Gilbert interrupted.

"I have never seen the necessity of it," Roger said.

"But aren't you curious to know what it's like? After all, it's a form of experience," Henry asked, looking at Roger with curiosity.

"Having scarlet fever is a form of experience, but I don't wish to know what it's like," Roger answered.

"My God, you are a prig, Roger!" said Gilbert simply.

"I know that," Roger answered. "That's why I don't get on with women. They find me out. No," he continued, "I've no experience of women in that way. I daresay I shall get experience some day, but in the meantime, I've got my job to do. . . ."

"We shall have a virgin Lord Chancellor on the woolsack," said Gilbert, "and then may God have mercy on all poor litigants!"

"We really ought to go to bed," Ninian protested.

"Not yet," Henry exclaimed.

He had recovered from his feeling of dejection, and he was eager to retrieve the good opinion which he thought he had lost.

"My own view," he said, beginning as they always began their oracular pronouncements, "my own view is that we make the mistake of thinking in masses instead of in individuals. Everybody who tries to reform the world, tries to make it uniform, but what we want is the most complete diversity that's obtainable. It's the variations from type that make type bearable! . . .''

"That's a good phrase, Quinny. Where'd you get it from?" Gilbert interrupted.

Henry flushed with pleasure. "I made it up," he answered. "All men are different," he went on, "and therefore the morals that suit one person are unlikely to suit another person. Roger doesn't bother about women. He looks upon them as a . . . a sideline. Don't you, Roger? He'll marry in due course, and he'll have one woman, and he'll have her all to himself. Won't you, Roger?"

"Probably," Roger replied, "but there's no certainty about these things."

Henry proceeded. "Gilbert wants lots and lots of women, but he doesn't want to talk about it, and he wants to keep his women and his work separate . . . in watertight compartments, as it were. As if you could do that! And Ninian wants to have a good old hearty coarse time like . . . like Tom Jones . . . and then he'll repent and praise God and lay his stick about the backsides of all the young sinners he meets!"

"No, I don't, . . ." said Ninian, but Henry, having started, would not let himself be interrupted. "I want to have lots and lots of women," he went on hurriedly, "but I don't care who knows about them. I like talking about my love-affairs. . . ."

"Well, why don't you talk about 'em?" Gilbert demanded.

Henry was nonplussed. His speech became hesitant. "I . . . I said I'd like to talk about them," he replied. "I didn't say I would do so. . . ." He hurried away from the subject. "But chiefly," he said, "I don't want anything permanent in my life. Now, do you understand? Roger's like the Rock of Ages . . . the same yesterday, to-day and forever, but I want to be different to-morrow from what I am to-day, and different again the day after. Endless variety for me!"

"It'll be an awful lot of trouble," said Gilbert.

"That doesn't matter. Now my argument is that I have a different nature from Roger and all of you, but I'm not a worse man than any of you are. . . ."

"No, no, of course not," they asserted.

"I'm just different, that's all. The man who loves one woman and cleaves to her until death do them part isn't a better man or a worse man than the chap who loves a different woman every year, and doesn't cleave to any of them. He's just different. You see," he continued, pleased with the way he was enunciating his opinions, "we are of all sorts. There are lustful men and there are men who have scarcely any sex impulse at all, and there are coarse men and refined men, and . . . and all sorts of men, and they're all necessary to the world. I say, why not recognise the differences between them and leave it at that? It's silly to try and fit us all with the same system of morals when nobody but a fool would try to fit us all with the same size hat!"

"You don't make any allowance for the views of women," Roger said.

"Oh, yes, I do," Henry retorted quickly. "There is as much variety among women as there is among men. Some of them are monogamous and some aren't. That's all!"

Gilbert stretched his legs out in front of him and then drew them back again. "Our little Quinny's got this world neatly parcelled out," he said. "Hasn't he, coves? There he sits, like a little Jehovah, handing out natures as if they were school-prizes. 'Here, my little lad, here's your set of morals. Now, run away and make a hog of yourself with the women!' 'Here, my little lad, here's your set of morals. Now, run away and be a bally monk!' "

"Exactly!" said Henry. "That's my view!"

"Well, all I can say," said Ninian, "is that it won't do. This may be a tom-fool sort of a world, but it gets along in its tom-fool way a lot better than it will in your neat arrangement of things. . . ."

"Besides," Roger said, taking up the argument from Ninian, "there is a common measure in life. Oh, I know quite well that there are differences between man and man, but there are resemblances, too, and what we've got to do . . . the Improved Tories, I mean . . . is to discover which is the more important, the resemblances of men or the differences of men. As a lawyer, of course, I only know what's in my brief, but as a man, I'm interested!"

"The question is," said Gilbert, "are women a damned nuisance that ought to be put down, or are they not? I say they are, but I like 'em all the same, and that only shows what a blasted hole I'm in. I like kissing them . . . it's no good pretending that I don't. . . ."

"Not a bit," said Ninian.

"And I kiss 'em whenever I get a chance," Gilbert continued, "but all the same I'd like to be a whopping big icicle so as to be able to ignore 'em . . . like Roger!"

Ninian got up, resolved on going to bed. "Come on," he said, stretching himself. "Our jaw about women doesn't appear to have solved anything!"

"It never will," Roger answered, rising too. "We shall still be jawing about them this day twelvemonth. . . ."

"D.V.," said Gilbert.

"But we won't get any forrarder!"

"Rum things, women!" said Ninian, moving towards the door, "but very nice . . . very nice, indeed!"

"My goodness me, I am tired," Gilbert yawned. "Oh, so tired! But we've settled everything, haven't we? The empire and women and so on? Great Scott," he exclaimed, "we forgot to say anything about God!"

"So we did," said Ninian, and he turned back from the door.

"The Improved Tories really ought to make up their minds about religion," Gilbert went on.

"Can't we leave that until to-morrow?" Roger complained. "We needn't talk about Him to-night, need we? I'm frightfully sleepy! . . ."

6

While Henry was undressing, he remembered how angry Gilbert had been with Ninian and Roger because they had mentioned the name of a girl for whom he had cared.

"Awfully rum, that!" he said to himself, sitting on the edge of his bed.

He tried to recall her name. "Lady something!" he said, and then said several times, "Lady . . . Lady . . . Lady! . . ." in the hope that the name would follow. But he could not remember it.

"Odd that I never heard of her before."

He put on his dressing-gown, and opened the door of his room. "I'll ask old Ninian," he said, as he went out.

Ninian, who had been yawning so heavily downstairs, was now sitting up in bed, reading a copy of the *Engineer*.

"Hilloa," he exclaimed as Henry entered the room in response to his "Come in!"

"I say, Ninian, what was the name of the girl that Gilbert was so gone on at Cambridge? Lady something or other! He was rather sick with you for mentioning her. . . ."

"Oh, Lady Cecily Jayne!"

"Is that her name? Who is she?"

"Society female," said Ninian. "Takes an interest in literature and art in her spare time, but she doesn't know anything about either of them. Her brother was in our college until he got sent down. That was how Gilbert met her. She came up one May week and made eyes at Gilbert. She wasn't married then! . . ."

"Is she married?" Henry interrupted.

"Oh, yes. She used to be Lady Cecily Blandgate . . . her father's the Earl of Bucklersbury. She's a big female. . . ."

"What do you mean? Fat?"

"No. Tall," said Ninian.

"Is she good-looking?"

"Yes, she is, and rather amusing, too, in a footling sort

of way. She's got a fearful appetite, and she thinks of herself all day long. I know because she damn near ruined me over cream buns once.''

"I suppose Gilbert was in love with her? . . .''

"I suppose so. He didn't tell me and I didn't ask, but he mooned about with her and looked awfully sloppy when he passed her things. You know what I mean. He'd hand her a plate of bread and butter, and look at her as much as to say, 'This is really my heart I'm handing you!' I never saw a chap look such an ass!''

"Has she been married very long?''

"Oh, a year or two. I don't know. I'm not very interested in her. Too much of a female for my taste. Extremely entertaining in the evening and the afternoon, but awfully boring in the morning! . . .''

"Sounds like sour grapes, Ninian!''

"Oh, I've been in love with her if that's what you mean. We all were, even old Roger. In fact, I kissed her once . . . or was it twice? She's the sort of woman a chap does kiss somehow. I couldn't think of anything else to do when I was with her. That's why she's so dull. She splashes her sex about as if she were distributing handbills. I'm surprised that you don't know her. She's a very well-known female. . . .''

"I've been in Ireland, Ninian. . . .''

"So you have. I'd forgotten that. Of course, if you will live in a place like that, you can't expect to be familiar with the wonders of civilisation. Ever see the *Daily Reflexion?*''

"Oh, yes, we get that in Ireland all right!''

"Do you, indeed! Well, praise God from Whom all blessings flow. If you buy a copy of to-morrow's *Daily Reflexion*, you'll probably see her photograph in it, or a paragraph about her. Roger says people pay to have themselves mentioned once a month in that sort of rag!''

"What's her husband like?'' Henry asked.

"God made him, but nobody knows why. I believe

chorus girls call him 'Chummie.' That's his purpose in life. I say, Henry, there's a ripping sketch of a new kind of engine in this paper. I wish you'd let me explain it to you. . . ."

"Who is her husband?" said Henry.

"Who is who's husband?"

"Lady Cecily Jayne's! . . ."

"Lordy God, man, you're not talking about her still, are you? Her husband is . . . let me see . . . oh, yes, he's Lord Jasper Jayne. His name sounds like the hero of a servant's novelette, but he doesn't look like that. He looks like a chucker-out in a back-street pub. His father's the Marquis of Dulbury. He's the second son. The eldest is sillier, but it's all been hushed up. Anything else you want to know?"

"I'm just interested, that's all!"

"Her brother . . . I told you, didn't I? . . . was at Cambridge with us. He came down a year before we did. As a matter of fact, he was sent down and told to stay down. He ducked a proctor in a water-butt and the dons were very cross about it. He's not a bad fellow. I think we'll ask him round here one evening. Lady Cecily's very fond of him . . . she used to come up to Cambridge to see him . . . before the affair with the proctor, of course . . . and Gilbert and I took her and another female out in a punt once!"

Henry, who had been sittting in an arm-chair while Ninian told him about Lady Cecily Jayne, got up and walked across the room.

"Gilbert was very upset when you mentioned her name," he said. "I suppose her marriage was a blow to him?"

"Oh, I don't know. Look here, Quinny, if you're going to jaw any more about this female, you can just hop off to your own room, but if you'd like to hear me explaining these diagrams to you, you can stay. . . ."

"Do you ever see Lady Cecily now?" Henry asked, ig-noring what Ninian had said.

"Now and again. Gilbert sees her quite often. . . ."

"Does he?" Henry said eagerly.

"Yes. At first nights. She goes to the theatre a lot. Do you want to meet her?"

There was some confusion in Henry's voice as he answered, "I should like to meet her. You see, I've never known a really beautiful woman. . . ."

"Aren't there any in Ireland?"

"Oh, yes. Plenty. Peasant girls, particularly!" He thought for a moment or two of Sheila Morgan, and then hurriedly went on. "But I've never known a really beautiful woman. You see, Ninian, ours is a fairly lonely sort of house, and I've spent most of my time either there or at T.C.D. or at Rumpell's, and somehow I've never got to know any one. . . ."

"Well, you'd better ask Gilbert to take you with him to a first-night. She's sure to be there, and you can ask him to introduce you to her. And now, you can hoof out, young fellow! . . ."

Henry went back to his own room and got into bed, but he did not sleep until the dawn began to break. His thoughts wandered vaguely about his mind, bumping up against one recollection and then against another. He remembered Sheila Morgan and the bright look in her eyes that evening when she had hurriedly come into the Language class out of the rain . . . and while he was remembering Sheila, he found himself thinking of Mary Graham and the way in which she would put up her hand and throw her long hair from her shoulders. Then came memories of Bridget Fallon . . . and almost mechanically he began to murmur a prayer to the Virgin. "Hail Mary, full of grace, the Lord is with thee. Blessed art thou among women, and blessed is the fruit of thy womb, Jesus! . . ."

He turned over on his side, pulling the bedclothes more closely about him. "Cecily Jayne," he murmured in a sleepy voice. "What a pretty name, that is!"

THE FOURTH CHAPTER

1

THEIR days were spent in work. Ninian and Roger left the house soon after nine o'clock, Ninian to go to the office of his engineering firm in Victoria Street, Roger to go to his chambers in the Temple, leaving Henry and Gilbert to work at home. In the evening, provided that there was not a "first-night" to call Gilbert to the theatre, they talked of themselves and of their future. Their egotism was undisguised. They had set their minds on a high destiny and were certain that they would achieve it, so they did not waste any energy, as Gilbert once said, in pretending that they were not remarkably able. In a short time, they gathered a group of friends about them who were, they thought, likely to work well and ably, and it became the custom for their friends to visit them on Thursday evening. Gilbert began the custom of asking some one to dine with them on Thursday, and the guest was expected to account for himself to the group that assembled after dinner. The Improved Tories, according to Gilbert, wanted heart-to-heart talks from people of experience. If a guest treated them to flummery, they let him know that they despised his flummery and insisted on asking him questions of a peculiarly intimate character. There were less than a dozen people in the group, apart from Roger and Ninian and Gilbert and Henry, but each of them had distinguished himself in some fashion at his college. Hilary Cornwall had taken so many prizes and scholarships that he had lost count of them, and when he entered the Colonial Office, it became a commonplace to say of him that he was destined to become Permanent Under-Secretary at a remarkably youthful age. Gerald Luke had produced two little books of poetry of such quality that people believed that he was in the line of great tradition. Ernest Carr had edited *Granta* so ably that he was invited to join the staff of the *Times.* Then there were Ashley Earls, who had had a play produced by the Stage Society, and Peter Crooks, the chemist, and Edward Allen, who was private secretary to a Cabinet Minister, and Goeffrey Grant, another journalist, and Clifford Dartrey, who spent his time in research work and had already produced a book on Casual Labour in the Building Trades in return for the Shaw Prize at the London School of Economics.

They called themselves the Improved Tories, although most of them would have voted at an election for any one but a Conservative candidate. Ashley Earls and Gerald Luke were Socialists and had only consented to join the group because they were told that the purpose of it was less political than sociological.

"You see," Gilbert said to them, "it isn't good for England to have a Tory Party so dense as this one is, and you'll really be doing useful work if you help to improve their quality. What is the good of an Opposition which can do nothing but oppose? Look at that fellow, Sir Frederick Banbury! What in the name of God is the good of a man like that? He doesn't make anything . . . he just gets in the way. Of course, that's useful . . . but he doesn't know when to get out of the way . . . which is much more useful. And there ought to be people who aren't content either to get in the way or just get out of it . . . there ought to be people who can shove things along. But there aren't . . . except Balfour, and he's getting old and anyhow he hasn't got much health. You see what I mean, don't you? There ought to be a strong Opposition, otherwise the Liberals will develop fatty degeneration of the political sense. . . . The trouble with a lot of these fellows is that they believe that twaddle that Lord Randolph Churchill talked about the duty of an Opposition being to oppose. Of course it isn't. The duty of the Opposition is to criticise and to improve, if they can. . . .''

And so Ashley Earls and Gerald Luke joined the group of Improved Tories, not as members, but as critics. It was they who induced the others to join the Fabian Society. "You can become subscribers . . . that won't commit you to anything . . . and then you'll be able to attend all the meetings and get all the publications. It'll be good for you! . . .''

The supply of political guests was not of the quality they desired. The eminent politicians were either too busy or too scornful to accept their invitations. F. E. Robinson was impertinent to them until he heard that Mr. Balfour was interested in their proceedings . . . had even asked to be introduced to Roger Carey . . . and then he offered to address them on Young Toryism, but they told him that they did not now wish to hear him. They had taken Robinson's measure very quickly. "Police-court lawyer!" they said, and ceased to trouble about him. Mr. Balfour never attended the group, but they consoled themselves to some extent by reading his book on Decadence and arguing about it among themselves. If, however, they were not able to secure many of the Eminent Ones, they were able to secure plenty of the Semi-Eminent, far more than they wanted, and for half a year, they listened to politicians of all sorts, Old Tories and Young Tories, Liberal Imperialists and Radicals, Fabian Socialists and Social Democrats, heckling them and being heckled by them. At the end of that six months, Gilbert revolted against politicians.

"These aren't the people who really matter," he said. "They don't start things. We want to get hold of the people with new ideas . . . the men who begin movements and the men who aren't always wondering what their constituents will say if they hear about it!"

Then followed a term with men who might have been called cranks. Bernard Shaw declined to dine with them . . . he preferred to eat at home. . . . "Voluptuous vege-

tarian!'' said Gilbert . . . but he talked to them for an
hour on ''Equality'' and tried to persuade them to advocate equal incomes for all, asserting that this was desir-
able from every point of view, biological, social and eco-
nomic. Following Bernard Shaw, came Edward Carpen-
ter, very gentle and very gracious, denouncing modern civilisation in words which were spoken quietly, but which,
in print, read like a thunderstorm. Alfred Russell Wal-
lace, whom they invited to talk on Evolution, came and
talked instead on the nationalisation of land. He sat, huddled in a chair, very old and very bright, with eyes that
sparkled behind his glasses . . . and suddenly, in the middle of his discourse on land, he informed them that he had
positive proof of the existence of angels. ''My God, he'll
want to make civil servants of 'em!'' Gilbert whispered to
Henry. . . . Sir Horace Plunkett dined with them one
night, eating so little that he scarcely seemed to eat at all,
and he preached the whole gospel of co-operation. It was
through him that they got hold of an agricultural genius
called T. Wibberley, an English-Irishman, who reorganised
the entire farming system on a basis of continuous cropping inside an hour and ten minutes.. Wibberley knew
Henry's father, and for the first time in his life Henry
learned that Mr. Quinn's agricultural experiments were of
value. . . . Then came H. G. Wells, smiling and very deprecating and almost inarticulate, to tell them of the enor-
mous importance of the novelist. They got him into a corner of the room, when he had finished reading his paper,
and persuaded him to make caricatures of them . . . and
while he was making the caricatures, he talked to them far
more brilliantly than he had read to them. G. K. Chesterton and Hilaire Belloc came to lecture and stayed to drink.
Chesterton's lecture would have been funny, they agreed,
if they had been able to hear it, but he laughed so heartily
at his jokes, as he, so to speak, saw them approaching, that
he forgot to make them. His method of speech was a mixture of giggle and whisper. ''Chuckle-and-squeak!'' Gil-

bert called it. Belloc whispered dark things about Influential Families and Hebrews and seemed to think that a man who changed his name only did so with the very worst intentions. He and Chesterton said harsh things about the Party System, and they babbled beatifically about the Catholic Church. ... "Two big men like that gabbling like a couple of priest-smitten flappers!" said Gilbert in disgust as he listened to them. "Them and their Cathlik Church!" he added, imitating Belloc's way of pronouncing the word "Catholic." Mouldy, grovelling, fat Papists! he called them, and vowed that he would resign from the Improved Tories if any more of that sort were asked to address them. That was because some one had suggested that Cecil Chesterton should also be invited to dine with them. "He's simply Belloc's echo," Gilbert protested. "I should feel as if I were listening to his master's voice. Besides, he's fatter than Belloc and he's a damned jiggery-pokery Papist too! Why don't these chaps go and cover themselves with blue woad and play mumbo-jumbo tricks before the village idol! That 'ud be about as intelligent as their Popery!" They intended to ask Lord Hugh Cecil to talk to them about Conservatism, but when they read his book on the subject they decided that such a Conservative was utterly damnable ... and so they asked his brother, Lord Robert, instead, and found that his point of view, although much more human and less logical than that of Lord Hugh, was antipathetic to theirs.

"Let's get Garvin!" Gilbert suggested, when they discussed the question of a more improved Tory than Lord Robert. "The Cecils are no good ... they're too superstitious!" which was his way of saying that they were too religious. "They're worse than priests: they're ... they're laymen! I propose that we ask Garvin to come and talk to us. He seems to be shoving the Tories all over the place!" So they invited the editor of the *Observer* to dine and talk with them, and he came, a quick, eager, intense man, with large, starting eyes, who spoke so quickly that his words became entangled and were wrecked on his teeth. They liked him, but they were dubious of his right to represent the Tory spirit. It seemed to them that this eager, thrusting-forward man, who banged the table in his earnestness, might carry a political party off its feet in his passion, but they were afraid that the feet would trail, that the party would be reluctant to be lifted. "He's Irish," said Roger in judgment.

"It isn't any good," Gilbert remarked, when Garvin had gone home, "trying to persuade the English to spread their wings. They haven't got any. Garvin 'ud do better if he'd hold a carrot in front of them . . . they'd follow that. Quinny," he added, "you ought to ask Garvin for a job on the *Observer*. They say he can't resist an Irishman!"

"I will," Henry replied.

"Oh, and there's a chance of doing book reviews on the *Morning Report!*" Geoffrey Grant said. "I told Leonard, the literary editor, about you, and he said he'd look at you if you went round one day!"

"I'll go and look at him," Henry answered.

2

While they were spending their evenings in this fashion, Henry, working steadily in the mornings, completely revised his novel. Gilbert, working less steadily than Henry, finished a new comedy and sent it to Sir Goeffrey Mundane, the manager of the Pall Mall Theatre, who utterly astounded Gilbert by accepting it.

"Quinny!" he shouted, running up to Henry's room with the letter which had been delivered by the mid-day post, "Mundane's accepted 'The Magic Casement'!"

"What's that?" said Henry, turning round from his desk.

"He's accepted it, Quinny! I always said he was a damned good actor, and so he is. My Lord, this is ripping! He says *it's a splendid comedy* . . . so it is . . . *as good as Oscar Wilde at his best* . . . oh, better, damn it, better . . . and will I *please come and see him on Friday morning at eleven o'clock* . . . I'll be there before he's out of bed! . . . I say, Quinny, we ought to do something, ought'nt we? Is it the correct thing to get drunk on these occasions?''

His joy was so extravagant that Henry felt many years older than Gilbert, and he patted him paternally on the shoulder and told him to develop the stoic virtues.

"I'm most frightfully pleased, Gilbert!" he said, when he had done with the paternal manner. "When's he going to put the play on?"

"He doesn't say. The thing he's doing now is no damn good, and he'll probably take it off soon. Perhaps he'll produce 'The Magic Casement' after that. Quinny, it *is* a good play, isn't it? Sometimes I get a most shocking hump about things, and I think I'm no good at all. . . ."

"Of course, it's a good play, Gilbert! . . ."

"Yes, but is it good enough?"

"I don't know. I don't suppose anything ever is. I thought 'Drusilla' was a great book until my father read it, and then I thought it was rubbish. . . ."

"It wasn't rubbish, Quinny, and the revised version is really good."

"I think that, too, but sometimes I'm not sure!"

"Isn't it damnable, Quinny, this job of writing? You never get any satisfaction out of it. I'd like to make cheeses . . . I'm sure people who make cheeses feel that they've just made the very best cheese that can be made . . . but I'm always seeing something in my work that might have been done better."

Henry nodded his head. "I suppose," he said, "it'll always be like that. I think," he went on, "Malden is going to take my novel. I saw Redder yesterday! . . ." Redder was his agent . . . "and he says Malden's the likeliest person. I shan't get much. Forty or fifty pounds on account of royalties, but it's a start!"

"The great thing," said Gilbert, "is to get into print. I wonder how much I'll make out of my play!"

"More than I shall make out of my novel," Henry answered. His talks with Mr. Redder had modified Henry's ideas of the profits made by novelists.

Gilbert started up from the low chair into which he had thrown himself. "I'm going to start on another play this minute!" he said. "My head's simply humming with ideas!" He stopped half way to the door, and turned towards Henry again. "You were working when I came in," he said. "What are you doing?"

"I've started another novel," Henry answered.

"Oh! Done much of it?"

"No, only the title. I'm calling it 'Broken Spears.'"

"Damn good title, too," said Gilbert.

3

The book was published long before Gilbert's play was produced; for Sir Geoffrey Mundane had taken fright at Gilbert's play. He was afraid that it was too clever, too original, too much above their heads, and so forth. "I'd like to produce it," he said. "I'd regard it as an honour to be allowed to produce it, but the Pall Mall is a very expensive theatre to maintain and I don't mind telling you, Mr. Farlow, that I lost money on that last piece, too much money, and I must retrieve some of it. Your play is excellent . . . excellent . . . in fact, it's a piece of literature . . . almost Greek in its form . . . Greek . . . yes, I think, Greek . . . remarkable plays those were, weren't they? . . . Have you seen this portrait of me in to-day's *Daily Reflexion* . . . quite jolly, I think . . . but it won't be popular, Mr. Farlow, and I must put on something that is likely to be popular!"

Gilbert found Sir Geoffrey's sudden changes of conversation curiously interesting, but the hint of disaster to

"The Magic Casement" disturbed him too much to let his interest absorb him.

"Then you've decided not to do the play?" he said, with a throb of disappointment in his voice.

Sir Geoffrey rose at him, fixing his eye-glass, and patted him on the shoulder. "No, *no*," he said. "I didn't mean *that*. I'll produce the play gladly . . . some day . . . but not just at present. If you care to leave it with me. . . ."

Gilbert wondered what he ought to say next. Sir Geoffrey might retain the play for a year or two, and then decide that he could not produce it.

"Perhaps," he said, "you'd undertake to do it within a certain time. . . ." He wanted to add that Sir Geoffrey should undertake to pay a fine if he failed to produce the play within the "certain time," but his courage was not strong enough. He was afraid that Sir Geoffrey might be offended by the suggestion and return the play at once. He wished that he had gone to Mr. Redder, as Henry had done, and asked him to place the play for him. "Redder'd stand no humbug," he said to himself.

Sir Geoffrey murmured something about the undesirability of committing oneself, and added that Gilbert should be content to wait for a year without any legal undertaking. "Of course," he said magnanimously, "if you can place the play elsewhere, don't let me stand in your way!" but Gilbert, alarmed, hurriedly said that he would be glad to leave the play with him for the time he mentioned. "I'd like you to take the part of Rupert Westlake," he said. "I don't think any one could play it so well as you could!" and Sir Geoffrey, still responsive to flattery, smiled and said he would be delighted to create the part.

The play which he produced instead of "The Magic Casement" ran for six weeks, bringing neither profit nor honour to Sir Geoffrey, who began to lose his head, with the result that he produced another play which was a greater failure than its predecessor. Then came a revival of an old play which had a moderate amount of success, and "I'll do your play next," he said to Gilbert. "I shall certainly do your play next!"

It was because of these delays in the production of "The Magic Casement" that Henry's novel, "Drusilla," was published much earlier than the play was performed. He had rewritten it so extensively that it was almost a new novel, very different from the manuscript which his father had read, and it received a fair number of reviews. The critics whose judgment he valued, praised it liberally, but the critics whose judgment he despised, either damned it or ignored it. Gilbert said it was splendid. "There's still some Slop in it," he said, "but it's miles better than the first version." Roger liked it. He said, "I like it, Quinny!" and that was all, but Henry knew that his speech was considerable praise. Ninian's praise was extravagant, and he was almost like a child in his pleasure at receiving an inscribed copy from Henry. He spent the better part of an afternoon in going to bookshops and asking the grossly ignorant assistants why they had not got "Drusilla" prominently placed in the window. The assistants were not humiliated by his charge of gross ignorance, nor were they impressed by his statement that the *Times* Literary Supplement had described the book as "remarkable." So many remarkable books are published in the course of a season that the assistants do not attempt to remember them; and so many friends of remarkable young authors wish to know why the works of these remarkable young men are not stacked in the window that the assistants have learned to look listlessly at the people who make the demands. Ninian bought three copies of the novel, and sent one to his mother and one to the Headmaster of Rumpell's and one to his uncle, the Dean of Exebury. "That ought to help the sales, Quinny!" he said. "I bought 'em in three different shops, and I stuffed the chaps that I'd been to other places to get it, but found they were sold out!"

"That'll make two copies Mrs. Graham'll have," Henry replied. "I've sent one to her to-day. . . ."

"Well, she can give the other one to Mary," said Ninian. The book was not a success. Including the number sold to the libraries, only three hundred and seventy-five copies were sold, but the financial failure of the book did not greatly depress Henry, for he had the praise of his friends to console him. His father's letter had heartened him almost as much as the review in the *Times*. "*It's great stuff*," he wrote, "*and I'm proud of you. I didn't think you could improve it so much as you have done. Hurry up and do another one!*"

His second book, "Broken Spears," was in proof before Sir Geoffrey Mundane decided to produce "The Magic Casement," and for a while he was at a loose end. He could not think of a subject for another story, although he had invented a good title: Turbulence. He sat at his desk, forcing himself to write chapters that ended ingloriously. He wrote pages and pages, and in the evening threw them into the wastepaper basket. "My God," he said to himself one morning, when he had been sitting at his desk for over an hour without writing a word, "I believe I've lost the power to write!"

He got up, terrified, and went to Gilbert's room.

"Hilloa, bloke!" said Gilbert, looking round at him as he entered.

"Are you busy, Gilbert?" he asked.

"I'm kidding myself that I am, but between ourselves, Quinny, I'm reading Gerald Luke's last book. That chap's a poet. He's as good as Alfred, Lord Tennyson. Listen to this! . . ."

But Henry did not wish to listen to Gerald Luke's poems.

"Gilbert," he said, "I believe I'm done!"

"Done?" Gilbert exclaimed, putting down the book of poems.

"Yes. I don't believe I shall ever do another book. . . ."

"Silly ass!"

"I can't think of anything. My mind's like pap. I keep on writing and writing, but I only get a pile of words. That was bad enough, but to-day I can't write at all. I simply can't write. . . ."

"Haven't you got a theme?"

"Vaguely, yes, but the thing won't come to life. The people lie about like logs, and . . . damn them, they won't move!"

"Look here," said Gilbert, "I'm tired of work. Let's chuck it for a while. You're obviously off colour, and a holiday'll do you good. Let's go out somewhere for the day anyhow. I've a first night this evening. We'll wind up with that!"

"What's the play?" Henry asked.

"A revival. They're bringing Wilde's 'The Ideal Husband' on at the St. James's again," Gilbert answered. "Alexander's very good in it. . . ."

"That's the fashionable theatre, isn't it?"

Henry's knowledge of London was still very limited, and he seldom visited the theatre, chiefly because Gilbert, who had to visit them all, spoke of the English drama with contempt.

"Yes," Gilbert replied. "All the Jews and dukes go there. Suppose we go for a row on the Serpentine, Quinny? You can pull the oars for an hour. It'll do you no end of good, and I'll lie in the bottom of the boat and watch you. That'll do me no end of good. Come on, let's get out of this!"

4

They came away from the boathouse, and as they walked towards Hyde Park Corner, a motor-car drove slowly past them.

"Who's that?" said Henry, as Gilbert raised his hat to the lady who was seated in the car.

"Lady Cecily Jayne," Gilbert answered.

"Oh! . . . She's very beautiful."

"Think so?"

"Yes."

"I'll introduce you to her to-night. She's certain to be at the theatre. We ought to make certain of getting a ticket for you, Quinny. Let's go down to the theatre and book a seat."

They came out of the Park and walked down Piccadilly to St. James's Street and presently turned the corner of the street in which the theatre is situated. Henry was able to secure a stall, but it was not next to Gilbert's. It was in the last row.

"Never mind," said Gilbert, "we can meet between the acts. My seat's at the end of a row, and you can easily get out of yours. If Cecily's in a box, she'll probably ask us to stay in it. She likes to have people about her!"

Henry wanted to talk about Lady Cecily to Gilbert, but the tone of his voice as he said, "She likes to have people about her!" prevented him from doing so. It was odd, he reflected, that Gilbert had never confided in him about her, odder still that there had been no talk of her in the Bloomsbury house since the night on which Henry and Ninian had discussed Gilbert's outburst of anger when her name was mentioned. Gilbert could be very secretive, Henry thought. . . .

"She's very beautiful," he said aloud.

Gilbert nodded his head.

"Very beautiful!" Henry repeated.

"You're an impressionable young fellow, Quinny!" said Gilbert. "I won't call you 'sloppy' again because I'm tired of telling you that, but really that's what you are. You've only got to see a beautiful woman for a couple of seconds and you start buzzing round her like a bumble bee. Of course, I'm sloppy myself. We're all sloppy. Damn it, here we are, two healthy young fellows who ought to be working hard, and we're wasting a fine morning in gabbling about women. . . ."

"Not women, Gilbert! Lady Cecily! . . ."

"Lady Cecily! Lady Cecily! . . ." He stopped suddenly and turned to Henry. "I suppose you know about her and me?" he said.

"Very little," Henry answered.

"Let's have some tea. We'll go in here!" The abrupt change disconcerted Henry for a moment or two, but he followed Gilbert into the tea-shop.

"I can see you're ready to fall in love with her," Gilbert said, as they drank their tea.

"Don't be an old ass!" Henry replied, feeling confused.

"She'll ask you to come and see her, and you'll waste a lot of time next week trying to meet her. . . ."

Henry laughed nervously. "You're rather ridiculous, Gilbert," he said. "I've never seen Lady Cecily before. I'm just interested in her because she's so beautiful. That's natural enough, isn't it?"

"Oh, yes, it's natural enough, and Lady Cecily will like your interest in her beauty!"

The bitterness of his tone was remarkable. Henry felt, as he listened to him, that there were open wounds. . . .

"Don't call her Cecily until you've known her two days," Gilbert went on. "She's very particular about that sort of thing. And don't fall too much in love. It'll take you longer to get over it than it took me!"

"I hate to hear you talking like that, Gilbert. Anybody'd think you were a dried-up old rip. You're frightfully cynical. . . ."

"That's because I'm so young, Quinny. I'm younger than you are, you know . . . six months . . . but I'll grow up. I *will* grow up, Quinny, I swear I will, and get full of the milk of lovingkindness. Pass the meringues. They play the devil with my inside, but I like them and I don't care . . . only Lord help the actors to-night!"

"I suppose Lady Cecily got tired of you, Gilbert," Henry said deliberately. He felt angry with him and tried to hurt him. The beauty of Lady Cecily had filled him

with longing to meet and know her, and he had a strange
sense of jealousy when he thought of Gilbert's friendship
with her.

"No," Gilbert answered, "I don't think she got tired
of me. I think she still cares for me as much as ever she
did! . . ."

"Damned conceit!" Henry exclaimed, laughing to cover
the jealousy that was in him.

"Oh, no, Quinny, not really. You'll understand that
soon, I expect!" He pushed his tea-cup away from him,
and sat back in his chair. "I suppose it is caddish to talk
of her like this," he went on. "One ought to bear one's
wounds in silence and feel no resentment at all . . . but
somehow she draws out the caddish part of me. There are
women like that, Quinny. There's a nasty, low, mean
streak in every man, I don't care who he is, and some
women seem to find it very easily. Here, let's get out of
this. You pay. I've had a sugary bun and a couple of
meringues. . . ."

5

Later in the evening they went to the theatre together. As they walked up the steps into the entrance
hall, Henry saw Lady Cecily standing in a small group of
men and women who were talking and laughing very
heartily.

"There she is!" he whispered to Gilbert.

"Who is?"

"Lady Cecily!"

"Oh, so she is. Let's find our seats!"

"Perhaps you could catch her eye, Gilbert. . . ."

"Catch my grandmother!" said Gilbert. "Come on!"

But if Gilbert were not willing to catch Lady Cecily's
eye, Lady Cecily was very willing to catch his. She saw
him walking towards the stalls, and she left her group of

friends and went over to him and touched his arm. "Hilloa, Gilbert!" she said, holding her hand out to him. "I thought I should see you here to-night!"

She spoke in louder tones than most women speak, and her voice sounded as if it were full of laughter. There was something in her attitude which stirred Henry, something which vaguely reminded him of a proud animal, stretching its limbs after sleep. Her thick, golden hair, cunningly bound about her head, glistened in the softened light, and he could almost see golden, downy gleams on her cheeks. She held her skirts about her, as she stood in front of Gilbert, and Henry could see her curving breasts rising and falling very gently beneath her silken dress. The odour of some disturbing perfume floated from her. . . . He moved a step nearer to her, wondering why Gilbert did not smile at her nor show any signs of pleasure at meeting her. It seemed to him to be impossible for any one but the most curmudgeonly of men to behave so ungraciously to so beautiful a woman, or to resist her radiant smiles. She turned to him as he moved towards her, and he saw that her eyes were grey. He heard Gilbert mumbling the introduction.

"So glad!" she said, shaking hands with him. He had expected her to bow to him, and had not been prepared for the offer of her hand. He inwardly cursed his clumsiness as he changed his gesture. "I saw you in the Park with Gilbert this afternoon, didn't I?" she added.

"Yes," he answered, and could say no more. Shyness had fallen on him, and he stood before her, grinning fatuously, and twisting a button on his waistcoat, but unable to speak. "Yes," he said, after a while, "I was with Gilbert in the Park this afternoon!"

"Speak up, you fool!" he was saying to himself. "Here's the loveliest woman you've ever met waiting for you to speak to her, and all you can do is to repeat her phrases as if you were a newly-breeched brat aping its parent. Speak up, you fool! . . ."

He felt his face turning red and hot. Almost before he
knew what he was saying his tongue began to wag, and he
heard himself saying, in a stiff, stilted voice, "It was very
nice in the Park this afternoon! . . ." *Oh, banal fool,* he
thought, *she will despise you now, as if you were a great,
gawky lout.* . . .

She turned away from him, and spoke to Gilbert. "I've
been at Dulbury," she said, "for six weeks. That's where
I got all this brown! . . ." She laughed and pointed to
her cheeks. "I'm so glad to get back. The country bores
me stiff. Nothing to see but the scenery. Oh dear!" She
almost yawned at her remembrance of the country. "And
things are always biting me or stinging me. I'm miserable
all the time I'm there!"

"Then why do you go?" said Gilbert.

"Jimphy wanted to go. Jimphy thinks it's his duty
to show himself to the tenants now and again. It's the
only return he can make, poor dear, for all that rent they
pay!"

Gilbert said "Hm!" and then turned to go to the
stalls. "It's Jimphy's birthday to-day," she said, and he
turned to her again. "That's why we're here to-night.
Together, I mean. He's treating me to a box. Come round
and talk to us, Gilbert, after the first act . . . and you, too,
Mr. . . . Mr! . . ."

She fumbled over his name. Gilbert, as is the custom
in England when introducing people, had spoken the name
so indistinctly that she had not heard it.

"Quinn!" he said.

"Of course," she replied. "Mr. Quinn. I'm awfully
stupid about names. You'll come, too?"

"I should like to!"

"Do. Gilbert, don't forget. Jimphy's very morose this
evening. He's thirty-one to-day, and he thinks that old
age is creeping over him!"

"All right," said Gilbert gloomily, and then he and
Henry went to their seats.

"Who is Jimphy?" said Henry, as they walked down the stairs into the auditorium.

"Her husband. Didn't you notice something hanging around in the vestibule while we were talking to her?"

"No. There were so many people about!"

"Well, if you had noticed something hanging around, that would have been Jimphy. His real name is Jasper, but Cecily never calls any one by his real name . . . except me. She can't think of a name for me!"

They entered the auditorium and stood for a moment looking about the theatre. People were passing quickly into their seats now, and the theatre was full of an eager air, of massed pleasure, and a loud buzz of conversation spread over the stalls from the pit where rows of young women whispered to each other excitedly as this well-known person and that well-known person entered.

"That's 'er, that's 'er!" one girl said in a frenzied whisper to her companion.

"Viola Tree?" the other girl, gazing vacantly into the stalls, replied.

"No, silly! Ellen Terry! Clap, can't you?"

And they clapped their hands as the actress went to her seat.

There was more clapping when Sir Charles Wyndham came in and took his seat.

"Is it Viola Tree?" the girl repeated.

"No, silly. It's Wyndham. Bray-vo! Seventy, if 'e's a day, an' don't look it. My word, I am enjoyin' myself, I can tell you! Everybody's 'ere to-night. Of course, it's St. James's, of course! . . . "

Popular criminal lawyers came in and sat next to racing marquises; and lords and ladies mingled with actresses who very ostentatiously accompanied their mothers. A few men of letters and a crowd of dramatic critics, depressed, unenthusiastic men, leavened the mass of the semi-great. The rest were the children of Israel.

"Jews to the right of us, Jews to the left of us! . . ."
Gilbert said.

"Anti-Semite!" Henry replied.

"Only in practice, Quinny, not in theory. I'll see you
at the interval!"

"If you nip out of your seat as the curtain goes down,"
said Henry, "we can both get up to her box before the
rush! . . ."

"There won't be any rush."

"Well, anyhow, we can get up to the box pretty quickly!"

Gilbert walked away without replying, and Henry sat
back in his seat and watched the boxes so that he might
see Lady Cecily the moment she entered. His stall was
in the last row, against the first row of the pit, and the girls
who had applauded Miss Terry and Sir Charles Wyndham were still identifying the fashionable people.

"I tell you it *is* 'im," said the more assertive of the two.

"I sawr 'is picture in the *Daily Reflexion* the time that
feller . . . wot's 'is name . . . the one that 'anged all 'is
wives in the coal-cellar . . . you know! . . ."

"I know," the other girl replied. "'Orrible case, I call
it!"

"Well, 'e defended 'im. I sawr 'is picture in the *Daily
Reflexion* myself. Very 'andsome man, eh? They do
say! . . ."

Lady Cecily came into her box, followed by her husband,
and Henry looked steadily up at her in the hope that she
would see him, but she did not glance in his direction. He
could see that she had found Gilbert in the audience, but
Gilbert was not looking at her. An odd sensation of jealousy ran through him. He suddenly resented her famil-
iarity with Gilbert. He remembered that she had called
him by his Christian name, that she distinguished between
him and other men by calling him by his proper name, and
not by some fanciful perversion of it. If only she would
call *him* by his Christian name! . . .

She was leaning on the edge of the box, and looking about the auditorium.

"That's Lydy Cecily Jyne!" he heard the assertive girl behind him saying.

"'Oo?"

"Lydy Cecily Jyne. *You* know!"

Her husband leant back in his seat, stifling a yawn as he did so, and Henry saw that he was a faded, insignificant-looking man whose head sloped so sharply that it seemed to be galloping away from his forehead; but he did not pay much attention to him. His eyes were fixed on Lady Cecily.

"A bit 'ot, she is," the girl behind him was saying. "Well, I mean to say! . . ."

But what she meant to say, Henry neither knew nor cared. The lights in the theatre were lowered, leaving only the bright, warm glow of the footlights on the heavy curtain. He could see Lady Cecily's face still golden and glowing even in the darkness.

"My dear," said the girl behind him, "the things I've 'eard . . . well, they'd fill a book!"

Then the curtain went up and the play began.

He saw her leaning forward eagerly to watch the stage, and presently he heard her laughing at some piece of wit in the play: a clear, joyful laugh; and as she laughed, she turned for a few moments and gazed into the darkened theatre. Her beautiful eyes seemed to him to be shining stars, and he imagined that she was looking straight at him. He smiled at her, and then jeered at himself. "Of course, she can't see me," he said.

He tried to interest himself in the traffic of the stage, but his thoughts continually wandered to the woman in the box above him.

"She's the loveliest woman I've ever seen," he said to himself.

THE FIFTH CHAPTER

1

SHE turned to greet them as they entered the box. "Come and sit beside me, Gilbert!" she said. "Mr. Quinn . . . oh, you don't know Jimphy, do you?" She introduced Henry to her husband who mumbled "How do!" in a sulky voice, and stood against the wall of the box twisting his moustache. The shyness which had enveloped Henry in the vestibule of the theatre still clung about him, and he felt awkward and tongue-tied. Lord Jasper Jayne did not help Henry to get rid of his shyness. There was a "Who-the-devil-are-you?" look about him that made easy conversation impossible and any conversation difficult. Lady Cecily was chatting to Gilbert as if she had been saving up all her conversation for a month past exclusively for his ears; and Henry could hear a recurrent phrase. . . . "But, Gilbert, it's ages since you've been to see me, and you know I like you to come! . . ." that jangled his temper and made him feel savage towards his friend. . . .

He made an effort to be chatty with Lord Jasper. "How do you like the play?" he said, as pleasantly as he could, for it was not easy to be chatty with Lord Jasper, whose coarse, flat features roused a sensation of repulsion in Henry.

"I don't like it," he replied. "Rotten twaddle!"

"Oh!" Henry exclaimed.

There did not appear to be anything more to say, nor did Lord Jasper seem anxious to continue the conversation; but just when it appeared that the effort to be pleasantly chatty was likely to be abortive, Lord Jasper

suddenly walked towards the door of the box. "Come
and have a drink!" he said.

Henry did not wish to go and have a drink, and he
paused irresolutely until Lady Cecily suddenly leant forward and said with a laugh, "Yes, do go with Jimphy, Mr.
Quinn. Gilbert and I have such a lot to say to each other,
and Jimphy's not in a good temper. Are you, Jimphy,
dear? You see," she went on, "he wanted to go to the
Empire, but I made him bring me here! . . . Do cheer up,
Jimphy, dear! Smile for the company! . . ."

Lord Jasper opened the door of the box and went out,
and Henry, raging inwardly, followed him. Before he
had quite shut the door again, Lady Cecily had turned to
Gilbert. Her hand was on his sleeve, and she was saying,
"But Gilbert, darling! . . ." He shut the door quickly
and almost ran after Lord Jasper. She was in love with
Gilbert, and Gilbert was in love with her. A woman would
not put her hand so affectionately on a man's arm and call
him "Gilbert, darling!" if she were not in love with him.
She had wished to be alone with Gilbert . . . had practically turned him out of the box so that she might be alone
with Gilbert . . . had not waited for him to close the door
before she began to fondle him . . . and Gilbert had spoken
so bitterly of her! . . .

He followed on the heels of Lord Jasper, passing through
a throng of men in the passages and on the stairs, until
he reached the bar. "Whisky and soda?" said Lord
Jasper, and Henry nodded his head.

"I hate theatres," Lord Jasper said.

"Oh!" Henry replied.

That seemed to be the only adequate retort to make to
anything that Jimphy said.

"Yes, I can't stand 'em. Cecily let me in to-night . . .
on a chap's birthday, too. She might have chosen the Empire!"

"You like music-halls then?"

"They're all right. Better than theatres anyhow. I like to see girls dancing and . . . and . . . all that kind of thing!"

A bell rang, warning them that the second act was about to begin.

"I suppose we ought to go back," said Henry, putting his glass down. He had barely touched the whisky and soda.

"No hurry," Lord Jasper replied. "No hurry. And you haven't drunk your whisky? Cecily's quite happy with that chap, Farlow. . . . I don't like him myself . . . oh, I say, he's a pal of yours, isn't he? Well, it doesn't matter now. I don't like him, and he doesn't like me. I know he doesn't. I can always tell a chap doesn't like me because I generally don't like him. Have another, will you?"

Henry shook his head.

"I think we ought to be getting back," he said, "I hate disturbing people after the curtain's gone up!"

"You don't want to see that rotten play, do you? Look here . . . I've forgotten your name! Sorry! . . ."

"Quinn. Henry Quinn!"

"Oh, Quinn! You're not English, are you?"

"I'm Irish."

"Are you? That's damn funny! Well, anyhow, what I was going to say was this. You don't want to see this rotten play, do you?"

"I do rather! . . ."

"No, you don't, Quinn. No, you don't. And I don't want to see it, either. Very well, then, what's to prevent you and me going to the Empire together, eh? We can come back for Cecily! . . ."

Henry stared at Lord Jasper. "But we can't do that," he protested.

"Oh, yes we can. Cecily won't mind. She'll be glad. We'll go and tell her . . . and look here, Quinn, I'll intro-

duce you to a girl I know . . . very nice girl . . . perfect
lady . . . lives with her mother as a matter of fact . . .
Eh?"

"I'd much rather see the play!"

"Oh, all right," Lord Jasper said sulkily. "All right!"

Henry moved towards the door of the bar, but Lord
Jasper made no attempt to follow him. "Aren't you coming?" he said, pausing at the door.

"No," Lord Jasper replied. "I don't want to see the
damn play. I shall have another drink, and then I shall
go to the Empire by myself. You better go back to Cecily
and . . . and that chap Farlow. She won't notice I'm not
there!"

"You'd better come and tell her yourself, hadn't you?"
Henry said.

Lord Jasper deliberated with himself for a few moments.

"All right," he said. "I will. I'll come presently.
You tell her, will you, that I'll come presently. P'raps
you'll change your mind, Quinn, and come with me to the
Empire after you've had another dose of this damn play.
A chap doesn't want to see a play on a chap's birth-
day! . . ."

It occurred to Henry that Lord Jasper Jayne was
slightly drunk. He had swallowed the second whisky and
soda rather more expeditiously than he had swallowed the
first, and no doubt he had dined well. There was a bleary
look in his eyes that signified a heated brain. . . .

"My God," Henry said to himself, "that beautiful
woman married to this . . . this swine!"

"I'm thirty-one to-day, ole f'la," Lord Jasper continued,
coming over to Henry and taking hold of his arm.
"Thirty-one. I'm getting on in years, ole f'la, that's what
I'm doing . . . sere and yellow, so to speak . . . and a
chap my age doesn't want to be bothered with a damn play.
He wants something . . . something substansl! . . ." He
fumbled over the word "substantial" and then fell on it.

"Something substansl," he repeated. "Now, if you come with me! . . ."

"I say, you mustn't talk so loudly," Henry warned him. "The curtain's gone up, and you'll disturb people. . . ."

"All right, ole f'la, all right. I won't say another word!"

They stumbled along the passages to the door of the box, and entered as quietly as they could. ,

"We thought you'd got lost," said Lady Cecily, smiling at Henry.

"No . . . no," he replied, "we didn't get lost!"

2

Gilbert was sitting in the seat where Jimphy had sat earlier in the evening. "Gilbert is going to stay here," said Lady Cecily. "Won't you stay, too, Mr. Quinn!"

"Won't I be crowding you? . . ." he said.

"Oh, no," she replied. "Jimphy doesn't want to see the play anyhow, and he'll be quite happy if he has some one to talk to in the bar between the acts! . . ."

He felt the blood rushing violently to his head, and in his anger he almost got up and walked out of the box. That she should use him to keep her sottish husband entertained while she made love to Gilbert, filled him with a sensation that came near to hatred of her. Gilbert had not spoken since they returned to the box, but it was clear from his manner that there had been love-making. . . . He crushed down his anger, and stood behind Lady Cecily while the play went on. Her bare shoulders had a soft, warm look, in the subdued light . . . he was conscious of beautifully shaped ears nestling in golden hair . . . and the anger in him began to die. Once she moved slightly in her seat, and looked round as if she wanted to speak. He leant over her.

"Do you want anything?" he asked.

"My wrap," she said.

He picked up the flimsy wrap and put it about her shoulders, and she turned to him and smiled and said, "Thank you!" and instantly all the anger in him perished. He had admired her before, admired her ardently, but now he knew that he loved her, must love her always. . . .

There was a sound of heavy breathing, and he turned to look at Jimphy.

"Wake him up," said Lady Cecily in a whisper. "Poor dear, he always goes to sleep when he's annoyed!"

He tiptoed across the box and shook the sleeper's arm.

"Eh? What is it?" Lord Jasper said, as he opened his eyes and gaped about him, and then, as he became conscious of his surroundings, he said, "Is it over yet?"

"No. The second act isn't finished yet!"

"Oh, Lord!" he groaned.

"It'll be over in a few minutes!"

"Thank God! I can't stick plays . . . not this sort anyhow. I don't mind a musical comedy now and again, although I think you can have too much of that. . . ."

Lady Cecily turned and waved her hand at her husband. "Ssh, Jimphy!" she whispered. "You're making a frightful row!"

The second act ended soon afterwards, and Lord Jasper scrambled to his feet . . . he had been sitting on the ground at the back of the box, yawning and yawning . . . and made for the door. "Come and have a drink, Quinn!" he said.

"No, thanks," Henry replied.

"Come on. Be a sport!"

"Do go with him, Mr. Quinn, please," Lady Cecily said. "He's sure to get lost or troublesome or something. Aren't you, Jimphy dear?"

"Aren't I what?"

"Aren't you sure to get lost or troublesome or something!"

Lord Jasper did not reply to his wife. "Come along,

Quinn!" he said. "Cecily thinks she's being comic! . . ."
Henry hesitated for a moment or two. He did not wish
to go to the bar, and he was sick of the sight of Lord Jasper.
He wished very much to stay with Lady Cecily, and he
felt hurt because she had urged him to accompany her husband. He would have to do as she had asked him, of
course. . . . While he hesitated, Gilbert got up quickly
from his seat and went to the door of the box. "I'll come
with you, Jimphy!" he said, and then, almost pushing
Lord Jasper in front of him, he went out, closing the door
of the box behind him. Henry stared at the door for a
second or two, nonplussed by the swiftness of Gilbert's
action, and then he turned to Lady Cecily. A look of vexation on her face instantly disappeared and she smiled at
Henry.

"Come and sit here," she said, "and tell me all about
yourself. I haven't really got to know you, have I? Gilbert says you're Irish!"

"Yes," he answered, sitting down.

"How jolly!" she said.

"Do you think so?"

"Oh, yes. It's supposed to be awfully jolly to be Irish.
All the Irish people in books seem to be very amused about
something. I suppose it's the climate. They say there's
a great deal of rain in Ireland. . . ."

"Yes," he answered vaguely, "there is some sometimes!"

She questioned him about Gilbert and Ninian Graham
and Roger Carey.

"It must be awfully jolly," she said, "to be living together like that, you four men!"

He noticed that Lady Cecily always spoke of things being
"awfully jolly" and wondered why her vocabulary should
be so limited in its expressions of pleasure.

"We get on very well together," he replied, "and it's
very lively at times. Gilbert's very lively. . . ."

"Is he?" she said. "He always seems so . . . so . . .
well, not lively. I don't mean that he's solemn or pom-

pous, but he's so . . . so anxious to have his own way, if you understand me. Now, I'm not like that!" She broke off and laughed. "Oh, I don't quite mean that. I *am* selfish. I know I am. I love having my own way, but if I can't have a thing just as I want it . . . well, I'm content to have it in the way that I can. Now, do you understand?"

Henry nodded his head.

"Gilbert isn't like me," she continued. "He says to himself, 'I must have this thing exactly in this way. If I can't have it exactly in this way, then I won't have it at all!' and it's so silly of him to behave like that!"

Henry looked up at her in a puzzled fashion. "What is it he wants? . . . I beg your pardon, I'm being impertinent!"

"Oh, no!" she replied, smiling graciously at him. "He wants . . . oh, he wants everything like that. Haven't you noticed?"

"No," Henry answered, "I haven't."

"Well, you will some day. My motto is, Take what you can get in the way you can get it. It's so much easier to live if you act on that principle!"

"Gilbert's an artist, Lady Cecily, and he can't act on that principle. No artist can. He takes what he wants in the way that he wants it or else he will not take it at all!"

"Exactly. That's what I've been saying. And it's so silly. But never mind. He's young yet, and he'll learn!"

She turned to gaze at the audience, and Henry, not knowing what else to do and having no more to say, looked too. He could think of plenty of fine things to say to her, but he could not get them on to his tongue. He wanted to tell her that he had scarcely heard a word of what was said in the first act of the play because he had filled his mind with thoughts of her, and had spent most of the time in gazing up at her as she sat leaning on the ledge of her box; but when he tried to speak, his mouth seemed to be parched and his tongue would not move.

3

"Do you like this play?" she asked.

"No," he replied.

"Why? I thought everybody admired Wilde's wit. It's clever, isn't it?"

"I don't like it!"

"But it's supposed to be awfully clever!" she insisted.

"It's a common melodrama with bits of wit and epigram stuck on to it!" Henry answered.

"Oh, really!"

"The wit isn't natural . . . it doesn't grow naturally out of the life of the play, I mean. It's stuck on like . . . like plaster images on the front of a house. The witty speeches aren't spontaneous . . . they don't come inevitably! . . . I'm afraid I'm not making myself very clear, but anyhow, I don't like the play. I don't like anything Wilde wrote, except 'The Ballad of Reading Gaol,' and even that's not true. That's really why I dislike his work. It isn't true, any of it. It's all lies. . . .'"

"How awfully interesting!"

"Do you know 'The Ballad of Reading Gaol'? he asked.

"No. . . . Oh, yes! I have read it. Of course, I have. Somebody lent it to me or I bought it or something. . . . Anyhow, I have read it, but I can't remember. . . .'"

"Do you remember the lines? . . .

> *For all men kill the thing they love,*
> *But all men do not die."*

"I seem to remember something . . ." she said vaguely.

"Well, that's a lie. All men don't kill the thing they love. Wilde couldn't help lying even when he was most sincere!"

"That's awfully interesting," Lady Cecily said. "Do you know I've never thought of that before. Won't you come and see me one afternoon, Mr. Quinn?"

"I should like to," he said, and as he spoke, the door of the box opened and Gilbert entered, followed by Lord Jasper.

Lady Cecily turned eagerly to Gilbert. "Oh, Gilbert," she said, "Mr. Quinn promised to come and see me one afternoon. You'll bring him, won't you? Come on Wednesday, both of you!"

"I should like to," Henry murmured again.

"I don't think I can come on Wednesday," Gilbert said.

"Oh, yes, you can," Lady Cecily exclaimed, "and if you can't, you can come some other day. You'll come, Mr. Quinn, won't you?"

"Yes, Lady Cecily! . . ."

"And. . . . Jimphy, dear, do be nice and ask them to come to supper with us after the play. We're going to the Savoy afterwards. I thought it would please Jimphy to go there because he'd be sure not to like the play. . . ."

"Yes, you come along, you chaps!" Jimphy said, willingly.

"I can't. I'm sorry," Gilbert replied. "I've got to go down to Fleet Street and write a notice of this play!"

"Can't you put it off for once, Gilbert!" Lady Cecily said.

Gilbert laughed. "I should like to see Dilton's face if I were to do that. . . ."

"Dilton! Dilton!! Who is Dilton?" she demanded.

"My editor. Very devoted to the human note, Dilton is. No, Cecily, I'm sorry, but I must go down to Fleet Street. Henry can go with you."

She paused for a moment, and then said, "How long will it take you to write the notice of the play?" she asked, adding before he could answer, "Can't you do it now?"

"Yes, Gilbert," Henry said, "you can do it now. You know the play, and you've seen the acting in two acts. . . ."

Gilbert looked at him very directly, and when he spoke, his voice was very firm. "No," he said, "I must go down to Fleet Street!"

Lady Cecily was cross and hurt, and she turned away pettishly.

"Oh, very well!" she said shortly.

There was a slight air of restraint among them . . . even Lord Jasper seemed to feel it. It was he who spoke next.

"You can come and join us at the Savoy after you've done your . . . whatyoumaycallit, can't you?" he said.

Gilbert paused for a moment. He looked as if he were undecided as to what he should say. Then he said, "Yes, I can do that . . . if I get away from the office in time!"

Henry was about to say, "Why, of course, you can get away in plenty of time!" but he checked himself and did not say it.

"Oh, that will do excellently," said Lady Cecily, all smiles again.

Then the lights of the theatre were lowered and the third act began.

4

When the play was over, they drove to Fleet Street in Lord Jasper's motor-car. Lady Cecily had suggested that they should take Gilbert to his newspaper office in order to save time, and he had consented readily enough.

"We might wait for you! . . ." she added, but Gilbert would not agree to this proposal. "It isn't fair to keep Jimphy from his birthday treat any longer," he said, "and I may be some time before I'm ready!"

She was sitting next to Gilbert, and Henry and Jimphy were together with their backs to the chauffeur. She did not appear to be tired nor had the sparkle of her beautiful eyes diminished. She lay against the padded back of the car and chattered in an inconsequent fashion that was oddly amusing. She did not listen to replies that were made to her questions, nor did she appear to notice that sometimes replies were not made. It seemed to Henry that she would have chattered exactly as she was now chattering if she had been alone. Neither Gilbert nor Jimphy answered her, but Henry felt that something ought to be said when she made a direct remark.

"Isn't Fleet Street funny at this time of night?" she said. "So quiet. I do hope the supper will be fit to eat. Oh, Gilbert, I wish you'd say something in your notice of Wilde's play about his insincerity. I felt all the time I was listening to the play that . . . that it wasn't true!"

Gilbert sat up straight in his seat and looked at her.

"Oh!" he exclaimed.

"Yes," she went on. "The wit seemed to be stuck on to the play . . . it wasn't part of it! . . ."

Gilbert leant back in his seat again. "You've been talking to Henry about Wilde, haven't you?"

She laughed lightly and turned towards Henry. "Oh, of course. Mr. Quinn, I always repeat what other people say. I forget that they've said it to me and think that I've thought of it myself!"

Henry professed to be pleased that she had accepted his ideas so completely.

"But, of course," she continued, "what you said was quite true. I've always felt that there was something wrong with Wilde's plays. . . ."

"I can't think what you all want to talk about a play for. I never see anything in 'em to talk about!" Jimphy murmured sleepily.

"Go to sleep, Jimphy, dear. We'll wake you when we get to the Savoy. . . ."

"Always ragging a chap!" Jimphy muttered, and then closed his eyes.

The car turned down one of the narrow streets that lead from Fleet Street to the Thames Embankment, and then turned again and stopped.

"Oh, is this your office, Gilbert?" Lady Cecily said. "Such an ugly, dark looking place! But I suppose it's interesting inside? Newspaper offices are supposed to be awfully interesting inside, aren't they?"

"Are they?" Gilbert replied, as he got out of the car. "I've never noticed it. Noisy holes where no one has time to think. Good-bye."

"Not 'good-bye,' Gilbert! We shall see you soon at the Savoy, shan't we?"

"Oh, yes. Yes. I'd almost forgotten that!"

The car drove off, threading the narrow steep street slowly. They could hear the deep rurr-rurr of the printing machines coming from the basements of the buildings, and now and then great patches of pallid blue light shot out of open windows. Motor-vans and horse-waggons were drawn up against the pavements in front of the office-doors, waiting for the newly-printed papers. Bundles of *Daily Reflexions* were already printed and were being thrown on to the cars and waggons for distribution.

"Are they printed already?" Lady Cecily said.

"Most of them were printed at nine o'clock," Henry replied. "The ha'penny illustrated papers go all over the country before the ordinary papers are printed at all!"

"How awfully clever of them!" she said.

The car turned into Fleet Street and quickly drove up to the Savoy.

"Thank God!" said Jimphy. "I shall get some fun out of my birthday now!"

"Jimphy loves his food," Lady Cecily exclaimed. "Don't you, Jimphy? Don't you love your little tum-tum? . . ."

They entered the hotel and found the table which had been reserved for them. There was a queer, hectic gaiety about the place, as if every one present were making a desperate effort to eat, drink *and* be merry. People greeted Lady Cecily as she passed them and muttered, "'loa, Jimphy!" Henry had never been to a fashionable restaurant before, and the barbaric beauty of the scene fascinated him. The women were riotously dressed, and the colours of their garments mingled and merged like the colours of a sunset. There was a constant flow of people through the room, and the chatter of animated voices and bursts of laughter and the jingling, sentimental music played by the orchestra made Jimphy forget how bored he had been at the theatre. The slightly fuddled air which he had had in the bar of St. James's had left him and he began to talk.

"Ripping woman, that!" he said to Henry, indicating a slight, dark girl who had entered the restaurant in company with a tall, flaxen-haired man. "Pretty little flapper, I call her! I like thin women, myself. Well, slender's a better word, isn't it? What you say, Cecily?"

Lady Cecily had tapped her husband's arm. "Ernest Lensley's just come in," she said. "He's with Boltt. Go and bring them both here. They can't find seats, poor dears!"

Ernest Lensley and Boltt were fashionable novelists. Lensley was an impudent-looking man with very blue eyes who had written a number of popular stories about society women who "chattered" very much in the way that Lady Cecily chattered. The heroine of his best-known book was modelled, so people said, on the wife of a Cabinet Minister, and thousands of suburban Englishwomen professed to have an intimate knowledge of the statesman's family life solely because they had read Lensley's novel. It was a flippant, vulgar book, the outcome of a flippant, vulgar mind. Boltt had a wider public than Lensley. Boltt, a tall, thin, stooping man, with peering eyes, had discovered "the human note" of which Gilbert's editor prated continually. He was a precise, priggish man, extraordinarily vain though no vainer than Lensley, who, however, had an easy manner that Boltt would never acquire. He spoke in the way in which one might expect a "reduced gentlewoman, poor dear!" to speak, and there was something about him that made a man long to kick him up a room and down a room and across a room and back again. His heroes were all big, burly, red-haired giants, who wore beards and old clothes and said "By God, yes!" when they admired the scenery, and led a vagabond life in a perfectly gentlemanly manner until they met the heroine. . . . His heroines constantly fell into situations which were extremely compromising in the eyes of a censorious world, but they were never completely compromised. The whole world knew, before the conclusion of the story, that the heroine had been falsely suspected. If she had spent the night in the hero's bedroom, she had done so with the best intentions, under the strictest chaperonage . . . usually that of her dear, devoted old nurse, God bless her! . . . whose presence in the bedroom had been hidden, until the middle of the penultimate chapter, from the heroine's friends and relatives. The hero, of course, poor, manly, broken giant, had been ill, suffering from a fever, and in his delirium had called for her, discontent until she had put her cool firm hand upon his hot brow, and the doctor had said that if she would stay with him, she would save his life. So she had flung her reputation to the winds and had hurried to his bedroom. . . . It was pretentious, flatulent stuff, through which a thin stream of tepid lust trickled so gently that it seemed like a stream of pretty sentiment, and it was written with such cleverness that young ladies in Bath and Cheltenham and Atlantic City, U. S. A., were tricked into believing that this was Life . . . Real Life. . . .

Lensley and Boltt followed Jimphy eagerly to Lady Cecily's table. Lensley was glad to sit with her: Boltt was glad to be certain of his supper. Lensley enjoyed listening to Cecily's babble because he could always be certain of getting something out of her speech that would just fit into his next novel: Boltt liked his contiguity to members of the governing class. They completely ignored Henry after they had been introduced to him.

"Mr. Quinn is writing a novel, too!" said Lady Cecily.

"Oh, yes!" said Lensley.

"Indeed!" Boltt burbled.

Thereafter they addressed themselves exclusively to Lady

Cecily and her husband. Lensley told Lady Cecily that she was to be the heroine of his next book. "I'm studying you now, dear Lady Cecily!" he said. "Jotting you down in my little book . . . all your little plaguey ways and speeches! . . ."

"How awfully exciting!" she replied, and her eyes seemed to become brighter, and she leant towards the novelist as if she meant to reveal herself more clearly to him.

"You'll be angry with me when you see the book," he said. "Dreadfully angry. You know poor Mrs. Maldon was very hurt about *'Jennifer'!*" Mrs. Maldon was the wife of the Cabinet Minister.

"I shan't mind what you say about me," Lady Cecily said, "so long as you make me the heroine of the book. What are you going to call it? . . ."

"The Delectable Lady!"

"How awfully nice! . . ."

5

Henry began to feel bored. He wished that Gilbert would come. Gilbert would soon rout this paltry little tuppenny-ha'penny Society novelist with his pretty-pretty chatter and his pretty-pretty blue eyes and his air of being a knowing dog. Lady Cecily seemed to have forgotten Henry altogether. . . . He turned to Lord Jasper who was trying hard not to yawn in Mr. Boltt's face. Mr. Boltt had been a surveyor at one period of his life, and his favourite theme of conversation was Renascence architecture. He was now telling Jimphy of the glories of French Cathedrals, and Jimphy, who cared even less for French Cathedrals than he cared for English ones, was wondering just how he could change the conversation to a discussion of the latest ballet at the Empire and particularly of a girl he knew who was a perfect lady and, as a matter of fact, lived with her mother. The supper party seemed likely to end dismally, and Henry, when he was not wishing that Gilbert would come, was wishing that he himself had not come. He could not understand why it was that he had so much difficulty in talking easily with strangers. Lensley was prattling as if he were determined to discharge an entire novelful of "chatter" at Lady Cecily, and Boltt's little clipped, pedantic voice recited a long rigmarole about a glorious view in France which he had lately seen while motoring in that country. Boltt admired Nature in the way in which any man of careful upbringing would admire a really nice woman. . . .

Henry had lately reviewed a book by Boltt for a daily paper, and he had expressed scorn for it and its stuffed dummies, masquerading as men and women . . . and Boltt, who took himself very seriously indeed, had written a letter of complaint to the editor of the paper. Henry wondered what Boltt would say if he knew that the review had been written by him, and an imp in him made him interrupt the long recital of the glories of France.

"The *Morning Report* had a good go at your last novel, Boltt!" he said.

The novelist looked reproachfully at Henry, as if he were rebuking him for indelicacy.

"I never see the *Morning Report*," he replied loftily.

"Oh, then, I suppose you didn't see the review. I thought you probably got clippings from a Press-cuttings agency! . . ."

"Yes, oh, yes, I do. I seem to remember that the *Morning Report* was unkind. Not quite fair, I should say!"

Lord Jasper began to take an intelligent interest in the conversation. "Have you published another book, Boltt?" he asked innocently.

"Yes . . . a . . . Lord Jasper . . . I have!" Mr. Boltt said, and there was some sniffiness in his tones. He was accustomed to lengthy reviews on the day of publication, and it annoyed him to think that there was some one in the world, some one, too, with whom he was acquainted, who did not know that the publication of one of his books was an event.

"I can't think how you writing chaps keep it up," said Jimphy. "I couldn't write a book to save my life! ..."

"No?" said Mr. Boltt, smiling in the way of one who says to himself, "God help you, my poor fellow, God help you!"

"I suppose it's all a question of knack," Jimphy continued. "You get into the way of it and you can't stop. Sometimes a tune gets into my head and I have to keep on humming it or whistling it. I'm not what you'd call a sentimental fellow at all, but that song . . . you know, about the honeysuckle and the bee . . . I *could not* get that song out of my head. I thought I should go cracked over it. Always humming it or whistling it . . . and I suppose if you get an idea for a yarn into your head, Boltt, well, it's something like that!"

Lady Cecily had exhausted the "chatter" of Mr. Lensley.

"What's that?" she exclaimed.

"Lord Jasper is describing the processes of literature to me, Lady Cecily," said Mr. Boltt sarcastically. "I have been greatly interested.

The man's conceit irritated Henry and he longed to disconcert him.

"Yes," he said. "It all began by my saying something about a review of Boltt's last novel in the *Morning Report!* . . ."

Mr. Boltt made motions with his hands. "Really," he said, "Lady Cecily isn't in the least interested in my effusions."

"Oh, but I am, Mr. Boltt," Lady Cecily interrupted. "What did the paper say? I'm sure it was very flattering! . . ."

"The reviewer said that the book would probably please

the vicar's only daughter, but that it wouldn't impose upon her when she grew up. . . ."

"Oh!" said Lady Cecily.

"Some rival, I'm afraid!" Mr. Boltt murmured. "Some one who dislikes me. . . ."

"The chief complaint was that your people aren't real. . . ." Henry continued, though Mr. Boltt frowned heavily.

"Yes. I don't think we need discuss the matter further, Mr. . . ."

"Quinn!!" said Henry.

He felt happier now that he had pricked the egregious fellow's vanity.

"Silly of 'em to say that," said Lord Jasper. "Boltt sells a tremendous number of books, don't you, Boltt? More than Lensley does. And that shows, doesn't it? If a chap can sell as many books as Boltt sells . . . well, he must be some good. I've never read any of 'em, of course, but then I'm not a chap that reads much. All the same, a chap I know says Boltt's all right, and he's a chap that knows what he's talking about. I mean to say, he's written books himself!"

Lady Cecily was no longer interested in the history of Mr. Boltt's novel. The meal was almost at an end, and Gilbert had not arrived. She glanced towards the door, looking straight over Mr. Lensley's head, and Henry could see that she was fidgeting.

"Gilbert's a long time," he said to her.

She did not answer, and before he could repeat his remark to her, Lord Jasper exclaimed, "I say, you know, we ought to be getting home, Cecily. It's getting jolly late! . . ."

"Let's wait a little longer," she said, "Gilbert hasn't come yet!"

"But I mean to say, this place'll be closing soon. . . ."

Mr. Boltt made a satirical remark on the ridiculously

early hours at which restaurants are compelled by law to close in England. In France, he said . . . but Lord Jasper did not wait to hear what is done in France.

"He won't come now," he said. "He wouldn't have time to eat any supper if he were to come . . . and it's getting jolly late, and I'm jolly tired!"

He got up from the table as he spoke. "Very well," said Lady Cecily, rising too.

The others followed her example, and Boltt and Lensley prepared to escort Lady Cecily to the door, but she gave her hand to them and said "Good-night!"

"It's so nice to have seen you both," she said. "No, don't trouble. Mr. Quinn will come with me!"

Lord Jasper had gone on in front to find his car, and Lady Cecily and Henry walked down the room together until they came to the courtyard where the car was waiting for them.

"Tell Gilbert I'm angry with him," she said. "He must come and see me soon and tell me how sorry he is. You'll come, too, perhaps, Mr. Quinn!"

He found his tongue suddenly. "I will, Lady Cecily," he said. "I'll come even if he doesn't. I've enjoyed to-night tremendously. . . ."

"Have you, Mr. Quinn?"

"Yes. . . ."

"I say, come along," Lord Jasper shouted to them.

"Poor Jimphy's getting fractious. You can tell me how much you've enjoyed to-night when we meet again!"

He took her to the car, and watched her as she gathered her skirts about her and climbed inside.

"Can't we drop you at your house?" said Lord Jasper. "It won't be any trouble to do so!"

"No, thanks," Henry replied. "I'd rather walk home. It's such a beautiful night!"

Lord Jasper followed Lady Cecily into the car. "You're a romantic chap, Quinn!" he said, and then, as an afterthought, he added quickly, "I say, we must arrange to go to the Empire together some evening. You're the sort of chap I like. . . ."

Lady Cecily waved her hand to him. As the car moved off he saw her beautiful face leaning against the side of the car, and he longed to take her in his arms and kiss her. Then the car turned, and drove quickly off. He stood for a moment or two looking after it, and continued to stand still even when it had swung out of the court-yard into the Strand. Then he walked slowly away from the restaurant. He had not gone very far when his arm was touched, and, turning round, he saw Gilbert.

6

"Hilloa," he said, "you're late!"

"No, I'm not," Gilbert replied.

"Yes, you are. The Jaynes have gone!"

"I saw them going. I've been here for over half-an-hour, waiting for you!"

"Over half-an-hour! What's up, Gilbert?"

Gilbert put his arm in Henry's and made him move out of the Savoy courtyard. "Come down to the Embank-ment," he said. "It's quieter there. I want to talk to you!"

"But hadn't we better go home? We can talk on the way. It's late. . . ."

"No. I want to go to the Embankment. Damn it all, Quinny, it's a sentimental place for a heart-to-heart talk, isn't it?"

"You aren't drunk, Gilbert, I suppose?"

"Never so sober in my life, Quinny. Besides, I don't get drunk. People who talk about beer and whisky as much as I do, never get drunk. Come along, there's a good chap!"

"Very well . . . only I'm not going to stay long. I'm no good for work the day after I've had a long night. . . ,"

"I won't keep you long. How did the supper-party go off?"

"Damnably. Two tame novelists turned up . . . Boltt and Lensley!"

"Those asses!"

"Yes. Lensley 'chattered' to Lady Cecily, and Boltt bored and bored and bored. . . . I took him down a bit. I rubbed in the *Morning Report* review. The little toad could hardly sit still! Of course, he affected the superior person attitude!"

"God be merciful to him, poor little rat! He wants to be a wicked, hell-for-leather fellow, but he hasn't got the stomach for it! What did Cecily say when I didn't turn up?"

"She looked rather cross. She told me as we came away to tell you she was angry with you. You're to go and apologise to her as soon as possible!"

"Did she?"

"Yes. I say, Gilbert, why didn't you turn up?"

They had reached the Embankment, and they crossed to the riverside and leant against the parapet.

"Because I was afraid to," said Gilbert.

"Afraid to!"

"Yes. Can't you see I'm in love with her?"

"Well, I guessed as much. . . ."

"I love her so much that she can do what she likes with me, and all she likes to do is to destroy me!"

"Destroy you?"

"Yes. If you love Cecily, she demands the whole of your life. Every bit of it. She consumes you. . . . Oh, I know this sounds like a penny dreadful, Quinny, but it's true. I've asked her to run away with me, but she won't come. She says she hates scandal and she likes her social position. My God, I feel sick when I see Jimphy with her . . . like a damned big lobster putting his . . . his claws about her. He isn't a bad fellow in his silly way, but I can't stand him as Cecily's husband!"

"I know what you mean," said Henry.

"I thought that if Cecily and I were to go away together, we could get our lives into some sort of perspective,
and then I could go on with my work and have her as
well, but she won't go away with me. She wants me to
hang around, being her lover . . . and I can't do that,
Quinny. It's mean and furtive, and I hate that. You're
always listening for some one coming . . . a servant or the
husband or some one . . . and I can't stand that. If I
love a woman, I love her, and I don't want to spend
part of my life in pretending that I don't. I loathe
myself when I have to change the talk suddenly or move
away when a door opens. . . . Do you understand,
Quinny?"

Henry nodded his head, but did not speak.

"Once when I'd been begging Cecily to go away with
me, Jimphy walked into the room . . . and I had to pretend to be talking about some nasturtiums that Cecily had
grown. I felt like a cad. That's what's rotten about loving another man's wife. It's the treachery of the thing,
the pretending. . . . I've often wondered why it is that
love of that sort seems so romantic and splendid in books
and so damnably mean when it comes into the Divorce
Court . . . but when I met Cecily I knew why . . . it's
because of the treachery and the deceit. I used to think
that it was beautiful in books because artists were able to
see the hidden beauty, and ugly in the Divorce Court
because ordinary people only saw the surface things . . .
but I'm not sure now."

He stopped speaking, but Henry did not speak instead.
He did not know what to say; he felt indeed that there was
nothing to be said, that he must simply listen. He watched
the electric signs on the other side of the river as they
spelt out the virtues of Someone's Teas and Another's
Whisky, and wondered how long it would be before Gilbert
said something else. He was beginning to be bored by the
business, and he felt sleepy. He was jealous too, when

he thought that Gilbert had kissed Cecily and had been held in her beautiful arms. . . .

"Cecily doesn't mind about the shabbiness of it," he heard Gilbert saying. "We've talked about that, and she says it doesn't matter a bit. All that matters to her is that she shan't be found out . . . too publicly anyhow! She called me a prig when I said that I was afraid of tainting my work. . . ."

"Tainting your work?"

"Yes. Perhaps it is priggish of me, but I feel that if I'm mean in one thing I may be mean in another. I'm terribly afraid of doing bad work, Quinny, and I got an idea into my head that if I let taint into my life in one place, I couldn't confine it and it would spread to other places. Do you see? If I let myself get into a rotten position with Cecily, I might write down. . . ."

"I don't see that," said Henry. "Because you love a married woman, it doesn't follow that you'll pot-boil."

"No, perhaps not. But I was afraid of it. I suppose it was priggish of me. That wasn't the only thing, however. I knew that if I did what Cecily wanted me to do, I'd spend most of my time with her or thinking about her. I can't work if I'm doing that, for I think of her and long for her. . . . Oh, let's go home. It isn't fair to keep you here listening to my twaddle!"

But they did not move. They gazed down on the swiftly-flowing river, and presently they heard Big Ben striking one deep note.

"One o'clock!" said Gilbert.

"What are you going to do about it, Gilbert?" Henry asked at last.

"I'm going away from London. I've chucked my job on the *Daily Echo*. . . ."

"Good Lord, man, what for?"

"Well, I'm fed-up with the English theatre to begin with, and I'm fed-up with journalism too . . . and it's the only way I can get free of Cecily. I must finish the

new comedy and I can't finish it if I stay in town and
see Cecily. She won't let me finish it. She'll make me
go here and go there with her. She'll keep me making
love to her when I ought to be working. God damn women,
Quinny!''

"You're excited, Gilbert!''

"Yes, I know I am. When I'm with Cecily, I'm like a
jelly-fish. She sucks the brains out of me. She doesn't
care whether I finish my comedy or not. She doesn't care
what happens to my work so long as I hang around and
love her and kiss her whenever she wants me to. My brains
go to bits when I'm with her. I'm all emotion and sensation . . . just like those asses Lensley and Boltt. Quinny,
fancy spending your life turning out the sort of stuff those
two men write. They've written about a dozen books each,
and I suppose they're good for twenty or thirty more. I'd
rather be a scavenger!''

They walked along the Embankment towards Waterloo
Bridge.

"I'm going to Anglesey,'' Gilbert said. "I shall go and
stay there until the end of the summer!''

"I shall miss you, Gilbert. So will Ninian and Roger!''

"I shall miss you three, but it can't be helped. I'm
the sort of man who succumbs to women . . . I can't help
it. If they're beautiful and soft and full of love . . . like
Cecily . . . they down me. Their femininity topples me
over, and there's no work to be got out of me while I'm
like that. But my work's of more consequence to me than
loving and kissing, Quinny, and if I can't do it while I'm
Cecily's lover, then I'll go away from her and do it!''

"What makes you think you could do it if she were to
go away with you?''

"I don't know. Hope, I suppose.''

They walked up Villiers Street into the Strand, and
made their way towards Bloomsbury.

"I suppose,'' said Gilbert, "you wouldn't like to come
to Anglesey too?''

Henry hesitated for a few moments. He had a vision of Lady Cecily's beautiful face leaning against the padded side of the car, and he remembered that she had smiled and waved her hand to him. . . .

"No," he replied, "I don't think so . . . not at present at any rate!" and then, added in explanation, "If I go, too, the house will be broken up. That would be a pity!"

"I forgot that," Gilbert answered. "Yes, of course!"

THE SIXTH CHAPTER

1

GILBERT did not leave London, as he had intended, for Sir Geoffrey Mundane definitely decided to produce ''The Magic Casement'' in succession to the play which was then being performed at his theatre. He had already discussed the caste with Gilbert, and on the morning after the scene on the Embankment, he telephoned to Gilbert, telling him that he had made engagements for the play, and would like to fix a date on which he should read the manuscript to the company. ''Any day'll suit me,'' Gilbert had informed him, and Sir Geoffrey thereupon settled that the reading should take place two days later. ''I suppose,'' he said, ''you'd like to attend the rehearsals?'' and Gilbert, forgetting his resolution to fly from Lady Cecily, said that he would. He thought that the experience would be very valuable to him. He became so excited at the prospect of seeing a play of his performed at a West End theatre that he was unable to sit still, and his language, always extravagant, became absurd. He broke every rule that Roger had invented. ''It'll take all the royalties you'll receive to pay off this score!'' Roger said, thrusting the fine-book before him.

''Poo!'' said Gilbert. ''I'll buy up the Ten Commandments with one night's royalty! Oh, it's going to be a success, I tell you. It'll run for a year . . . more than that . . . two years! . . .'' He began to estimate the number of performances the play would receive. ''Six evening performances and two matinées every week for fifty-two weeks! Eight times fifty-two, Roger . . . you were a Second Wrangler, you ought to know that! Four hundred

273

and sixteen! Lordy God, what a lot! And if I get ten pounds every time it's done . . . Oh-h-h! Four thousand, one hundred and sixty pounds! And then there'll be American rights and provincial rights. . . . I'll tell you what I'll do, coves! I'll buy you all a stick of barley-sugar each, or a penn'orth of acid-drops . . . which 'ud you like? . . .''

It was during the rehearsals of "The Magic Casement" that "Broken Spears" was published.

"It isn't as good as 'Drusilla,'" they said to Henry, when they had read it, "but it'll be more popular!"

It was. The critics who had praised "Drusilla" were not impressed by "Broken Spears," but the critics who had been indifferent to "Drusilla" praised "Broken Spears" so extravagantly that six thousand copies of it were sold in six months, apart from the copies which were sold to the lending libraries, and the sale of "Drusilla," in consequence of the success of "Broken Spears," increased from three hundred and seventy-five copies to one thousand five hundred and eighty. Mr. Quinn, in thanking Henry for a copy of it, merely said, in direct reference to the book, *"I see you've been tickling the English. Don't go on doing it!"* and the effect of this criticism was so stimulating that Henry destroyed the three chapters of "Turbulence" which were in manuscript and started to rewrite the book. Literary agents now began to write to him, telling him how charmed they were with his work and how certain they were of their ability to increase his income considerably; and a publisher of some enterprise and resource wrote to him and said that he would like to see his third book.

"You look as if you were established, Quinny!" said Roger, and Henry blushed and murmured deprecatingly about himself.

"How's the Bar?" he said.

"Oh, it's not bad. I got a fellow off to-day who ought to have had six months hard," Roger answered. "And a new solicitor has given me a brief. We ought to ask him to dinner and feed him well. F. E. Robinson always tells his butler to bring out the second-quality wine for solicitors. Snob!''

''We seem to be getting on, don't we, coves?'' Gilbert interjected. ''Look at all these press-cuttings! . . .''

He held out a fistful of slips which had come that evening from a Press-Cutting Agency. ''All about me,'' he said, ''and the play. Mundane knows more about the preliminary puff than any one else in England. He calls me 'this talented young author from whom much may be expected.' I never thought I should get pleasure out of a trade advertisement, but I do. I'm lapping up this stuff like billy-o. I saw a poster on the side of a 'bus this afternoon, advertising 'The Magic Casement.' Mundane's name was in big letters, and you could just see mine with the naked eye. I hopped on to the 'bus and went for a fourpenny ride on it, so's I could touch the damn thing . . . and I very nearly told the conductor who I was. It's no good pretending I'm not conceited. I am, and I don't care. Where's Ninian?''

''Not come in yet. How'd the rehearsals go to-day?'' Roger answered.

''Better than any other day. They're beginning to feel their parts. It's about time, too. I felt sick with fright yesterday, they were so wooden. Mundane might have been the village idiot, instead of the fine actor he is . . . but they're better now. Ninian's late!''

''Is he? He'll be here presently. By the way, my Cousin Rachel's coming to town to-morrow. She's been investigating something or other . . . factory life, I think. I thought I'd bring her here to dinner. She may be interesting.''

''Do,'' said Gilbert, and then, as he heard the noise of the street-door being closed, he added, ''There's Ninian now!''

Ninian, on his way to his room, stopped for a moment

or two, to shout at them, "I say, the mater and Mary've come up from Devon. I got a wire this afternoon. I'm not grubbing with you to-night. They want to go to a theatre, and I've got to climb into gaudy garments and go with them. . . ."

He closed the door and ran up the stairs, but before he reached the first landing, Gilbert called after him, "I say, Ninian!"

"Yes," he answered, pausing on the stairs.

"Bring them to dinner to-morrow night. Roger's Cousin Rachel is coming, and we may as well make a party of it. Gaudy garments and liqueurs. Do you think they'll stay for the first night of my play?"

"That's one of the reasons why they've come up," Ninian answered.

2

Rachel Wynne and Mrs. Graham and Mary dined with them on the following evening, and it seemed to Henry when he saw Mary entering Ninian's sitting-room that she was a stranger to him. He had known her as a child and as a young, self-conscious girl, but this Mary was a woman. He felt shy in her presence, and when, for a few moments, he was left alone with her, he hardly knew what to say to her. They had been "Quinny" and "Mary" to each other before, but now they avoided names. . . . He spoke tritely about her journey to London, reminding her of the slowness of the train between Whitcombe and Salisbury, and wondered whether she liked London better than Bovey-hayne. His old disability to say the things that were in his mind prevented him from re-establishing his intimacy with her. He tried to say, "Hilloa, Mary!" but could not do so, and his shyness affected her so that she stood before him, fingering her fan nervously, and answering "Yes" and "Oh, yes!" and "No" and "Oh, no!" to all that he said. He liked the sweep of her hair across her brow and the soft flush in her cheeks and the slender lines of her neck and the gleam of a gold chain that held a pendant suspended about her throat. He thought, too, that her eyes shone like lustres in the light, and suddenly, as he thought this, he felt that he could speak to her with his old freedom. He moved towards her, shaping his lips to say, "Oh, Mary, I . . ." but the door opened before he could speak, and Rachel Wynne entered the room with Roger and Mrs. Graham.

"Yes, Quinny?" Mary said, saying his name quite easily now.

He laughed nervously and looked at the others. "I've forgotten what I was going to say," he said, and went forward to greet Mrs. Graham.

"My cousin, Rachel Wynne," said Roger, introducing her to him.

Rachel Wynne was a tall, thin girl, with a curious tightened look, as if she were keeping a close hold on herself. When she held out her hand to him, he had a sensation of discomfort, not because her clasp was firm, but because she seemed to be looking, not through him, but into him. He was very sensitive to the opinion of people about him, feeling very quickly the dislike of any one who did not care for him, and in a moment he knew that Rachel Wynne was antipathetic to him. Henry was always rude to people whom he disliked . . . he could not be civil to them, however hard he might try to be so, but his feeling in the presence of people who disliked him, was one of powerlessness: he was tongue-tied and nervous and very dull, and his faculties seemed to shrivel up. There was a look of cold efficiency about Rachel Wynne that frightened him. She seemed to be incapable of wasting time or of waywardness. Her career at Newnham, Roger had told him, had been one of steady brilliance. "There wasn't a flicker in it," he had said to Henry. "Rachel's always well-trimmed!"

There were no ragged edges about Rachel Wynne. Her

frock was neatly made, so neatly that he was unaware of it, and her hair was bound tightly to her head by a black velvet ribbon. She had a look of cold tidiness, as if she had been frozen into her shape and could not be thawed out of it; but she was not cold in spirit, as he discovered during dinner when the conversation shifted from generalities about themselves to the work she had lately been doing. They had been talking about Gilbert's play, and then Mrs. Graham had turned to Henry and told him how much she liked his novels. Her tastes were simple, and she preferred "Broken Spears" to "Drusilla." "Of course, 'Drusilla' is very clever!" she said a little deprecatingly, and then she turned to Rachel and asked her whether she had read Henry's novels.

"No," Rachel answered. "I very seldom read novels! . . ."

He felt contempt for her. Now he knew why he had been chilled by her presence. She belonged to that order of prigs which will not read novels, preferring instead to read "serious" books. Such a woman would treat "Tom Jones" as a frivolous book, less illuminating than some tedious biography or history book. She might even deny that it had any illumination at all. . . . He could not prevent a sneer from his retort to her statement that she seldom read novels.

"I suppose," he said, "you think that novels are not sufficiently serious?"

"Oh, no," she answered quickly. "I just haven't time for novel-reading!"

That seemed to him to be worse than if she had said that she preferred to read solid books. A novel, in her imagination, was a light diversion in which one only indulged in times of unusual slackness. No wonder, he thought to himself, all reformers and serious people make such a mess of the social system when they despise and ignore the principal means of knowing the human spirit.

"That's a pity," he said aloud. "I should have thought

that you'd find novels useful to you in your work. I mean,
there's surely more chance of understanding the people
of the eighteenth century if you read Fielding's 'Tom
Jones' than there is if you read Lecky's 'England in the
Eighteenth Century.'"

"Is there?" said Rachel.

"Of course, there is," Gilbert hurled at her from the
other side of the table. "Fielding was an artist, inspired
by God, but Lecky was simply a fact-pedlar, inspired by
the Board of Education. Why even that dull ass, Richard-
son, makes you understand more about his period than
Lecky does!"

"Perhaps," said Rachel, in a tone which indicated that
there was no doubt in her mind about the relative values
of Lecky and Fielding. She turned to Henry. "I wish
you'd write a book about the factory system," she said.
"That would be worth doing!"

He disliked the suggestion that "Broken Spears" and
"Drusilla" had not been worth doing, and he let his
resentment of her attitude towards his work affect the
tone of his voice as he answered, "I don't know anything
about factories!"

"You should learn about them," she retorted.

No, he did not like this woman, aggressive and assertive.
He turned to speak to Mary . . . but Rachel Wynne had
not finished with him.

"I've spent six months in the north of England," she
said, reaching for the salted almonds. "I've seen every
kind of factory, model and otherwise!"

"Oh, yes," he answered, vaguely irritated by her. He
wished that she would talk to her other neighbour and
leave him in peace with Mary. As an Improved Tory, he
knew that he ought to get all the information about factories out of her that he could, but as Henry Quinn, he had
no other desire than to be quit of her as quickly as possible.

"And I think the model factories are no better than the
rotten ones," she went on.

"What's that you say?" Roger called to her from the other side of the table.

She repeated her remark. "I went over a model factory last week . . . a cocoa and chocolate works . . . and I'd rather be a tramp than work in it," she went on.

"But isn't it rather wonderfully organised?" Roger asked.

"Oh, yes, it's marvellously arranged. There are baths and gymnasia and continuation classes and free medical inspection and model houses and savings banks and all the rest of it . . . but I'd rather be a tramp, I tell you. . . . You see, even with the best of employers, genuinely philanthropic people eager to deal justly with the workers who make their fortunes for them, the factory system remains a rotten one. You can't make a decent, human thing out of it because it's fundamentally vile! . . ."

"My dear Rachel! . . ." Roger began, but she would not listen to interruptions.

"They look just as pale and 'peeked' in model factories as they do in bad ones. They're cleaner, that's all. The firm sees that they wash, but it can't prevent them from becoming ill, and they're all ill. They don't look any better than the people in the bad factories. They look worse, because they're cleaner and you can see their illness more easily. But that isn't all. They have no hope of ever controlling the firm . . . they'll never be allowed to own the factory . . . that will always belong to the Family. The best that the clever ones can look forward to is a little managership. Most of them can't look forward to anything but being drilled and washed and medically inspected and modelly housed and morally controlled. . . . Oh, it isn't worth it, it isn't worth it. I'd rather be a dirty, insanitary tramp!"

A kind of moral fury possessed her, and they sat still, listening to her without interrupting her.

"I saw three girls at a machine," she went on, "and one of them did some little thing to a chocolate box and then

passed it on to the second girl who did a further little thing
to it and then passed it to the third girl who did another
little thing to it, and then it was finished, and that was all.
They do that every day, and the man who took me round
told me that the firm had to catch 'em young, otherwise
they can't acquire the knack of it. I saw girls putting
pieces of chocolate into tinfoil so quickly that you could
hardly see their movements; and they do that all day. And
they have to be caught young . . . before they've properly
tasted life. They wouldn't do it otherwise, I suppose.
That's your factory system for you! And think of the
things they produce. Chocolate boxes full of sweets!
There was one girl who spent the whole of her working
days in pasting photographs of grinning chorus girls on to
box-lids. I should go mad if I had to look at that soppy
grin all day long. . . ."

Mrs. Graham murmured gently, but her words were not
audible. Rachel would not have heard them if they had
been.

"Well," said Gilbert, "what do you want to do about
it?"

"I'm a reactionary," Rachel answered. "I'm against
all this . . . this progress. We're simply eating up people's lives, and paying meanly for them. I'd destroy all
these factories . . . the whole lot. They aren't worth the
price. And I'd go back to decent piggery. What is the
good of a plate when it means that some girl has been
poisoned so that it can be bought cheaply?"

"But we must have plates?" Henry said.

"Why?" she retorted.

"Well!" he rejoined, smiling at her as one smiles at a
foolish child.

"Oh, I know," she went on, "you think I'm talking
wildly. I've heard all about your Improved Toryism.
Roger's told me about it. You all think that you are the
anointed ones, and that the bulk of people are born to do
what they're told. You won't have whips for your slaves

. . . you'll have statutes. You won't sell them . . . you'll socialise them. Cogs in wheels, you'll make them! Oh, it isn't worth while living like that. You don't even let a man do a whole job . . . you only let him do a part of one, and you're trying to turn him into an automaton more and more every day. He's to press a button . . . and that's all. Presently, he'll *be* a button! . . ."

"My dear Rachel," Roger said, "you don't imagine, do you, that the whole world's going to turn back to . . . piggery as you call it? We've spent centuries in creating this civilisation. . . ."

"Is it worth while?" she demanded.

"Yes. . . ."

"Prove it," she insisted.

"Well, of course, that's a job, isn't it? I can't prove it in a few minutes. . . ."

"You can't prove it, Roger," she interrupted. "If all this civilisation were worth while, you wouldn't need to prove it: it would be obvious. We'd only have to look out of the door to see the proof."

"I don't say that the factory system is satisfactory at present. It isn't; but it can be improved. . . ."

"No, it can't, Roger. It's unimprovable. I dare you to go to any model factory in England and study it with an honest mind and then say that it is worth while. It makes the people ill . . . they get no pleasure out of their work. . . ."

"We could shorten the hours in factories," Henry suggested.

"If you do that, you admit that the thing is rotten, and can only be endured in short shifts!" she retorted. "And who wants his hours reduced? A healthy man wants to work as long as he can stand up. I don't want my hours reduced. I'll go on working until I drop . . . but I wouldn't work for two seconds if I didn't like the job!" She turned again to Henry. "Why don't you write a book exposing the factory system. It would be much more

useful than all this lovey-dovey stuff. I'd give the world
for a book like that . . . as good as Tolstoy's 'War and
Peace' or 'Dickens's 'Oliver Twist'! . . .''

3

Mary had not spoken at all while Rachel harangued them
on the question of the factory system, but that was not
surprising, for Rachel had not given any of them a chance
to say more than two or three words. In Ninian's sitting-
room, when Gilbert turned to her and asked her what she
thought of factories, she blushed a little, conscious that
they had all turned to look at her, and answered that she
had never seen a factory.

"Never seen a factory!" Rachel exclaimed, and was off
again in denunciation.

Henry went and sat beside Mary while Rachel told tales
of sweaters that caused Mrs. Graham to cry out with pain.

"Mary!" he said to her under his breath.

"Yes, Quinny," she answered, turning towards him and
speaking as softly as he had spoken.

He fumbled for words. "It's . . . it's awfully nice to
see you again," he said.

"It's nice to see you all again," she replied.

"You're . . . you're so different," he went on.

"Am I?" She paused a moment, and then, smiling at
him, said, "So are you."

"Am I very different?" he asked.

"In some ways. You're quite famous now, aren't you?"

"Famous?" he said vaguely.

"Yes. Your novels. . . ."

He laughed. "Oh, dear no, not anything like famous!"

"Well-known, then."

"Moderately well-known. That's all. But what's the
point?"

"Well, that's the point," she replied. "You were only

'Quinny' before, but now you're the moderately well-known novelist, and I'm afraid of you. . . ."

"Don't be absurd, Mary!"

"But I am, Quinny. I read a review of one of your books in some paper, and it called you a very wise person, and said you knew a great deal about human nature or something of that sort. Well, one feels rather awful in the presence of a person like that. At least, I do!"

He felt that she was chaffing him, and he did not want to be chaffed by her. He liked the "Quinny" and "Mary" attitude, and he wished that she would forget that he had written "wise" books.

"You're making fun of me," he said.

"Oh, no, I'm not," she answered quickly. "I'm quite serious!"

He did not answer for a few moments. He could hear Rachel's passionate voice saying, "They get seven shillings a week . . . in theory. There are fines . . ." and he wondered why it was that she repelled him. Her sincerity was palpable . . . it was clear that she was hurt by the miseries of factory girls . . . but in spite of her sincerity, he felt that he could not bear to be near her. "If she'd only talk of something else," he thought . . . and then returned to Mary.

"Do you remember that time at Boveyhayne?" he said.

"Which time?" she asked.

"The first time."

"Yes."

He swallowed and then went on. "Do you remember what I said to you . . . on the platform at Whitcombe?"

She spoke more quickly and loudly as she answered him. "Oh, yes," she said, "we got engaged, didn't we? We *were* kids! . . ."

Mrs. Graham caught the word "engaged."

"Who's engaged?" she asked.

"No one, mother," Mary answered. "Quinny and I were talking about the time when we were engaged! . . ."

He felt a frightful fool. What on earth had possessed her that she should treat the matter in this fashion?

"Were you engaged, dear?" Mrs. Graham said.

"Oh, yes, mother. Don't you remember? Of course, we were kids then! . . ."

Why did she insist on the fact that they were "kids" then?

"I remember it," Ninian interjected. "Old Quinny was frightfully sloppy over it. Oh, I say, I met Tom Arthurs to-day. He's going to Southampton to-morrow. The *Gigantic's* starting on her maiden trip, and he's going over with her. I wish to goodness I could go too!"

"Why don't you?" Mrs. Graham said. It seemed to her too that if Ninian wished to do anything that was sufficient reason why he should be allowed to do it.

"I can't get away," he answered. "We're busier than we've ever been. But I'm going to Southampton to see the *Gigantic* start. The biggest boat in the world! My goodness! Tom's awfully excited about it. You'd think the *Gigantic* was his son! . . ."

Henry thanked heaven that at last the conversation had veered from factories and his engagement to Mary. He tried to fasten it to the *Gigantic*.

"What are you so busy about that you can't go with Tom?" he asked.

"Oh, heaps of things! Old Hare's keen on building a Channel Tunnel, and he's spent a good deal of time working the thing out!"

Mrs. Graham had always imagined that the proposal to build a Tunnel between France and England was a joke, and she said so.

"Good heavens, mother!" Ninian exclaimed. "Old Hare isn't a joke. The thing's as practicable as the Tuppenny Tube. People have been experimenting for half-a-century with it. Joke, indeed! They've made seven thousand soundings in forty years! . . ."

"Really!" said Mrs. Graham.

"And borings, too . . . lots of them . . . in the bed of the Channel. They've started a Tunnel, two thousand yards of it from Dover, under the sea, and there isn't a flaw in it. Hardly any water comes through, although there isn't a lining to the walls . . . just the bare, grey chalk. I was awfully sick when I was told I couldn't go to Harland and Wolff's, but I don't mind now. Building a Channel Tunnel is as big a job as building the *Gigantic* any day, and Hare is as brainy as Tom Arthurs!"

He became oratorical about the Channel Tunnel, and he told them stories of remarkable borings on both sides of the sea.

"There's a big thick bed of grey chalk all the way from England to France," he said, "and the water simply can't get through it. They've made experimental tubes from our side and from the French side, and they let people into them, and it was all right. No mud, no water, no foul air . . . perfectly sound!"

He quoted Sartiaux, the French engineer, and Sir Francis Fox, the English engineer. "They don't fool about with wildcat schemes, I can tell you. Why, Fox built the Mersey Tunnel and the Simplon Tunnel . . . and the Channel Tunnel is as easy as that!"

There were to be two tubes, each capable of carrying the ordinary British railway, bored through a bed of cenomian chalk, two hundred feet thick on an average.

"We could have an extra tunnel for motor-cars, if necessary!" said Ninian. "Just think of the difference there'd be if we had the Tunnel. You could buzz from London to Paris in five or six hours without changing, and you'd never get seasick! . . ."

"That would be nice," said Mrs. Graham.

"And you'd be safer in the Tunnel than you'd be on the Channel. There'd be a hundred and fifty feet of watertight chalk between you and the sea!"

They argued about the Tunnel. How long would it take to construct? "Oh, six or seven years!" Ninian answered airily. "What about War? Supposing England and France went to War with each other?"

"We could flood a long section of the Tunnel from our side, and they couldn't pump the water out from theirs," he answered. "Of course, I don't know much about it, but when you get chaps like Hare and Sartiaux and Fox talking seriously about it, you listen seriously to them. Anyhow, I do. Old Hare told me yesterday I was getting on nicely! . . ."

Mrs. Graham was delighted. "Did he, dear?" she burbled at Ninian.

"Yes," Ninian answered, "he said I wasn't such an ass as he'd thought I was. Oh, I'm getting on all right!"

4

Henry sat back in his chair while they talked, and let his mind fill with thoughts of Mary. She was listening to Ninian, not as if she understood all that he was saying, but as if she were proud of him, and while he watched her, he felt his old affection for her surging up in his heart. He had described a young, fresh girl in "Drusilla," and he had fallen in love with his description. Now, looking at Mary, he realised that unconsciously he had drawn her portrait. "I must have been in love with her all the time," he thought, "even when I was running after Sheila Morgan!"

He looked·at her so steadily that she felt his gaze, and she turned to look at him. She smiled at him as she did so, and he smiled back at her.

"Isn't it interesting to hear about the Tunnel?" she said.

"Eh? . . . Oh, yes! Yes. Awfully interesting. . . ."

5

"You know," said Roger when Mrs. Graham and Mary and Rachel had gone, "we really haven't talked enough about this factory system. Rachel's wild about it, of course . . . she's a girl . . . but she's got more sense on her side than we have on ours. It really isn't any good ignoring it. It's too big to be overlooked. I think we ought to have a course of talks about the whole thing. We could get people to come and tell us all they know. Rachel's got a lot of information. We could pick it out of her. And then there's that woman . . . what's her name . . . Mc something . . . who knows all about factories . . . Mc Mc Mc . . ."

"Mary McArthur," said Gilbert.

"Yes. That's her name. I wonder if she'd come and dine with us. You know, we haven't had any women. That's an oversight, isn't it?" He walked towards the door as he spoke. "I'm going to bed now," he said. "I've got a county court case in the morning at Croydon, and I shall have to get up early. Good-night!"

"Good-night, Roger!" they murmured sleepily.

"Oh, by the way," he added, "Rachel and I are engaged. I thought I'd tell you!"

He shut the door behind him.

6

They sat up, gaping at the closed door.

"What'd he say?" said Ninian.

"He says he's engaged to that blooming orator!" Gilbert answered.

"But, damn it, why?" said Ninian.

"And we've got the lease of this house for another two years!" Henry exclaimed. "I suppose he'll want to get married and . . . all that!"

They were silent for a while, contemplating this strange disruption of their affairs.

"Of course, people do get engaged!" said Ninian, and then he relapsed into silence.

"I've been in love myself," Gilbert said, "but . . . this is excessive. We ought to do something. Can't we get up a memorial or something? . . ."

Ninian sat upright, pointing a finger at them. "You know, chaps," he exclaimed, "Roger's ashamed of himself. He didn't tell us 'til he'd got to the door, and then he damn well hooked it!"

"He's been trapped," Gilbert said. "Females are always trapping chaps! . . ."

"We ought to save him from himself!" Ninian stood up as he spoke.

"But supposing he doesn't want to be saved?" Henry asked.

"We'll save him all the same," Ninian answered.

"Let's go on a deputation to him," Gilbert suggested. "We will put it reasonably to him. We'll tell him that he mustn't do this thing. . . . Oh, Lord, coves, it's no good. This house is doomed. A female has done it!"

"If it had been you, Gilbert, or Quinny," said Ninian, "I'd have thought it was natural. You're that sort! But old Roger . . . well, there's no doubt about it, God moves in a mysterious way, His wonders to perform. Let's go to bed. I'm fed-up with everything!"

7

Henry switched off the light and got into bed. He shut his eyes and tried to sleep, but sleep would not come to him. He lay blinking at the ceiling for a while, and then he got up and went into his sitting-room and got out his manuscript and began to write. He wrote steadily for half-an-hour, and then he put down his pen and read over what he had written.

"No," he said, crumpling the paper and throwing it into the wastepaper basket, "that won't do!"

He walked about the room for a few minutes, and then he went back to bed, and lay there with his hands clasped about his head.

"I don't see why I shouldn't get married myself," he said, and then he went to sleep.

THE SEVENTH CHAPTER

1

In the morning, Ninian and Roger rose early, for Ninian was going to Southampton to see the *Gigantic* start on her maiden voyage to America, and Roger had a case at a county court outside London. In a vague way, Ninian had intended to talk to Roger about his engagement, to reason with him, as he put it. Gilbert had pointed out that the chief employment of women is to disrupt the friendships of men. "Men," he had said to Ninian and Henry after Roger had gone to bed, "take years to make up a friendship, and then a female comes along and busts it up in a couple of weeks!" Ninian did not intend to let Miss Rachel Wynne break up *their* friendship, and he planned a long, comprehensive and settling conversation with Roger on the subject of females generally and of Rachel Wynne particularly. In bed, he had invented an extraordinarily convincing argument, before which Roger must collapse, but by the time he had finished shaving, the argument had vanished from his mind, and his convincing speech shrivelled into a halting, "I say, Roger, old chap, it's a bit thick, you know!" and even that ceased to exist when he saw Roger, with the *Times* propped against the sugar bowl, eating bacon and eggs as easily as if he had never betrothed himself to any woman.

"Hilloa, Roger!" said Ninian, sitting down at the table, and reaching for the toast.

"Hilloa, Ninian!" Roger murmured, without looking up.

Magnolia entered with Ninian's breakfast and placed it before him.

"Anything in the *Times?*" Ninian said, pouring out coffee.

"Usual stuff. The bacon's salt! . . ."

The time, Ninian thought, was hardly suitable for a few home-thrusting words on the subject of marriage, so he reminded Roger that he was going to Southampton.

"Tom Arthurs has promised to show me over as much of the *Gigantic* as we can manage in a couple of hours. That won't be as much as I'd like to see, but I'll try and go over her when she comes back from New York. Any mustard about?"

"You'll be back again to-night, I suppose?"

"Probably. You're right . . . this bacon is salt, damn it!"

Roger rose from the table and moved to the window where he stood for a while looking out on the garden. It seemed to Ninian that in a moment or two he would speak of his engagement, and so he sat still, waiting for him to begin.

"Well," said Roger, turning away from the window and feeling for his watch, "I must be off. So long, Ninian!"

He went out of the room quickly and in a little while, Ninian heard the street door banging behind him.

"Damn," he said to himself, "I've just remembered what I was going to say to him!"

He had finished his breakfast and left the house before Gilbert and Henry came down from their rooms. Henry was too tired to talk much, and Gilbert, finding him uncommunicative, made no effort to make conversation. He picked up the *Times* and contented himself with the morning's news, while Henry read a letter from John Marsh which had come by the first post.

"*I'm interested in your Improved Tories,*" he wrote, "*I think the scheme is excellent. You sharpen your wits on other people's, and you keep in touch with all kinds of opinions. That's excellent! Your father, and you, too, used to say we were rather one-eyed in Dublin, and I think*

*there's a good deal of truth in that, so I'm trying to get
a group of people in Dublin to form a society somewhat
similar to your Improved Tories. Did you ever meet a man
called Arthur Griffiths when you were here? He is a very
able, but not very sociable, man, and so people do not know
him as well as they ought to . . . and his tongue is like a
flail . . . so that most of the people who do know him,
don't like him. The Nationalist M.P.'s detest him. Well,
several years ago he founded a society which he called the
Sinn Fein Movement, and the principle of the thing is excellent up to a point. Do you remember any of your
Gaelic? Sinn Fein means 'we ourselves,' and that is the
principle of the society. The object is to induce Irishmen
to do for themselves, things that are done for them by
Englishmen. It ought to appeal to your father. Griffiths
got the idea, I think, from Hungary. We're to withdraw
our representatives from the English parliament and start
an Irish Government on the basis of a Grand Council of
the County Councils. We're to have our own consular
service, our own National Bank and Stock Exchange and
Civil Service, and a mercantile marine so that we can trade
direct with other countries. And we're to nationalise the
railways and canals and bogs (which are to be reclaimed)
and take over insurance and education and so forth. All
this is to be done by the General Council of the County
Councils in opposition to anything of the sort that is done
by the English Government in preparation for the day
when there is an Irish Government when, of course, the
General Council will be merged in the Government. Oh,
and we're to have Protection, too! It seems rather a lot,
doesn't it? but the idea is excellent and, if modified considerably, fairly practical. Griffiths has antiquated notions
of economics, however, and some of the things he says prevent me from joining him. His great idea is to attract
capital to Ireland by telling capitalists how cheap Irish
labour is. That seems to me to be an abominable proposal,
likely to lead to something worse than Wigan and all those*

*miserable English towns your father dislikes so heartily.
And probably, of all his proposals, it is the most likely to
succeed. That's why I'm opposed to him at present. I
cannot bear the thought of seeing England duplicated in
Ireland. But the scheme has merit, and Galway and I are
plotting to capture the movement from Griffiths. We think
that if we could graft the Sinn Fein on to the Gaelic
League, we'd be on the way to establishing Irish independ-
ence. Our people are becoming very materialistic, and we
must quicken their spirits again somehow. Douglas Hyde
is the trouble, of course. He wants to keep the Gaelic
League clear of politics. As if you can possibly keep politics out of anything in Ireland! We want to make every
Gaelic Leaguer a conscious rebel against English beliefs and
English habits. I wish you'd come over and join us. It'll
be very hard, but exhilarating, work. You've no notion of
how sordid and money-grubbing and English the mass of
our people are becoming. It's a man's job to destroy that
spirit and revive the old, careless, generous, God-loving
Irish one. . . ."*

"Still harping on that old nationality," Henry thought
to himself, when he had finished reading the letter.

He was in no mood for thoughts on Ireland. His mind
was still full of the idea that had come into his head the
previous night. *Why should he not get married?* The
idea attracted and repelled him. It would, he thought, be
very pleasant to live with . . . with Mary, say . . . to love
her and be loved by her . . . very pleasant . . . but one
would have to accept responsibilities, and there would probably be children. He would dislike having to leave Ninian
and Roger and Gilbert, particularly Gilbert, and his share
in the meetings of the Improved Tories would begin to
dwindle. On the other hand, there would be Mary. . .
If he were to lose his friends and the careless, cultured life
they led in the Bloomsbury house, he would gain Mary,
and perhaps she would more than compensate for them. . . .

Gilbert interrupted his thoughts.

"Rum go, this about Roger, isn't it?" he said.

Henry nodded his head. "I hadn't any idea of it," he replied. "I'd never even heard of her until he said she was coming to dinner!"

"I had," Gilbert said, "but I didn't think he was going to let the life force catch hold of him. Close chap, Roger! He never gives himself away . . . and that's the sort that's most romantic. You and I are obviously sloppy, Quinny, but somehow we miss all the messes that reticent, close chaps like Roger fall into. You don't much like her, do you?"

"Well, I'm not what you might call smitten by her, but that's because she seems to think I'm wasting time in writing novels. She's too strenuous for me. I like women who relax sometimes. She'll orate to him every night, just as she orated to us, about people's wrongs. . . ."

"Mind, she's clever!" said Gilbert.

"Oh, I don't deny that. That's part of my case against her. Really and truly, Gilbert, do you like clever women?"

"Really and truly, Quinny, I don't. Perhaps that's not the way to put it. I like talking to clever women, but I shouldn't like to marry one of them. I'm clever myself, and perhaps that's why. There isn't room for more than one clever person in a family, and I think a clever man should marry an intelligently stupid woman, and vice versa. You can argue with clever women, but you can't kiss them or flirt with them. All the clever ones I've ever known have had something hard in them . . . like a lump of steel. Men aren't like that! They can be hard, of course, but they aren't always exhibiting their hardness. Clever women are."

Henry tossed Marsh's letter across the table to Gilbert. "Read that," he said, "while I look through the *Times!*"

They both rose from the table, and sat for a while in the armchairs on either side of the fireplace.

"You know, Quinny," said Gilbert, as he took Marsh's letter out of its envelope, "I often think we're awfully young, all of us!"

"Young?"

"Yes. Immature . . . and all that. We're frightfully clever, of course, but really we don't know much, and yet you're writing books and I'm writing plays and Ninian's building Tunnels and Roger's playing ducks and drakes with the law . . . and not one of us is thirty yet. Lord, I wish Roger hadn't got engaged. That sort of thing makes a man think!"

He read Marsh's letter and then passed it back to Henry.

"Seems all right," he said. "It's a pity those Irish fellows haven't got a wider outlook. Sitting there fussing over their mouldy island when there's the whole world to fuss over! I must be off soon. There's a rehearsal of my play this morning. . . ."

"I say, Gilbert," Henry interrupted, "do you think I ought to go and join this Irish Renascence business?"

"How can I tell? It probably won't amount to much. I should take an intelligent interest in it, if I were you. Perhaps you can induce Marsh to come over and talk to the Improved Tories about it. What are you doing this morning?"

"Oh, working!"

"Well, so long!"

"So long, Gilbert. You'll be back to lunch, I suppose?"

"I don't think so. The rehearsals are very long now. You see, the play's to be done on Wednesday. . . ."

2

When Gilbert had gone, Henry, having glanced through the *Times*, went up to his room and began to write, but he did not continue at his manuscript for very long. The words would not roll lightly off his pen: they fell off and lay inertly about the paper. He was accustomed now to periods during which his mind seemed to have lost its power to operate, and he was not alarmed by them. He knew that it was useless to attempt to do any work that morning, so he left his room and, telling Mrs. Clutters that he would not return to lunch, went out of the house and wandered about the streets for a while without any purpose. It was not until he saw the sign on a passing motor-'bus that he decided on what he should do. "Hyde Park Corner" was on the sign, and he called to the conductor and presently mounted to the roof of the 'bus and was driven towards the Park.

"I wonder," he thought to himself, "whether I shall see Lady Cecily to-day!"

Lady Cecily had curiously disappeared from their lives. Gilbert, absorbed in the production of his play, had not spoken of her again, nor had he made any mention of his proposal to leave London and go to Anglesey. He had resigned from the staff of the *Daily Echo*, and, since he no longer attended first-nights at the theatre, he had not seen Lady Cecily since the night on which "The Ideal Husband" was revived. Henry had said to himself on several occasions that he would go and see Lady Cecily, but he had not done so. He did not care to go alone, and he cared less to ask Gilbert to go with him . . . but to-day, as suddenly as she had quitted his thoughts, Lady Cecily came into them again, and, as he sat on top of the omnibus, he hoped that he would see her in the Park. "If not," he said to himself, "I'll call on her this afternoon!"

He descended from the 'bus at Hyde Park Corner and hastily entered the Park. He crossed to the Achilles monument and debated with himself as to whether he should sit down or walk about, and decided to sit down. If Lady Cecily were in the Park, he told himself, she would pass his chair some time during the morning. He chose a seat near the railings and sat down and waited. There was a continual flow of carriages and cars, but none of them contained Lady Cecily, and when he had been sitting for al-

most an hour, he told himself that he was not likely to see
her that morning. He rose, as he said this to himself, and
turned to walk across the grass towards Rotten Row, and
as he turned, he saw Jimphy. He was not anxious to meet
Jimphy again, and he pretended not to see him, but Jimphy
came up to him, smiling affably, and said "Hilloa, Quinn,
old chap!" so he had to be as amiable as he could in response to the greeting.

Jimphy wanted to know why it was that he and Henry
had not met again since the night that "Cecily let a chap
in for a damn play," and reminded him of their engagement to visit the Empire together. "Anyhow," he said,
"you can come and lunch with us. Cecily'll be glad to see
you. I said I'd come home to lunch if I could find some
one worth bringing with me, so that's all right!"

"How is Lady Cecily?" Henry asked, as he and Jimphy
left the Park together.

"Oh, I expect she's all right," Jimphy answered. "I
forgot to ask this morning, but if she'd been seedy or anything she'd have told me about it, so I suppose she's all
right!"

"When's this play of Farlow's coming on?" Jimphy
asked on the doorstep of his house.

"Wednesday," Henry answered.

"Cecily's made me promise to go and see it with her.
What sort of a piece is it?"

They entered the house as he spoke.

"It's excellent. . . ."

"Is it comic?"

"Well, I suppose it is. He calls it a comedy," Henry
said.

"So long as there's a laugh in it, I don't mind going to
see it. I can't stand these weepy bits. 'Hamlet' and that
sort of stuff. Enough to give a chap the pip! Oh, here's
Cecily!"

Henry turned to look up the stairs down which Lady
Cecily was coming, and then he went forward to greet her.

"How nice of you," she said. "Has Gilbert come, too?"
"No," he answered, chilled by her question. "He has
a rehearsal this morning!"
"Oh, yes, of course," she said. "His play! I forgot.
We're going to see it on Wednesday. I hope it's good!"
"It's very good," Henry replied.

3

Jimphy left them after lunch. He was awfully sorry,
old chap, to have to tear himself away and all that, but the
fact was he had an appointment . . . an important appointment . . . and of course a chap had to keep an important appointment. . . .
"We'll forgive you, Jimphy!" Lady Cecily said, and
then he went away, begging Henry to remember that they
must go to the Empire together one night.
"Well?" said Lady Cecily when her husband had gone,
"how are you all getting on?"
She was reclining on a couch, with her feet resting on
a cushion, and as she asked her question she pointed to another cushion lying on a chair. He fetched it and put it
behind her back.
"Splendidly," he answered. "Is that right?"
She settled herself more comfortably. "Yes, thanks,"
she said. "I read your novel," she went on.
"Did you like it?"
"Oh, yes. Of course, I liked it. I suppose you're writing another book now!" He nodded his head, and she
went on. "I wish I could write books, but of course I
can't. Mr. Lensley says I live books. Isn't that nice of
him? Do you put real people in your books, or do you
make them all up? Do you know, I think I'll have another cigarette!"
He passed the box of cigarettes to her and held it while
she made up her mind whether she would smoke an Egyp-
tian or a Turkish. Her delicate fingers moved indeci-

sively from the one brand to the other. "You like Turkish, don't you?" he said, wishing that he could take her
slender hand in his and hold it forever.

"Choose one for me," she said, capriciously, lying back
and clasping her hands about her head.

He took a cigarette from the box and offered it to her,
but she did not hold out her hand to take it, and he understood that he was to place it between her lips. His fingers
trembled as he did so, and he turned hurriedly to find the
matches.

"Behind you," she said, and he turned and picked them
up.

He lit a match and held it to her cigarette, and while he
held it, her fingers touched his. She had taken hold of the
cigarette to remove it from her lips. . . . He blew out the
light and threw the match into the ash-tray, and then went
and sat down in the deep chair in which he had been sitting
when she asked him to get the cushion for her.

"Why didn't you call before?" she said, lazily blowing
the smoke up into the air.

It was difficult to say why he had not called before, so
he answered vaguely. There had been so much to do of
late. . . .

"And Gilbert? He doesn't rehearse all day long, does
he?"

"No, not all day, but he's pretty tired by the time he
gets home."

"Why didn't he come to the Savoy that night?" she
asked.

He wished she would not talk about Gilbert. He could
not tell her the real reason why Gilbert had not kept his
promise to join the supper-party and he was a poor hand
at inventing convincing lies.

"There was some trouble at his office, I think," he said,
"and he couldn't get away until too late! . . ."

"He didn't write or come to see me!" she protested.

It was probable that Gilbert forgot his duty in the excitement of hearing that his play was to be produced. . . .

"I suppose so," she said.

She talked to him about his books and about Ireland. She had been to Dublin once and had gone to the Viceregal Lodge . . . Lady Dundrum had taken her to some function there . . . and she was eager for the tittle-tattle of the Court. Was it true that Lord Kelpie was indifferent to his lady? . . . Henry knew very little of the Dublin gossip. "I haven't been there since I left Trinity," he said, in explanation, "and the only people who write to me don't take any interest in Court functions!"

He rose to go, but she asked him to stay to tea with her, and so he remained.

"I don't suppose any one will call," she said, "but in case . . ."

She told a servant that she was "not at home" to any one, and Henry, wondering why she had done so, felt vaguely flattered and as vaguely nervous. Her beauty filled him with desire and apprehension and left him half eager, half afraid to be alone with her. He understood Gilbert's fear that if he yielded to Cecily, she would destroy him. There was something in this woman that overpowered the senses, that made a man as will-less as a log, and left him in the end, spent, exhausted, incapable. He saw the danger that had frightened Gilbert, but he could not make up his mind to run away from it. There was something so exquisitely sensual in her look as she lay on the couch, looking at him and chattering in the Lensley style, that he felt inclined to yield himself to her, even if in yielding he should lose everything.

"Of course," he said to himself, "this is all imagination. She doesn't want me at all . . . she wants Gilbert!"

She asked for another cigarette, and he took one and placed it in her lips and lit it for her, and again his fingers touched hers, and again he trembled with unaccountable emotion. As he bent over her, holding the match to the cigarette, he felt the blood rushing to his head and for a moment or two his eyes were blurred and he could not see clearly. Then his eyes cleared and he saw that she was looking steadily at him, and he knew that she understood what was passing in his mind. He dropped the match on to the ash-tray and bent a little nearer to her. He would take her in his arms, he said to himself, and hold her tightly to him. . . .

"Won't you sit down," she said, pointing to his chair.

He straightened himself, but did not move away. His eyes were still intent on hers, as if he could not avoid her gaze, and for a while neither of them spoke or moved. Then she smiled at him.

"You're a funny boy," she said. "Won't you sit down!" and again she pointed to the chair.

His answer was so low that he could hardly hear himself speak, and at first he thought she had not heard him. "I'd better go," he said.

"Not yet," she answered. "You needn't go yet!"

"I'd better. . . ."

She put out her hand and made him sit down.

"There's no hurry," she said.

He leant back in his chair, resting his elbows on the arms of it and folding his fingers under his chin.

"You look frightened," she said.

"I am," he answered.

"Of me?" He nodded his head, and she laughed. "How absurd!" she said. "I'm not a bit terrifying. . . ."

He was not trembling now. He felt quite calm, as if he had resigned himself to what must be.

"No, I . . . I know you're not," he said, "only . . ."

"Only what?"

"I don't know!"

She put her cigarette down and turned slightly towards him.

"Funny boy!" she said. "Funny Irish boy!"

He smiled foolishly at her, but did not answer. He knew

that if he spoke at all, he would say wild things that could not be withdrawn or explained away.

"Funny scared Irish boy!" she said, and he could see the mockery in her eyes. "Such a frightened Irish boy! . . ."

He could hold out no longer. She had put her hand out towards him . . . why he could not tell . . . and impulsively he seized it and clasped it tightly in his. His grasp must have hurt her, for she cried a little and tried to withdraw her hand, but he would not let go his hold of it until, kneeling beside her, he had put his arms about her and kissed her.

"I love you," he said. "You know I love you. . . ."

"Don't!"

"I loved you the minute I set eyes on you, and I wanted to meet you again . . . and then I was jealous of Gilbert because you took so much notice of him and so little of me, and . . . I love you, I love you!"

She thrust him from her. "You're hurting me," she said, and she panted as she spoke.

"I want to hurt you," he answered.

"But you mustn't. . . ."

He did not let her finish her sentence. He pressed his lips hard on hers until his strength seemed to pass away from him. He felt in some strange way that her eyes were closed and that she was moaning. . . .

He put his arms about her again, and drew her head gently on to his breast. "My dear," he said softly, bending over her and kissing her hair.

She lay very still in his arms, so still that he thought she had fallen asleep. Her long lashes trembled a little, and then she opened her eyes, sighing contentedly as she did so. He smiled down at her, and she smiled in response. Then she put her hand up and stroked his cheek and ruffled his hair.

"Funny Irish boy!" she said again.

4

He climbed on to a 'bus which bore him eastwards. It was impossible, in his state of exaltation, to go home and eat in the company of the others. Ninian would probably be back from Southampton, unbalanced with admiration for Tom Arthurs and the *Gigantic,* and then Gilbert would tell him how Sir Geoffrey Mundane had behaved during the rehearsal and how exasperating Mrs. Michael Gordon, the leading lady, had been. "She's brilliant, of course," he had said about her once, "but if I were her husband I'd beat her!" He could not endure the thought of spending the evening in the customary company of his friends. They would want to talk, they would draw him into the conversation, and he neither wished to talk nor to listen. His desire was only to remember, to go over again in his mind that long, passionate afternoon with Cecily. . . . So he had telephoned to Mrs. Clutters telling her that he would not be in to dinner, and then, climbing on to a 'bus, had allowed himself to be carried eastwards, not knowing or caring whither he was being carried.

He paid no heed to the other passengers on the 'bus, nor did he interest himself in the traffic of the streets. When the conductor came, demanding fares, he asked for a ticket to the terminus, but did not bother to ask where the terminus was. His mind was full of golden hair and warm, moist lips and soft, disturbing perfume and the touch of a shapely hand. Cecily had insisted on calling him "Paddy" because he was Irish and because so many Englishmen are called "Henry," and when he had left her, she had offered her lips to him and, when he had kissed her, had told him she would see him again soon. "When Gilbert's play is done," she said, and added, "Tell Gilbert I shall expect him to come and talk to me after the first act!"

He had been jealous when she said that. "You don't

really care for me," he had said. "You really love Gilbert!"

"Of course I love Gilbert," she had answered, laughing at him and patting his cheek, "but I love you, too. I love lots of people! . . ."

Then, ashamed of himself, he had left her. It was caddish of him to speak of Gilbert to her, for Gilbert was his friend and her lover. If one were to try and take a friend's mistress from him, one should at least be silent about it. But how could he help these outbursts of jealousy? He cared for Gilbert far more than he cared for any man . . . but he could not prevent himself from raging at the thought that Gilbert had but to hold out his arms and Cecily would run to be clasped in them. "I'm a makeshift," he said to himself. "That's all!"

But even if he were only a makeshift, that was better than being shut away from her love altogether. "I daresay," he thought, "she's as fond of me as she is of any one!" and he wondered whether she really loved Gilbert. It was difficult for him to believe that she could yield so easily to him and love Gilbert deeply, and he soothed his conscience by telling himself that Cecily was one of those women who are in love with love, ready to accept kisses from any ardent youth who offers them to her. He remembered his contribution to the discussion on women and the way in which he had insisted on infinite variety of experiences. Cecily was, as a woman, what he had wished to be as a man. We had to recognise the differences of nature, he had said, but somehow he did not greatly care to see his principle put into practice by Cecily. There was something very fine and dashing and Byronic and adventurous in a man with a spacious spirit, but after all, women were women, and one did not like to think of adventuring women. He wanted to have Cecily to himself . . . he did not wish to share her with Gilbert or with Jimphy or with any one, and it hardly seemed decent that Cecily should wish to spread her affections over three men. "And there may be others, too!" All this talk about sex-equality had an equitable sound . . . his intellect agreed that if men were to have amorous adventures, then women should have them too; if men were to be unfaithful without reproach, then women should be equally without reproach in their infidelity . . . but his instinct cried out against it. He wanted his woman to himself even though he might not keep himself for her alone.

"And that's the beginning and the end of the sex-question," he said. "We simply aren't willing to let women live on our level. In theory, the man who goes to a prostitute is as bad as she is, but in practice, we don't believe it, and women don't believe it either, and nothing will ever make us believe it. And it's the same with lovers and mistresses. It simply doesn't seem decent to a man who keeps a mistress that his wife should have a lover. You can't help having instincts! . . ."

5

The 'bus drove over London Bridge and presently he found himself in the railway station. It was too early yet to eat, and he made up his mind to go for a walk through Southwark. None of them had ever been in the slums. They had set their minds against suggestions that they should live in Walworth or Whitechapel or Bethnal Green in order that they might get to know something of the lives of the very poor. "That's simply slush," Gilbert had said. "We shouldn't live like them. We'd have four good meals every day and baths every morning, and we'd only feel virtuous and 'smarmy' and do-good-to-the-poor-y. My object is to get rid of slums, not to go and live in the damn things and encourage slum-owners by paying rent regularly. All those Settlement people . . . really, they're doing the heroic stunt for their own ends. They'll go into parliament and say they have intimate knowledge of the

way in which the poor live because they've lived with them
. . . and it's all my eye, that stuff!''

The notion had made a faint appeal to Henry, but he
had not responded to it because of the way in which the
others had sneered at it and because he liked pleasant surroundings. Once, in Dublin, he had wandered out of St.
Stephens's Green and found himself in the Combe, and
the sights he had witnessed there had sickened him so that
he had hurried away, and always thereafter had been careful not to enter side streets with which he was not familiar. Now, he felt that he ought to see a London slum.
One had to have a point of view about poor people, and
it was difficult to have a point of view about people of
whom one was almost totally ignorant.

He walked slowly up the Borough High Street, uncertain of himself and of the district. He would want something to eat presently, and if he were to venture too far
into the slums that lay hidden behind St. George's Church
and the Elephant, he might have difficulty in finding a
place where he could take a meal in comfort. He stood
for a few moments outside the window of a shop in which
sausages and steaks and onions were being fried. There
was a thick, hot, steamy odour coming from the door that
filled him with nausea, and he turned to move away, but
as he did so, he saw two sickly boys, half naked, standing
against the window with their mouths pressed close to the
glass. They were eyeing the cooking food so hungrily that
he felt pity for them, and he touched one of them on the
shoulder and asked him if he would like something to eat.
The boy looked at him, but did not answer, and his companion came shuffling to his side and eyed him too.

"Wouldn't you like some of that . . . that stuff!''
Henry said, pointing to a great slab of thick pudding,
padded with currants.

One of the boys nodded his head, and Henry moved
towards the door of the shop, bidding them both to follow
him.

"Give these youngsters some of that pudding!" he said to the man behind the counter: a fat, flaccid man with a wet, steamy brow which he periodically wiped with a grimy towel.

" 'Ere!" said the man, cutting off large pieces of the pudding and passing it across the counter to the boys who took it, without speaking, and began to gnaw at it immediately.

"Wod you say for it, eih?" the man demanded.

They mumbled unintelligibly, their mouths choked with the food.

"Pore little kids, they don't know no better! Nah, then, 'op it, you two! That'll be fourpence, sir!"

Henry paid for the pudding and left the malodorous shop. The children were standing in the shadow outside, one of them eating wolfishly, while the other held the pudding in front of him, gaping at it. . . .

"Don't you like it?" Henry said, bending down to him.

" 'E can't eat it, guv'nor!" the other boy said.

"Can't eat it!"

"No, guv'nor, 'e can't. I'll 'ave to eat it for 'im. . . ."

"But why can't you eat?" Henry asked, turning to the boy who still gaped helplessly at the pudding.

The child did not answer. He stared at the pudding, and then he stared at Henry, and as he did so, the pudding fell from his hands, and he became sick. . . .

" 'Ere, wod you chuckin' it away for?" the other boy said, dropping quickly to the ground and picking up the pudding.

"He's ill," Henry said helplessly.

" 'E's always ill," the boy answered, stuffing pieces of the recovered pudding into his mouth.

A policeman was standing at the corner, and Henry went to him and told him of the child's plight.

"Sick is 'e?" the constable exclaimed.

"Yes," Henry answered. "He looked hungry, poor little chap, and so I bought him some of the pudding they sell in that shop!"

The policeman looked at him for a few moments. "Well, of course, you meant it kindly, sir!" he said, "but if I was you I wouldn't do that again. If you'll excuse me sayin' it, sir, it was a damn silly thing to do!"

"Why?"

"Why! 'Alf the kids about 'ere is too 'ungry to eat. That kid ought to be in the 'ospital by rights. Don't never give 'em no puddin' or stuff like that, sir. Their stomachs can't stand it. Nah, then," he said to the sick child, "you 'op 'ome, young 'un. You didn't ought to be 'angin' about 'ere, you know, upsettin' the traffic an' mykin' a mess on the pyvement. Gow on! Git aht of it!"

The boys ran off, leaving Henry staring blankly after them. " 'E'll be all right, sir!" said the policeman. "It's no good tryin' to do nothink for 'em. They're down, guv'nor, an' that's all about it. I seen a lot of yooman nature down about 'ere, an' you can tyke it from me, them kids is down an' they'll stay down, an' that's all you can say about it. Good-night, sir!"

"Good-night!" said Henry.

He moved away, feeling sick and miserable and angry. "It's beastly," he said to himself. "That's what it is. Beastly!"

6

His mind was occupied by violent thoughts about the two children whom he had fed with currant pudding, and he did not observe what he was doing or where he was going. He was in a wide, dark street where there were tram-lines, but he could not remember seeing a tramcar pass by. He was tired and although he was not hungry, he was conscious of a missed meal, and he was thirsty. "I'd better turn back," he said to himself, turning as he did so. He won-

dered where he was, and he resolved that he would ask the
first policeman he met to tell him in what part of London
he now was and what was the quickest way to get out of it.

"It was silly of me to come here at all," he murmured,
and then he turned quickly and stared across the street.

A woman had screamed somewhere near by . . . on the
other side of the street, he thought . . . and as he looked,
he saw figures struggling, and then they parted and one
of them, a woman, ran away towards a lamppost, holding
her hands before her in an appealing fashion, and crying,
"Oh, don't! Don't hit me! . . ." The other figure was
that of a man, and as the woman shrank from him, the man
advanced towards her with his fist uplifted. . . .

Henry could feel himself shrinking back into the shadow.

"He's going to hit her," he was saying to himself, and
he closed his eyes, afraid lest he should see the man's fist
smashing into the woman's face. He could hear a foul
oath uttered by the man and the woman's scream as she retreated still further from him . . . and then, trembling
with fright, he ran across the street and thrust himself
between them. "Oh, my God, what am I doing?" he
moaned to himself as he stood in the glare of the yellow
light that fell from the street lamp. He felt rather than
saw that the woman had risen from the ground and run
away the moment the man's attention was distracted from
her, and a shudder of fear ran through him as he realised
that he was alone. He could see the man's brutal face and
his blazing, drink-inflamed eyes, and in the middle of his
fear, he thought how ugly the man's eyebrows were . . .
one long, black line from eye to eye across the top of his
nose. The man, his fist clenched and raised, advanced towards him. "He's going to hit me now," Henry thought.
"He'll knock me down and . . . and kick me! . . . These
people always kick you! . . ."

He stood still waiting for the blow, mesmerised by the
man's blazing eyes; but the man, though his fist was still
clenched, did not strike him. He reeled up to him so

closely that Henry was sickened by the smell of his drink-sodden breath. "Fight for a woman, would you?" he shouted at him. "Eih? P'tect a woman, would you? . . ."

Henry wanted to laugh. The man was repeating phrases from melodramas! . . .

"Tyke a woman's part, eih? I know you, you bloody toff! You . . . you think you're a bloody 'ero, eih, p'tectin' a woman from 'er 'usband!" He pushed Henry aside, almost falling on the pavement as he did so. "I've a goo' mind to break your bloody neck for you, see, bloody toff, interferin' . . . 'usband an' wife. See? Thash what I'll do! . . ."

He came again at Henry, but still he did not strike. He mumbled his melodramatic phrases, swaying in front of Henry, and threatening to break his neck and punch his jaw and give him a thick ear, but he did no more than that, and while he threatened, a crowd gathered out of the shadows, and a woman, with bare arms, touched Henry's arm and drew him away from the drunken man. "You 'op it, mister," she said, "or you'll get 'urt!" She pushed him out of the crowd, slapping a lad in the face who had jostled him and said, "Gawblimey, look at Percy!" and when she had got him away from them, she told him again to 'op it.

"Thank you! . . ." he began.

"Don't you wyste no time, mister, but 'op it quick," she interrupted, giving him a push forward.

"But I don't know where I am," he replied.

"Dunno w'ere you are! . . . Well, of course, you look like that! You're in Bermondsey, mister, an' if you tyke my advice you'll go 'ome an' sty 'ome. People like you didden ought to be let out alone! You go 'ome to your mother, sir! The first turnin' on the right'll bring you to the trams. . . ."

He did as she told him, hurrying away from the dark street as quickly as he could. He was trembling. Every nerve in his body seemed to be strained, and his eyes had the tired feel they always had when he was deeply agitated.

"My God," he said, "what an ass I was to do that!"

7

Gilbert and Roger were sitting together when he got home.

"Hilloa, Quinny!" Gilbert exclaimed as he looked at Henry's white face. "What have you been up to?"

He told them of his adventure in Bermondsey.

"You do do some damn funny things, Quinny!" said Gilbert, going to the sideboard and getting out the whisky. "Here, have a drop of this stuff. You look completely pipped!"

"I don't think I should make a habit of knight-errantry, if I were you," said Roger. "Not in slums at all events!"

"Has Ninian come back yet?" Henry asked, sipping the whisky.

"He's gone to bed. The *Gigantic* got off all right, but there was trouble at the start. She fouled a cruiser or something. Ninian's full of it. He'll tell you the whole rigmarole in the morning. You'd better trot off to bed when you've drunk that, and for God's sake, Quinny, don't try to be heroic again. You're not cut out for that sort of job! . . ."

THE EIGHTH CHAPTER

1

MRS. GRAHAM and Mary and Rachel Wynne dined with them on the first night of "The Magic Casement." Rachel, fresh from a Care Committee, composed mostly of members of the Charity Organisation Society and the wives of prosperous tradesmen, was inclined to tell the world what she thought of it, but they diverted her mind from the iniquities of the Care Committee by congratulating her on her engagement to Roger. She blushed and gave her thanks in stammers, looking with bright, proud eyes at Roger; and when they saw how human she was, they forgot her hard efficiency and her sociological angers, and liked her. Gilbert ·urged her to tell them tales of the C.O.S. and the Care Committee, and rejoiced loudly when she described how she had discomfited a large, granitic woman . . . the Mayor's wife . . . who had committed a flagrant breach of the law in her anxiety to penalise some unfortunate children whose father was an agitator. "If I were poor," Rachel said, "I'd hit a C.O.S. person on sight! I'd hit it simply because it was a C.O.S. person! That would be evidence against it!" She enjoyed calling a C.O.S. person, "it," and Henry felt that perhaps some of the difficulty with the Mayor's wife was due to the pleasure that Rachel took in rubbing her up the wrong way. He suggested that tactful treatment. . . .

"You can't be tactful with that kind of person," she asserted instantly. "You can only be angry. You see, they love to badger poor people. It's sheer delight to them to ask impertinent questions. There's a big streak of

Torquemada in them. They'd have been Inquisitors if
they'd been born in Spain when there were Inquisitors!''
She paused for a second or two, and then went on rapidly.
''I never thought of that before. Why, of course, that's
what they are. They've been reincarnated . . . you know,
transmigration of souls . . . and that fat woman, Mrs.
Smeale. . . .'' Mrs. Smeale was the Mayor's wife . . .
''was an Inquisitor before she was . . . was dug up again.
I can see her beastly big face in a cowl, and hot pincers
in her hands, plucking poor Protestants' flesh off their
bones . . . and she's doing that now, using all the rotten
rules and regulations as hot pincers to pluck the spirit
out of the poor! Of course, she does it all for the best!
So did the Inquisitors! She doesn't want to undermine
the moral character of the poor, and they didn't want to
let the poor heretic imperil his soul. . . . I'd like to inquisit her! . . .''

''There isn't a word 'inquisit,' Rachel!'' said Roger.

''Well, there ought to be,'' she answered.

Henry pictured her, in her committee room, surrounded
by hard women, opposing herself to them, fighting for
people who were not of her class against people who were,
and it seemed to him that Rachel was very valiant, even if
she were tactless, much more valiant than he could be.
Rachel belonged to the fearless, ungracious, blunt people
who are not to be deterred from their purpose by ostracism
or abuse, and Henry realised that such courage as hers must
inevitably be accompanied by aggressiveness, a harsh insistence on one's point of view, and worst of all, a surrender of social charm and ease and the kindly regard of
one's friends. ''I couldn't do that,'' he thought to himself. It was easy enough to sneer at such people, to call
them ''cranks,'' but indisputably they had the heroic spirit,
the will to endure obloquy for their opinions. ''I suppose,'' he reflected, ''the reason why one feels so angry
with such people is partly that nine times out of ten they're
in the right, and partly that ten times out of ten they've

got the pluck we haven't got!'' And he remembered that Witterton, a journalist whom he had met at the office of the *Morning Record,* had climbed on to the plinth in Trafalgar Square during the Boer War and made a speech in denunciation of Chamberlain and the Rand lords, and had been badly mauled by the mob. "By God, that's courage!" he murmured. That was the sort of person Rachel was. He could see her opposing herself to mobs, but he could not see himself doing so. Probably, he thought, he would be on the fringe of the crowd, mildly deprecating violence and tactlessness. . . .

He came out of his ruminations to hear Mrs. Graham telling Rachel how pleased she was to hear that Roger and she were engaged. "My dear," she said, "I'm very glad!" and then she kissed Rachel.

"Come here, Roger," she added, and when he had ambled awkwardly up to her, she took his head in her hands and kissed him too. . . .

"I've a jolly good mind to get engaged myself," said Gilbert.

"Well, why don't you?" Mrs. Graham retorted.

"I would, only I keep on forgetting about it," he answered. "Couldn't you kiss me 'Good-luck' to my play?"

"I could," she replied, and kissed him.

Then they insisted that she should kiss them all, and she did as they insisted. She was very gracious and very charming and her eyes were bright with her pleasure in their youth and spirits . . . so bright that presently she cried a little . . . and then they all talked quickly and kicked one another's shins under the table in order to enforce tactful behaviour.

2

They sat in one of the two large boxes of the Pall Mall Theatre. Gilbert was nervous and restless, and after the play began, he retreated to the back of the box and sat down in a corner.

"What's up, Gilbert?" Henry whispered to him. "Are you ill?"

"Ill!" Gilbert exclaimed, looking up at Henry with a whimsical smile. "Man, Quinny, I'm dying! Go away like a good chap and let me die in peace. Tell all my friends that my last words were. . . ."

Henry went back to his seat beside Mary and whispered to her that Gilbert was too nervous and agitated to be sociable . . . "some sort of stage fright! . . ." and they pretended not to notice that he was huddled in the darkest corner of the box. "Thank goodness," Henry said to the others, "a novelist doesn't get a storm of nerves on the day of publication!" Leaning over the edge of the box, he could see Lady Cecily sitting in the stalls, with Jimphy by her side . . . and for a while he forgot the play and Mary and Gilbert's agitation. She was sitting forward, looking intently at the stage, and as he watched her, she laughed and turned to Jimphy as if she would share her pleasure with him, but Jimphy, lying back in his stall, was fiddling with his programme, utterly uninterested. She glanced up at the box, her eyes meeting his, and smiled at him.

"Who is it?" said Mary, leaning towards him.

"Oh . . . Lady Cecily Jayne!" he answered, discomposed by her question.

"She's very beautiful, isn't she?"

"Yes."

They turned again to the stage and were silent until the end of the first act. There was a burst of laughter, and then the curtain descended, to rise again in quick response to the applause.

"Cheering a chap at his funeral!" said Gilbert, groaning with delight as he listened to the shouts and handclaps.

They turned to him and offered their congratulations.

"Five curtain-calls," said Roger. "Very satisfactory!"

"It's splendid, Gilbert," Mrs. Graham exclaimed. "I'm sure it'll be a great success!"

"Oh, dear, O Lord, I wish it were over!" Gilbert replied.

"Let's fill him with whisky," said Ninian, rising and taking hold of Gilbert's arm, and he and Henry took him and led him to the bar where they met Jimphy, looking like a lost rabbit.

"Hilloa, Jimphy!" they exclaimed, and he turned gleefully to welcome them. Here at all events was something he could comprehend. He congratulated Gilbert. "Jolly good, old chap! Have a drink," he said, and insisted that they should join him at the bar. "Of course," he added privately to Henry, "this sort of stuff isn't really in my line . . . jolly good and all that, of course . . . but still it's not in my line. All the same, a chap has to congratulate a chap. Oh, Cecily wants you to go and talk to her. You know where she is, don't you?"

He turned to listen to Ninian who was describing the accident which had happened when the *Gigantic* started on her first trip to America. "She jolly near sank a cruiser," he was saying as Henry moved away from the bar. "That was the second accident. The first time, she broke from her moorings. . . ."

He pushed his way through the crowd of drinking and gossiping men, and entered the stalls. Lady Cecily saw him coming, and she beckoned to him.

"Who is that nice girl in the box?" she asked, as he sat down in Jimphy's seat. "She sat beside you. . . ."

"Oh, Ninian's sister," he replied. "Mary Graham."

"She's very pretty, isn't she?"

"Yes. . . ,"

He would have said more, but it suddenly struck him as comical that Lady Cecily should speak of Mary almost in the words that Mary had used when she spoke of Lady

Cecily. He looked up at the box and saw that Mary was talking to her mother, and something in her attitude sent a pang through his heart.

"I *do* love Mary." he said to himself, "but somehow . . . somehow I love Cecily too!"

Lady Cecily was speaking to him and he turned to listen.

"I want you to introduce me to Ninian's sister," she said.

"Yes," he answered reluctantly, though he could not have said why he was reluctant to introduce her to Mary.

"After the next act," she went on, and he nodded his head.

Then Jimphy returned, and Henry got up and left her, and hurried back to the box. The second act had begun when he reached it, and he tiptoed to his seat and sat down in silence. Mary looked round at him, smiling, and then looked back at the stage, and again he felt that odd reluctance to bring Lady Cecily and her together.

3

At the end of the second act, he turned to Mary and said, "Lady Cecily wants to be introduced to you. I said I'd bring her here after this act!"

"Do," Mary answered.

As he walked towards the door of the box, he remembered Gilbert and he bent towards him and said quietly, "Oh, Gilbert, I'm going to fetch Lady Cecily. She wants to talk to Mary! . . ."

"Righto!" Gilbert replied, without looking up.

Henry hesitated. "You . . . you don't mind, do you?" he said, and then wished that he had remained silent.

"Mind!" Gilbert looked up. "Why should I mind?"

"I thought perhaps . . . but of course if you don't mind, that's all right!"

He hurried out of the box, feeling that he had intruded into private places. He had intended to be considerate and had achieved only the appearance of prying. "That's like me!" he thought, as he descended the stairs that led to the stalls. "I wonder why it is that I'm full of sympathy and understanding and tact in my books, and such a clumsy fool in life!"

He entered the stalls, and as he did so, Lady Cecily rose to join him. Jimphy had already gone to the bar. He held the curtain for her and she passed through. "Isn't it clever?" she said, speaking of the play, and he nodded his head. The passage leading up from the stalls was full of chattering people, but when they reached the narrow corridor which led to the box, there was no one about. . . .

"Cecily!" he said in a low voice.

"Yes, Paddy!" she answered, looking back over her shoulder.

He put his hands on her shoulders and turned her towards him.

"Some one will see you," she said.

"No, they won't," he replied, "and I don't care. . . ." He kissed her ardently. "My dear!" he murmured with his lips on hers.

She pushed him from her. "You *are* a fool," she said.

"I couldn't help it!"

Their voices were low lest the people in the box should hear them.

"You must never do that again," she said. "I'd never have forgiven you if any one had seen us!"

"What are you afraid of, Cecily?" he asked.

She made a gesture of despair. "Haven't you *any* sense?" she said.

She turned to go towards the box again, but he caught hold of her hand and held her.

"Cecily," he whispered, "you know I love you, don't you?"

"Yes, yes," she answered impatiently, snatching her hand from his, "but you needn't tell everybody about it!"

"And you love me, too. Don't you?"

"Let's go and join the others! . . ."

He held her again. "No, Cecily," he said, "you must listen to me!"

"Well, what is it?"

"Cecily!" He was breathing hard, and it seemed to him that he could only speak by forcing words out of himself. "Cecily . . . come with me! . . ."

"That's what I want to do, but you keep me hanging about here. If any one were to see us! . . ."

"I don't mean that," he interrupted. "You know quite well what I mean! . . ."

"What *do* you mean? I don't know! . . ."

He went closer to her, trying to waken her passion by the strength of his. "I want you to leave Jimphy and come away with me," he said.

"Leave Jimphy!"

"Yes. You're not happy . . . you're not suited to each other. Come with me!"

"Like this?" she said, holding out her hands and mocking him.

"That doesn't matter," he urged. "We'll go somewhere. . . ."

"Fly to Ireland, I suppose, in evening dress! Poor Paddy, you're so Irish, aren't you? Please don't be an idiot!"

She went on towards the door of the box, and he followed after her. "Cecily!" he said.

"Not to-night," she answered. "I want to be introduced to that nice girl, Mary Graham, and I really must congratulate Gilbert . . . I suppose he's here . . . it's such a clever play!"

She opened the door of the box and went in, and, hesitating for a moment, he went after her.

4

She stayed in the box, sitting between Mrs. Graham and
Mary, until the end of the play. The curtain had gone
down to applause and laughter and had been raised again
and a third and fourth time, and then the audience had
demanded that the author should appear. Somewhere in
the gallery, they could hear the faint groan of the man
who attends all first nights and groans on principle. "I'd
like to punch that chap's jaw!" Ninian muttered, glancing up at the gallery indignantly. There was more applause and a louder and more insistent shout of "Author!
Author!" and the curtain went up, and Gilbert, very
nervous and very pale, came on to the stage and bowed.
Then, after another curtain call, the lights were lowered
and the audience began to disperse.

There was to be a supper party at the Carlton, because
the Carlton was nearer to the Pall Mall than the Savoy,
and Sir Geoffrey Mundane and Mrs. Michael Gordon had
accepted Gilbert's invitation to join them. "It'll cost
a hell of a lot," Gilbert said to Henry, "but what's money
for? When I die, they'll put on my tombstone, *'He was
born in debt, he lived in debt, he died in debt, and he
didn't care a damn. So be it!'* He extended his invitation to Jimphy and Lady Cecily.

"You didn't come to Jimphy's birthday party," she
objected.

"Didn't I?" he replied. "Well, both of you come to
my party . . . that'll make up for it!"

Gilbert did not appear to be affected by Cecily's presence. He had greeted her naturally, behaving to her in
as friendly a way as he would have behaved if she had
been Mrs. Graham. Henry, remembering the scene on
the Embankment, had difficulty in understanding Gilbert's
easy manner. Had he been in Gilbert's place, he knew that
he would have been awkward, constrained, tongue-tied.
Undoubtedly, Gilbert had *savoir faire*. So, too, had Cecily.

Her look of irritation with Henry had disappeared as she entered the box. He, following after her, had been nervous and self-conscious, feeling that the flushed look on his face must betray him to his friends; but Cecily had none of these awkwardnesses. She behaved as easily as if the scene with Henry had not taken place. "You'd think she hadn't any feelings," he murmured to himself, and as he did so, it seemed to him that in that moment he knew Cecily, knew her once and for all. *She had no feelings, no particular feelings for any one, not even for Gilbert.* She was a beautiful animal, eager for emotional diversions, but indifferent to the creature that pleased her after it had pleased her. If Henry were to quit her now and never return to her, she might some day say, "I wonder where poor Paddy is!" and turn carelessly to a new lover; but that would be all. Gilbert had piqued her, perhaps, but he had done no more than that, though probably it was more than Henry could ever hope to do, and she had yawned a little with the tedium of waiting for him, and then had decided to yawn no more. . . .

He fell among platitudes. "Like a butterfly," he said to himself. "Just like a damned butterfly!"

Well, he thought, mentally cooler because of his revelation, that is an attitude towards life that has many advantages. One might call Cecily a stoical amorist, an erotic philosopher. "Love where you can, and don't bother where you can't!" might serve her for a motto. "And, really, that's rather a good way of getting through these plaguey emotions of ours!" he told himself. "Only," he went on, "you can't walk in that way just because you think it's a good one!"

He sat between Lady Cecily and Mary at supper, but he did not talk a great deal to either of them, for Mary was chattering excitedly to Sir Geoffrey Mundane, and Cecily was persuading Ninian that engineering had always been the passion of her life. "I quite agree," she was saying, "a Channel Tunnel would be very useful and . . . and so

convenient, too. I've often said that to Jimphy, but dear
Jimphy doesn't pretend to understand these things!"
She had turned to him once and, in a whisper, had said,
"Which of you is in love with Mary?" but he had pre-
tended to be wooden and hard of understanding.

"My dear Paddy," she said, raising her eyebrows, "I
believe you're sulking . . . just because I wouldn't run
away with you. You're as bad as Gilbert!"

"You're perfectly brutal," he said under his breath.

"Aren't you exaggerating?" she replied. "And if I had
gone off with you, we'd have missed this nice supper.
Do be sociable, there's a dear Paddy, and perhaps I'll run
away with you next Tuesday!"

There was a babble of conversation about them, and
much laughter, for Gilbert, reacting from his fright, was
full of bright talk, and Sir Geoffrey, reminiscent, capped
it with entertaining tales of dramatists and stage people.
It was easy for Cecily and Henry to carry on their
conversation in quiet tones without fear of being overheard.

"You treat me like a boy," he said reproachfully.

"You are a boy, Paddy dear, and a very nice boy!"

"I suppose," he retorted, "it's impossible for you to
understand that I love you. . . ."

"Indeed, it isn't," she interrupted. "I understand
that quite easily. What I can't understand is why you
wish to spoil everything by silly proposals to . . . to
elope! . . ."

"But I love you," he insisted. "Isn't that enough to
make you understand?"

She shook her head, and turned again to Ninian.

"You see," Ninian said, "you bore through this big bed
of chalk from both sides. . . ."

"But how do you know the two ends will meet?" she
asked.

"Oh, engineers manage that sort of thing easily," Ninian
answered. "Think of the Simplon Tunnel! . . ."

"Yes?" she said, to indicate that she was thinking of it. "Well, that met, didn't it?"

"Did it?" she replied. "Oh, but of course it must have met. I've been through it! . . ."

"There was hardly an inch of divergence between the two ends," he went on. . . .

"Hell's flames!" Henry said to himself.

5

"I must see you," he said to her when the party had broken up and she was going home. "I must see you alone!"

"I do hope you're not going to be a nuisance, Paddy!" she replied.

He put her cloak about her shoulders. "Will you meet me at the suspension bridge over the lake in St. James's Park to-morrow at eleven? . . ."

"That's awfully early, Paddy, and St. James's Park is such a·long way from everywhere. Couldn't you come to lunch? Jimphy'll be glad to see you. He seems to like you for some reason!"

"I want to talk to you alone, and we're not likely to be disturbed in St. James's Park. You must come, Cecily!"

"Oh, all right," she answered. "But I shan't be there before twelve. You can take me to lunch somewhere. . . ."

"Very well," he said. "I'll be at the bridge at twelve, and I'll wait for you . . . only, come as soon as you can, Cecily!"

"I can't think why you want to behave like this, Paddy. It's so melodramatic. Gilbert was just the same! . . ."

He felt that he could hit her when she said that, and he turned away from her so quickly that her cloak slipped from her shoulders.

"Oh, Paddy!" she exclaimed.

"I beg your pardon!" he answered, turning again and picking the cloak from the ground.

"You're so . . . so selfish," she said. "You want everything to be just as you like it. You're just like Gilbert . . . where is Gilbert? . . . I must say good-night to him . . . and that nice girl, Mary. I think it's a very clever play, and she's such a nice girl, too. Oh, Gilbert, there you are! Good-night! I've enjoyed everything so much . . . a nice play and a nice supper. Good-night, and do come and see me soon, won't you. Why not come to-morrow with Paddy? . . ."

"Paddy?" said Gilbert.

"Yes, Henry Quinn. I call him Paddy. It seems natural to call him Paddy. He's so Irish. Do come with him to-morrow, and bring all your press cuttings with you and read them to me. Paddy wants to talk to me. . . ."

Henry walked away from them. What sort of woman was this? he asked himself. Was she totally insensitive? Was it impossible for her to realise that she was hurting him? . . .

"Good-night, Quinny!"

He turned quickly to take Mary's hand.

"We're going back to Devonshire the day after to-morrow," she said.

"Are you?" he murmured vaguely.

"Yes. Good-night, Quinny!"

"Aren't you tired?" he asked.

"Oh, no," she answered. "I've enjoyed myself awfully much. Here's Ninian! He's taking us back to our hotel. Good-night, Quinny!"

He hesitated for a moment or two. He wanted to suggest that he should go with her instead of Ninian, but before he could speak he saw Cecily moving down the room towards the street.

"Good-night, Mary!" was all he said.

6

Roger had taken Rachel home, and so, when Ninian had gone off with his mother and Mary, there were only Henry and Gilbert left.

"Let's go home, Quinny," Gilbert said. "I'd like to walk if you don't mind!"

"Very well," Henry replied.

They left the hotel and strolled across the street towards the National Gallery.

"I wish it were the morning," Gilbert said. "I want to see the newspapers!"

"It doesn't greatly matter what they say, does it?" Henry answered. "The play's a success. The audience liked it."

"I want to read the notices all the same. Of course, I want to read them. I shall spend the whole of to-morrow reading and re-reading them. Just vanity!"

They walked past the Gallery, and made their way through the complicated streets that lie behind the Strand, about Covent Garden, towards Bloomsbury. They did not speak for some time, for they were tired and their minds were too full of other things. Once indeed, Gilbert began to speak . . . "I think I could improve the second act a little . . ." but he did not finish his sentence, and Henry did not ask him to do so. It was not until they were nearly at their home that Henry spoke to Gilbert about Cecily.

"Are you going to Lady Cecily's to-morrow?" he said.

"Eh?" Gilbert exclaimed, starting out of his dreams. "Oh, no, I think not! Why?"

"I only wondered. She asked you, you know!"

They walked on in silence until they reached the door of their house.

"I say, Quinny," said Gilbert, while Henry opened the door, "you seem to be very friendly with Cecily!"

Henry fumbled with the key and muttered, "Damn this door, it won't open!"

"Let me try! . . ."

"It's all right now. I've done it! What were you say-ing, Gilbert?"

They entered the house, shutting the door behind them, and stood for a while in the hall, removing their hats and coats.

"Oh, nothing," Gilbert replied. "I was only saying you seemed very friendly with Cecily!"

"Well, yes, I suppose I am, but not more than most people. Are you going to bed now or will you wait up for Ninian and Roger?"

"I shan't sleep if I go to bed . . . I'm too excited. I shall read for a while in my room . . . unless you'd like to jaw a bit!"

Henry shook his head. "No," he said, "I'm too tired to jaw to-night. See you in the morning. Good-night, Gilbert!"

"Good-night, Quinny!"

Henry went to his bedroom, leaving Gilbert in the hall, and began to undress. His mind was full of a flat rage against Cecily. She had consented to meet him in St. James's Park, and then, almost as she had made her promise, she had turned to Gilbert and had invited him to call on her, in his company, at the time she had appointed for his private meeting with her. He did not wish to see her again. "She's fooling me," he said, throwing his coat on to a chair so that it fell on to the ground where he let it lie. "I've not done a stroke of work for days on her account, and she cares no more for me than she does for . . . for anybody. I won't go and meet her to-morrow, damn her! I'll send a messenger to say I can't come, and then I'll drop her. It isn't worth while going through this . . . this agony for a woman who doesn't care a curse for you!"

"I'm not going to be treated like this," he went on to himself while he brushed his teeth. "I'm not going to hang about her and let her treat me as she pleases. She can get somebody else, some one who is more complacent than I am, and doesn't feel things. I hope she goes to the Park and waits for me. Perhaps that'll teach her to understand what a man feels like. . . ."

But of course she would not go to the Park and wait for him. He would send an express messenger with a note to tell her that he was unable to keep the appointment.

"I'll write it now," he said to himself and he stopped in the middle of washing his face and hands to find note-paper. "Damn, my hands are wet," he said aloud, and picked up a towel.

"*Dear Lady Cecily*," he wrote, when he was dry, using the formal address because he wished to let her know that he was ill friends with her, "*I am sorry I shall not be able to meet you to-day as we arranged last night.*" He wondered what excuse he should make for breaking off the appointment, and then decided that he would not make any. "I won't add anything else," he said, and he signed himself, "*Yours sincerely, Henry Quinn.*" "She'll know that I'm sick of this . . . messing about. I don't see why I should explain myself to her!"

He sealed the envelope and put the letter aside, and sat for a while drumming on his table with the pen.

"Mary's worth a dozen of her," he said aloud, getting up and going to bed.

THE NINTH CHAPTER

1

THEY all rose early the next day. Ninian had been out of the house before any of them had reached the breakfast room, and when he returned, his arms were full of newspapers.

"What's Walkley say?" said Gilbert. "That's all I want to know!"

They opened the *Times*, and then, when they had read the criticism of "The Magic Casement," they murmured, "Charming! Splendid! Oh, ripping!" while Gilbert, sitting back in his chair, smiled beatifically and said, "Read it again, coves. Read it aloud and slowly!"

While they were reading the notices, Henry went off to a post office, and sent his letter to Lady Cecily by express messenger. "That's settled," he said, as he returned home, for he had been afraid that he might change his mind. As he was shaving that morning, he had faltered in his resolution. "I'd better go," he had said to himself, and then had added weakly, "No, I'm damned if I will!" Well, it was settled now. The letter was on its way to her. She would probably be angry with him, but not as angry as he was with her, and perhaps they would not meet again for a long while. So much the better. Now he could get on with his book in peace. Gilbert was right. Women *do* upset things. Well, this particular woman would not upset him again. . . .

They had read all the notices when Henry returned, and were now at breakfast. Roger was relating the latest legal jest about Mr. Justice Kirkcubbin, a poor old man who per-

sisted in clinging to the Bench in spite of the broadest
hints from the *Law Journal,* and Ninian was making mysterious movements with his hands.

"What's the matter, Ninian?" Henry asked, as he sat
down at the table.

Ninian, while searching for the notices of Gilbert's play,
had seen a sentence in a serial story in one of the newspapers. . . . *"Her hands fluttered helplessly over his
breast"* . . . and he was trying to discover exactly what
the lady had done with her hands. "She seems to have
just flopped them about," he said, and he turned to Gilbert.
"Look here, Gilbert," he said, "you try it. I'll clasp you
in my arms as the hero clasped this female, and you'll let
your hands flutter helplessly over my breast!"

"I'll let my fist flutter helplessly over your jaw, young
Ninian! . . ."

"I don't believe she let her hands do anything of the
sort," Ninian went on. "She couldn't have done it. An
engineer couldn't do it, and I don't believe a female can
do what an engineer can't do!"

"I suppose," he added, getting up from the table, "Tom
Arthurs is half way across now. I wish I could have gone
with him. What a holiday!"

"Talking of holidays," Gilbert said, "I'm going to take
one, and as you don't seem in a fit state to do any work,
Quinny, you'd better take one too, and come with me!"

"Where are you going?" Roger asked. "Anglesey?"

"No. I thought of going there, but I've changed my
mind. I shall go to Ireland with Quinny."

"Ireland!" Henry exclaimed, looking across at Gilbert.

"Yes. Dublin. We can go to-night. I've never been
there, and I'd like to know what these chaps, Marsh and
Galway, are up to. That whatdoyoucallit movement you
were telling me about? . . . you know, the thing that
means 'a stitch in time saves nine' or something of the
sort!"

"Oh, the Sinn Fein movement!"

"Yes. That's the thing. The Improved Tories ought to know about that. . . ."

"That reminds me," said Roger, "of an idea I had in the middle of the night about the Improved Tories. We ought to publish our views on problems. The Fabians do that kind of thing rather well. We ought to imitate them. We ought to study some subject hard, argue all round it, and then tell the world just how we think it ought to be solved. I thought we might begin on the problem of unemployment. . . ."

"Good Lord, do you think we can solve that!" Ninian exclaimed.

"No, but we might find a means of palliating it. My own notion. . . ."

"I thought you had some scheme in your skull, Roger!" said Gilbert. "Let's have it!"

"Well, it's rather raw in my mind at present, but my idea is that the way to mitigate the problem of unemployment, perhaps solve it, is to join it on to the problem of defence. Supposing we decided to create a big army . . . and we shall need one sooner or later with all these ententes and alliances we're forming . . . the problem would be to form it without dislocating the industrial system. My idea is to make it compulsory for every man to undergo military training, about a couple of months every year, and call the men up to the camp in times of trade depression. You wouldn't have to call them all up at once . . . trades aren't all slack at the same time . . . and you'd arrange the period of training as far as possible to fit in with the slack time in each job. I mean, people who are employed in gasworks could easily be trained in the summer without dislocating the gas industry . . . colliers, too, and people like that . . . and men who are slack in the winter, like builders' men, could be trained in the winter. That's my idea roughly. There'd be training going on all the year round, and of course you could vary the duration of the period of training . . . never less than two months, but longer if trade were badly depressed. You'd save a lot of misery that way . . . you'd keep your men fit and fed and their homes going . . . and you'd have the nucleus of a large army. I don't see why we shouldn't bring the Board of Education in. If we were to raise the school age to sixteen, and then make it compulsory for every boy to go into a cadet corps or something of the sort for a couple of years, you'd relieve the pressure on the labour market at that end enormously, and you'd make the job of getting the army ready much easier in case of emergency. A couple of years' training to begin with, followed by a couple of months' further training every year, would make all the difference in the world to us militarily, and it would do away, largely, with the unemployed!''

"How about apprentices?'' said Gilbert. "If you raise the school age to sixteen and then make all the boys go into training until they are eighteen, you're going to make a big difficulty in the way of getting skilled labour!''

"I don't think so. As far as I can make out the period of apprenticeship is much too long. Five or six years is a ridiculous time to ask a boy to spend in learning his job, and any trade unionist will tell you that every apprentice spends the first year or two in acting as a sort of messenger: fetching beer and cleaning up things. I suppose the real reason why the period of indenture is so long is because the Unions don't want to swamp the labour market with skilled workers. Well, why shouldn't we reduce the period of apprenticeship by giving the boy a military training? You see, don't you, what a problem this is? I thought of talking about it to the Improved Tories, and when we'd argued it over a bit, we'd put our proposals into print and circulate them among informed people, and invite them to come and tell us what they think of the notion from their point of view . . . Trade Union secretaries and military men and employers and people like that . . . and then, we might publish a book on it. Jaurés wrote a book on the French Army . . . a very good book, too . . . so there isn't anything remarkably novel about the notion, except, perhaps, my idea of linking the military problem on to the unemployment problem. You and Quinny could write the book, Gilbert, because you've got style and we want the book to be written so that people will read it without getting tied up. Of course, if you must go to Ireland, you must, but it seems a little needless, doesn't it?"

"This business will take time," Gilbert replied. "Tons of time. I don't think our visit to Ireland will affect it much. You'll come with me, won't you, Quinny?"

Henry nodded his head. "At once, if you like," he answered, hoping indeed that Gilbert would suggest an immediate departure. If Lady Cecily were to hear that he had left London. . . .

"To-night will do," said Gilbert.

2

"Are you going to work?" Gilbert said to Henry, when the others had gone.

"I think so," Henry replied. "I haven't written a word for days. You?"

"I'll go and have a squint at the Pall Mall . . . just to make sure that last night wasn't a dream. I'll come back to lunch. It 'ud be rather jolly to go on from Dublin and see your father, Quinny?"

"Yes . . . that's a notion. I'll write and tell him we're coming. Bring back the afternoon papers when you come, Gilbert, I'd like to see what they say about the play!"

"Righto!" said Gilbert.

Henry sat on in the breakfast room, after Gilbert had gone, reading the criticisms of "The Magic Casement," and then, when he had finished, he went up to his room and began to work on "Turbulence." He wrote steadily for an hour, and then read over what he had done.

"This is better," he murmured to himself, pleased with what he had written, and he prepared to go on, but before he could start again, there was a knock on the door, and Magnolia came in.

"You're wanted on the telephone, sir!" she said.

"Who is it?"

"I don't know, sir. They didn't say!"

He went downstairs and took up the receiver. "Hilloa!" he said.

"Is that you, Paddy?" was the response.

"Cecily!"

"Yes. I've just had your letter. Are you very cross, Paddy?"

He felt perturbed, but he tried to make his voice sound as if he were indifferent to her.

"No," he replied, "I'm not cross at all. . . ."

"Oh, yes, you are, Paddy. You're very cross, and you're going to teach me a lesson, aren't you?"

He could hear her light laugh as she spoke.

"I can't *make* you believe that I'm not cross at all," he said.

"No, you can't. Paddy!" Her voice had a coaxing note as she said his name.

"Yes."

"Come to lunch with me. Jimphy's gone off for the day somewhere. . . ."

"I'm sorry! . . ."

"Do come, Paddy. I want you to come. I do, really!"

He paused for a second or two before he replied. After all why should he not go? . . .

"I'm sorry," he said, "but I really can't lunch with you. I'm going to Ireland! . . ."

"Going where?"

"Ireland. To-night! I'm going with Gilbert!"

"But you can't go this minute. Paddy, you *are* cross, and you're spiteful, too. If you aren't cross, you'll come and lunch with me. You ought to come and say 'good-bye' to me before you go to Ireland. . . ."

"I've got a lot to do . . . packing and things!"

"You can do that afterwards!" Her voice became more insistent. "Paddy, I want you to come. You must come! . . ."

He hesitated, and she said, "Do, Paddy!" very appealingly.

It would be weak, he told himself, to yield to her now . . . she would think she had only to be a little gracious and he would be at her feet immediately; and then he thought it would be weak not to yield to her. "It'll look as if I were afraid to meet her . . . running away like this. Or that I'm sulking . . . just petulant!"

"All right," he said to her, "I'll come!"

"Come now!"

He nodded his head, forgetting that she could not see him, and she called to him again, "You'll come now, won't you?"

"Yes," he replied. "I'll come at once!"

He put up the receiver and reached for his hat. "I wonder what she wants," he thought. "Perhaps she really does love me and my letter's frightened her!" His spirits rose at the thought and he went jauntily to the door and opened it, and as he did so, Ninian, pale and miserable, panted up the steps.

"My God, Quinny!" he exclaimed, almost sobbing, "the *Gigantic's* gone down!"

"The what?"

"The *Gigantic's* gone down! It's in the paper. Look, look!" He was unbalanced by grief as he thrust the *Westminster Gazette* and the *Globe* into Henry's hands.

"But, damn it, she can't have gone down," Henry said, "she's a Belfast boat . . . she can't have gone down!"

"She has, I tell you, and Tom Arthurs . . . oh, my God, Quinny, he's gone down too! The decentest chap on earth and . . . and he's been drowned!"

Henry led him into the house. "I went out to get the evening papers to see about Gilbert's play," he went on, "and that's what I saw. I saw her at Southampton going

off as proud as a queen . . . and now she's at the bottom
of the Atlantic. And Tom waved his hand to me. He was
going to show me over her properly when he came back.
Isn't it horrible, Quinny? What's the sense of it . . .
what the hell's the sense of it?''

"She can't have gone down . . ." Henry said, as if that
would comfort Ninian.

"She has, I tell you. . . ."

Henry went to the sideboard and took out the whisky.

"Here, Ninian," he said, pouring out some of it, "drink
that. You're upset! . . ."

"No, I don't want any whisky. God damn it, what's
the sense of a thing like this! A man like Tom
Arthurs! . . ."

There was a noise like the sound of a taxi-cab drawing
up in front of the house, and presently the bell rang, and
then, after a moment or two, the door opened, and Mrs.
Graham came hurrying into the room.

"Ninian! Where's Ninian?" she said wildly to Henry.

"He's here, Mrs. Graham!"

She went to him and clutched him tightly to her. "Oh,
my dear, my dear," she said.

"What is it, mother?" he asked, calming himself and
looking at her.

"I telephoned to your office, but you weren't there,
so I came here to find you. I couldn't rest content till I'd
seen you!"

"What is it, mother?"

"That ship, Ninian. If you'd been on it . . . you
wanted to go, and I said why didn't you . . . oh, my dear,
if you'd been on it, and I'd lost you!"

He put his arms about her and drew her on to his
shoulder. "I'm all right, mother!" he said.

Henry left the room hurriedly. He went to the kitchen
and called to Mrs. Clutters. "I won't be in to lunch," he
said. "Don't let any one disturb Mrs. Graham and Mr.
Graham for a while. They . . . they've had bad news!"

Then he went out of the house. The taxi-cab in which
Mrs. Graham had come was still standing outside the door.
"I ain't 'ad me fare yet," said the driver.
"All right!" said Henry. "I'll pay it."
He gave Cecily's address to the man, and then he got
into the cab.

3

He could hear the newspaper boys crying out the news
of the disaster as he was driven swiftly to Cecily's house.
The sinking of the great ship had stunned men's minds and
humiliated their pride. This beautiful vessel, skilfully
built, the greatest ship afloat, had seemed imperishable, the
most powerful weapon that man had yet forged to subdue
the sea, and in a little while, recoiling from the hidden iceberg, she had foundered, broken as easily as a child's toy,
carrying all her vanity and strength to the bottom. . . .
"It isn't true," he kept on saying to himself as if he
were trying to contradict the cries of the newsvendors.
"She's a Belfast boat and Belfast boats don't go
down. . . ."
He felt it oddly, this loss. The drowning of many men
and women and children affected him merely as a vague,
impersonal thing. "Yes, it's dreadful," he would say when
he thought of it, but he was not moved by it. When he
remembered Tom Arthurs he was stirred, but less than
Ninian had been. He could see him now, just as he had
stood in the shipyard that day when John Marsh and
Henry had been with him, and he had watched the workmen pouring through the gates. "Those are my pals!"
he had said. . . . Poor Tom Arthurs! Destroyed with the
thing that he had conceived and his "pals" had built! But
perhaps that was as he would have wished. It would have
hurt Tom Arthurs to have lived on after the *Gigantic* had
gone down. . . . It was not the drowning of a crowd of
people or the drowning of Tom Arthurs that most affected

Henry. It was the fact that a boat built by Belfast men had foundered on her maiden trip, on a clear, cold night of stars, reeling from the iceberg's blow like a flimsy yacht. He had the Ulsterman's pride in the Ulsterman's power, and he liked to boast that the best ships in the world were built on the Lagan. . . .

"By God," he said to himself, "this'll break their hearts in Belfast!"

The cab drew up before the door of Cecily's house, and in a little while he was with her.

"Have you heard about the *Gigantic?*" he said, as he walked across the room to her.

"Oh, yes," she answered, "isn't it dreadful? Come and sit down here!"

He had not greeted her otherwise than by his question about the *Gigantic,* and she frowned a little as she made room for him beside her on the sofa.

"That great boat! . . ." he began, but she interrupted him.

"I suppose you're still cross," she said.

"Cross?"

"Yes. You haven't even shaken hands with me!"

He remembered now. "Oh!" he said in confusion, but could say no more.

"Are you really going to Ireland?" she asked, putting her hand on his arm.

"Yes," he answered, feeling his resolution weakening just because she had touched him.

"But why?"

"You know why!" he said.

Her hand dropped from his arm. "I don't know why," she exclaimed pettishly, and he saw and disliked the way her lips turned downwards as she said it.

"I can't bear it, Cecily," he exclaimed. "I must have you to myself or . . . or not have you at all!"

"Perfectly absurd!" she murmured.

"It isn't absurd. How can you expect me to feel happy

when I see you going off with Jimphy? Can't you understand, Cecily? Here I am with you now, but if Jimphy
were to come into the room, I should have to . . . to give
way, to pretend that I'm not in love with you!"

"I can't see what difference it makes," she said.
"Jimphy and I don't interfere with each other. It's ridiculous to make all this fuss. I don't see any necessity to
go about telling everybody! . . ."

"I didn't propose that," he interrupted.

"Yes, you did, Paddy, dear! You asked me to run away
with you, and what's that but telling everybody?"

He felt angry with her for what seemed to him to be
flippancy. "I'm in earnest, Cecily!" he said. "I'm not
joking!"

"I'm in earnest, too. I don't want to run away with
you . . . not because I don't love you . . . I do love you,
Paddy, very much . . . but it's so absurd to run away
and make a . . . a mountain out of a molehill. We should
be awfully miserable if we were to elope. We'd have to
go to some horrid place where we shouldn't know anybody
and there'd be nothing to do. Really, it's much pleasanter
to go on as we are now, Paddy. You can come here and
take me to lunch sometimes and go to the theatre with me
when Jimphy wants to go to a music-hall, and . . . and
so on!"

He could not rid himself of the notion that she was
"chattering" in the Lensley style.

"It would be decenter to go away together," he said.

She moved away from him angrily. "You're a prig,
Paddy!" she exclaimed. "You can go to Ireland. I don't
care!"

He got up as if to go, but did not move away. He stood
beside her irresolutely, wishing to go and wishing to stay,
and then he bent over her and touched her. "Cecily," he
said, "come with me!"

"No!" she answered, keeping her back to him.

"Very well," he said, and he walked across the room

towards the door. His hand was on the handle when she called to him.

"Aren't you going to stay to lunch?" she said.

"You told me to go! . . ."

"Yes, but I didn't mean immediately. I shall be all alone."

He went back to her very quickly, and sat down beside her and folded her in his arms.

"I loathe you," he cried, with his lips pressed against her cheek. "I loathe you because you're so selfish and brutal. You don't really care for me. . . ."

"Oh, I do, Paddy! . . ."

"No, you don't. You were making love to Ninian last night! . . ."

" So that's it, is it? . . ."

"No, it isn't. Ninian doesn't care about you or about any woman. He's not like me, a soft, sloppy fool. You don't love me. If I were to leave you now, you'd find some one to take my place quite easily. Lensley or Boltt! . . ."

"They're too middle-aged, Paddy!"

He pushed her away from him. "Damn it, can't you be serious!" he shouted at her.

"You're very rude," she replied.

"I'd like to beat you! I'd like to hurt you! . . ."

She smiled at him and then she put her arms about his neck and drew him towards her. "You don't loathe me, Paddy," she said softly, soothing him with her voice, "you love me, don't you?"

"Will you come away with me? Now?"

"No!" She kissed him and got up. "Let's go to lunch," she said.

He felt that he ought to leave her then, but he followed her meekly enough.

"I don't think I'll stay to lunch," he said weakly.

"Yes, you will!" she replied. "You can take me to a picture gallery afterwards! . . ."

4

They did not go to a picture gallery. The spring air was so fresh that she declared she must go for a drive. "Let's go to Hampstead!" he said, signalling to a taxi-driver. "We'll have tea at Jack Straw's Castle!"

"Yes, let's!" she exclaimed.

She had tried to persuade him not to return to Ireland, but he had insisted that he must go because of his promise to Gilbert.

"Do you care for Gilbert more than you care for me?" she had asked, making him wonder at the casual way in which she spoke Gilbert's name. It seemed incredible, listening to her, that Gilbert had been her lover. . . .

"It's hardly the same thing," he replied.

Then, after more pleading and anger, she had given in. "Very well," she said, "I won't ask you again, and don't let's talk about it any more. We'll enjoy to-day anyhow!"

The taxi-cab carried them swiftly to Hampstead.

"We'll get out at the Spaniards' Road," he said, "and walk across the Heath. It's beautiful now!"

"All right," she answered.

They did as he said, and walked about the Heath for nearly an hour. The fresh smell of spring exhilarated them, and they sat for a little while on a seat which was perched on rising ground so that they were able to see far beyond the common. Young bracken fronds were thrusting their curled heads upwards through the old brown growth; and the buds on the blackened boughs were bursting from their cases and offering delicate green leaves to the sunlight; and the yellow whins shone like little golden stars on their spiky stems. Henry's capacity for sensuous enjoyment was fully employed, and he would willingly have sat there until dusk, drawing his breath in with as much luxurious feeling as a woman has when she puts new linen on her limbs. He would have liked to strip and bathe his naked body in the Highgate Ponds or run with bare feet over the wet grass . . . but Cecily was tired of the Heath.

"Isn't it time we got some tea?" she said, getting up and looking about her as if she were searching for a teashop.

"I suppose it is," he answered reluctantly, and he rose too. "We go this way," he said, moving in the direction of Jack Straw's Castle. "Let's come back to the Heath," he added, "after we've had tea!"

"But why?" she asked.

"Oh, because it's so beautiful."

"I thought it was getting chilly," she objected.

5

"I don't see why you want to go to Ireland," she exclaimed, as she handed a cup of tea to him.

"I've told you why," he said.

"Oh, but that isn't a reason. And why does Gilbert want to go? He isn't Irish."

"I suppose! . . ."

"It's so absurd to go rushing about like this. I should have thought Gilbert would want to stay in town now that his play is on. Is it a success? I haven't looked at the papers, but then I never do. I can't read newspapers . . . they're so dull. This tea is nice. And it's much nicer in town now than it can possibly be in Ireland. Besides, I don't want you to go!"

He let her chatter on, hoping that she would exhaust her interest in his visit to Ireland and begin to talk of something else, but he did not know that Cecily had greater tenacity than might appear from the incoherence of her conversation. She held on to a subject until it was settled irrevocably. She looked very charming as she sat opposite to him, and he wondered how Jimphy could be so careless of her loveliness. The sunlight shining through the window above her head kindled her hair so that the

ripples of it shone like gold, and the delicate sunburnt
flush of her cheeks deepened in the soft glow. He put out
his hand and touched her fingers. "Beautiful Cecily!" he
said, and she smiled because she liked to be told how
beautiful she was.

"But you're going to Ireland," she said.

He did not answer.

"You say you'd do anything for me," she proceeded,
"but when I ask you not to go to Ireland, you refuse. If
you really love me! . . ."

"I do love you, Cecily!"

"Well, why don't you stay in town? It's so queer to
go away the moment you get to know me!" She began to
laugh.

"What's the joke?" he asked.

"Oh, I've just remembered how little we know of each
other. You kissed me the first time you came to my
house!"

"I loved you the moment I saw you . . . that day in
the Park when I was with Gilbert . . . I loved you then.
I didn't know who you were, but I loved you. I couldn't
help it, Cecily. You were looking at Gilbert and then your
eyes shifted and you looked at me, and I loved you, dear.
I worried Gilbert to tell me about you! . . ."

"What did he say?" she interrupted eagerly, leaning
her elbows on the table and resting her chin in the cup
of her hands.

"He told me who you were," Henry answered awkwardly.

"But didn't he say anything else? . . . didn't he? . . ."

"I've forgotten what he said. . . . Then I saw you at
the St. James's . . . he told me you often went to first-
nights, and I went specially, hoping to see you! . . ."

"Dear Paddy," she said, "and you were so shy!"

"And so jealous and angry because you talked all the
time to Gilbert, and ignored me. You made me go out of

the box with Jimphy, and as I went, I saw you putting your hand out to touch Gilbert, and I heard you calling him, 'Gilbert, darling.' . . ."

She laughed, but did not speak.

"And I was frightfully jealous. Gilbert's my best friend, Cecily, but I hated him that night. I suppose . . . oh, I don't know!"

"What were you going to say?" she asked.

He looked at her intently for a few moments. Her grey eyes were full of laughter, and he wondered whether she would answer his question seriously.

"Well?" she said.

"Do you still love Gilbert, Cecily? Am I . . . just some one to fill in the time . . . until Gilbert! . . ."

She sat back in her seat, and the laughter left her eyes.

"Let's go!" she said.

But he did not move. "You do love him," he persisted, "and you don't love me. . . ."

"Are you going to Ireland with him?" she demanded.

"Yes!"

"Very well, then!" The tightened tone of her voice indicated that there was no more to be said, but he would not heed the warning, and persisted in demanding explanations.

"If you go to Ireland with Gilbert," she said, "I'll never speak to you again!"

She closed her lips firmly, and he saw the downward curve of them again, and while he pondered on what she had said, the thought shot across his mind that that downward curve would deepen as she grew older. "She'll get very bad-tempered! . . ."

"I mean it," she said, interrupting his thought and compelling him to pay heed to her. "I'll never speak to you again if you go away now."

"But I've promised, Cecily!" he protested.

She shrugged her shoulders. "I don't see what that's got to do with it," she answered.

6

They came out of the inn, and stood for a few moments before the door.

"Shall we go back to the Heath?" he said.

"No," she replied. "Let's go home."

"Very well!"

He felt broken and crushed and tongueless. Cecily did not speak to him as they walked towards the Spaniards' Road, nor did he speak to her. The angry look on her face deterred him.

He hailed a taxi, and they got into it and were driven down Fitzjohn's Avenue and homewards. Once she turned to him and said again, "Are you going to Ireland with him?" but when he answered, "I must, Cecily, I said I would!" she turned away again and did not speak until the taxi drew up before her door.

"Perhaps you'd rather I didn't come in?" he said, expecting that she would dismiss him, but she did not do so.

"Jimphy may be at home," she said, "and probably he'd like to see you!"

"I thought he'd gone away for the day!"

"He may have returned."

She went up the steps of the house while he paid the driver of the taxi-cab, and spoke to the servant who had opened the door.

"He's not in," she said to Henry when he joined her.

"Then I won't . . ."

"Come in," she interrupted. "I want to say something to you!"

He followed her into the hall and up the stairs to the drawing-room, where she left him while she went to her room to take off her outdoor garments. He moved aimlessly about until she returned. She had changed her clothes, and was wearing a loose golden silk teagown with a girdle round it, and the gold in her hair seemed to be enriched by the gold in her dress. She went up to him quickly, putting her hands on his shoulders and drawing him close to her.

"Paddy!" she said, and her voice was very tense.

"Yes?" he answered.

"I've never asked you to do anything for me, have I?" She put her arms round his neck and kissed him. He tried to answer her, but could not because her lips were tightly pressed on his.

"You won't go, will you?" she murmured, closing her eyes and tightening her hold on him.

He struggled a little. . . . "Why don't you want me to go with Gilbert?" he said.

But she did not answer his question. She drew him back to her again, whispering, "I love you, Paddy, I love you. I don't love any one else but you!"

He threw his arms about her, and they stood there forgetful of everything. . . .

She moved a little, and he led her to the sofa where they sat down together. She laid her head on his shoulder, and he put his arms around her and drew her warm, yielding body close to his. He could feel the beating of her heart. . . .

"You won't go, will you, Paddy?" she whispered.

"No," he answered, bending over her and kissing her.

She drew herself closer to him. "Dear Paddy!" she said.

7

He went up to Gilbert's room immediately after he returned home. All the way back from Lady Cecily's, he had told himself that he must tell Gilbert at once that he was not going to Ireland because he was in love with Cecily "and because she's in love with me!" and he had repeated his resolution many times to himself in the hope that by thinking exclusively of it, there would be no opportunity for other thoughts to come into his head. He shrank from the meeting with Gilbert, for his conscience hurt him because of his betrayal of Gilbert's love and friendship. He had palliated his conduct by saying to himself that Gilbert had given Cecily up, but the excuse would not serve to absolve him from the sense of unfriendly behaviour.

"I'm making excuses for myself," he murmured. "That's all I'm doing. The decent thing is to go to Gilbert and tell him everything . . . or . . . or I could write it. I could write a long letter to him and get Magnolia to give it to him. . . . Perhaps that 'ud be better than telling him. It'll be difficult to get a chance to say anything to him with Roger and Ninian about. . . ."

He broke off his thoughts and spoke out loud. "You're funking it," he said. "Damn you, you're funking it!"

"I must tell him myself," he went on. "I must stand up to some one. I can't go on funking things forever. . . ."

It was odd, he thought, that he had no feeling for Jimphy. He had not any sense of shame because he had made love to Jimphy's wife. Jimphy appeared to him only in a comic light. Yet Jimphy had professed friendship for him. "Of course," he said, "they don't love each other!" but in this mood of self-confession which held him, he admitted that he would have felt no contrition even if Jimphy had been devoted to Cecily.

"He's a born cuckold!" he went on. "I might be afraid to take his wife from him, but I wouldn't be ashamed to do it. No one would. . . ."

He had opened the door and gone quickly up the stairs, hoping that he would not meet any of the others. Gilbert would probably be in his study or in his bedroom, and so he could talk to him at once and get the thing over. He knocked on the study door, and then, receiving no answer, opened it and looked in. Gilbert was not there. He went to the bedroom and called "Are you in, Gilbert?" but there was no response. "I suppose he's downstairs," he said to himself, and he walked part of the way down to the dining-room, stopping midway when he saw Magnolia.

"Tell Mr. Farlow I want to speak to him," he called to her. "Up in my study!"

He went to his room, and stood staring out of the window until Gilbert came.

"Hilloa, Quinny, what's up?" Gilbert said, as he entered the study.

Henry turned to him. He could *feel* the pallor of his cheeks, so nervous was he.

"Gilbert," he said desperately, "I want to talk to you!"

"Yes? . . ."

"I'm not going to Ireland with you!"

"Not going! . . . Why?"

He moved mechanically towards Gilbert and stopped at the table where he wrote. He stood for a few moments, fingering things, turning over pieces of foolscap and tapping the table with a paper knife.

"What is it, Quinny?" Gilbert said again, and as he spoke, he came up to Henry and touched him. "Is it . . . is it anything about Cecily?" Henry nodded his head. "I thought so," Gilbert continued. He moved away and sat down. "Well, tell me about it," he said.

"I'm in love with her, Glibert!"

"Yes."

"I . . . I asked her to run away with me! . . ."

Gilbert laughed. "You have hustled, Quinny," he said. "And she wouldn't, eh?"

"No!" Gilbert's laughter stimulated him, and he spoke more fluently. "But she's in love with me. She told me so. I've just come from her. And she wants me to stay in town."

"To be near her?"

"Yes. Yes, I suppose so. I had to tell you. I felt that I must tell you. Gilbert, I'm ashamed, but I can't help it. I love her so much that I'd . . . I'd do anything for her."

Gilbert did not move nor did he speak. He sat in his chair, looking very intently at Henry.

"I can't understand myself," Henry went on. "My feelings are hopelessly mixed up. I want to do decent things and I loathe cads, but all the same I do caddish things myself. I want to be straight, but I'm not straight. . . . It's awfully hard to explain what I mean, but there's something in me that seems to keep pulling me out of line, and I haven't enough force in me to beat it. I suppose it's the mill in my blood. My grandfather was a mill-owner."

Gilbert shook his head and smiled. "I don't think your notions of heredity are sound, Quinny. Is that all you have to confess?"

"All?"

"Yes. There isn't anything else?"

"No. I wanted to tell you that I'm ashamed, but I must tell you, too, that although I'm ashamed, I shan't stop loving Cecily. I can't. . . ."

Gilbert got up and went over to him. He sat on the edge of the table so that Henry, when he looked up, had to gaze straight at him.

"You're a rum bloke, Quinny," he said. "I'm always telling you that, aren't I? But you were never so rum as you are now. It's no good pretending that I don't feel . . . feel anything about Cecily. I do. But I've known about you and her for some while. I knew you'd fall in love with her that day in the Park when you were excited about her beauty and were so anxious that I should introduce you to her. Of course, I knew you'd fall in love with her. I'm not a dramatist for nothing. So what you say isn't news. I mean, it doesn't surprise me. Quinny, I'm awfully fond of you, old chap, much more than I am of Ninian or Roger. I expect it's because you're such a blooming baby. I'm not really upset about your being in love with Cecily. That had to be. But I'm awfully upset about you!"

"Me, Gilbert?" Henry said, looking up in astonishment.

"Yes. You haven't got much resolution, have you? Cecily has only got to blub a little or kiss you a few times,

and you're done for . . . she can do what she likes with
you. You haven't got the courage to run away from her,
and you haven't the power to stand up to her and say 'Be-
damned to you'!"

"No, I know that!"

"So, I think I'll just kidnap you, Quinny. I think I'll
make you come to Ireland with me. . . ."

"You can't do that, Gilbert!"

"Can't I, by God!" Gilbert's voice had changed from
its bantering note to a note of resolve. "Do you think
I'm going to let my best friend make an ass of himself, and
do nothing to prevent him? Quinny, you're an ass!
You're too fond of running about saying you can't help
this and you can't help that . . . and spilling over! And
what do you think's going to be the end of this business?
I suppose you imagine that Cecily'll change her mind some
day, and run away with you? Do you think she'll run
away with *you* when she wouldn't run away with me?
Damn you, you've got a nerve to think a thing like
that. . . ."

"I don't think that, Gilbert," Henry interjected.

"Oh, yes, you do! Of course, you do! That's natural
enough. I wouldn't mind so much if I thought there were
a chance that she would run away with you, but she
won't!"

"You wouldn't mind! . . ."

"No. Why should I? If she won't run away with me,
she couldn't do better than run away with you. And
there'd be a chance then that you'd get on with your job.
You'd soon shake down into some sort of balance if you
were together, but you'll never get level if you go on in
the way you're going now. You'll run up into one emotional crisis and down into another, and you'll spend the
time between them in . . . in recovering. That's all.
And your work will go to blazes. I *know*, Quinny. You
see, I was your predecessor. . . ."

"But Cecily's proud of my work. . . ."

"She was proud of mine. So she said. Look here, Quinny, *buck up!* How much of your new novel have you written since you knew her?"

"Not very much, of course, but! . . ."

"Exactly. I couldn't work either when . . . when I was your predecessor. Cecily's greedy, Quinny! She wants *all* of you . . . and she has the power to make you give the whole of yourself to her. If you think that 'all for love and the world well lost' is the right motto for a man . . . then Cecily's your woman. But is it? Hang it all, Quinny, you haven't done your work yet . . . you've only begun to do it!"

He got off the table and began to search among Henry's papers.

"What are you looking for?" Henry asked.

"I want the manuscript of 'Turbulence.' Where is it?"

"I'll get it. What do you want it for?"

He opened a drawer and took out the few sheets of the novel that were written.

"Is that all?" said Gilbert.

"Yes," Henry answered.

"Cecily doesn't seem to inspire you, Quinny, does she, any more than she inspired me? You haven't written a whole chapter yet. . . . Do you remember what we swore at Rumpell's?"

"We swore a whole lot of things! . . ."

"Yes, but the most important thing? We swore we'd become Great. I don't know that any of us ever will be Great. . . . I get the sensation now and then that we're frightfully crude, even Roger, but we can become something better than one of Cecily's lovers, can't we?"

"I don't know that I want to be anything else. . . ."

"For shame, Quinny!"

Gilbert put the manuscript back into the drawer from which Henry had taken it.

"You'll come to Ireland with me?" he said.

"No, Gilbert, I won't!"

"You will. I'll break your jaw if you don't come. I'll
knock the stuffing out of you if you don't come. We can
catch the night train and be in Dublin to-morrow morning! . . ."

"I promised Cecily I wouldn't go. . . ."

"And you promised me you would go. I've packed all
the things I want, and it oughtn't to take you long to pack
a trunk. I'll come and help you after dinner . . . there's
the gong . . . we'll just have time if you hop round
quickly. Ninian can telephone for a taxi to take us to
Euston!"

"It's no good, Gilbert. . . ."

"Come on. I can smell onions, and I'd risk my immortal soul for onions. Boiled, fried, stewed or roasted,
Quinny, there's no vegetable to beat them. . . ."

8

"I'm not going, Gilbert! . . ."

"You are going!"

They had finished dinner and were now in Henry's bedroom. Gilbert had instructed Ninian to telephone for a
taxi. Then, shoving Henry before him, he had climbed the
stairs to Henry's room and started to pack his trunk.

"You can't make me go! . . ."

Gilbert took an armful of shirts from the chest of draw-
ers and dropped them into the trunk. "Once, when I was
wandering in Walworth," he said, "I heard a costermonger threatening to give another costermonger a thick
ear, a bunged-up eye and a mouth full of blood. That's
what you'll get if you don't hop round. What suits do
you want?"

Henry did not answer. He walked to the window and
stood there, peering out at the trees in the garden. A
taxi-cab drove up to the door and presently Ninian came
bounding up the stairs to tell them of its arrival.

"Tell him to wait," said Gilbert, and Ninian hurried back to do so. "If you won't choose your suits yourself," he went on to Henry, "I shall have to do it for you. Socks, socks, where the hell do you keep your socks?..."

It seemed to Henry that he could see Cecily's face shining out of the darkness. He could feel her arms about him and hear her beautiful voice telling him that she loved him. "I won't go," he said to himself. "I won't go!..."

"If you'd only help to pack, we'd save heaps of money," Gilbert grumbled. "It's sickening to think of that taxi sitting out there totting up tuppences. Come and sit on the lid of this trunk, will you?"

Henry did not move from the window. Gilbert straightened himself. For a moment or two he could not see clearly because he was giddy with stooping. Then he crossed the room and took hold of Henry's arm.

"Come on, Quinny," he said, pulling him towards the trunk.

"What's the good of fussing like this, Gilbert, when I've told you I won't go...."

"Well, sit on the trunk anyhow. I may as well close the thing now I've filled it...."

9

He called Ninian, and between them they carried the luggage downstairs to the cab.

"Now then, Quinny!" said Gilbert.

"I'm not going, I tell you...."

"Get into the cab, damn you. Go on!"

He shoved him forward so that he almost fell against the step of the taxi, and Ninian caught hold of him, and they lifted him and heaved him into the taxi.

"Get in, Ninian," said Gilbert. He turned and shouted up the hall to Roger. "Come on, Roger! You'd better come and see us off!"

None of them spoke during the short drive to Euston. Henry sulked in a corner of the cab, telling himself that it was monstrous of Gilbert to treat him in this fashion, and vowing that nothing would induce him to get into the train . . . and then, his mind veering again, telling himself that perhaps it would be a good thing to go to Ireland for a while. Cecily had chopped and changed with him. Why should he not chop and change with her? . . . Neither Ninian nor Roger made any remark on the peculiarity of the journey to Ireland. They had known in the morning that Gilbert and Henry were going away that night, but it was clear that something had happened since then, that Gilbert was more intent on the journey than Henry. . . . No doubt, they would know in good time. Probably, Ninian thought to himself, that woman Jayne is mixed up in it. . . .

"You get the tickets, Ninian," Gilbert said when they reached Euston. "Firsts. Democracy's all right in theory, but I don't like it in a railway carriage!"

"Where's the money?" said Ninian.

"Money! What do you want money for? All right! Here you are! You can pay me afterwards, Quinny!"

They had only a few minutes in which to get into the train, and Gilbert, putting his arm in Henry's and hurrying him towards the Irish mail, was glad that the wait would not be long.

"It's ridiculous to behave like this," said Henry, as they shoved him into a carriage.

"I know it is," Gilbert answered. He turned to Roger. "We may want grub during the night. Get some, will you! Sandwiches will do and hard-boiled eggs, if you can get 'em. . . ."

He turned to Henry. "You're my friend, Quinny," he said, "I can't let you make a mucker of everything, can I?"

Henry did not answer.

"I know exactly how you feel," Gilbert went on. "I

should feel like it myself if I were in your place, but if I were, Quinny, I'd be damned glad if you'd do the same for me!"

10

"Good Lord!" Gilbert exclaimed, as the train drove out of London, "I forgot to pack your toothpaste. . . ."

THE THIRD BOOK
OF
CHANGING WINDS

        . . . quitted all to save
A world from utter loss.
                    PARADISE LOST.

THE FIRST CHAPTER

1

As the boat turned round the end of the pier and moved up the harbour to her berth, Gilbert, eyeing the passengers, caught sight of Henry and instantly hallooed to him. The passage from Kingstown had been smooth, and Henry, heartened by the sea air and sunshine, pressed eagerly through the throng of passengers so that he might be near the gangway and so be among the first to descend from the steamer. He called a greeting to Gilbert, and then, the boat being berthed, hurried forward to the gangway. He could not get off the steamer as quickly as he wished for the number of passengers on board was very large, and he fidgeted impatiently until he was able to get ashore.

"We'll send this bag on by the waggonette," Gilbert said, when they had shaken hands and congratulated each other on their healthy looks, "and walk over to Tre'Arrdur, and we'll gabble on the way. Here," he added, taking a letter out of his breastpocket, "you can read that while I find the man. It's from Ninian. It came this morning! . . ."

He seized Henry's bag and hurried off with it, leaving Henry to follow slowly or remain where he was, as he pleased, and then, before Henry had time to do more than take the letter from its envelope and glance carelessly at the first page of it, he came quickly back. "Come up," he said, putting his arm in Henry's. "You can read it as you go along. There's not much in it!"

They left the pier and passed through the station into the street.

"Holyhead," said Gilbert, "is a good place to get drunk in! We won't linger! . . ."

They took the lower road to Tre'Arrdur Bay because it was quieter than the upper road, and as they walked, Henry read Ninian's letter.

"He seems to like South America," he said, returning the letter to Gilbert when he had finished with it.

Gilbert nodded his head. "That old Tunnel of his doesn't get itself built, does it? But it must be great fun building a railway in a place like that. There's a revolution on the first and third Tuesdays of the month, and the President of the Republic and the Emperor of the Empire are in power for a fortnight and in exile for another one. So Ninian says. He told Roger in his last letter that he had had to kick the emperor's backside for him for interfering with the railway contract. . . . Oh, by the bye, Rachel's produced an infant. She says it's like Roger, but Roger hopes not. He says it's like nothing on earth. He came to see me off from Euston yesterday and when I asked him to describe it to me, he said he couldn't . . . it was indescribable. It looks *raw*, he says. It must be frightfully comic to be a father, Quinny!"

"I don't see anything comic about it," Henry replied. "I'd rather like to be a father myself."

"Well, why don't you become one. They say it's easy enough. First, you get a wife. . . ."

"What sort of an infant is it? Is it a boy or a girl?"

"Great Scott!" said Gilbert, "I forgot to ask that. That was very careless of me. Look out, Quinny, here's a motor, and that's Holy Mountain on the right. We'll go up it to-morrow, if you like. It's not much of a climb. Just enough to jig you up a bit. There's a chap in the hotel who scoots up mountains like a young goat. He asked me to go up Snowdon with him, but when I asked him what the tramfare was, he was slightly snorty in his manner. How's the novel getting on?"

"It'll be out in September. I corrected the final proofs last month. I think it's rather good."

"Better than 'Turbulence' or 'The Wayward Man'?"

"Yes, I think so. I'm calling it 'The Fennels.' That's the name of the people it's about. I've taken an Ulster family and . . . well, that's what I've done. I've taken an Ulster family and just shown it. My father likes it much better than anything else I've done, although he was very keen on 'Turbulence.' "

"How is your father?"

"Oh, much better, thanks, but still a bit shaky. He hates all this Volunteer business in Ireland. You remember John Marsh, don't you, and Galway? You saw them in Dublin that time! . . ." Gilbert nodded his head and so Henry did not complete his sentence. "Well, they're up to their necks in the opposition Volunteers. I saw John in Dublin yesterday for a few minutes. He was very excited about the gun-running in Ulster! Damned play-acting! He could hardly spare the time to say 'How are you?' to me, he was so anxious to be off to his drilling. He hasn't done any writing for a long time now. He's become very friendly with Mineely! . . ."

"Is that the Labour man?"

"Yes. I liked him when I met him, but he's frightfully bitter since the strike. He's got more brains than all the others put together, and he influences John tremendously. I don't wonder at his bitterness. The employers *were* brutal in that strike, Gilbert, and Mineely will never forget it. He'll make trouble for them yet, and they'll deserve all they get. He said to me 'They won't deal reasonably with us, so they can't complain if we deal unreasonably with them. They set the police on to us. . . .' "

"What's he going to do then?"

"I don't know, but he's drilling his men as hard as ever he can. He means to hit back. After he'd spoken about the police, he said, 'The next time we go to them, we'll have guns in our hands. Mebbe they'll listen to us then!' He's like John . . . he doesn't care what happens to himself. All those people, John and Galway and Mineely, have a contempt for death that I can't understand. I loathe the thought of dying . . . but they don't seem to mind. It's their religion partly, I suppose, but it's something more than religion. If they were poor, like the slum people, I could understand it better. You can't frighten *them* by threatening to kill them. Their life is such a rotten one that they'd be much better off if they were dead, even if there were no heaven, and I suppose they feel that . . . and of course the Catholic religion teaches them to despise life! But it isn't all religious fervour or the apathy of people who're too poor to mind whether they live or die. Marsh and Galway and Mineely are moved by a sort of nationalistic ecstasy . . . Marsh and Galway more than Mineely, I think, because there's a bitterness in him that isn't in them. They think of Ireland first, and he thinks of starving workmen first. They're Ireland mad. They really don't value their lives a happorth. They'd love to be martyrised for Ireland. It's a kind of lust, Gilbert. They get a sensual look on their faces . . . almost . . . when they talk of dying for Ireland.''

''It's a little silly of us English people who love life so much to try and govern a people like that,'' said Gilbert.

2

Much had happened to them in the two years that had elapsed since the day on which Gilbert carried Henry off to Dublin. The Bloomsbury household had come to an end. Suddenly and, as it seemed to them, inexplicably, Mrs. Clutters had died. It had never occurred to any of them that Mrs. Clutters could die. They seldom saw her. The kitchen was her domain, and Magnolia was her messenger. If they had any preferences or prejudices concerning food, they made them known to Magnolia, and Magnolia made them known to Mrs. Clutters. Ninian returning home in an epicurean mood, might announce that he had seen mushrooms in a greengrocer's window. ''Magnolia,'' he would

say, "let there be mushrooms!" and Magnolia would answer, "Yes, sir, certainly, sir!" and behold in the morning
there would be mushrooms for breakfast. Or Gilbert would
give their opinion of a dish. "Magnolia, we do not like
scrambled eggs. We like our eggs boiled, fried, poached,
beaten up in milk, Mr. Graham even likes them raw, but
none of us like them scrambled! . . ." and Magnolia would
say, "Yes, sir, certainly, sir!" and so scrambled eggs ceased
to be seen on their breakfast table. Magnolia always said,
"Yes, sir, certainly, sir!" If they had informed her
that the Judgment Day was to begin that afternoon
at three o'clock, Magnolia, they felt sure, would say, "Yes,
sir, certainly, sir!" and go on with her work. . . . There
seemed to be no adequate excuse for Mrs. Clutters' death
. . . "an' everythink goin' on so nice an' all!" as Magnolia said . . . and yet she had died. There had been delay in serving breakfast, and Roger, anxious to catch a
train, had been impatient.

"Magnolia!" he shouted from the door, "Magnolia!"

"Yes, sir!" Magnolia answered in an agitated voice.

They waited for her to add "Certainly, sir!" but she
did not do so, and they looked oddly at each other, feeling
that something unusual had happened.

"We're waiting for breakfast," Roger said in a less
impatient voice.

"Yes, sir, I'm comin', sir! . . ."

Magnolia appeared at the door, very red in the face and
very worried in her looks, and placed a covered dish in
front of Roger who was the father of the four, appointed
to carve and to serve.

"What's this?" Roger demanded when he had removed
the cover.

"Please, sir, it's eggs, sir! Fried eggs, sir! That's what
it's supposed to be, sir!" Magnolia replied dubiously.

"It's a bad imitation, Magnolia!" Gilbert said. "I
think I'll just have bread and marmalade this morning!"

He reached for the marmalade as he spoke, and Henry,

eyeing the eggs with disrelish, murmured, "After you, Gilbert!"

"Tell Mrs. Clutters I want her," Roger said to Magnolia.

"Please, sir, she's not very well in herself this mornin'. . . ."

"Not very well!"

"Do you mean to say she's ill?" Ninian shouted.

"Yes, sir. It was me fried the eggs, sir!"

"But . . . but she can't be ill," Ninian continued.

"Well, she is, sir. That's what she says any'ow. 'You'll 'ave to cook the breakfis yourself,' she says to me, an' when I said I didn't know 'ow, she said 'Well, you must do the best you can, that's all!' an' I done it, sir. She don't look well at all! . . ."

"How long has she been ill?" Roger asked.

"I don't know, sir. She didn't tell me. She was groanin' a bit yesterday an' the day before, but she wouldn't give in. I said to 'er, 'If I was you, Mrs. Clutters, I'd 'ave a doctor an' chance it!' an' she told me to 'old me tongue, so of course I wasn't goin' to say no more, not after that. I mean to say, I can take a 'int as good as any one. . . ."

"We'd better send for a doctor," Roger said, interrupting Magnolia. "I'll telephone to Dunroon. He lives quite near!" Then he remembered his county court case. "You'd better telephone, Quinny! I *must* catch this train. Take these . . . eggs away, Magnolia. We won't say anything more about them. You did your best!"

"Yes, sir, I did, but I told 'er I didn't know 'ow. . . ."

"All right!" said Roger, passing the dish to her.

3

Dr. Dunroon suggested that they should send for Mrs. Clutters' friends.

"Is it serious, doctor?" Henry asked, and the doctor nodded his head. "She's dying," he said.

"Dying!"

Magnolia, disregarding the conventions, had stood by, openly listening to what they were saying, and when she heard the doctor say that Mrs. Clutters was dying, she let a howl out of her that startled them. The doctor turned to her quickly.

"Hold your tongue," he said, "or she'll hear you. Anybody 'ud think you were dying by the noise you're making!"

Magnolia blubbered away. "I 'ate to 'ear of anybody dyin'," she said. "I never been in a 'ouse before where it's 'appened, an' besides she's been good to me!" Her mind wandered off at a tangent. "Any'ow," she said, wiping her eyes, "I done me best. No one can't never say I ain't done me best, an' the best can't do no more!"

"Has she got any friends, Magnolia? . . ."

It seemed to them to be extraordinary that this woman had lived in their house, had worked and cared for them, and yet was so much a stranger to them that now, in this time of her coming dissolution, they did not know where her friends were to be found, whether indeed, she had any friends. "That's very English," Henry thought; "in Ireland we know all about our servants!"

"Well, I *think* 'e's 'er 'usband," Magnolia replied. "Any'ow, 'e was drunk when 'e come! . . ."

They had assumed that Mrs. Clutters was a widow, a childless widow. . . .

"I've seen 'im 'angin' about two-three times, an' when I said to 'er, 'Mrs. Clutters, there's your friend 'angin' about the corner of the street, she tole me to mind me own business, an' then she 'urried out. Of course, it 'adn't got nothink to do with me, 'oo 'e was, an' when she tole me to mind me own business, I took the 'int. . . ."

"Do you know where he lives?" Gilbert asked.

"No, sir, I don't. When she told me to mind me own business! . . ."

The approach of Death had made Magnolia amazingly garrulous. She said more to them that morning than she had said to them all the rest of the time she had been in their service . . . and mixed up with her reminiscences of what Mrs. Clutters had said to her and what she had said to Mrs. Clutters, there was a continual statement of her fear and dislike of death, followed by the assertion that no one 'ad ever died in a house she'd worked in before.

"You'd think she was blaming us for it," Gilbert said afterwards.

"Well, you'd better go and ask her to tell you where her husband lives," Henry said to her, but she shrunk away from him when he said that.

"Oh, I couldn't go near no one what was dyin'," she said. "I ain't used to it, an' I don't like it!"

Ninian shoved her aside. "I'll go," he said.

"We'd better get some one to look after her," Gilbert proposed when Ninian had gone. "Magnolia's no damn good! . . ."

"No, sir, I ain't . . . not with dead people I ain't!"

"Clear out, Magnolia!" Gilbert shouted at her. "Go and make the beds or sit in the kitchen or something!"

"Yes, sir, certainly, sir!" Magnolia answered, and then she left the room.

"I've never felt such a helpless ass in my life before," Gilbert went on when she had shut the door behind her. "I simply don't know what to do!"

"We can't do anything," Henry murmured. "Dunroon said he'd come in again in a short while. Perhaps if we were to get a nurse or somebody. There's sure to be a Nurses' Home near to. Can't we ring up somebody?"

He got hold of the telephone book and began to turn over the pages rapidly.

"What are you looking for?" Gilbert asked.

"Nursing Homes," he answered.

"That's no good. Let's send round to Dunroon's! . . ."

"He won't be there!"

"Some one'll be there. We'll ring 'em up! . . ."

Dr. Dunroon's secretary was there, and she knew exactly what to do. "Oh, very well," she said in a voice so calm that Gilbert felt reassured. "I'll send some one round as soon as possible!"

Ninian came down the stairs before they had finished telephoning to Dr. Dunroon's secretary.

"I'm going to fetch her husband," he whispered to Henry, and then he left them.

4

"Let's go out," Gilbert said suddenly to Henry.

The nurse had arrived, and was busy in attendance on Mrs. Clutters. Magnolia, full of the antagonism which servants instinctively feel towards nurses, was maintaining a grievance in the kitchen. "Givin' 'er orders, as if she was some one!" she was mumbling to herself. "Too bossy, she is! . . ."

"It's no good trying to do any work to-day," Gilbert went on. "I . . . I couldn't make up things with her . . . up there!"

They told Magnolia that they would have their meals out, and that she need not trouble to cook anything for them, and they sent for the nurse and explained their circumstances to her. "That's all right," she said cheerfully, "I'll look after myself!"

They set off towards Hampstead, but after a while they found themselves returning to Bloomsbury. They could not keep away from the house. . . . They tried to eat a meal at the Vienna Café, but they could not swallow the food, so they paid their bill and went away. They wandered into the British Museum, and tried to interest themselves in Egyptology. . . .

"This female," said Gilbert, pointing to the mummy of

the Priestess of Amen-Ra, "is supposed to bring frightful
ill-luck to you if you squint at her. There was a fellow at
Cambridge who was cracked about her . . . used to come
here in vac. and make love to her . . . sit here for hours
spooning with a corpse. I often wanted to smack his face
for him!"

"Pose, I expect!" Henry replied. "I should have
thought it was rather dull to get smitten on a woman who's
as dead as this one is. . . ."

They remembered Mrs. Clutters. . . .

"Let's go back and see what's happened," Gilbert said,
turning away from the case which held the Priestess. . . .

Ninian met them in the hall. "She's dead," he said.
"Her husband's in the kitchen. I found him in a lodging-
house in Camden Town, and I should say he's a first-class
rotter!"

5

They sat together that evening without speaking. There
was to have been a meeting of the Improved Tories to talk
over Roger's plan for enlarging the Army and mitigating
the problem of unemployment. They could not get messages
to people in time, and so part of the evening was spent in
whispered explanations at the door to those who turned
up.

"I think I'll go to bed," Ninian said, but he did not
move, nor did any of them move. It was as if they wished
to keep together as long as possible.

Magnolia, red-eyed from weeping, had come to them
earlier in the evening, declaring that she was frightened.

"What are you afraid of?" Roger snapped at her.

" 'Er!" she answered.

"But she's dead! . . ."

"Yes, sir," Magnolia said, "that's why! I don't like
goin' upstairs be meself, sir! . . ."

"Oh, rubbish, Magnolia!" Roger exclaimed.

"I can't 'elp bein' afraid, sir. I know she's dead an'
can't do me no 'arm . . . not that she'd want to do me any
'arm . . . I will say that for 'er . . . but some'ow I'm
afraid all the same, sir. I can't 'elp it!''

"I want to get a book out of my room," Henry interjected, "so I'll go upstairs with her!"

"Oh, thank you, sir," said Magnolia gratefully. "I
know she wouldn't 'arm me if she could 'elp it, not if
she was alive any'ow, but they're different when they're
dead! . . ." She broke down, blubbering hopelessly.
"Oh, I wish I was 'ome," she moaned.

"Come on, Magnolia!" Henry said, opening the door for
her.

"That girl's getting on my nerves," Gilbert murmured
when she had gone.

Magnolia followed Henry upstairs. They had to pass the
room in which the dead woman lay, and Magnolia, when
she reached the door, gave a little squeal of fright and ran
forward, thrusting past Henry. . . . "Don't be a fool,
Magnolia!" he said, catching hold of her arm and steady-
ing her.

"I'm frightened, sir!" she moaned, looking up at him
with dilated eyes.

"There's nothing to be afraid of. Come along!"

He took her to her room and opened the door for her.

"You're all right now, aren't you?" he said, switching
on the light.

"Yes, thank you, sir!"

"Good-night, then!"

"Good-night, sir!"

When she had shut the door, he heard her turning the
key in the lock, and he smiled at her precaution. "That
wouldn't hinder Mrs. Clutters' ghost if she . . . if she
started to walk!" he thought to himself, as he descended
the stairs to his room. He had switched off the light on
Magnolia's landing, but there was a light showing dimly
up the stairs from the landing beneath. It shone faintly

on the door of the room in which Mrs. Clutters' body was lying. He went down the stairs towards the door, and then, half-way down, stopped. He could not look away from the door . . . he felt that in a moment or two it would open, and Mrs. Clutters, in her grave-clothes, would stand in the shadow and look at him with fixed eyes. . . .

"Don't be a fool!" he said aloud, shaking his head and dashing his hand across his eyes as if he were trying to sweep something away. "I'm nervy, that's what it is," he went on, still speaking aloud. "I'm worse than Magnolia! . . ."

He descended the rest of the stairs, determined not to show any sign of fear, and then, as he passed the door, he shut his eyes and hurried by. He ran down the next flight of stairs, afraid to look back, and did not pause in his running until he had reached the ground floor. He stood still in the hall for a few minutes to recover himself, and then he entered the room where the others were sitting.

They looked up at him.

"All right?" Ninian asked, and Henry nodded his head.

"You haven't brought the book," Roger said.

"No," he answered, "No . . . I changed my mind. I didn't really want the book. I just said that to . . . to get Magnolia out of the room!"

6

Mrs. Clutters' husband insisted on seeing them after the funeral because, he said, he wished to thank them for all they had done for " 'er!" He made a jerk over his shoulder with his thumb when he said " 'er," and they gathered that he was indicating the direction of Kensal Green cemetery. He was very maudlin and drunk, and Ninian thought that he ought to be kicked.

"I'm shorry," he said, "to be thish con . . . condish'n, gemmem, but y'see it's like this. A gemman said to me, y'see, 'Bert,' 'e says . . . thash my name . . . Bert, called

after Queen's 'usban' . . . Gaw' bless 'er! . . . Alber'
the Goo' they called '*im* . . . not me, oh, Lor' no! . . .
thish gemmam, 'e says to me, 'Bert,' 'e says, 'come an' 'ave
one!' an' so o' course I '*ad* to 'ave one. Thash 'ow 'twas,
see! Shorry to be in thish disgrashful state . . . thish
sad occas'n, gemmem. Very shorry! *I* thank you!'' He
turned to leave them, staggering towards the door. ''I
ain't been a good 'usban' to 'er,'' he went on, again making the jerking gesture over his shoulder with his thumb.
''Thash a fac'. I ain't. But I 'pologise. I'm shorry!
Can't say no more'n that, can I? Goo'-ni', gemmem!''

And then he staggered out.

''Somebody ought to do him in,'' said Ninian, going to
see that he left the house as quickly as possible.

''Well,'' said Roger, when Ninian had returned, ''what
are we going to do next?''

''Sack Magnolia,'' said Gilbert.

''And then?'' Roger went on.

''I don't know,'' Gilbert replied.

''I suppose we can get another housekeeper,'' Henry
suggested.

''Yes, we could do that,'' said Gilbert.

Roger got up and moved about the room for a few moments. ''I think I shall get married,'' he said at last.
''I've got to get married some time, and I might as well
get married now. This . . . this business seems to provide an opportunity, don't you think?''

''It's a pity to break up the house,'' Gilbert murmured.

''It'll have to be broken up some day,'' Roger retorted.

Ninian joined in. ''There's talk of a big railway contract in South America, and I might have to go. Hare
spoke of sending me. In about six months' time. . . .''

''We might let the house furnished for the remainder of
the lease,'' Roger went on. ''Perhaps some one would take
the furniture over altogether. . . . I could use some of it,
of course, for my house when I get married!''

''You've settled it then?'' said Gilbert.

"Not exactly. I haven't said anything to Rachel yet. The idea occurred to me in the chapel while the parson was saying the Burial Service!"

"I could have hit that fellow," Gilbert exclaimed. "Gabbling it off like that! I suppose he was in a hurry to get home to tea!"

They sat in silence for a while, each of them conjuring up the vision of the cold little service in the cemetery chapel. Magnolia, clothed in black, had sobbed loudly, while Mr. Clutters sniffed and said "A-men" very emphatically, and the parson, regarding the little group of mourners with the curiosity of a man who is bored by death and the ritual of burial, gabbled away: *NowisChristrisen fromthedeadandbecomethefirstfruitsofthemthatsleptforsince Bymancamedeathbymancamealso Theresurrectionofthedead.* . . .

"It means breaking up everything," Gilbert still protested.

"Things are always breaking up," said Roger.

"I suppose so," Gilbert replied.

Henry had not taken part in the conversation, but had lain back in his chair, with his hands clasped behind his head, lazily listening to what they were saying.

"I don't think I'd like to go on living here," he exclaimed, "particularly if Roger and Ninian go away. Perhaps we could share a flat or something, Gilbert?"

"That's a notion," Gilbert answered.

"There's no reason why the Improved Tories should collapse just because I'm going to get married," Roger asserted. "This house really isn't the most convenient place to meet. We might hire a room in a hotel near the Strand and meet there. . . ."

7

The house was let unfurnished. The incoming tenant was willing to take on the remainder of their lease and con-

tinue in occupation of the house after its expiry, but he
had furniture of his own, and so he had no use for theirs.
Roger took his furniture to a small house in Hampstead,
and offered to buy most of what was left, but they would
not listen to his proposals. "We'll give it to you as a
wedding present," they insisted. "If there's anything
you don't want, we'll sell it!" Magnolia was presented
with a couple of months' wages and a new dress, and bidden to get another home as soon as she could conveniently
do so . . . and then the house was abandoned.

"It's funny," said Gilbert, as they shut the door behind them for the last time, "it's funny that we hardly
ever thought of that old woman, and yet, the minute she
dies, we sort of go to pieces. We didn't even know she'd
got a husband. Her name was Jennifer. I saw it on the
coffin lid! . . ."

Their arrangements for quitting the house were not completed for a month after the burial of Mrs. Clutters, and
before they finally settled their affairs, Ninian was told
that he was to proceed to South America with the junior
partner. He was to have a couple of months' leave . . .
"I shall go down to Boveyhayne," he said . . . after which
he would leave England for a lengthy while. "And then
there were three!" said Gilbert, when Ninian told them
of his appointment. "Three little clever boys," he went
on, "going up to fame. One little clever boy got married
and then there were two! . . ."

Until they could make some settlement of their future,
they decided to live in a boarding house in Russell
Square.

"We shall loathe it," Gilbert said, "but that will be
good for us!"

8

And then Roger and Rachel got married. They walked
into a Registrar's office, with Gilbert and Ninian and

Henry to bear them company, and made their declarations
of fealty to each other.

"My father would have been horrified," Roger said at
luncheon afterwards. "If he'd been alive, Rachel, we'd
have had to get married in a church!"

Rachel smiled. "I shouldn't have minded, Roger!" she
answered. "You'll laugh, I know, when I tell you that
half-way through the service I began to long for a surplice and the Voice that Breathed O'er Eden. A marriage
in a church is a lot prettier than one in a Registrar's
office! . . ."

"If only the Mayor of the Borough had performed the
ceremony," Gilbert lamented. "In his nice furry red
robes and cocked hat, joining you two together in the name
of the Borough of Holborn, he'd have looked rather jolly!
Roger, we ought to get the Improved Tories to consider
the question of Civil Marriage. We want more beauty in
it. Rachel, my dear, I haven't kissed you yet. I look
upon myself as Roger's best man, and I ought to kiss you!"

"Very well, Gilbert," she answered, turning her face
towards him.

"You've deceived us all, Rachel," he said as he kissed
her. "We'd made up our minds to hate you because you
were taking our little Roger from us, and at first we
thought we were right to hate you because you were so
aggressive to us, but you've deceived us. We don't hate
you. We like you, Rachel!"

"Do you, Gilbert?" She turned to Ninian and Henry.
"Do you like me, too?" she said.

"I shouldn't mind marrying you myself," Ninian replied.

"I don't see why Gilbert should get all the kisses," said
Henry. "After all, I more or less gave you away, didn't
I? I was there anyhow! . . ."

So she kissed Ninian and Henry too. Then, a little
later, Roger and she went off to spend a honeymoon in
Normandy.

9

"I feel horribly lonely somehow," said Gilbert to Henry. Ninian, in a hurry to catch the train for Boveyhayne at Waterloo, had left them at Charing Cross.

Henry nodded his head.

"This marrying and giving in marriage is the devil, isn't it?" Gilbert went on. "We ought to cheer ourselves up, Quinny!"

"We ought, Gilbert!"

"Let's go and see my play. Perhaps that'll make us feel merry and bright! . . ."

"No," said Henry. "It wouldn't. It 'ud depress us. We'd keep thinking of Ninian and Roger. I think we ought to get drunk, Gilbert, very and incredibly drunk. . . ."

"I should feel like Mrs. Clutters' husband if I did that," Gilbert answered. "Aren't there any other forms of debauchery? Couldn't we go to a music-hall or a picture-palace or something? Or we might discuss our future! . . ."

"I'm sick of this boarding house we're in," Henry exclaimed.

"So am I, but I don't feel like setting up house again. I'm certain you'd go and get married the moment we'd settled into a place. . . ."

"I'm not a marrying man, Gilbert," Henry interrupted.

"Well, what are you, Quinny?"

"I don't know!"

They were wandering aimlessly along the streets. They had drifted along Regent Street, and then had drifted into Oxford Street, and were going slowly in the direction of Marble Arch.

"Quinny!" said Gilbert after a while.

"Yes?" Henry answered.

"Have you . . . have you seen Cecily since you came back?"

"Yes. Twice!"

Gilbert did not ask the question which was on the tip of his tongue, but Henry was willing to give the answer without being asked.

"She didn't appear to know I'd been away," he said.

"She knew all the same! . . ."

"She just said, 'Hilloa, Paddy!' and went on talking to the other people who were there too. I tried to outstay them, but Jimphy came in the first time, and there was a painter there the second time, who wouldn't budge. He's painting her portrait. I've not seen her since. . . ."

"You're glad, aren't you, that I kidnapped you, Quinny?"

"In a way, yes!"

"You got on with your book, anyhow. You'd never have done that if you'd stayed in town, trailing after Cecily!"

"I can't quite make you out, Gilbert," Henry said, turning to his friend. "Are you in love with Cecily?"

Gilbert nodded his head. "Of course, I am, but what's the good? Cecily doesn't love me any more than she loves you. She doesn't love any man particularly. She's . . . just an Appetite. You and I are no more to her than . . . than the caramel she ate last Tuesday. The only hope for us is that we shall grow out of this caramel state or at all events get the upper hand of it. . . . In the meantime, what are we going to do?"

"Work, I suppose. 'Turbulence' is nearly finished, and I'm itching to get on with a new story I've thought of. I'm calling it 'The Wayward Man.' . . ."

"We might go into the country. . . ."

"Or hire a furnished flat for a while. . . ."

"Or do something. . . . Lordy God, Quinny, we're getting frightfully vague and loose-endy. We really must pull ourselves together. There's a bun-shop somewhere about. Suppose we have tea?"

10

They took a furnished flat in Buckingham Street, and lived there while Henry completed "Turbulence" and saw it through the press. Gilbert had finished another comedy soon after the production of "The Magic Casement," and Sir Geoffrey Mundane had asked for a first option on it. "The Magic Casement" was not a great popular success, but it "paid its way," as Sir Geoffrey said. It was performed for a hundred and twenty times in England, and for three weeks in America, where it failed lamentably. "I never did think much of a republic!" Gilbert said when he heard of the play's failure.

Roger and Rachel had settled in their house in Hampstead soon after Gilbert and Henry had taken the furnished flat, and after a while, some of the old routine of their lives, except that part of it represented by Ninian, went on as before. Most of Ninian's leave was spent in quelling his mother's alarms about his journey to South America. "It's a splendid chance for me, mother!" he insisted. "It's jolly decent of old Hare to give it to me!"

"But it's so far away, Ninian, dear, and if anything were to happen to you! . . ."

"Nothing'll happen to me, mother . . . nothing serious anyhow. Heaps of chaps go off to places like that without turning a hair!"

"But I've only got you, Ninian!" Mrs. Graham objected.

"You've got Mary, too, and I shall come back to you!"

One evening, as they walked along the road that leads to Sidmouth, she put her arm in his, and drew him near to her.

"Ninian, dear," she said very softly and hesitatingly as if she were afraid to say all that was in her mind.

"Yes, mother!"

"Ninian, I sometimes wish . . ."

Again she hesitated, and again he said, "Yes, mother?"

Her speech took another direction. "There have been Grahams at Boveyhayne for four hundred years, dear, and there's only you left now."

He looked at her uncomprehendingly. "Well, mother! . . ."

"My dear, we can't let it go away from us. It's us, and we're it, and if anything were to happen to you, and a stranger were to come here!"

"But, my dear mother," he interrupted, "nothing's going to happen to me, and no one's going to get Boveyhayne away from us. Why should any one? . . ."

She put her free hand on his sleeve. "When Roger married Rachel," she said, "I wished . . . I wished that you were Roger, Ninian!"

"You want me to get married, mother?"

She did not answer, but her clasp on his arm tightened.

"A chap can't marry a girl just for the sake of getting married, mother! . . ."

"No, dear, I know, but . . ."

"I've not seen a girl yet that I wanted particularly. You see, I've been awfully busy at my job! . . . I know how you feel, mother, about Boveyhayne, and I feel like that myself sometimes. I used to think it was rather rot all this talk about Family and keeping on and . . . and that kind of thing, but I can't help feeling proud of . . . of all those old chaps who went before me, and . . . all that, and I'd hate to break the line . . . only I can't just go up to a girl and . . . and say, 'We want some . . . some babies in our house!' . . ."

"No, dear, you can't say *that*, of course, but there are plenty of nice girls about, and if you would just . . . just think of some of them, instead of always thinking of works and tunnels and things! . . . Of course, I know that tunnels are very interesting, Ninian, but . . . but Boveyhayne! . . ."

She did not say any more. She stood by the gate of a field, looking over the valley of the Axe to the hilly country that separates Dorset from Devon, seeing nothing because her eyes were full of tears. He slipped his arm from hers and put it round her waist and drew her close to him. "All right, mother!" he said.

"My dear!" she said, reaching up and kissing him.

11

They dined together on Ninian's last night in England. Rachel, with fine understanding, insisted that they should dine alone, although they urged her to join them.

"I say, you chaps," Ninian said to them, "you might go and see my mater sometimes. She'd be awfully glad. Quinny, you haven't been to Boveyhayne for centuries. . . . If you'd go, now and then, you'd cheer the mater up. She's awfully down in the mouth about me going!"

"Righto, Ninian!" said Gilbert.

"Mary was saying what a long time it was since you were there, Quinny," Ninian went on.

"Did she?" Henry answered.

"Yes. I hope you'll go down sometime."

"I will," he said.

THE SECOND CHAPTER

1

MRS. GRAHAM invited Gilbert and Henry to spend Christmas at Boveyhayne, and they gladly accepted her invitation, but a week before they were due to go to Devonshire, Mr. Quinn fell ill, and Henry, alarmed by the reports which were sent to him by Hannah, wrote to Mrs. Graham to say that he must travel to Ireland at once. He hurried home to Ballymartin, and found that his father was more ill even than Hannah had hinted.

"I wouldn't have let her send for you, Henry!" he said, apologetically, "only I was afraid . . . I mightn't see you again!"

He tried to cheer his father by protesting that in a little while he would be astride his horse again, directing the farm experiments as vigorously as ever, but Mr. Quinn shook his head. "I don't think so, Henry!" he said. "I'll not be fit for much anyway. You'll have to lend a hand with the estate, my son."

"I'll help all I can, father, but I'm not much of an agriculturist! . . ."

"Well, you can't be everything. That new book of yours . . . the one you sent me the other day! . . ."

" 'Turbulence,' father?"

"Aye. It's a gran' book, that. I'd like well to be able to write a book of that sort. I'm proud of you, Henry!"

Henry blushed and turned away shyly, for direct praise always embarrassed him, but he was very pleased with his father's praises which gave him greater pleasure than the praises of any one else, even Gilbert.

"You'll stay home a while, now you're here, Henry, son, won't you?"

"Yes, father, as long as you like!"

"That's right. You'll be able to work away here in peace and quietness. Nobody'll disturb you. I suppose you're started on another book?"

Henry told him of "The Wayward Man." . . .

"That's a great title," he said. "You're a gran' one at gettin' good titles for your books, Henry. I was readin' a bit in the paper about you the other day, an' I near wrote to the man an' told him you were my son, I was that pleased. Ease this pillow under my head, will you? Thanks, boy!"

He took Henry's hand in his. "I'm right an' glad to have you home again," he said, smiling at him. "Right an' glad!"

2

The whole of "The Wayward Man" was completed before Mr. Quinn was well enough to move about easily. Henry spent the morning and part of the afternoon on his novel, giving the rest of the day to his father. Sometimes, in his walks, Henry met young farmers and labourers returning from the Orange Hall where they had been doing such drill as can be done indoors. On Saturday afternoons, they would set off to join other companies of the Ulster Volunteer Force in a route march. Jamesey McKeown had begun to learn wireless telegraphy and was already expert with flag-signals and the heliograph. Peter Logan, who had married Sheila Morgan, had been promoted to be a sergeant. . . . "I suppose Sheila's a nurse?" Henry said to him the first time he met him.

"She's nursin' a wean, Mr. Henry!" Logan replied,

winking heavily. "We've a couple already, an' there'll be another afore long. She's as punctual as the clock, Sheila. She's a great woman for fine, healthy childher!"

"Well, that's what you want, isn't it?" Henry said.

"Aye, you're right, sir. You are, indeed. There's nothin' til beat a lot of young childher about the house. Will you come an' see the drill? . . ."

Henry went to see a display in a field just outside Bally-martin. The men marched and counter-marched, and charged and skirmished, and did physical drill until they were tired and sweating, while their women looked on in pride and pleasure. Sheila was there, too, and Henry went to her and sat beside her while the military man-œuvres took place. She made no impression on him now . . . he saw her simply as a countrywoman in the family way . . . a little blowsy and dishevelled and red with exertion.

"For dear sake, Henry!" she said in greeting, holding out her hand to him.

"Well," he said, "when does the war begin?"

"Aw, now," she answered, "don't ask me! Sure, I'm never done coddin' Peter about it. But it's the grand health, Henry. You'd never believe the differs it's made to that wee lad, Gebbie, that serves in Dobbin's shop. I declare to my God, he had a back as roun' as a hoop 'til they started these Volunteers, but now he's like a ramrod. He's a marvel, that lad! Teeshie Halpin's taken a notion of him since he straightened up, an' as sure as you're living she'll have him the minute they can scrape a few ha'pence thegether to buy a wheen of furniture. Well, if the Volunteers never does no more nor that, they'll have done well, for dear knows, Andy Gebbie was an affront to the Almighty, an' him stoopin' that way!"

"But are they going to fight, Sheila? . . ."

"Ah, get away with you, man!" said Sheila. "What in the name of all that's good an' gracious, would they be fightin' for? Sure, they're lettin' on, to frighten the Eng-

lish out of their wits!'' She changed the talk to more
interesting discourse. "I've two childher now," she said.
"So Peter was telling me," he answered.
"A wee boy an' a wee girl. An' terrible wee tories they
are, too! They're about somewhere with their aunt Kate.
An' how an' all are you, Henry?''
"I'm very well, Sheila."
"You're lookin' gran'. I hear you write books, but I
never read noan of them!''
"Would you like to read them?'' he askea.
"I would, fine. Dear, oh, I often wonder how anybody
can write books. I never was no hand at writin' anything, not even a letter. But I suppose there's a knack in
it, an' once you learn it, you're all right!''
"Yes," he replied, "that's about it. I'll send my books
to you. I'd have sent them before if I'd thought you'd
care to read them!''
"You might 'a' knowed rightly, I'd be glad to have
them. . . .''

3

But Sheila's good-natured scorn for the Ulster Volunteer
Force did not convince Henry. One could not look at these
drilling men, and feel satisfied that they were pretending
to be angry or that they did not mean what they said, when
they declared that they would die in the last ditch rather
than consent to be governed by Nationalists. Mr. Quinn
spent much time in denouncing Sir Edward Carson and
his friends, but he did not doubt for a moment that the
followers would fight. He had very little faith in the sincerity of the politicians. "That fellow, F. E. Smith," he
exclaimed wrathfully, "what in hell is he doin' over here,
I'd like to know? I'd like to kick his backside for him, an'
pack him back to wherever he come from!'' And there
was F. E. Robinson, too, bounding about Ulster like a
well-polished young gentleman from the Gaiety chorus,

and delivering historical orations that filled the crowd with amazement.

"He's the great cod, that lad!" Mr. Quinn said. "He's worse nor Smith. He come down here to Ballymartin, an' he made a speech all about King James's foreign policy, and mentioned a whole lot of people that the Or'ngemen never heard tell of. It would 'a' done well for a lecture at the Queen's College . . . you should 'a' seen the men nudgin' one another, an' askin' who he was, an' what in the name of God he was talkin' about! 'Why doesn't he curse the Pope an' 'a' done wi' it!' one fellow said to another. 'That lad curse anybody!' says the other one. 'Sure, he'd hear boak[1] himself if he done the like of that!' Aye, there's a lot of bletherin' about the Volunteers, but all the same I don't like the look o' things, an' if they're not careful there'll be bother. It'll take the men at the top all their time to hold the bottom ones down. It ought never to have been allowed to begin with. The minute they started their drillin' an' palaver, they ought to 'a' been stopped. Have you seen John Marsh lately, Henry?"

"I saw him when I was in Dublin a few months ago with Gilbert Farlow. He's drilling, too! . . ."

"It's fearful, that's what it is. Fightin' an' wranglin' like that! I wish I could get him up here a while. I'd talk to him, an' try an' put some sense into him. Do you think would he come if I was to ask him?"

"I daresay, father. Shall I write to him for you?"

"Aye, do, Henry. I like that fellow quaren well, an' I'd be sorry if any harm come to him. He's the sort gets into any bother that's about! Write to him now, will you, an' you'll catch the evenin' mail!"

Henry got writing materials and wrote the letter in his father's room. "Will that do?" he said, passing it to Mr. Quinn for inspection.

"That'll do fine," Mr. Quinn replied, when he had finished reading it. "Matier'll take it to the letter-box!"

"I don't know what the world's comin' to," he went on,
a little fractiously. "There's a fellow wouldn't harm a
fly, drillin' and gettin' ready to shoot people. An' Irish
people, too! One lot of Irishmen wantin' to shoot another
lot! . . . They're out of their minds, that's what's wrong
wi' them. There's Matier . . . you'd think at his age, he'd
have more sense, but nothin'll do him but he must be off
of an evenin' formin' fours. And what for? I'd like to
know. I says to him, 'William Henry, who do you want
to kill?' 'The Home Rulers an' the Papishes!' says he.
'Quit, man,' says I, 'an' talk sense.' 'I am talkin' sense,'
says he. 'You're not,' I says to him. 'D'you mean to
stan' there an' tell me you want to kill Hugh Kearney?'
'I do not indeed,' says he. 'What put that notion in your
head?' 'Isn't he a Catholic an' a Home Ruler?' says I.
I had him properly when I said that, for him an' Hugh
Kearney is like brothers to one another. 'Would you kill
him?' I says to Matier. 'No, sir, I wouldn't,' he answers
me back. 'I'd shed me heart's blood for him!' And he
would, too! . . . I've always been against Home Rule,
Henry, an' you know well why, but I'm more against this
sort of thing than I am against that, and anyway I'm
not so sure it wouldn't be better in the long run. There's
too much Socialism in England, an' we have to put
up with the results of it because of the Union. The Socialists get this law an' that law passed, an' we have
to suffer it in Ireland because we're tied up to England. . . ."

4

John Marsh came to Ballymartin. Henry had sent a
private note to him, urging him to accept his father's
invitation. *"He's very ill,"* he wrote, *"and he would like
to see you. I'm afraid he may not get better, although
there's a chance. . . ."*

"There you are, John Marsh!" Mr. Quinn said to him, as he entered the bedroom. "An' what damned nonsense are you up to now, will you tell me?"

John smiled at him. "You're to get well at once," he answered. "We can't have you lying ill at a time like this!"

"An' aren't you an' the like of you enough to make any man ill? Come here to me, an' let me have a look at you. I can't see you rightly in that light. . . . You're lookin' pale on it, John. What ails you?"

"I'm tired, that's all. I shall be all right in the morning. . . ."

"You're workin' yourself to death! That's what you're doin'. Sit down there by the side of the bed till I talk to you!"

John drew a chair up to the old man's bedside, and sat down on it as he had been bidden. Henry, anxious lest his father should overtax his strength, sat at the foot of the bed.

"An' what are you drillin' for?" Mr. Quinn demanded of John.

"We must defend ourselves, Mr. Quinn. . . ."

"Defend me granny! An' who's goin' to harm you?" Henry made a motion as if he would quieten his father, but the old man shook him off. "Leave me alone, Henry," he said, "an' let me have my say!" He turned again to John Marsh. "Isn't there the English Army to defend you if anybody tries to injure you? What call have you to start another lot of damned volunteers to be makin' ill-feelin' in the country for?"

"We must be prepared to defend ourselves," John insisted. "We can't trust the English. . . ."

And so they wrangled until Mr. Quinn, too tired to continue, sent Henry and Marsh from his room.

"Take him away an' talk to him, Henry!" he said. "He'll not be happy 'til he's in bother, that lad. Away on with you, John! . . ."

5

It was while John Marsh was at Ballymartin, that the mutiny at the Curragh Camp took place. The soldiers had been ordered to Ulster to maintain order . . . and their officers had refused to go.

"I thought you said we could depend on the English Army," John exclaimed to Mr. Quinn in very excited tones. "This looks like it, doesn't it? If they'd been ordered to march on *us*, they'd have done it quick enough. That's why we're drilling, Mr. Quinn. We've got to defend ourselves. Supposing the Ulster Volunteers attack us! . . ."

"They won't," Mr. Quinn snapped at him.

"But supposing they do, are we to sit down and let them do it? I tell you we daren't trust to the English. They'll promise everything and give nothing. That's the nature of them. They're a treacherous race! . . ."

"I wish to my God you had some sense, John Marsh," said Mr. Quinn.

"Oh, I know you think I'm a madman, but you can't deny facts, and the facts are that the English have systematically betrayed the Irish throughout their history. If there's a war on, they go down on their hands and knees and ask us to win it for them . . . they offer us the sun and the moon and the stars for our help . . . but the minute they've got over their fright, they start plotting to get out of their promises. They've done it before and they'll do it again. I want our Volunteers to be more than a defensive organisation. I want them to be an offensive organisation. If we don't look out very sharply we'll find that the English have ruined Ireland again. They've started to do it openly now. You've heard, haven't you, about the Cunard Line and Queenstown? . . ."

It appeared that the Cunard Line had abandoned Queenstown as a port of call for American liners. . . . That means absolute ruin for Queenstown! . . . Casement tried to get the Hamburg-Amerika line to send their boats instead, and they'd agreed to do so . . . all the preparations were made to welcome the first of their boats . . . and then the scheme was abandoned by the Germans. The English Foreign office got at them! . . . Oh, of course, it's only Ireland, and Irish people and Irish interests can be neglected and ruined without a blush so long as the English interests are safe. . . . More and more I'm convinced that we've got to separate from them. They're a common-minded people. You know they are! They're hucksters . . . they think in . . . in ha'porths! . . ."

6

The attempt to bring John Marsh to reason was a failure, and he went back to Dublin more resolved to make the Volunteers an offensive body than he had been when he arrived. He had seen a review of the Ulster Volunteer Force in Belfast and the setness of the men impressed him. "They'll fight all right," he said. "I don't suppose their leaders have any stomach for fighting, but the men have plenty. By God, I wish they were on our side!"

"Well, why don't you try to get them on your side?" Henry demanded. "Your notion of conciliating them is to start getting ready to fight them!"

"We have tried to conciliate them," Marsh replied. "When Carson formed his Provisional Government, some of us asked him to extend it to the whole of Ireland. Do you think we wouldn't rather have Carson than Redmond? He's got *some* stuff in him anyhow, but Redmond! . . ."

He made a gesture of contempt. "I've no use," he said, "for a man who looks so like Napoleon without being Napoleon!"

"But Carson wouldn't," he went on. "It's all very well to say 'Conciliate Ulster!' but Ulster won't let us conciliate her. The Ulster people have nothing but contempt for us, and they ram Belfast down our throats until we're

sick of it. And a lot of their prosperity is just good luck
and . . . and favour. They've been well looked after by
the English, and they're near everything . . . coalfields
and Lancashire. Do you think if Galway was where Belfast is, it wouldn't be as prosperous? If they're so almighty clever as they say they are, why don't they come
and lead us, instead of clinging on to England like a pam-
pered kid? . . .''

Henry listened patiently to John. There must, he
thought, be some powerful motive for so much passion.
He had come to look upon nationality as a contemptible
thing, a fretful preoccupation with little affairs, but when
he faced the fury of John Marsh, he could not deny that
this passion, whether it be little or big, will bring the world
to broils until it be satisfied. He did not now feel that
irritation which he had formerly felt when John derided
the English or called them by opprobrious names. He could
make allowances for the anger of the dispossessed. ''That
kind of talk,'' he thought, ''kills itself. Marsh has only to
let himself go along enough, and he'll let himself go altogether. He'll exhaust his abuse. . . .''

He remembered that when Gilbert and he had arrived
in Dublin after their flight from London, they had tried
to discover just what Marsh and his friends meant to do
with Ireland when they had gained control of the country
. . . but Marsh and his friends had no plans. They talked
vaguely of the national spirit and of self-government, but
they could not be induced to name a specific reform to
which they would set their minds. Some one had given a
copy of Dale's Report of Irish Elementary Education to
Henry, and he had read it with something like horror. It
seemed to him that here was the whole Irish problem, that
when this was solved, everything was solved . . . but when
he spoke of it to Marsh and his friends he found that
most of them had never heard of Dale's Report, were
scarcely aware of the fact that there was an Irish education problem. ''We'll deal with that after we've got

Home Rule," they would say, waving their hands in the airy fashion in which futile people always wave their hands. And so it was with everything else. They would deal with that *after* they had got Home Rule. Gilbert and Henry had explored the Combe and the dreadful swamp of slums reaching up from Ringsend and spilling almost into the gardens of Merrion Square. . . .

"But don't they know about this?" Gilbert asked in amazement. "I mean, haven't they any eyes . . . or noses?"

"They'll deal with that *after* they've got Home Rule," Henry answered miserably.

They had gone back to their lodgings in a state of deep depression. Wherever one went in Dublin, one was followed by little whining children, demanding alms in the cadging voice of the professional beggar, and many of them were hopelessly diseased. . . .

"I thought the Irish were very religious and moral?" Gilbert said once, as they passed a group of sickly children sitting at the entrance to a court of Baggot Street.

"Why?" Henry replied.

"These kids are syphilitic," Gilbert answered. "The place is full of syphilis!"

"Dublin is a garrison town and a University town," said Henry, with a shrug of his shoulders. "There are eight barracks in Dublin . . . it's the most be-barracked city in the Kingdom. . . . Oh, we're terribly moral, we Irish. As moral as ostriches. If you pick up a Dublin newspaper, it's a million to one you'll see a reference to 'the innate purity of the Irish women,' written probably by a boozy reporter. No, Gilbert, you're wrong about these kids. They're not syphilitic. . . . Good Lord, no! That's English misgovernment. Wait 'til they've got Home Rule . . . and those kids won't be syphilitic any more! . . ."

They had met a man at Ernest Harper's who wore the kilt of the Gael, and had listened to him while he bleated about the beautiful purity of the Irish women. He was a convert to Catholicism and Nationalism and anti-Englishism, and he had the appearance of a nicely-brought-up saint. "He looks as if he had just committed a miracle, and is afraid he may do it again!" Gilbert whispered to Henry. This man purred at them. "The priests have kept Ireland pure," he murmured. "Many harsh things have been said about them, but no one has ever denied that they have kept Ireland pure!"

"I do," said Henry, full of desire to shock the Celt.

"You do? . . ."

"Anybody can keep a man pure by putting him in prison. That's what the priests have done. They've put the Irish people in gaol! . . ."

The kilted Celt shrank away from him. He was sorry, but he could not possibly sit still and listen to such conversation. He hoped that he was as broad-minded as any one, but there were limits. . . . Very wisely, he thought, the Church! . . .

"Blast the Church!" said Henry, and the kilted Celt had gone shivering away from him.

"That kind of person makes me foam at the mouth," Henry muttered to Gilbert. "The Irish people aren't any purer than any other race. It's all bunkum, this talk about their 'innate purity.' If you clap the population into gaol, you can keep them 'pure,' in act anyhow, and if the priests won't let the sexes mingle openly, they can get up a spurious purity just like that. If a girl gets into trouble in Ireland, she goes to the priest and confesses, and the priest takes jolly good care that the man marries her. That's why the rate of illegitimacy is so low. And anyhow, the bulk of the people are agricultural, and country people are more continent than any other people. It's the same in England, but the English don't go about bleating of their 'innate purity.' I tell you, Gilbert, the trouble with this country is self-consciousness. . . ."

"Home Rule ought to cure that!" said Gilbert.

"That's why I'm a Home Ruler," Henry replied. "If

you chaff these people, they get angry and want to fight. If anybody were to get up in a public hall and say about the Irish one-quarter of the things that Bernard Shaw says in public about the English, the audience would flay him alive and wreck the building. They're too little to stand chaff easily. It takes a big people to bear criticism good-naturedly. . . . All the same, Gilbert, your damned countrymen are to blame for all this!"

"I know that," said Gilbert, "but your damned countrymen seem determined to remain like it!"

8

Mr. Quinn and Henry had talked of Ireland and of John Marsh, after John had returned to Dublin.

"Sometimes," said Mr. Quinn, "I think that the best thing for Ireland would be to let the two sides fight. That might bring them together. One damned good scrap . . . and they might shake hands and become reconciled. There was as much antagonism and bitterness between the North and South in America as there is between the North and South in Ireland . . . and on the whole, I think the Civil War did a lot of good!"

"It's a damned queer country, Henry!" he went on, lying down and drawing the bedclothes up about his neck. "Damned queer!"

"I suppose they all know what they're up to," he continued, looking intently at the ceiling. "But I don't!"

"Are you comfortable, father?" Henry asked, bending anxiously over Mr. Quinn who had a grey, tired look on his face.

"Yes, thank you, Henry, I'm . . . I'm comfortable enough!" He turned his head slightly and gazed at Henry for a few moments without speaking. Then he smiled at him. "I tried hard to make an Irishman out of you, Henry," he said.

"I am an Irishman, father!"

"Aye, but a *very* Irishman. Many's a time I wonder what you are. What are you, Henry? You're not English an' you're not Irish. What are you?"

"I don't know, father. I'm very Irish when I'm in England, and I'm very English when I'm here!"

"That's no good, Henry. All you do is to make both sides angry. You should be something all the time!"

"I try to be fair," said Henry.

"That'll not lead you very far. Well, well, the world's the world, and there's an end of it!"

9

Sitting in the garden that evening, looking towards the hazy hills, Henry wondered, too, what he was. Indeed, he told himself, he loved Ireland, but then he loved England, also. Once, when he was in Trinity, he had trudged up into the mountains, and had sat on a stone and gazed down on the city and, beyond it, to the sea, and while he had sat there, a great love of his country had come into his heart, and he had found himself irrationally loving the earth about him, just because it was Irish earth. He had tried to check this love which was conquering him, and he had scraped up a handful of earth and rubbed his fingers in it. "Soil," he had murmured aloud. "Just soil . . . like any other soil!" and then, suddenly, overpoweringly, irresistibly, something had quickened in him, and while he was murmuring that the earth he had scraped up was "just soil," he had raised it to his lips and had kissed it. . . . And as quickly as the impulse to kiss the earth came to him, came also revulsion. "That was a sloppy thing to do," he said to himself, and he flung the earth away from him.

He had stayed there until the evening, lulled by the warm wind that blew about the mountains, and soothed by the soft, kindly smell of burning turf. There was an odour of smouldering furze near by, and the air was full of pleasant sounds: the rattle of carts, the call of a man to a dog, the whinnying of horses and the deep lowing of cows. He turned on his side and looked seawards. The sun had set in a great field of golden cloud, throwing splashes of light down the sides of the mountains and turning little rain-pools into pools of fire; but now the dusk was settling down, and as Henry looked towards the sea, he saw lights shining out of the houses, making warm and comforting signals in the dark. Dublin lay curled about the Bay, covered by smoke that was pierced here and there by the chimney-stacks of factories. There, beneath him, were little rocking lights on the boats and ships that lay in Kingstown Harbour or drifted up and down the Irish Sea, and over there, across the Bay, the great high hump of Howth thrust itself upwards. A tired ship sailed slowly up to the city, trailing a long line of white foam behind her. . . . He stood up and looked about him; and again the love of Ireland came into his heart, and this time he did not try to check it. He yielded to it, giving himself up to it completely. . . .

"You can't help it," he murmured to himself. "You simply can't help it! . . ."

But he loved England, too. There had been nights when he had loved London as a man might love his mother . . . when the curve of the Thames, and the dark shine of its water against the arches of Waterloo Bridge, and the bulging dome of St. Paul's rising proudly out of the haze and smoke, and the view of the little humpy hills at Harrow that was seen from the Hampstead Heath . . . when all these became like living things that loved him and were loved by him. Once, with Gilbert, he had wandered over Romney Marsh, from Hythe to Rye, and had felt that Kent and Sussex were as close to him as Antrim and Down. And Devonshire, from north and south, was friendly and native to him. He had tramped about Exmoor and had seen the red deer running swiftly from the hunt, and had climbed a bare scarp of Dartmoor, startling the wild ponies so that they ran off with their long tails flying in the air, scattering the flocks of sheep in their flight. The very names of the Devonshire rivers were like homely music to him, and he would say the names over to himself for the pleasure of their sound: Taw and Tamar and Torridge, the Teign and the Dart and the Exe, and the rivers about Boveyhayne, the Sid and the Otter, the Coly, the Axe and the Yarty. . . .

"I'm not de-nationalised," he insisted. "I love Ireland and England. I'm part of them and they are part of me, and we shall never be separate. . . ."

10

He had stayed at Ballymartin until he had completed "The Wayward Man." His father's health had varied greatly, but soon after the publication of the new novel, it mended and, although he did not recover his old strength and vigour, he was well enough to move about and superintend the work on his farm.

"You can go back to London now, Henry!" he said to his son one morning, after breakfast. "I know you're just itchin' to get back there, an' I'm sure I'm sick, sore an' tired of the sight of you. Away off with you, now!" And Henry, protesting that he did not wish to go, had gone to London. Gilbert's second comedy, "Sylvia," had been produced by Sir Geoffrey Mundane and, like "The Magic Casement," had achieved a fair amount of success. "But I haven't done anything big yet," Gilbert complained to Henry. "My aim's better than it was, but I'm still missing the point. Perhaps the next one will hit it. . . ."

In London, Henry began "The Fennels," but after he had written a couple of chapters, he found himself unable to proceed with it.

"I must go back to Ireland," he said to Gilbert. "I want the feel of Ulster. I can't get it into this book unless

I'm there, somehow!'' And so, sooner than he had anticipated, he returned to Ballymartin, where ''The Fennels''
was finished, and there he stayed until Gilbert wrote and
asked him to join him at Tre'Arrdur Bay.

''You can't get much nearer to Ireland than that,''
he wrote: ''You hop into the boat at Kingstown and hop
out of it again at Holyhead and there you are! . . .''

''I shall be back again in a month, father!'' he had
said to Mr. Quinn, and then he had taken train to Belfast, where he was to change for Dublin and thence go to
Wales.

In Belfast, there was great excitement because the Ulster
Volunteers had successfully landed a cargo of guns that
were purchased in Germany. The Volunteers had seized
the coastguard stations at Larne and at Donaghadee and
Bangor, overawing the police, and there had been much
jocularity. It was all done in excellent taste. Had it not
been for the death of a coastguard through heart failure,
there would have been nothing to mar the jolly entertainment. . . .

11

''I suppose John Marsh was sick about the gun-running
in Ulster?'' said Gilbert to Henry, as they approached the
hotel at Tre'Arrdur Bay at which they were to stay.

''No, I don't think so. He seemed to think it was rather
fine of the Ulstermen to do it. You see, it's put the Government in a hole, and that pleases him. He was very
mysterious in his talk, and full of hints! . . .''

''Are they going to run guns, too?'' Gilbert asked.

''I shouldn't be surprised,'' said Henry. ''One of
these days a gun'll go off, and then they'll stop playing
the fool, I suppose!''

THE THIRD CHAPTER

1

"ROGER'S getting all his facts in fine trim for the book on a National Army," Gilbert said after lunch. "The thing's been much bigger than any of us imagined, but Roger's a sticker, and he's got a lot done!"

"I'd nearly forgotten about that business," Henry replied.

"Roger hasn't forgotten. He's been spending a great deal of time in Bermondsey lately, and I shouldn't be surprised if the local Tories adopt him as their candidate at the next election. I don't suppose he'll get in. It'll be a pity if he doesn't. Rachel's making it easier for him. Roger says she's popular with the girls in the jam factories . . . and of course that's very useful. You see, Rachel tells the girls to tell their mothers to tell their fathers to vote for Roger when the time comes, and the fathers'll have to do it or they'll get a hell of a time from their women. I can tell you, Quinny, Rachel knows what's what. She's going to ask some of the jam-girls out to tea and show them the baby! . . ."

"Good old British Slop, Gilbert! Do you remember how we swore that we would never have anything to do with Slop? . . ."

"We've had a lot to do with it. Roger was right. The Slop is there and you've got to make allowances for it, and after all, why shouldn't Rachel show her baby to the girls? Damn it all, a baby is a remarkable thing, when you come to think of it. All that wriggle and bubble and squeak and kick . . . and Lord only knows what'll come

out of it! We ought to get married, Quinny, and father
a few brats. My own notion is to get hold of a nice,
large, healthy female of the working-class and set her up
in a very ugly house in a very ugly suburb, near a municipal park, and give her three pounds a week for herself,
and an allowance for every child she produces. I could
have all the pride and pleasure of parenthood without
the boredom and nuisance of being a husband, and the
youngsters would probably be young giants. The girl
wouldn't mind how many she had, and she'd feed 'em
herself. There'd be no damned bottle and no damned lim-
itation. And I'd put all the boys in the Navy, and I'd
make cooks out of the girls . . . *cooks*, Quinny, not food-
murderers, and I'd call the first boy Michael John, and
the second boy Patrick James and the third boy Peter
William and the fourth boy Roger Henry Gilbert Ninian. . . ."

"And what would you call the girls?"

"Wait a minute! I haven't done with the boys yet.
And I'd call the fifth boy Matthew. I'd call the first girl
Margaret, and the second girl Bridget, and the third girl
Rachel, and the fourth girl Mary, and I'm damned if I
know what I'd call the fifth girl, so I'd let her mother
choose her name. And they'd all know how to swim, and
manage a boat, and box, and whistle with two fingers in
their mouths, and the girls' chief ambition would be to
get married and have babies. They'd have a competition
to see who could have the most. And their husbands would
all be big, hearty men. Margaret would marry a black-
smith, and Bridget 'ud marry a fisherman, and Rachel 'ud
marry a farmer, and Mary'd marry a soldier and the
other one would marry a sailor. Mary's man 'ud be a
sergeant-major, a fat sergeant-major, and the other one's
'ud be a boatswain or a chief gunner. I'd have so
many grandchildren that I'd never be able to remember
which were mine and which belonged to the man next
door! . . ."

"You'd want a great deal of money for that lot, Gilbert!"

"I suppose I would. But I think that men of quality ought to have children by strong, healthy women of the working-class. I think there's a lot to be said for the right of the lord, don't you? It was good for the race . . . kept up the quality of the breed! I shall have to think seriously about this. . . ."

"You'd better look out for a farmer's daughter while you're here," Henry suggested.

"What! A Welshwoman! Good God, no!! My goodness, Quinny, you ought to bring that fellow, John Marsh, to Wales for a few months. That 'ud cure him of his Slop about nationality. I came to Wales, determined to like the Welsh, and I've failed. That's all. I've failed hopelessly. I told myself that it was absurd to believe that a whole nation could be as bad as English people say the Welsh are . . . but it isn't absurd . . . of the Welsh anyhow. They're all that everybody says they are, only about ten times worse. I've been all over this country one time and another, and they're simply . . . mean. They're a dying race, thank heaven! They've kept themselves to themselves so much that their blood is like water, and so they're simply perishing. They wouldn't absorb or be absorbed . . . and so they're just dying out. Your lot were wiser than the Welsh, Quinny!"

"The Irish?"

"Yes. They absorbed all the new blood they could get into their veins, and so, whoever else may perish, the Irish won't. This nationality business is all my eye, Quinny. You don't want one strain in a country. You want hundreds of strains. You want to mingle the bloods. . . . I don't believe there's a pure-blooded Irishman in Ireland or out of it. . . . Oh, the Welsh! Oh, the awful Welsh! Inbreeding in a nation is the very devil . . . and it makes 'em so damned uncivil. Oh, a shifty, whining race, the Welsh! . . ."

2

There are many bays on that coast, and in one of these, where they could easily get to deep water, they bathed every morning, drying themselves in the sun when they were tired of swimming. They would haul themselves out of the sea by clutching at the long tassels of sea-weed, and then lie down on the bare, warm rocks while the sun dried the salt into their skins. Once, while they were lying in this fashion, Gilbert turned to Henry and said, "Have you been to Boveyhayne at all since Ninian went away?"

"No," Henry answered. "I was to have gone with you that Christmas, but my father's illness prevented me, and I haven't been since."

"Why don't you go? They'd be glad to see you, and Ninian'd like it."

"I must go one of these days. How is Mrs. Graham? I suppose you've seen her lately?"

"She was all right when I saw her. Mary's rather nice!"

Henry did not say anything, and Gilbert, having waited for a while, went on.

"I always thought you and Mary. . . ."

He broke off suddenly and sat up. "It's getting a bit chilly," he said. "I think I'll dress!"

"There's no hurry, Gilbert," Henry answered. "You didn't finish what you were saying."

"It's none of my business. I've no right to. . . ."

"Oh, yes, you have, Gilbert," Henry interrupted, sitting up too. "Go on!"

"Well, I always thought that you and Mary were . . . well, liked each other. That was why I was so puzzled when you got fond of Cecily. I felt certain that you'd marry Mary. Why don't you, Quinny? She's an awfully nice girl, and you and she are rather good pals, aren't you?"

"I don't know, Gilbert. I think I love Mary better

than any one I've ever met, and yet I seem to lose touch
with her very easily!"

"Oh, I shouldn't count Cecily. Cecily is anybody's
sweetheart! . . ."

"But it wasn't only Cecily. There was a girl . . . a
farm-girl in Antrim. I never told you about her. Her
name was Sheila Morgan . . . she's married now . . . and
I went straight from Mary to her. Of course, I was a kid
then, but still I'd told Mary I was fond of her, and we'd
arranged to get married when we grew up . . . and then
I went home and made love to Sheila Morgan!"

"None of these women held you, Quinny!" said Gilbert.

"No, that's true, and Mary has, although I seldom see
her. I thought that I could never love anybody as I
loved Sheila Morgan . . . until I met Cecily . . . and
then I thought I should never love any one as I loved her
. . . but somehow Cecily doesn't hold me now, and Mary
does. I can't tell you when I ceased to love Cecily . . .
I don't really know that I have ceased to love her . . . it
just weakened, so gradually that I did not notice it weakening. All the same, if I were to see Cecily now, I should
probably want her as badly as ever."

"You might, Quinny, but you wouldn't go on wanting
her. You see, she wouldn't want you for very long, and
my general opinion is that you can't keep on giving if you
get nothing in return . . . unless, of course, you're a one-
eyed ass. A healthy, intelligent man, if he loves a woman
who doesn't love him . . . well he goes off and loves some
one else . . . and quite right, too. These devoted fellows
who cherish their blighted affections forever . . . damn it,
they deserve it. They've got no imagination! I don't
think Cecily'd hold you now, Quinny, not for very long
anyhow. I wish you'd marry Mary. You quite obviously
love her, and she quite obviously loves you. . . . Oh, Lordy
God, I wish I could love somebody. I wish I were a young
man in a novelette, with a nice, clear-cut face and crisp,
curly hair and frightfully gentlemanly ways and no brains

so that I could get into the most idiotic messes. . . . Why aren't there any aphrodisiacs for men who cannot love any one in particular, Quinny! If you'd had the sense to have a sister, I should probably have married her. Roger's family runs to nothing but males, and Rachel can't honestly recommend any of her female relatives to me. If I thought Mary'd have me, I'd marry her, but I know she wouldn't. I used to think it was awful to want to believe in God and not be able to believe in Him, but it's a lot worse to want to love and not be able to love. I shall have to marry an actress. That's all!"

They dressed in the shelter of the rocks, and then went back to the hotel to lunch.

"I'd like to marry Mary! . . ." Henry began.

"Why don't you, then?" Gilbert interrupted.

"Because I feel that I must go to her absolutely undivided, Gilbert. Do you know what I mean? I want to be able to go to her, knowing that no other woman can sway me from her for a second. It would be horrible to be married to her and feel something lurking inside me, just waiting for a chance to spring out and . . . and make love to some one else!"

"You've changed a lot, Quinny, since the days when you pleaded for infinite variety. You wanted a wife for every mood! . . ."

Henry laughed. "We did talk a lot of rot when we first went to London," he said, putting his arm in Gilbert's.

"It wasn't all rot. My contributions to the discussion were very sensible. I wonder what's the excitement up there! The papers are in! . . ."

There was a group of visitors sitting on the seats in front of the hotel and they were reading the newspapers which had just been sent out from Holyhead.

"Let's go and ask," Henry exclaimed, and they both went on more quickly.

"Any news?" Gilbert shouted as they mounted the steps
leading from the carriage-way to the terrace.

"Yes. Bad news from Ireland," a visitor answered.

"From Ireland!" Henry said.

"Yes. The Nationalists landed some guns at
Howth! . . ."

"Yes, yes!" Henry said excitedly.

"And there was a scrap between the people and soldiers! . . ."

"The soldiers!"

The visitor nodded his head. "Some damned ass," he
said, "had ordered the soldiers out, and . . . well, there
was a row. The crowd stoned the soldiers . . . and soldiers are human like anybody else . . . they fired on the
crowd! . . ."

"Fired on them?"

"Yes. Several people were killed. It's a bad business,
a damned bad business! . . ."

3

There was an unreasonable fury in Henry's heart. "It's
a clever joke when the Ulster people do it," he said, raging at Gilbert. "And everybody agrees to look the other
way, but it's a crime when the Nationalists do it, and it
can only be punished by . . . by shooting. I suppose it's
absolutely impossible for the English to get any understanding into their thick heads! . . ."

"Don't be an old ass, Henry. You're not going to improve a rotten bad business by hitting about indiscrim-
inately. I daresay the people who were responsible for the
thing were Irishmen. I've always noticed that when anything really dirty is done in Ireland, it's an Irishman who
does it. . . ."

"A rotten Unionist! . . ."

"Irish, all the same! The only thing that you Irish

are united about is your habit of blaming the English for
your own faults and misbehaviour. If I had the fellow
who was responsible for this business I'd shoot him out of
hand. I wouldn't think twice about it. If a man is such
an ass as all that, he ought to be put out of the world
quick. But then I'm English. The Irish'll make a case out
of him. They'll orate over him, and they'll get frightfully cross for a fortnight, and then they'll do nothing.
You know as well as I do, Quinny, that the English aren't
unfriendly to the Irish, that they really are anxious to do
the decent thing by Ireland. It isn't us: it's you. We're
not against you . . . you're against yourselves. There are
about seventy-five different parties in Ireland, aren't there,
and they all hate each other like poison?"

"I wonder if John Marsh was hurt! . . ."

"I don't suppose so. There'd have been some reference to him in the paper if he'd been hurt."

"This was what he was hinting at when I saw him in
Dublin," Henry went on. "He talked about 'doubling
it' and said that two could play at that game!"

He was calmer now, and able to talk about the Dublin
shooting with some discrimination.

"I don't know why they want to 'run' guns at all," he
said. "The tit-for-tat style of politics seems a fairly foolish one. . . . I think I shall go back to Ireland to-morrow,
Gilbert. I feel as if I ought to be there. This business
won't end where it is now. I know what John Marsh and
Galway and Mineely are like. Whatever bitterness was in
them before will be increased enormously by this. Mineely's an Ulsterman, and he'll make somebody pay for
this. He doesn't say much . . . he's like Connolly . . .
Connolly's the brains behind Larkin . . . but he keeps
things inside him, deep down, but safe, so that he can
always get at them when he wants them!"

"What sort of man is he, Quinny?" Gilbert asked. "I
didn't see him when we were in Dublin."

"He looks like a comfortable tradesman, and he's a

kindly sort of chap. You'd never dream that he was an
agitator or that he'd want to lead a rebellion. I don't
believe he likes that work, either. I think that inside him
his chief desire is for a decent house with a garden, where
he can grow sweet peas and cabbages and sit in the evening
with his wife and children. He has more balanced knowledge than most of the people he works with. Marsh and
Galway have had a better education than Mineely, but they
haven't had his experience or his knowledge of men, and
so they can't check their enthusiasm. He was in America
for a long while, and he's lived in England, too. He wrote
a quite good book on the Irish Labour Movement that would
have been better if he'd made more allowance for the
nature of the times. If the employers hadn't behaved so
brutally over the strike, Mineely might have become the
solvent of a lot of ill-will in Ireland; but they made a bitter man out of him then, and I suppose it's too late now.
He'll go on, getting more and more bitter until. . . . Do
you remember that story by H. G. Wells, Gilbert, called
'In the Days of the Comet'?''

"Is that the green vapour story?"

"Yes. Well, we want a green vapour very badly in
Ireland, something to obliterate every memory and leave
us all with fresh minds!''

"Miracle-mongering won't lead you very far, Quinny.
It's no good howling for a vapour to heal you. You've
just got to take your blooming memories and cure 'em yourselves, by the sweat of your brows! And, look here,
Quinny, there doesn't seem any good reason why you
should dash back to Ireland because of this business. I
always think that the worst row in the world would never
have come to anything if people hadn't done what you
propose to do, rushed into it just because they thought
they ought to be there. They congest things . . . they
use up the air and make the place feel stuffy . . . and then
they get cross, and somebody shoves somebody else, and
before they know where they are, they're splitting each

other's skulls. If they'd only remained dispersed. . . ."

"But I'd like to be there! . . ."

"I know you would. We'd all like to be there, so's we could say afterwards we'd seen the whole thing from beginning to end. That's just why we shouldn't be there. It isn't the principals in the row that make all the trouble, Quinny . . . it's the blooming spectators! . . ."

4

He let himself be persuaded by Gilbert to stay in Wales, and they spent the next two or three days in tramping about the island of Anglesey. The days were bright and sunny, and the rich sparkle of the sea tempted them frequently to the water. There were many visitors at the hotel, some of whom were Irish people from Dublin, but mostly they came from Liverpool and Manchester; and with several of them, Gilbert and Henry became friendly. There was a schoolmaster who made a profession of mountain-climbing and a hobby of religion; and a doctor who told comic stories and talked with good temper about Home Rule, to which he was opposed; and a splendid old man, with his wife, who was interested in co-operation and was eager to limit armaments; and a wine merchant from Liverpool who had come to the conclusion that the world, on the whole, was quite a decent place to live in; and a dreadful little stockbroker who belonged to the Bloody school of politicians and talked about the Empire as if it were a music-hall; and an agent of some sort from Manchester who had reached that stage of prosperity at which he was beginning to wonder whether, after all, Nonconformity was not a grievous heresy and the Church of England a sure means of salvation. And there were others, vague people of the middle class, kindly and comfortable and inarticulate, with no particular opinions on anything except the desirability of four good meals every day and a month's holiday in the summer. There were daughters, too . . . all sorts and conditions of daughters! Some that were hearty and athletic, living either in the sea or on the golf-links; and others that were full of their sex, unable to forget that men are men and women are women, and never the two shall come together but there shall be wooing and marrying. . . . There were a few who were eager to use their minds . . . and they quoted their parents and the morning papers to Gilbert and Henry. . . .

Surprisingly, their feeling about the Howth gun-raid became cool. In that exquisite sunlight, beneath the wide reach of blue sky, it was impossible to experience rancour or maintain anger. They swam and basked and swam again, and let their eyes look gladly on young shapely girls, running across the grassy tops of the piled rocks, and were sure that there could be nothing on earth more beautiful than the spectacle of pink arms gleaming through white muslin, unless it might be the full brown ears of wheat now bending in the ripening rays of sunshine. . . . And again, after dinner, they would sit in a high, grassy corner of the bay, listening to the lap of the sea beneath them, while the stars threw their faint reflections on the returning tide. . . .

Exquisite peace and quiet, long days of rich pleasure and sweet nights of rest, kindliness and laughter and the friendly word of casual acquaintances . . . and over all, the enduring beauty of this world.

THE FOURTH CHAPTER

1

GILBERT looked up from the paper as Henry came out of the hotel.

"I say, Quinny," he said, "I think there's going to be a war!"

"A what?" Henry exclaimed.

"A war! . . ."

"But where?"

Henry sat down on the long seat beside Gilbert, and looked over his shoulder at the paper.

"All over the place!" Gilbert answered. "The Austrians want to have a go at the Serbians, and the Russians mean to have one at the Austrians, and then the Germans will have to help the Austrians, and that'll bring the French in, and . . . and then I suppose we shall shove in somewhere!"

Henry took the paper from Gilbert's hands. "But what have we got to do with it?" he said, hastily scanning the telegrams with which the news columns were filled.

"I dunno! . . ."

"It's ridiculous. . . . What's there to fight about? Damn it all, my novel's coming out in a month! What's it about?"

"You remember that Archduke chap who got blown up the other day! . . ."

"Yes, I remember!"

"Well, that's what it's about!"

"But, good God, man, they can't have a war about a thing like that. . . ."

"It looks as if they thought they could. Anyhow, they're going to try!" said Gilbert.

"Just because an Archduke got killed! Damn it, Gilbert, that's what they're for! . . ."

There was a queer look of fright in the faces of the visitors to the hotel. The boy from Holyhead had been slow in coming with the papers, and the first news that came to them came from a man who had been into the town that morning.

"There's going to be a war," he had shouted to the group of people sitting on the terrace.

"Don't be an ass!" they had shouted back at him.

"Yes, there is. The whole blooming world'll be scrapping presently!" He spoke with the queer gaiety of a man who has abandoned all hope. "Just as I was getting on my feet, too!" he went on. He suddenly unburdened himself to a man who had only arrived at the hotel late on the previous evening . . . they had never seen each other before . . . but now they were revealing intimacies. . . .

"Just getting on my feet," the man who had brought the news went on.

"It'll be very bad for business, I'm afraid! . . ."

"Bad. Goo' Lor', man, it's ruin . . . absolute ruin! I'll be up the pole, that's where I'll be. And I was thinking of getting married, too. Just thinking of it, you know . . . nothing settled or anything . . . and now . . . damn it, what they want to go and have a war for? We don't want one!"

Then the boy with the newspapers appeared, and they rushed at him and tore the papers from his bag. . . .

"By Jove!" they said, "it's . . . it's true!"

"I told you it was true. You wouldn't believe me when I told you. You know, it's a Bit Thick, that's what it is. I've been a Liberal all my life, same as my father . . . and then this goes and happens! What is a chap to do? . . ."

He wailed away, filling the air with prophecies of doom and disaster. They could hear him, as he rushed about the hotel telling the news, taking people into corners and informing them that it was a Bit Thick. There was something pitiful about him . . . he had climbed to a comfortable competence from a hard beginning . . . and something comical, too, something that made them all wish to laugh. The veneer of manners which he had acquired with so much trouble had worn off in a moment, and the careful speech, the rigid insistence on aspirates, so to speak, took to its heels. He appeared to them suddenly, carrying an atlas.

"Where the 'ell is Serbia anyway?" he demanded. "I can't find the damn place on the map!"

2

They stood about, gaping at each other, unable to realise what had happened to them. One of the windows of the drawing-room was open, and the subdued buzz of women's voices came through it to the terrace. Monotonously, exasperatingly, one querulous voice sent a fretful question through the bewildered speeches of the women . . . "But what's it about? That's what I want to know. I've asked everybody, but nobody seems to know!" Some one made an inaudible reply to the querulous voice, and then it went on: "Serbia! That's what some one else said, but we aren't Serbia. We're England, and I don't see what we've got to do with it. If they want to go and fight, let them. That's what I say! . . ."

Gilbert and Henry sat in the middle of the group on the terrace, listening to what was being said about them. They had thrown the newspapers aside . . . there was hysteria in the headlines . . . and were sitting in a sort of stupor, wondering what would happen next. The buzzing voice, demanding to be told what the war was about, still droned through the window, irritating them vaguely until the man who had first brought the news got up from his seat, and went to the window and shut it noisily.

"Damn 'er," he said, as he came back to his seat. " 'Oo cares whether she knows what it's about or not! What's it got to do with 'er any'ow. She won't 'ave to do none of the fightin'!"

Fighting!

Henry sat up and looked at the man. Why, of course, there would be fighting . . . and perhaps England would be drawn into the war, and then! . . .

A girl came out of the hotel, with towels under her arm, and called to them. "Coming to bathe?" she said.

They looked at her vacantly. "Bathe!" said Henry.

"Yes. It's a ripping morning!"

They stood up, and looked towards the sea that was white with sunshine . . . and then turned away again. It seemed to Henry as if, down there by the rocks, in a splash of sunlight, a corpse were lying . . . festering. . . . He sat down again, mechanically picking up a newspaper and reading once more the telegrams he had already read many times.

"Come along," the girl said. "You might just as well bathe!"

Gilbert looked up at her and smiled. "I was just wondering," he said, "what one ought to do!"

3

The banks had closed, and there was an alarm about money and a deeper alarm about food. . . . Panic suddenly came upon them, and in a short while, visitors began to pack their trunks in their eagerness to get home. The women felt that they would be safer at home . . . they wanted to be in familiar places. "I really ought to be at home to look after my house," a man said to Henry.

"They're a rough lot in our town, and if there's any short-age of food . . . they'll loot, of course! I don't like breaking my holiday, but! . . ."

He did not complete his sentence . . . no one ever com-pleted a sentence then . . . but went indoors. . . .

And telegrams came incessantly, telegrams calling people home, telegrams announcing that others were not coming, telegrams containing information of the war. . . .

"I suppose," said Gilbert, "if anything comes of this, we'll have to do something! . . ."

"Do something?" Henry murmured.

"Yes, I suppose so. . . ."

Perkins came to him, Perkins who had an agency in Man-chester.

"You know," he said, "I don't call this place safe. It's right on the coast . . . slap-up against the sea . . . and you know, if a German cruiser was to drop a shell right in the middle of us, we'd look damn silly, I can tell you!"

"We have a navy too," said Gilbert.

"Yes, I know all about that, but that wouldn't be much consolation to me if I was to get blown up, would it? You know, I do think they ought to draw the blinds down at night so's the light won't show out at sea. I mean to say, there's no sense in running risks, is there?"

"No . . . no, of course not!"

"I think I'll go and suggest that to the proprietor. I've just been up to Manchester to see how things are going on there. Bit excited, of course. Nobody seems to know what to do, so they just sit down and cancel everything. Silly, I call it. I went to my office to get my letters, and every blessed one was cancelling an order. I mean to say, that's no way to go on . . . losing their heads like that. And you know they'll need my stuff later on . . . if we go in!"

"Your stuff?" Henry said.

"Yes. I deal in black! . . ."

"Christ!" said Gilbert, getting up and walking away.

"Your friend seems a bit upset, doesn't he?" Mr. Perkins murmured to Henry.

4

They went into Holyhead, and wandered aimlessly about the station. Marvellously, men in uniform appeared everywhere. The reservists, naval and military, had been called up, and while Gilbert and Henry stood in the station, a large number of them went away, leaving tearful, puzzled women on the platform. That morning the boots at the hotel had been called up to join his Territorial regiment. He had been carrying a trunk on his back, when the call came to him, and, chuckling, he dropped the trunk, and skipped off to get ready. "I'm wanted," he said . . . and then he went off.

And still people went about, bemused and frightened, demanding what it was about. . . .

"We'll have to go in," some one said in the station. "I can't see how we can stay out! . . ."

"I can't see that at all," his neighbour replied. "We've got nothing to do with it!"

"If the Germans won't leave the Belgians alone! . . ."

Perkins interrupted again. "We've got a Belgian cook in our hotel," he said. "It . . . it sort of brings it all home to you, that!"

There were rumours that the working-people were resolute against the war. . . .

"And so are the employers," said Perkins. "I can tell you that. I've not met anybody yet who wants a war!"

And as the rumours flew about, they grew. One could see a rumour begin and swell and change and increase.

"I tell you what," said Perkins. "These Germans have been damn well asking for it, and I hope they'll damn well get it. I know a few Germans . . . Manchester's full of 'em . . . and I don't like 'em. As a nation, I don't like 'em. They . . . they get on my nerves, that's what they do!''

There was talk about German organisation, German efficiency, German militarism. . . .

"They don't think anything of a civilian in Germany. The soldier's everything. And women . . . oh, my God, the way they treat women! I've seen German officers . . . I've seen 'em myself . . . chaps that are supposed to be gentlemen . . . going along the street, and shoving women off the pavement! . . .''

"You know," said Perkins, "I don't really think much of the Germans myself. I mean to say, they got no initiative. That's what's the matter with 'em. Do you know what a German does when he wants to go across the street? He goes up to a policeman and asks him. And what does the policeman do? Shoves him off the pavement! . . . I'd break his jaw for him if he shoved me!''

They stayed on, wondering sometimes why they stayed, and then at midnight, a troop train steamed into the station, and a crowd of tired soldiers alighted from the carriages and prepared to embark.

"My God, it's begun!" said Perkins. "Where you chaps going to?" he asked of a soldier.

"I dunno," the soldier answered. "Ireland, I think. I 'eard we was goin' to put down these bleedin' Orangemen that's bin makin' so much fuss lately, but some'ow I don't think that's it. 'Ere, mate," he added, thrusting a dirty envelope into Perkins's hand. "That's my wife's address. I 'adn't time to write to 'er . . . we was sent off in a 'urry . . . you might just drop 'er a line, will you an' say I'm off! . . .''

"Right you are," said Perkins.

"Tell 'er I think I'm off to France, see, on'y I don't know, see! There's a rumour we're goin' to Ireland, but I don't think so. You better tell 'er that. An' I'm all right, see. So far any'ow! . . .''

"God!" said Perkins, as the soldiers moved towards the

transport, "don't it make you feel as if you wanted to cry! . . ."

In the morning, they knew that England had declared war on Germany.

"Of course," said Gilbert, "we couldn't keep out of it. We simply had to go in!"

They had gone down to the bay to bathe. "This'll be my last," Gilbert muttered as they stripped, "for a while anyhow!"

"But you're not going yet," Henry said.

"I think so," Gilbert replied. "I don't know how the trains are running, but I shall try to get back to London to-night."

"But why? . . ."

"Oh, I expect they'll need chaps. Don't you think they will?"

"Do you mean you're going to . . . enlist?"

"Yes. That seems the obvious thing to do. They're sure to need people," Gilbert answered.

"I suppose so," said Henry.

"I don't quite fancy myself as a soldier, Quinny. I'm not what you'd call a bellicose chap. I shan't enjoy it very much, and I expect I shall be damned scared when it comes to . . . to charging and that sort of thing . . . but a chap must do his share. . . ."

"I suppose so," Henry said again.

It seemed to him to be utterly absurd that Gilbert should become a soldier, that his sensitive mind should be diverted from its proper functions to the bloody business of war.

"I've always jibbed a bit when I heard people talking about England in the way that awful stockbroker in the hotel talks about it," Gilbert was saying, "and I loathe the Kipling flag-flapper, all bounce and brag and bloodies . . . but I feel fond of England to-day, Quinny, and nothing else seems to matter much. And anyhow fighting's such a filthy job that it ought to be shared by everybody that can take a hand in it at all. It doesn't seem right somehow to do your fighting by proxy. I should hate to think that I let some one else save my skin when I'm perfectly able to save it myself. . . ."

"But you've other work to do, Gilbert, more important work than that. There are plenty of people to do that job, but there aren't many people to do yours. Supposing you went out and . . . and got . . . killed? . . ."

"There's that risk, of course," said Gilbert, "but after all, I don't know that my life is of greater value than another man's. A clerk's life is of as much consequence to him as mine is to me."

"I daresay it is, Gilbert, but is it of as much consequence to England? I know it sounds priggish to say that, but some lives are of more value than others, and it's silly to pretend that they're not."

"I should have agreed with you about that last week, Quinny. You remember my doctrine of aristocracy? . . . Well, somehow I don't feel like that now. I just don't feel like it. Those chaps we saw at Holyhead, going off to France . . . I shouldn't like to put my plays against the life of any one of them. I couldn't help thinking last night, while I was lying in bed, that there I was, snugly tucked up, and out there . . . somewhere! . . ." He pointed out towards the Irish Sea . . . "those chaps were sailing to . . . to fight for me. I felt ashamed of myself, and I don't like to feel ashamed of myself. You saw that soldier giving his wife's address to Perkins? Poor devil, he hadn't had time to say 'Good-bye' to her, and perhaps he won't come back. I should feel like a cad if I let myself believe that my plays were worth more than that man's life. And anyhow, if I don't write the plays, some one else will. I've always believed that if there's a good job to be done in the world, it'll get done by somebody. If this chap fails to do it, it'll be done by some other chap. . . . Will you come into Holyhead with me and enquire about trains? There's a rumour that a whole lot of

them have been taken off. They're shifting troops
about. . . .''

6

Gilbert was to travel by the Irish mail the next day.
He had made up his mind definitely to go to London and
enlist, and Henry, having failed to dissuade him from his
decision, resolved to go to London with him. They had
talked about the war all day, insisting to each other that
it could not be of long duration. There was a while, during the first two or three days' fighting, when the Germans
seemed to have been held by the Belgians, that they had the
wildest hopes. "If the Belgians can keep them back, what
will happen when the French and British get at them?"
But that time of jubilee hope did not last long, and again
the air was full of rumours of disaster and misfortune.
The Black Watch had been cut to pieces. . . .

There was a sense of fear in every heart, not of physical
cowardice, but of doubt of the stability of things. This
horrible disaster had been foretold many times, so frequently, indeed, that it had become a joke, and novelists
had written horrific accounts of the ills that would swiftly
follow after the outbreak of hostilities. Credit would disappear . . . and all that pretence at wealth, the pieces of
paper and the scrips and shares, would be revealed at last
as . . . pieces of paper. Silver, even, would be treated with
contempt, and there would be a scramble for gold. And
people would begin to hoard things . . . and no one would
trust any one else. There would be suspicion and fear and
greed and hate . . . and very swiftly and very surely,
civilisation would reel and topple and fall to pieces. . . .
At any moment that might happen. So far, indeed, things
were still steady . . . calamity had not come so quickly as
imaginative men had foretold . . . but presently, when the
slums . . . the rich man's reproach . . . had become hun-

grier than they usually were, there would be rioting . . .
and killing. . . . One began to be frightfully conscious of
the slums . . . and the rage of desperate, starving people.
One imagined the obsessing thought in each mind: *Here we
are, eating and drinking and being waited upon . . . and
perhaps to-morrow!* . . .

But no one, in forecasting the European Disaster, had
made allowance for the obstinacy of man or taken into account the resisting power of human society. As if man,
having built up this mighty structure of civilisation, would
let it be flung down in a moment without trying to save
some of it! As if man, having in pain and bloody sweat
discovered his soul, would let it get lost without struggling
to hold and preserve it! . . .

Gilbert and Henry came into the drawing-room, where
the women were whispering to each other. Inexplicably,
almost unconsciously, their voices had fallen to whispers
. . . as if they were in church or a corpse were above in a
bedroom. . . . Four of the women were playing Bridge,
but none of them wished to play Bridge; and as Gilbert
and Henry entered the room, they put down their cards
and looked round at them.

"Is there any more news?" one of them said, and Gilbert told them of the rumours that had been heard in Holyhead.

"They say the Black Watch have been cut to pieces,"
he said.

The whispering stopped. . . . They could hear the
clock's regular tick-tick. . . .

"Oh, the poor men . . . the poor men!" an old woman
said, and her fingers began to twitch. . . .

Almost mechanically, the Bridge players picked up their
cards. "It's your lead, partner!" one of them said, and
then she threw down her cards, and rising from her chair,
went swiftly from the room.

"Oh, the poor men . . . the poor men!" the old woman
moaned.

7

They sat on the rocks after tea and while they sat there, they saw a great ship sailing up the sea, beautiful and proud and swift; and they jumped up and climbed to the highest point of the cliff to watch her go by. They knew her, for there had been anxiety about her for two days, and as they watched her sailing past, they cheered and waved their hands although no one on the great vessel could see them. A girl came running to them. . . .

"What is it?" she said.

"It's the *Lusitania*," they answered. "She's dodged them, damn them!"

"Oh, hurrah!" the girl shouted. "Hurrah! Hurrah!"

8

And then the strain lifted. The *Lusitania* had won home to safety. The Germans, greedy for this great prize, had failed to find her. Civilisation still held good . . . if the world were to go down in the fight, it would go down proudly, hitting hard, hitting until the last. . . .

THE FIFTH CHAPTER

1

It was odd, that journey from Holyhead to London, odd and silent; for all the way from Wales to Euston they passed but one train. They drove through the long stretch of England, past wide and windy fields where the harvesters were cutting the corn, through the dark towns of the Potteries, by the collieries where the wheels still revolved as the cages were lowered and raised, and then, plunging into the outer areas of London, they drove swiftly up to the station. In the evening, they went to Hampstead to see Roger and Rachel, and found them reading newspapers.

"I don't seem able to do anything else," said Roger. "I buy every edition that comes out. I read the damn things over and over, and then I read them again. . . ."

Rachel nodded her head. "So do I," she said.

A girl came in, a friend of Rachel, who had been in Finland when the war began. She had hurried home by Berlin, where she had spent an hour or two, while waiting for a train, before England declared war on Germany. . . .

"What were they like?" Gilbert asked.

"Wild with excitement. We went to a restaurant to get something to eat, and while we were there, the news came that Russia was at war with them. . . . My goodness! There was a Russian in the room, and they went for him! . . . I had my aunt with me, and I was afraid she'd get hurt, so we cleared out as quickly as we could, and when we got to the station, we had to fight to get into the train. My aunt fainted . . . and they were beastly to us, oh, beastly! I tried to get things for her, but they wouldn't give us anything! They kept on telling us we'd be shot,

and threatening us! . . . They were frightened, those big
fat men were frightened. If you'd touched them suddenly, they'd have squealed . . . like panic-stricken rab-
bits! . . ."

They sat and talked and talked, and gloom settled on
them. What was to be the end of this horrible thing which
no one had desired, but no one was able to prevent.

"I believe they all lost their nerve at the last," Roger
said, "and they just . . . just let things rip. They call
it a brain-storm in America. They lost their heads . . .
and they let things rip. My God, what a thing to have
happened!"

They sat in silence, full of foreboding, and then the girl
who had come from Finland went home.

"It's all up with the Bar, I suppose!" said Roger, when
he had let her out. "Whatever else people want to do, they
won't want to go to law. Having a youngster makes things
awkward! . . ."

"If you should need any money, Roger," said Gilbert,
"you might let me know!"

"And me, Roger!" said Henry.

"Thanks awfully!" Roger replied. "I won't forget.
I've got some, of course, and Rachel has a little. I daresay we'll manage. It can't last long. A couple of months,
perhaps! . . ."

"I can't see how it can last longer. It's too big, and
. . . oh, it can't last longer!"

"Kitchener says three years! . . ."

"He wants to be on the safe side, I suppose, but my God,
three years of . . . of that! . . ."

2

Rachel got up suddenly. "You haven't seen my baby
yet," she said.

"So we haven't," Gilbert exclaimed. "Where is it?"

"She's upstairs asleep. You must come quietly! . . ."

"It's a girl, then?" said Henry.

Rachel nodded, and led the way upstairs to the bedroom where the baby lay in her cot.

"Isn't she a darling?" she said, bending over the child.

They did not answer, afraid, as men are in the presence of a sleeping child, that they might disturb her; and while they stood looking at the cot, Rachel bent closer to her baby, and lightly kissed her cheek.

They moved away on tiptoe.

"What do you call her?" Henry whispered to Roger, as they left the bedroom.

"Eleanor," he answered. "That was my mother's name. Jolly little kid, isn't she?"

Gilbert turned and went back to the bedroom. Rachel was still bending over the baby, and she looked up at him warningly. He went up to the cot and, leaning towards Rachel, whispered, "Do you mind if I kiss her, too, Rachel? I'm going to enlist to-morrow, and perhaps I won't get so good a chance as this! . . ."

She stood up quickly and put her arms round him. "Oh, Gilbert!" she said, and then she drew him down, so that he could kiss the baby easily.

3

Henry told Roger of Gilbert's intention, while Rachel and Gilbert were in the bedroom with the baby.

"Enlist?" said Roger.

Henry nodded his head.

"Well, of course! . . ." Roger began, and then he stopped. "I suppose so," he said, moving towards the tray which Rachel had brought into the room earlier in the evening. "Whisky?" he said.

"No, thanks, Roger!" Henry answered. "He's going down to-morrow!"

"He'd better wait a few days. There's been a hell of a scrum already to join. Queues and queues of chaps, stand-

ing outside Scotland Yard all day. He'd better wait 'til
the rush is over. . . ."
"I think he'd rather like to be in the rush," Henry said.
Then Rachel came into the room, followed by Gilbert.
"Roger," she said, "Gilbert's going to enlist! . . ."
"So Quinny's just been telling me. Have a whisky,
Gilbert?"
"No, thanks, old chap," said Gilbert, "but if you have
a cigarette! . . ."
"I'll get them," Rachel exclaimed.
She brought the box of cigarettes to him, and while he
was choosing one, she said to Roger, "I was so excited when
he told me, that I got up and hugged him!"
"Good!" said Roger.

4

They walked home to Bloomsbury, where they had easily
obtained rooms, for the sudden withdrawal of Germans and
Austrians had left Bloomsbury in a state of vacancy. As
they went down Haverstock Hill towards Chalk Farm, an
old man lurched against them.
"All the young chaps," he mumbled thickly. "Thash
wot sticks in my gizzard! All the young chaps! Gawblimey, why don't they tyke the ole ones! . . ."
"Steady on," Gilbert exclaimed. catching his arm and
holding him up. "You'll fall, if you're not careful!"
"Don't marrer a damn wherrer I do or not!" He reeled
a little, and Gilbert caught hold of him again. "I woul'n
be a young chap," he muttered, "not for . . . not for nothink. You . . . you're a young chap, ain't you? Yesh
you are! You needn't tell me you ain't! I can see as
wellsh anythink! You're a young chap ri' enough. Well
. . . well, Gawd, 'elp you, young feller! Thash all I got
to sy . . . subjec!' Goo-ni', gen'lemen!" He staggered
off the pavement, and went half way across the deserted
street. Then he turned and looked at them for a few mo-

ments. "Ain't it a bloody treat, eih?" he shouted to them.
"*Ain't* it a bloody treat?"

"Drunk," said Gilbert.

Henry did not reply, and they walked on through Chalk
Farm, through Camden Town, into the tangle of mean
streets by Euston, and then across the Euston Road to
Bloomsbury. They did not speak to each other until they
were almost at their destination.

"It's awfully quiet," said Henry, turning and looking
about him.

"I don't see any one," Gilbert answered, "except that
old fellow ahead of us! . . ."

"No!"

They walked on, and when they came up to the old man,
who walked slowly, and heavily in the same direction, they
called "Good-night!" to him. He looked round at them,
an old, tired, bewildered man, and he made a gesture with
his hands, a gesture of despair. "Ach, mein freund!" he
said brokenly, and again he made the suppliant motion
with his hands.

"Poor old devil!" Gilbert muttered almost to himself.

5

They went to their rooms at once, too tired to talk to
each other, and Henry, hurriedly undressing, got into bed.
But he could not sleep. "I suppose I ought to join, too!"
he said to himself, as he lay on his back, staring at the
ceiling. "Gilbert and I could go together! . . ."

But what would be the good of that? The war would
be over quite soon. Even Roger thought it would be over
in a couple of months, and if that were so, there would be
no need for him to throw up his work and take to soldier-
ing. "It'll be over before Gilbert's got through his training. Long before! . . ."

"Anyhow, I can wait until the rush is over. I might as
well go on working as stand outside Scotland Yard all day,

waiting to be taken on. . . . Or I could apply for a commission! . . ."

He lay very still, hoping that he would fall asleep soon, but sleep would not come to him. He sat up in bed, and glanced about the room.

"I suppose," he said aloud, "they're fighting now!"

He lay down again quickly, thrusting himself well under the bedclothes and shut his eyes tightly. "Oh, my God, isn't it horrible?" he groaned.

He saw again that crowd of hurried soldiers detraining at Holyhead, thinking that perhaps they were going to Ireland, but not quite sure . . . and he could see them stumbling up the gangways of the transport, each man heavily accoutred; and sometimes a man would laugh, and sometimes a man would swear . . . and then the ship sailed out of the harbour, rounding the pier and the breakwater, churning the sea into a long white trail of foam as she set her course past the South Stack. . . . They could see the lights on her masthead diminishing as she went further away, and then, as the cold sea wind blew about them, they shivered and went home. . . . Now, lying here in this stillness, warm and snug, Henry could see those soldiers, huddled together on the ship. He could imagine them, murmuring to one another, "I say, d'ye think we *are* goin' to Ireland?" and hear one answering, "You'll know in three hours. We'll be there *then*, if we are!" and slowly there would come to each man the knowledge that their journey was not to Ireland, but to France, and there would be a tightening of the lips, an involuntary movement here and there and then. . . . "Well, o' course, we're goin' to France! 'Oo the 'ell thought we was goin' anywhere else?" The ship would carry them swiftly down the Irish Sea and across the English Channel . . . and after that! . . .

"Some of them may be dead already," he murmured to himself.

Torn up suddenly from their accustomed life, hurried

through the darkness along the length of England, and then, after long, cold nights on the sea, landed in France and set to slaying. . . .

"And they won't know what's it for?"

But did that matter? Would it be any better if they were aware of the cause of the fight? One lived in a land and loved it. Surely, that was sufficient?

In his mind, he could still see the soldiers, but always they were moving in the dark. He could see very vividly the man who had asked Perkins to write to his wife . . . and it seemed to him that he was still demanding of passers-by that they should write to her. "Tell 'er I'm all right," he kept on saying. "So far, any'ow! . . ."

He turned over on his side, dragging the clothes about his head, and tried to shut out the vision of the soldiers marching through the fields of France, but he could not shut it out. They still marched, endlessly, ceaselessly marched. . . .

6

When they got to Scotland Yard, there was a great crowd of men waiting to be enlisted.

"You'd better come again, Gilbert," Henry said. "You'll have to hang about here all day, and then perhaps you won't be reached!"

"I think I'll hang about anyhow," Gilbert answered.

He had become queerly quiet since the beginning of the War. The old, light-hearted, exaggerated speech had gone from him, and when he spoke, his words were abrupt and colourless. He took his place at the end of the file of men, and as he did so, the man in front of him, a fringe-haired, quick-eyed youth with a muffler round his neck, turned and greeted him. " 'Illoa, myte!" he said with the cheery friendliness of the East End. "You come too, eih?"

Gilbert answered, "Yes, I thought I might as well!"

"We'll 'ave to wyte a 'ell of a time," the Cockney went on. "Some of 'em's bin 'ere since six this mornin'. Gawblimey, you'd think they was givin' awy prizes. I dunno wot the 'ell I come for. I jus' did, sort of!..."

Some one standing by, turned to a recruiting sergeant and whispered something to him, pointing to the gutter-snipes in the queue.

"Fight!" said the recruiting sergeant. "Gawd love you, guv'nor, they'd fight 'ell's blazes, them chaps would!"

Henry tried again to induce Gilbert to fall out of the queue and wait until there was more likelihood of being enlisted quickly, but Gilbert would not be persuaded.

"You'll have to get something to eat," Henry urged. "They'll never get near you until this evening, and if you've got to fall out to get food, you might as well fall out now!"

"I think I'll wait," Gilbert repeated. "Perhaps," he went on, "you'll get me some sandwiches. Get a lot, will you. This chap in front of me doesn't look as if he'd brought anything!"

"You could get a commission, Gilbert, easily," Henry said.

"I don't think I should be much good as an officer, Quinny. . . . Go and get the sandwiches like a decent chap!"

Henry went away to do as Gilbert had bidden him, and after a while, he returned with a big packet of sandwiches and apples.

"I shan't wait, Gilbert," he said. "I can't stand about all day. I'll come back when the rush is over. . . ."

"But why, Quinny?"

"I'm going to join, too, with you!..."

"You're going to join? . . . That's awf'lly decent of you, Quinny!"

"Decent! Why? It isn't any more decent than your joining is!"

"P'raps not, but I always think it's very decent of an Irishman to fight for England. If there doesn't seem any chance of my getting in to-day, I'll come back to tea. There's a fellow here says this is the second day he's been waiting!"

Henry went away. He walked along the Embankment towards Blackfriars, and when he had reached the Temple, he turned up one of the steep streets that link the Embankment to Fleet Street.

"I'll go and see Delap," he said to himself.

Delap was the editor of a weekly paper for which Henry had sometimes written articles. Delap, however, was not at the office, but Bundy, the manager of the paper, who was also the financier, was there.

"It's all up with us," said Bundy. "We're closing down next week!"

"Closing down!"

"Yes. We're bust. Damn it, we're getting on splendidly, too. Just turning the corner! We should have had a magnificent autumn if it hadn't been for this. . . ."

He came away from Bundy, and walked aimlessly down Fleet Street. "Lots of other people would have had a fine autumn if it hadn't been for this," he thought to himself, and then he saw Leadenham and Crowborough, who worked on the *Cottenham Guardian*. They were very pale and tired-looking.

"Hilloa!" he said, slapping Leadenham on the back.

Leadenham jumped . . . startled! "Oh, it's you," he said, smiling weakly.

"Yes. What's up? You look frightened!" He turned to greet Crowborough.

"Well, we're all rather jiggered by this," Leadenham replied. "We're going to get something to eat. Come with us!"

They went into a tea-shop and sat down. "Is the *Guardian* all right?" Henry asked.

"Oh, yes," said Leadenham wearily, "as right as anything is. Nobody in Fleet Street knows how long his job'll last. Half the men on the *Daily Circle* have had the sack. Some of our chaps have gone! Fleet Street's full of men looking for jobs. About fifty papers have smashed up since the thing began . . . sporting papers mostly. It frightens you, this sort of thing! . . ."

He came away from Fleet Street as quickly as possible. The nervous, hectic state of the journalists made him feel nervous too.

"I'd better get among less jumpy people," he said to himself, and he hurried towards Charing Cross. And there he met Jimphy. He did not recognise him at first, for Jimphy was in khaki, and he would have passed on without seeing him, had Jimphy not caught hold of his arm and stopped him.

"Cutting a chap, damn you!" said Jimphy. . . .

"Good Lord, I didn't know you!"

"Thought you didn't. Where you going?"

"Oh, nowhere. Just loafing about. Gilbert's down at Scotland Yard trying to enlist."

"Is he, begad? Everybody seems to be trying to enlist. He'd much better try to get a commission. I'm going home now. You come with me, Quinny. Hi, hi! . . ." He hailed a taxi-cab, and, without waiting to hear what Henry had to say, bundled him into it.

"Lord," he exclaimed, as he leant back in the cab, "it's years an' years an' years since I saw you. Well, what do you think of this for a bally war, eh? Millions of 'em . . . all smackin' each other. I'm going out soon!" He leant out of the window and shouted at the driver, "Hi, you chap, hurry up, will you!

"I don't seem able to get anywhere quick enough nowadays," he said as he sat back again in his seat. "You know," he went on, "we've never been to the Empire yet, you an' me. Damned if we have! Never mind! We'll go when the War's over!"

7

There were half a dozen women in the drawing-room with Cecily when Henry and Jimphy entered it. In addition to the women, there were a photographer and Boltt. The photographer had finished his work and was preparing to depart, and Boltt was talking in his nice little clipped voice about the working-class. It appeared that the working-class had not realised the seriousness of the situation. The other classes had been quick to understand and to offer themselves, but the working-class. . . . No! Oo, noo! Boltt had written an article in the *Evening Gazette* full of gentle reproach to the working-class, but without effect. The working-class had taken no notice. "Democracy, dear ladies," said Boltt, with a downward motion of his fingers. "Democracy!" A newspaper, a Labour newspaper, had been rather rude to Boltt. It had put some intimate, he might say, impertinent, questions to Boltt, but Boltt had borne this impertinent inquisition with fortitude. He had not made any answer to it. . . .

"Hilloa, Paddy!" Lady Cecily called across the room to Henry. "Aren't you at the war?"

"Well, no, I only got to London. . . ."

"Oh, but everybody's going. Jimphy and everybody! Except Mr. Boltt, of course. He's unfit or something. Aren't you, Mr. Boltt?"

"Ah, if I were only a young man again, Lady Cecily! . . ."

"But he's writing to the papers, and that's something, isn't it?" Cecily interrupted. "And I'm making mittens for the soldiers. We're all making mittens. Except Mr. Boltt, of course."

"Who was the johnny who's just gone out?" Jimphy demanded. "Was he the chap who sells the stuff you make the mittens out of? . . ."

"Oh, no, Jimphy, he was a photographer. We're all to have our photographs in the *Daily Reflexion*. . . ."

"Except Mr. Boltt?" Henry asked maliciously.

"No, Mr. Boltt's to be in it too. Holding wool. I've been photographed in three different positions . . . beginning to knit a mitten, half-way through a mitten, and finishing a mitten. I was rather anxious to be taken with a pile of socks, but I can't knit socks! . . ."

"You can't knit mittens either," said Jimphy.

It appeared that Lady Cecily's maid was allowed to undo her mistress's false stitches and finish the mittens properly. . . .

"Well, of course, I'm not really a knitter," Cecily admitted, "but I feel I must do something for the country. I've a good mind to take up nursing. I met Jenny Customs this morning, and she says it's quite easy, and the uniform is rather nice. . . ."

"But don't you require to be trained?" Henry asked dubiously.

"Oh, yes, if you're a professional. But I'm not. I'm doing it for the country. Jenny Customs went to a First Aid Class, and learnt quite a lot about bandaging. She can change sheets while the patient is in bed, and she says he can scarcely tell that she's doing it. I should love to be able to do that. She told me a lot of things, and I really know the first lesson already. I can shake a bottle of medicine the proper way! . . ."

"Can't we have tea or something?" said Jimphy. "Oh, by the way, Cecily, Quinn says that chap Gilbert Farlow's hanging about Scotland Yard. . . ."

"Goodness me, what for?" Cecily demanded in a startled voice. "He hasn't done anything, has he?"

"No, of course he hasn't. He's trying to enlist!"

"Enlist!" she said.

"Yes. Silly ass not to ask for a commission!" said Jimphy.

Boltt burbled about the priceless privilege of youth. If only he were a youngster once again! . . .

They drank their tea, while Jimphy discoursed on the

war. Henry had entered Cecily's house with a feeling of alarm, wondering whether she would be friendly to him, wondering whether he would be able to look into her eyes and not care . . . and now he knew that he did not care. There was something incredibly unfeeling and trivial about Cecily, something . . . vulgar. While the world was still reeling from the shock of the War, she was arranging to be photographed with mittens that she had not made and could not make. The portrait would be reproduced in the *Daily Reflexion* under the title of "Lady Cecily Jayne Does Her Bit." . . . But she was beautiful, undeniably she was beautiful. As he looked at her, she raised her eyes, conscious perhaps of his stare, and smiled at him. . . .

"She'd smile at anybody," he said to himself. "If she had any feeling at all for me, she'd be angry with me!"

She came to him. "I wish you'd tell Gilbert to come and see me," she said, sitting down beside him.

"Very well," he answered, "I will!"

"I'm sure he'll look awfully nice in khaki. And I should love to see him saluting Jimphy. He'll have to do that, you know, if he's a private. . . ."

8

He got away as soon as he could decently do so, and went back to Bloomsbury. "That isn't England," he told himself, "that mitten-making, posturing crew!" and he remembered the great queues of men, standing outside Scotland Yard, struggling to get into the Army, and suffering much discomfort in the effort.

"Perhaps," he said to himself, "Gilbert's at home now. I wonder if he managed to get in!"

A man and a woman were standing at the corner of a street, talking, and he overheard them as he passed.

" 'Illoa, Sarah," the man said, "w'ere you goin', eih?"

· "Goin' roun' the awfices," she answered, "to see if I kin get a job o' charin'!"

"Gawblimey!" said the man, laughing at her.

"Well, you got to do somethink, 'aven't you? No good sittin' on your be'ind an' 'owlin' because there's a war on, is there?"

There was more of the spirit of England in that, Henry thought, than in Cecily's mitten-making. . . .

Gilbert was not at home when he reached the Bloomsbury boarding-house. "Still trying, I suppose," Henry thought.

There was a telegram for him. His father was ill again, "seriously ill," was the message, and he was needed at home.

He hurriedly wrote a note to be given to Gilbert when he returned, in case he should not see him again, but before he had begun his packing, Gilbert came in.

"It's all right," he said. "I've joined. I've had a week's leave. . . . I'm damned tired!"

"My father's ill again, Gilbert. I've just had a telegram, and I'm going back to-night! . . ."

"I'm awf'lly sorry, Quinny!" Gilbert said, quickly sympathetic.

"I met Jimphy at Charing Cross. He's in khaki. He took me back to tea. Cecily's making mittens! . . ."

"She would," said Gilbert.

"She told me to tell you to go and see her!"

"Did she, indeed?"

"You'll stay here, I suppose," Henry went on, "until you're called up?" Gilbert nodded his head. "Let me know what happens to you afterwards, will you?"

"Righto!"

"I'll come back as soon as I can, Gilbert!"

THE SIXTH CHAPTER

1

Mr. Quinn died at Christmas. The old man, weakened by his long illness, had been stunned by the War, and when his second illness seized him, he made no effort to resist it. He would lie very quietly for a long while, and then a paroxysm of fury would possess him, and he would shake his fist impotently in the air. "If they wanted a war," he shouted once, "why didn't they go and fight it themselves. They were paid to keep the peace, and . . . and! . . ."

He fell back on his pillow, exhausted, and when Henry, hurrying up the stairs to him the moment he heard the shout, reached him, he was gasping for breath. "It's all right, son!" he said when he had recovered himself. "It's all right! . . ."

"It's foolish of you, father, to agitate yourself like that," Henry said to him, putting his arms round him and lifting him into a more comfortable position. ·

"I can't help it, Henry, when I think of . . . of all the young lads! . . . By God, they'd no right to do it! . . ."

"Hush, father! . . ."

"They'd no right to do it! You'd think they were greedy for blood . . . young men's blood!" He pointed to an English newspaper lying on the floor. "Did you read that paper?" he said.

"Yes."

"Houndin' them into it," the old man went on. "Yellin' for young men! By God, I'd be ashamed . . . parsons an' women an' old men that can't fight themselves,

434

houndin' young men into it! If they'd any decency, they'd shut up. . . ."

"All right, father!"

"The man that owns this paper . . . whatshisname! . . ."

"It doesn't matter, does it? Lie still and be quiet!"

"I can't be quiet. Like a damned big monster, yellin' for boys to eat. Has he any childher, will you tell me? . . ."

"I don't know, father!"

"Of course he hasn't. An' here he is, yelpin' in his damned rag every day, 'Fee-fo-fum, I smell the blood of a young man!' Why don't they shove him at the Front . . . the very front!"

"You must keep quiet, father!"

"All right, Henry, all right!"

He was silent for a few minutes, and then he began again, in a quieter voice. "I'd have put the men that made it, the whole lot of them, in the front rank, and let them blow themselves to blazes. Old men sittin' in offices, an' makin' wars, an' then biddin' young men to pay the price of them! By God, that's mean! By God, that's low! . . ."

"But old men couldn't bear the strain of it, father!" Henry interjected, and he recalled some of the horrors of the trenches where the soldiers had stood with the water reaching to their waists; but Mr. Quinn insisted that the old men should have fought the war they made.

"Who cares a damn whether they can bear it or not," he said. "Let 'em die, damn 'em! They're no good!" He turned quickly to Henry, and demanded, "What good are they? Tell me that now!" but before Henry could make an answer to him, he went off insistently, "They're no good, I tell you. I know well what they're like . . . sittin' in their clubs, yappin' an' yappin' an' demandin' this an' demandin' that, an' gettin' on one another's nerves; an' whatever happens it's not them that suffers for it: it's

the young lads that pays for everything. Look at the way
the old fellows go on in Parliament, Henry! By God, I
want to vomit when I read about them! Yappin' an' yappin' when they should be down on their knees beggin' God's
forgiveness. . . ."

He spoke as if he were not himself an old man, and it
did not seem strange to Henry that he should speak in that
fashion, for Mr. Quinn's spirit had always been a young
spirit.

"An' these wee bitches with their white feathers," he
went on, "ought to be well skelped. If I had a daughter,
an' she did a thing like that, by God, I'd break her skull
for her!"

"I suppose they think they're doing their duty, father,
and they're young! . . ."

"There's women at it, too. I read in the paper yesterday mornin' that there was grown women doin' it. There's
nobody has any right to bid a man go to that except them
that's been to it themselves. If the women an' the parsons an' the old men can't fight for their country, they
can hold their tongues for it, an' by God they ought to
be made to hold them. . . ."

He asked continually after Gilbert.

"He's a sergeant now, father. He's been offered a commission, but he won't take it! . . ."

"Why?"

"Oh, one of his whimsy-whamsies, I suppose. He says
the non-commissioned officers are the backbone of the Army,
and he prefers to be part of the backbone. You remember Ninian Graham, father?"

"I do, rightly! . . ."

"He's come home to join. He's in the Engineers!"

Mr. Quinn did not make any answer to Henry. He
slipped a little further into the bed, and lay for a long
while with his eyes closed, so long that Henry thought he
had fallen asleep; but, just when Henry began to tiptoe

from the room, he opened his eyes again, and suddenly they were full of tears.

"The fine young fellows," he said. "The fine young lads!"

2

And at Christmas, he died. He had called Henry to him that morning, and had enquired about "The Fennels," which had lately been published after a postponement and much hesitation, and about the new book on which Henry was now working.

"That's right," he said, when he heard that Henry was working steadily on it. "It'll keep your mind from broodin'. How's the Ulster book goin'?"

" 'The Fennels'?"

"Ay. You had hard luck, son, in bringing out your best book at a time like this, but never matter, never matter! . . ."

"I don't know how it's doing. It's too soon to tell yet. The reviews have been good, but I don't suppose people are buying books at present!"

"You've done a good few now, Henry!"

"Five, father."

"Ay, I have the lot there on that ledge so's I can take them down easily an' look at them. I feel proud of you, son . . . proud of you!"

He began to remind Henry of things that had happened when he was a boy. His mind became flooded with memories. "Do you mind Bridget Fallon?" he would say, and then he would recall many incidents that were connected with her. "Do you mind the way you wanted to go to Cambridge, an' I wouldn't let you," and "Do you mind the time you took the woollen balls from Mr. Maginn's house? . . ."

Henry remembered. Mr. Maginn, the vicar of Ballymartin, had invited Henry to spend the afternoon with his nephew and niece and some other children. They had played a game with balls made of coloured wool, and while they were playing, Henry, liking the pattern of one of them, had put it into his pocket. It had been missed, and there had been a search for it, in which Henry had joined. He was miserable, and he wanted to confess that he had the ball, but every time he opened his lips to say that he had it, he felt afraid, and so he had refrained from speaking. He felt, too, that every one knew that he had taken it, but still he could not confess that he had it, and when they said, "Isn't it queer? I wonder where it's gone!" he had answered, "Yes, isn't it queer?" They had abandoned the search, and had played another game, but all the pleasure of the party was lost for Henry. He kept saying to himself, "You've got it. *You've* got it! . . ."

He had hurried home after the party was over, and when he reached the shrubbery, he dug a hole and buried the ball in it. He had closed his eyes as he took it out of his pocket, so that he should not see the bright colours of it, and had heaped the earth on to it as if he could not conceal it quickly enough . . . but burying it had not quieted his mind. He felt, whenever he met Mr. Maginn, that the vicar looked at him as if he were saying to himself, "You stole the woollen ball! . . ." At the end of the month, he had gone to his father and told him of it, and Mr. Quinn had cocked his eye at him for a moment and considered the subject.

"If I were you, Henry," he had said, "I'd dig up that ball and take it back to Mr. Maginn and just tell him about it!"

Henry could remember how hard it had been to do that, how he had loitered outside the gates of the vicarage for an hour, trying to force himself to go up to the door and ask for the vicar . . . and how kind Mr. Maginn had been when, at last, he had made his confession!

Oh, yes, he remembered! . . .

"You were a funny wee lad, Henry," Mr. Quinn said, taking his son's hand in his. "Always imaginin' things!" He thought for a second or two. "I suppose," he went on, "that's what makes you able to write books . . . imaginin' things! Ay, that's it!"

They sat in quietness for a while, and then Mr. Quinn fell asleep, and Henry went down to the library and worked again on his new novel, for which he had not yet found a title; and in his sleep, Mr. Quinn died.

3

Henry had finished a chapter of the book, and he put down his pen, and yawned. He was tired, and he thought gratefully of tea. Hannah would bring a tray to his father's room. There would be little soda farls and toasted barn-brack, and perhaps she would have made "slim-jim," and there would be newly-churned butter and home-made jam, which Hannah, in her Ulster way, would call "Preserve." . . .

He got up from the table and went into the hall.

"Will tea be long, Hannah?" he called down the stairs, leading to the kitchens.

"Haven't I it near ready?" she answered.

He had gone up the staircase at a run, and had entered his father's room, expecting to see him sitting up. . . .

"Hilloa," he said, stopping sharply, "still asleep!" and he went out of the room and called softly to Hannah, now coming up the stairs, to take the tray to the library. "He's asleep, Hannah!" he said almost in a whisper.

"He's never asleep at this hour," she answered.

And somehow, as she said that, he knew. He went back into the room and leant over his father, listening. . . .

"Is he dead, Master Henry?" Hannah said, as she came into the room. She had left the tray on a table on the landing.

Henry straightened himself and turned to her. "Yes,
Hannah!" he said quietly.

The old woman threw her apron over her head and let a
great cry out of her. "Och, ochanee!" she moaned, "Och,
och, ochanee! . . ."

4

He had none of the terror he had had when Mrs. Clutters lay dead in the Bloomsbury house. He went into the
room and stood beside his father's body. The finely
moulded face had a proud look and a great look of peace.
"I don't feel that he's dead," Henry murmured to himself. "I shall never feel that he's dead!"

"I wasn't with him enough," he went on. "I left him
alone too often. . . ."

Extraordinarily, they had loved each other. Under-
neath all that roughness of speech and violence of statement, there was great tenderness and understanding. He
spoke his mind, and more than his mind, but he was generous and quick to retract and quicker to console. "I'm an
Ulsterman," he said once. "Ulster to the marrow, an'
begod I'm proud of it!"

"But I'm Irish too," he added, turning to John Marsh
as he said it, fearful lest he should have hurt John's feelings. "Begod, it's gran' to be Irish. I pity the poor
devils that aren't! . . ."

He was a great lover of life, exulting in his strength and
vigour, shouting sometimes for the joy of hearing himself
shout. "And shy, too," Henry murmured to himself, "shy
as a wren about intimate things!"

The sight of his father's placid face comforted him. One
might cry over other people, but not over *him*. Henry
felt that if he were to weep for his father, and the old man,
regaining life for a moment were to open his eyes and see
him, he would shout at him, "Good God, Henry, what are

you cryin' about? Go out, man, an' get the fresh air
about you!..."
He put his hand out and touched the dead man.
"All right, father!" he said aloud. ...

5

There was much to do after the burial, and it was not
until the beginning of the Spring that Henry left Ballymartin. He had completed his sixth novel, and had asked
that the proofs should be sent to him as speedily as possible so that he might correct them before he left Ireland,
and while he was waiting for them, he had travelled to
Dublin for a few days, partly on business connected with
his estate and partly to see his friends. Mr. Quinn had
spent a great deal of money on his farming experiments,
the more freely as he found that Henry's books brought
him an increasing income, and so Henry had decided to
let the six hundred acres which Mr. Quinn himself had
farmed. At first, he had thought of selling the land, but
it seemed to him that his father would have liked him to
keep it, and so he did not do so. He settled his affairs with
his solicitors, and then returned to Ballymartin; but before
he did so, he spent an evening with John Marsh, whom he
found still keenly drilling.
"But why are you drilling now?" he asked. "This
hardly seems the time to be playing at soldiers, John!"
"I'm not playing, Henry. I *am* a soldier!"
It was difficult to remember how many armies there
were in Ireland. The Ulster Volunteers still sulked in
the North. The National Volunteers had split. The
politicians, alarmed at the growth of the Volunteer Movement among their followers, had swooped down on the
Volunteers and "captured" them. John Marsh and Galway and their friends had seceded, and, under the presi-
dency of a professor of the National University, John Mac-

Neill, had formed a new body, called the Irish Volunteers. The politicians, failing to understand the temper of their time, worked to discourage the growth of the Volunteer Movement, and the result of their efforts was that the more enthusiastic and courageous of the National Volunteers seceded to the Irish Volunteers.

"We're growing rapidly," John said to Henry. "They're flocking out of the Nationals into ours as hard as they can. We've got Thomas MacDonagh and Patrick Pearse and a few others with us, and we're trying to link up with Larkins' Citizen Army. Mineely's urging Connolly on to our side, but Connolly's more interested in the industrial fight than in the national fight. But I think we'll get him over!"

Their objects were to defend themselves from attack by the Ulster Volunteers if attack were made, to raise a rebellion if the Home Rule Bill were not passed into law, and to resist the enactment of conscription in Ireland. The burden of their belief was still the fear of betrayal. "But you're going to get Home Rule," Henry would say to them, and they would answer, "We'll believe it when we see the King opening the Parliament in College Green. Not before. We know what the English are like. . . ."

Henry had suggested to them that they should offer the services of their volunteers to the Government in return for the immediate enactment of the Bill, but they saw no hope of such an offer being accepted and honoured. "The minute they'd got us out of the way, they'd break their word," said Galway. "Our only hope is to stay here and make ourselves as formidable as we can. You can't persuade the English to do the decent thing . . . you can only terrorise them into it. Look at the way the Ulster people have frightened the wits out of them! . . ."

"But the Ulster people haven't frightened the wits out of them. I can't understand you fellows! You sit here with preconceived ideas in your heads, and you won't check

them by going to see the people you're theorising about.
You keep on saying the same thing over and over again,
and you won't listen to any one who tells you that you've
got hold of the wrong end of the stick! . . ."

"My dear Henry," said John, "our history is enough
for us. Even since the war, the English have tried to be-
little the Irish. They've done the most inept, small things
to annoy us. They'd have got far more men from Ireland
than they have done, if they'd behaved decently; but they
couldn't. They simply couldn't do the decent thing to
Ireland. That's their nature. . . . I'd have gone myself! . . ."

"You?"

"Yes. I think the Germans are in the wrong. I think
they've behaved badly, and anyhow, I don't like their
theory of life. But the English couldn't treat us properly.
We wanted an Irish Division, with Irish officers, and Irish
colours, and Irish priests . . . but no! They actually
stopped some women in the South from making an Irish
flag for the Irish regiments! . . . What are you to do
with people like that. If they aren't treacherous, they're
so stupid that it's impossible to do anything with them,
and we'd much better be separate from them!"

"I should have thought that Belgium showed the folly
of that sort of thing," said Henry. "A little country can't
keep itself separate from a big one. It'll get hurt if it
does."

"Belgium fought, didn't she?" John answered. "I
daresay we should get beaten, too, but we could fight,
couldn't we?"

Henry went away from them in a state of depression. It
seemed impossible to persuade them to behave reasonably.
Fixed and immovable in their minds was this belief that
England would use them in her need . . . and then betray
them when her need was satisfied.

He went back to Ballymartin and corrected his proofs.

"I'll go over to England next week," he said to himself when he had revised the final proofs and posted them to his publishers.

6

Mrs. Graham had written to him when his father died. *"My dear Henry,"* she wrote, *"I know how you must feel at the death of your father, and I know, too, that you will not wish to have your sorrow intruded on. A letter is a poor thing, but, my dear, I send you all my sympathy. I never saw your father, but Ninian has often spoken of him to me, and I know that his loss must be almost unbearable to you. Perhaps he was glad, as I should be glad, to slip away from the thought and memory of this horrible war, and that may bring comfort to you. If you feel lonely and unhappy at home, come to Boveyhayne for a while. You know how glad we shall be to have you. It is very quiet here now, more than a hundred of our men have gone into the Navy or the Army, and the poor women are full of anxiety about them. Ninian has just been moved to Colchester. I daresay he has written to you before this. If you would like to come to Boveyhayne just send a telegram to me. That will be sufficient. Believe me, my dear Henry, Your sincere friend, Janet Graham."*

He remembered Mrs. Graham's letter now, and he went to his writing desk and took it from the notes of condolence he had received. Ninian and Gilbert and Roger had written to him, short, abrupt letters that he knew were full of kindly concern for him, and Rachel had written too. There was a letter from Mary.

Dear Quinny, you don't know how sorry I am. It must be awful to lose your father when you and he have been such chums. I can only just remember my father, and how I cried when he was taken away, and so I know how hard it must be for you. Your friend, Mary.

He read Mrs. Graham's note, and Mary's several times, and as he read them, he had a longing to go to Boveyhayne again. The house at Ballymartin was so lonely, now that his father's heavy footsteps no longer sounded through the hall. Sometimes, forgetting that he was dead, Henry would stop suddenly and listen as if he were listening for his father's voice. Since his return from Dublin, he had felt his loss more poignantly than he had before he went away. In the old days, his father would have been at the station to meet him. There would have been a hearty shout, and. . . .

"I must go," he said to himself, "I must go. I can't bear to be here now."

He went down to the village and telegraphed to Mrs. Graham telling her that he would be with her two days later, and while he was in the post office, the *Belfast Evening Telegraph* came in.

"I'll take my copy with me," he said to the post-mistress, and he opened it at once to read the news. There was a paragraph in a corner of the paper, which caught his eye at once. It announced the death in action of Lord Jasper Jayne.

"My God!" he said, crumpling the paper as he gaped at the announcement.

"Is it bad news, sir?" the post-mistress asked.

"A friend of mine," he answered, turning to her. "Killed at the Front!"

"Aw, dear," she said. "Aw, dear-a-dear! An' there'll be plenty more, sir. There's young fellas away from the village, sir. My own nephew's away. You mind him, don't you, sir! Peter Logan! . . ."

"Peter Logan!"

"Ay, he used to keep the forge 'til he married Matt Hamilton's niece, an' then he took to the land. Nothin' would stop him, but to be off. Nothin' at all would stop him. I toul' him myself the Belgians was Catholics an' the Germans was Protestants, but nothin' would stop him. . . ."

"Sheila Morgan's husband," Henry murmured.

"Ay," she answered, "that was her name before she was married. He's trainin' now, an' in a while, I suppose, he'll be off like the rest of them. Och, ochanee, sir, isn't this a terr'ble world, wi' nothin' but fightin' an' wringlin'? Will that be all you're wantin', sir?"

"Yes, thanks," he said.

Poor old Jimphy! They had all been contemptuous of him . . . and now! . . .

Cecily would be free now! Oh, but what of that? Poor Jimphy! He had not wished for much from life . . . and sometimes it had seemed that he had got much more than he needed. . . .

"The best of us can't do more than he did," Henry thought as he walked home. "A man can't give more than he's got, and Jimphy's given everything!"

7

He started up, and looked about the room, and while he listened, he could hear the big clock in the hall sounding three times. He was shivering, though he was not cold. In his dream, he had seen Jimphy, all bloody and broken. . . .

"Oh, my God, how horrible!" he groaned.

He got up and went to the window, but he could not see beyond the high trees, which swayed and moaned and took strange shapes in the wind. His dream still held his mind, and as he looked into the darkness and saw the bending branches yielding and rebounding, it seemed to him that he saw the soldiers rushing forward and heard their cries, hoarse with war lust or stifled by the blood that gushed from their mouths as they staggered and fell . . . and as he had seen him in his dream, so he saw Jimphy again, running forward and shouting as he ran, until suddenly, with a queer wrinkled look of amazement on his face, he stopped, and then, clasping his hands to his head, tumbled in a shapeless heap on the ground . . . but now it seemed to him that as Jimphy fell, his face changed: it was no longer Jimphy's face, but his own.

"My God, it's me!" he cried, shrinking away from the window, and clutching at the curtains as if he would cover himself with them. "My God, it's *me!*"

He shut his eyes tightly and stumbled back to bed. He bruised himself against a chair, but he was afraid to open his eyes, and he rolled into bed, covering himself completely with the clothes, and buried his face in his folded arms. In his mind, one thought hammered insistently: *I must live! I must live! I must live!*

8

"I'm run down," he said to himself in the morning. "That's what's the matter with me. I'm run down!"

His father's death had affected him, he thought, far more than he had imagined. He would be all right again after a rest in Devonshire. It was natural that he should be in a nervous state . . . quite natural. He would go straight to Boveyhayne from Liverpool. He could catch the Bournemouth Express, and change at Templecombe. . . . "That's what I'll do," he said, and he hurried downstairs to prepare for his journey.

THE SEVENTH CHAPTER

1

He changed his mind at Liverpool. "I'll go to London first," he said, "and see Roger and Rachel. I might as well hear anything there is to hear!" And so he had telegraphed to Roger who met him at Euston.

"Gilbert's going out in a few days," Roger said, when they had greeted each other.

"Out?"

"Yes. He's going to the Dardanelles! . . . This job's serious, Quinny!" he added grimly. "Our two months' estimate was a bit out, wasn't it? I suppose you haven't heard from Ninian lately? He hasn't written to me for a good while."

"Not lately," Henry answered, "but I shall hear of him to-morrow when I get to Boveyhayne. I'll write and let you know!"

"My Big Army book's gone to pot, of course!" Roger went on. "At present anyhow! . . ."

"The War's done for the Improved Tories, I suppose?"

"Absolutely. They've all enlisted. Ashley Earls is in the R.A.M.C. He went in last week. He couldn't go before . . . he was ill. You remember Ernest Carr. He tried to enlist when the War began, but he was so crippled with rheumatism that they hoofed him out. Well, he's been living like a hermit ever since to get himself cured, and he says he's going on splendidly. He thinks he'll be able to join before long. . . ."

"I wonder if I ought to join," he went on, more to himself than to Henry. "I've thought and thought about it . . . but I can't make up my mind. I've got a decent connexion at the Bar now, and if I go into the Army, I shall lose it. The fellows who don't go will get my work. And if the War lasts as long as Kitchener reckons, I shall be forgotten by the time I get back . . . and I shall have to begin again at an age when most men have either established themselves or cleared out of the profession altogether. I want to do what's right, but I can't reconcile my two duties, Quinny. I've a duty to England, of course, but I think I have a bigger duty to Rachel and Eleanor. If they'd only conscript us all, this problem wouldn't arise . . . not so acutely anyhow. I suppose the Government is having a pretty hard time, but they do seem to act the goat rather! There's a great deal of talk about a man's duty to England, but very little talk about England's duty to the man. However! . . ." He did not finish his sentence, but shrugged his shoulders and looked away.

"I don't feel happy," he went on after a while, "when I see other men joining up, but I've got to think of Rachel and Eleanor. . . . When I was going to meet you, Quinny, I passed a chap on crutches. His leg was off! . . . He made me feel damned ashamed. I suppose that's why they let the wounded go about in uniform so freely; to make you feel ashamed of yourself. That's what I'm afraid of. I'm afraid I shall rush off to the recruiting office in a burst of emotion . . . and I must think of Rachel and Eleanor! . . ."

"I don't see why you should go before I do, Roger," Henry interjected.

"Are you going, Quinny?"

Henry flushed. It hurt him that there should be any question about it.

"Yes," he said.

"I don't think of you as a soldier, Quinny!"

"I don't think of myself as one!" He paused for a moment, and then, impetuously, he turned to Roger.

"Roger," he said, "do you think I'm . . . neurotic? Would you say I'm . . . well, degenerate?"

"Don't be an ass, Quinny!"

"I'm serious, Roger. I'm not just talking about myself, and slopping over!"

"You're highly strung, of course, but I shouldn't say you were neurotic. You're healthy enough, aren't you?"

"Oh, yes, I'm healthy enough, but I'm such a damned coward, Roger, and sometimes some perfectly uncontrollable fear seizes me . . . silly frights. I never told you, did I, how scared I was when Mrs. Clutters died? . . ." He told Roger how he had trembled outside the door of the dead woman's room. "Things like that have happened to me ever since I was a kid. I make up my mind to join the Army, and then I suddenly get panicky, and I can almost feel myself being killed. I'm continually seeing the War . . . me in it, crouching in a trench waiting for the order to go over, and trembling with fright . . . so frightened that I can't do anything but get killed . . . and it's worse when I think of myself killing other people . . . I feel sick at the thought of thrusting a bayonet into a man's body . . . squelching through his flesh . . . My God! . . ."

"Yes, I know, Quinny!" Roger said. "One does feel like that. But when you're there, you don't think of it . . . you're more or less off your head . . . you couldn't do it if you weren't. They work you up to a kind of frenzy, and then you . . . just let yourself go!"

"But afterwards? Don't you think a man 'ud go mad afterwards when he thought of it? I should. I know I should. I'd lie awake at night and see the men I'd killed! . . ."

A passenger in the train had told a story of the trenches to Henry, who now repeated it to Roger.

"One of our men got hold of a German in a German trench, and he bayonetted him, but he did it clumsily. There wasn't enough room to kill him properly . . . he couldn't withdraw the bayonet and stick it in again and finish the man . . . and there they were, jammed together

. . . and the German was squealing, oh, horribly . . . and
our men had to come and haul the British soldier out of
the trench. He'd gone off his head! . . ."

"One oughtn't to think of things like that, Quinny!"

"But if you can't help it? What terrifies me is that I
might turn funk . . . let my lot down! . . ."

"You wouldn't. You're the sort that imagines the worst
and does the best. I shouldn't think of it any more if I
were you. A month at Boveyhayne'll pull you all right
again. . . ."

"It's dying that I'm most afraid of. Some of these
papers write columns and columns of stuff about 'glorious
deaths' at the front, but it doesn't seem very glorious to
me to be dead before you've had a chance to do your job
. . . killed like that . . . blown to bits, perhaps . . . so
that they can't tell which is you and which is some one
else! . . ."

Roger nodded his head. "Our journalists contrive to see
a great deal of glory in war . . . from Fleet Street, don't
they, Quinny?"

"Sometimes," Henry proceeded, "I think that the worst
kind of cowardice is to love life too much. That's the kind
of coward I am. I love living. I used to cry when I was
a kid at the thought that I might die and not be able to
run about and look at things that I liked! And that makes
you funky. You're afraid to take risks, for fear you should
lose your life and have to give up the pleasure of living.
I suppose that's what the Bible means when it says that
'whosoever shall lose his life, shall find it.' This hunt for
security melts the marrow in your backbone! . . ."

"Perhaps," said Roger. "Where you go wrong, I think,
is in imagining that courage consists in hurling yourself
recklessly on things . . . in not caring a damn. I don't
think that that's courage . . . it's simply insensibility . . .
a sort of permanent imperceptiveness. Really, Quinny, if
you don't feel fear, there's not much of the heroic in your
acts. That kind of man isn't much braver when he's plung-

ing at Germans than he is when he's plunging at a motor-
omnibus or getting into a 'scrum' at Rugger. He simply
doesn't see any difference. It's something to plunge at,
and so he plunges. I haven't much faith in the Don't-
Care-a-Damn Brigade. They're more anxious to get V.C's
than to get victories. Their courage is just egoism . . .
they're thinking, not of their country, but of themselves.
The real hero, I think, is the man who makes himself do
something that he's afraid to do, who goes into a thing,
trembling with fright, but nevertheless goes into it. Did
you ever meet Léon Lorthiois?" he said quickly.

"You mean the French painter who used to hang about
the Café Royal?" Henry replied.

"Yes. He was killed the other day in France."

"I hadn't heard. Poor chap!"

"I think he showed extraordinary courage. He started
off from London to join the French Army . . . all his
friends dined him jolly well . . . and wished him good-
luck, and so on, and then he went off. And a week later,
he turned up again with a cock-and-bull story about having
been arrested as a deserter. He said he'd escaped from
prison and, after a lot of difficulty and hardship, got back
to England. But he hadn't done anything of the sort.
He'd funked it at the last. He got as far as Dover, and
then he turned back . . . frightened. He stayed in London for a while . . . and then he tried again . . . and this
time he didn't funk it! They say he was fighting splendidly when he was killed. Men have got the V.C. for less
heroic behaviour than that. He'd conquered himself. I
used to despise that fellow because he wore eccentric
clothes and had his hair cut in a silly fashion . . . but I
feel proud now of having known him!"

2

Mary met him at Whitcombe, and they walked home,
sending his trunk and portmanteau on in the carriage with

Widger. He had anticipated their meeting with strange emotion, feeling as if he were returning to her after a time of misunderstanding, richer in knowledge, more capable of sympathy. He had not seen her since the first performance of "The Magic Casement," and very much had happened to them since then. His desire for Cecily seemed to have died. He had not troubled to visit her in London . . . he could have found time to do so, had he been anxious to see her . . . but he had not the wish. He had not written to her about Jimphy . . . he could not bring himself to do that . . . and the thought that she might wish to see him did not stir his mind. He felt for her what a man feels for a woman he has loved, but now loves no more: neither like nor dislike, but, occasionally, curiosity that did not last long. She moved him as little as Sheila Morgan had done when he saw her in the field at Ballymartin, big with child, watching her husband drilling.

"There are permanent things in one's life, and there are impermanent things . . . and you can't turn the one into the other," he thought to himself, as the little branch railway drove down the Axe Valley. "I wanted Cecily . . . and then I didn't want her. There's no more to be said about it than that!"

There were very few people waiting on the platform when the train drew into Whitcombe, and so Henry and Mary saw each other immediately, and when he saw her, standing on the windy platform, with her hand to her hat, he felt more powerfully than he had ever felt it, his old love for her surging through him. Nothing could ever divert him from her for very long . . . inevitably he would return to her . . . whatever of permanence there was in his life was centred in her. He led her out of the station and they walked along the road at the top of the shingle . . . and as they walked, suddenly he turned to her and, drawing her arm in his, told her that he loved her.

"I haven't much to offer you, Mary . . . I'm a poor sort of fellow at the best . . . but I need you, and! . . ."

She did not answer, but she looked up at him with shining eyes. . . .

"My dear!" he said, and drew her very close to him.

3

They went up the path over the red cliffs and then
climbed the steep steps that led to the top of the White
Cliff. The night was beginning to gather her clouds about
her, but still they did not hurry homewards. Far out,
they could see the trawlers returning to the Bay, dipping
and rising and plunging and reeling before the wind as
from a heavy blow, and then, when it seemed that they must
fall, righting themselves and moving swiftly homewards.
Beneath them, the sea splashed in great thick waves that
tossed their spray high in the air, and the gulls and jack-
daws spun round and up and down or huddled themselves
in the shelter of the cliffs.

"Mary!" he said, putting his arm about her.

"Yes, Quinny!" she answered so quietly that he could
not hear her above the noise of the sea and the wind.

He raised her lips to his and kissed her.

"My dear!" he said again.

4

There was news of Ninian for them when they reached
the Manor. Mrs. Graham, with his letter in her hand, met
them at the door.

"He's coming home on leave," she said. "He'll be here
to-morrow night. Then he's going out! . . ."

She turned away quickly, after she had spoken, and they
followed her silently into the drawing-room. She stood for
a while at the window, gazing down the avenue where the
oaks and the chestnuts mingled their branches and made a
covering for passers-by.

"I'll just go upstairs," Henry began, but before he could

leave the room, Mrs. Graham turned away from the window and went to him.

"I've put you in your old room, Henry," she said. "How are you? You don't look well!"

"I'm tired . . . but I shall be all right presently. I'll just go upstairs now! . . ."

He left her hurriedly, for Mary was anxious to tell her mother of their betrothal, and he wished her to know as quickly as possible. He dallied in his room so that she might have plenty of time in which to learn Mary's news. He sat on the wide window-seat and let his mind roam over his memories. It was in this room that he had first told himself that he loved Mary . . . it was at this very window he had stood while he resolved that he would marry Sheila Morgan, and again had considered what Ninian and Gilbert had said about men who marry out of their class. Almost he expected to hear the door opening as Gilbert walked in, just as he had done then. . . .

"It's no good mooning like this," he said to himself, and then he went downstairs again.

Mary was sitting beside her mother, holding her hand, and as he entered she turned to look at him, and smiled so that he knew what he must do, and so, without hesitation, he crossed the room to Mrs. Graham and kissed her.

"I'm very glad, Henry!" she said. "Sit down here!"

She moved so that he could sit beside her, and when he had settled himself, she put her hand on his shoulder. "It's nice to have you back again," she said.

They spent the time until dinner in desultory talk that sometimes lapsed into lengthy silence. A high wind was blowing up from the sea, and when they had dined, they drew their chairs close to the fire, and sat quietly in the warmth of it. They could hear the heavy rustle of the leaves as the trees swayed in the wind, and now and then raindrops fell down the chimney and sizzled in the hot coals. The lamps were left unlit, and the firelight made long shadows round the room, flickering over the old

polished furniture and the silverware and the dim por-
traits of dead Grahams. . . .

Mary moved from her chair and, placing a cushion on the
floor between Henry and her mother, she sat down and
leant her head against him. He bent forward slightly, and
placed his hand on her shoulder, and as he did so, she put
hers up and took hold of it and so they sat in exquisite
peace and quietness until the rising wind, gathering itself
together in greater strength, flung itself heavily on the
house and shook it roughly. In the lull, they could hear
the rain beating sharply on the windows . . . and as they
listened to the noise of the storm, their minds wandered
away, and in their imagination they could see the soldiers
in France, crouching in the dark trenches, while the wind
and rain beat about them without pity; and in the mind
of each of them, probing painfully, was this persistent
thought: Here we are in this comfort . . . and there they
are *in that!*

5

When Mary had gone to bed, Mrs. Graham began to talk
of her to Henry.

"I always knew that she and you would marry, Henry,"
she said, "even when you seemed to have forgotten about
her. You . . . you were very fond of Lady Cecily Jayne,
weren't you, Henry?" He nodded his head. He wanted
to explain that that was over now, that it had been a passing thing that had no durability, but he could not make the
explanation, and so he did not say anything. "I thought
her a very beautiful woman," Mrs. Graham went on. "If
I'd been a boy I think I should have loved her, too. Boys
are like that!"

She was so gentle and kind and understanding that he
lost his shyness, and he confided in her as he would like to
have confided in his mother if she had been alive.

"Inside me," he said, "I always loved Mary, even when

I was obsessed by . . . by some one else. I can't tell you
how happy I am, Mrs. Graham. I feel as if I'd got home
after a long and bitter journey . . . and I don't want to
go away again ever. Just to look at Mary seems sufficient
. . . to know that she's there . . . that I can put out my
hand and touch her. . . .''

"Ninian will be glad, too," she said, speaking quickly
to cover up the difficulty he had in finishing his speech.

"We've been awfully good friends, we four," he replied,
"Ninian and Roger and Gilbert and I. I've always felt
about them that we could go on with our friendship just
where we left off, even if we were separated from each other
for years. We're all proud of each other. I used to think,
when we first lived in that house in Bloomsbury, that we'd
never separate . . . that we'd form a sort of brotherhood
of work and friendship . . . Roger always preached about
The Job Well Done . . . but, of course that was impossible.
We were bound to diverge and separate . . . all sorts of
things compel men to do that. Roger married, and now
Gilbert and Ninian are soldiers. . . .''

"I feel proud and afraid," Mrs. Graham said. "I'm
glad that Ninian has joined . . . I think I should hate it
if he hadn't . . . and yet I wish too that . . . that he
weren't in it. I'm not much of a patriot, Henry. I love
my son more than I love my country. I've never been able
to understand those women one reads about who offer their
sons gladly. I don't offer Ninian gladly. I offer him . . .
that's all. I know that men have to defend their country,
and I love England and I'm proud to be English . . . but
when I've said all that, it's very little when I remember
that I love Ninian. I suppose that that's a selfish thing to
say . . . but I don't care whether it is or not! . . .'' She
stopped for a moment or two, and then, with a change of
voice, she said, "Do you think the war will last long,
Henry?"

"I don't know," he replied. "Nobody seems able to
form any estimate. When it began I thought it couldn't

possibly last for longer than two months, but it looks like
going on for a very long time yet. We move forward and
we move back . . . and more men are killed. That's
the only result of anything at present!"

"It's strange," she murmured, "how indifferent one becomes to the death lists. I thought my heart would break
when I saw the first Devon casualties, but now one simply
doesn't feel anything . . . just a vague regret. Sometimes I think I'm growing callous. I can't feel anything
when I read that thousands of men have been killed and
wounded. It's almost as if I were saying to myself, 'Is
that all? Weren't there more? . . .' I'm not the only
one like that. People don't like to admit it, but I've heard
people confessing . . . I confess myself . . . that I get a
. . . kind of shocked pleasure out of a big casualty list!
. . . Oh, isn't it disgusting, Henry? One gets more and
more coarse every day, less sensitive! . . ."

"Yes," he said, nodding his head and staring into the
fire which was now burning down.

And everywhere, it seemed to him, that coarsening process was going on, a persistent blunting of the feelings,
an itching desire for more and grimmer and bloodier details. One saw it operating in kindly women who visited
soldiers in hospital or took them for drives . . . an uncontrollable wish to hear the ghastlier things, a greedy anxiety
for "experiences." . . . And the soldiers loathed these prying women in whom lust had taken a new turn: the love
lust had turned to blood lust, and those who had formerly
itched for men (and even those who had not) itched now
for horrors, more and more horrors. . . . "Tell me, now,"
they would say, "did you kill any Germans? I suppose
you saw some awful things. . . ."

One saw this coarsening process operating on men with
incredible swiftness. Their tastes became edgeless . . .
they entertained themselves with big, splashy things, asking
for noise and glare and an inchoate massing of colour, and
crowds and crowds of bare girls. There was a demand for

Nakedness, not the nakedness of cleanly, natural things, but the Nakedness that is partly covered, the Nakedness that hints at Nakedness. . . .

"That's inevitable, I suppose," Henry thought to himself.

The sloppier journalists made a cult of blasphemy and foul speech. The drill-sergeant was regarded as the most entertaining of humourists, and decent men who had never done more than the normal and healthy amount of swearing, began to believe that it was impossible to be manly unless one bloodied every time one spoke: and swearing, which is a good and wholesome and manly and picturesque thing, suddenly became like the gibbering of an idiot. . . . One was led to believe that the drill-sergeant spent his time in ordering men to "bloody well form bloody fours!" It was immaterial to the sloppier journalists that the drill-sergeant did not do anything of the sort . . . and so the legend grew, of a great Army going into battle, not with the old English war-cries on their lips or with new cries as noble, but with "Bloody!" for their watch-word, and "Who were you With Last Night?" for their war-song. . . .

6

"I often wonder what things will be like when the war is over," Mrs. Graham said. "Men can't live like that without some permanent effect. Their habits will be rougher, more elementary, I suppose, and they'll value life less highly. I don't see how they can help it. You can't see men killed in that careless way . . . and feel any sanctity about life. I think life will be harsher for women after the war than it was before. . . ."

She remembered that Ninian's father had always declared that the Franco-German War had brutalised Germany.

"He'd lived in Germany for a long while," she said,

"and people admitted that Germany had changed after the War . . . grown coarser and less kindly! . . ."

They talked on in this strain until the clock chimed twelve. The storm still blew over the house, but the rain had ceased, and when they looked out of the window, they could see a rift in the clouds, through which the moon tore her way.

"Good-night, Henry," she said, bending towards him, and he kissed her cheek and then opened the door for her.

"Good-night!" he said.

7

Ninian came home on the next day, and when they had told him the news of Henry's engagement to Mary, he was full of cheers. "Good!" he said. "Now I shall be able to keep you in order, young fellow. I shall be a Relation! . . ."

"Oh, I've a note for you," he exclaimed, as they drove home. "It's from Gilbert. I met him in town. He'll be on his way out before I get back. He'd like to have come down here, but he couldn't manage it. He sent his love to you, Mary, and you, mother! He looks jolly fit . . . never seen him look fitter!"

He handed Gilbert's note to Henry who put it in his pocket. He would read it, he told himself, when he was alone.

"We're hopping off to France next week," Ninian said. "I suppose," he added, turning again to Henry, "you saw that Jimphy Jayne was killed. Rough luck, wasn't it? I met a fellow who was in his regiment . . . home on sick-leave . . . and he says Jimphy fought like fifty. Gilbert says Cecily's bearing up wonderfully!"

"He's seen her then?" Henry asked.

"Yes. She met him in the street . . . and as he says, she's bearing up wonderfully. He didn't say a great deal, but I imagine he didn't admire the attitude much. Rum woman, Cecily!'' He had grown together more since he had been to South America, and his figure, that was always loose-looking and a little hulking, had been tightened up by his training.

"I don't like your moustache, Ninian," his mother said, looking with disfavour at the "tooth-brush" on his upper lip.

"Nor do I," he replied, "but you have to wear something on your face . . . they don't think you can fight if you don't . . . and this sort of thing is the least a chap can do for his king and country. When are you two going to get married?''

His conversation jumped about like a squib.

"Oh, not yet," Mrs. Graham hurriedly exclaimed. "There's plenty of time. . . .''

"I should like to get married at once," said Henry.

"No, not yet," Mrs. Graham insisted. "I won't be left alone yet awhile. . . .''

There was a learned discourse from Ninian on lengthy engagements which filled the time until the carriage drove up to Boveyhayne House, where it was dropped as suddenly as it was begun.

Indoors, Henry read Gilbert's letter.

"My dear Quinny," he wrote, *"I'm writing this in Soho with a pen that was made in hell."* Then there was a splutter of ink. *"There,"* the letter went on, *"that's the sort of thing it does. I believe this pen was brought to Soho by the first Frenchman to open a café here, and it's been handed down from proprietor to proprietor ever since. Ninian and I have been dining together, and as he's going down to Boveyhayne to-morrow, I thought I might as well write to you because I shan't see you again for a while. I'm off to Gallipoli in a day or two. I dined with Roger and Rachel last night, and they told me that you looked rather pipped before you went to Devonshire. I hope you'll soon be all right again. I wish we could have met,*

*but it can't be helped. We must just meet when we can.
It seems a very long while, doesn't it, since we were at
Tre'Arrdur together? It'll be jolly to be there again when
the war's over. You've no idea how interested I've become in this job, far more interested than I ever imagined
I should be. And I've changed very largely in my attitude towards the War. I 'joined up' chiefly because I felt
an uncontrollable love for England that made me want to
do things that were repugnant to me, and also because I
thought that the Germans had behaved very scurvily to the
Belgians; but I don't feel those emotions now particularly.
I do, of course, feel proud of England, and the sight of a
hedgerow makes me want to get up on my hindlegs and
cheer, but I've got something else now that had never
entered into my calculations at all . . . and that is an extraordinary pride in my regiment and a strong desire to
be worthy of it. I've just been reading a book about it, a
history of the regiment, and it's left me with a sense of
inheritance . . . as I should feel if I were the heir of an
old estate. This thing has a history and a tradition which
gives me a feeling of pride and, perhaps more than that,
a sense of responsibility. . . . 'You mustn't let it down'
I keep telling myself, and I feel about all the men who
served in the regiment from the time it was formed, that
they are my forefathers, so to speak. I feel their ghosts
about me, not the alarming sort of spook, but friendly,
sympathetic ghosts, and I imagine them saying to me,
'Sergeant Farlow, you've got to live up to us!' I've not
told any one else about this, because I'm afraid of being
called a sloppy ass . . . and perhaps it is sloppy . . . but
you'll understand what I feel, so I don't mind telling you.
I shall write to you as often as I can, and you must write
to me and tell me what you're doing. I wish we could have
gone out together. Sometimes I get a creepy-crawly sort
of feeling that nearly turns me inside out . . . a feeling
that this is good-bye for good, but I suppose most fellows
get that just before they go out. I began another play*

*about a month ago, and I think it will be good, much better
than anything else I've done. I wish I had time to finish
it before leaving home. This is rather a mess of a letter,
and I must chuck it now, for Ninian is getting tied up in
an effort to cultivate a cordial understanding with the
waiter, and I shall have to rescue them both or there'll be
a rupture between the Allies. Give my love to Mary and
Mrs. Graham. I'd have gone to Boveyhayne to see them
if I possibly could, tell them. So long, old chap!*

"*Yours Ever,*
"*Gilbert Farlow.*"

He showed the letter to Mary, and as he gave it to her,
he felt a new pleasure in his love for her, the pleasure
of sharing things, of having confidences together.

"Gilbert's a dear," she said, when she had finished reading the letter. "It would be awfully hard not to be fond
of him!"

He took the letter and put it in his pocket, and then he
put his arm in Mary's and led her to the garden where the
spring flowers were blowing. "I've had great luck," he
said. "I have Gilbert for my friend and I have you, Mary,
to be my wife, and I don't know that I deserve either!"

"Silly Quinny!" she said affectionately.

8

They spent the days of Ninian's leave in visiting all the
familiar places about Boveyhayne. It seemed almost that
Ninian could not see enough of them. He would rise early,
rousing them with insistent shouts, and urge them to make
haste and prepare for a long walk; and all day they
tramped along the roads, up the combes and down the
combes, over commons, through woods, lingering in the
lanes to pluck the wildflowers that grew profusely in the
hedgerows, or listening to the mating birds that flew continually about them. They walked along the Roman Road

to Lyme Regis in the east, and along the Roman Road again to Sidmouth in the west, returning in the dark, tired and hungry; and sometimes they went into the roadside public-houses because of the warm, comfortable smell they had, and because they liked to listen to the slow, burring voices of the labourers as they drank their beer and cider and talked of the day's doings. There was a corner of the Common, near the edge of the cliff, where they could lie when the sun was warm, and look out over the Channel to where the Brixham trawlers lay in a line along the horizon. Westwards, the red clay cliffs ran up and down in steeply undulating lines as far as they could see, and near at hand, in a wide valley beyond the gloomy combe that leads to Salcombe Regis, they could very plainly see the front of Sidmouth. In the east, they could look up the wooded valley of the Axe, and, beyond the vari-coloured Haven Cliff, see the Dorset Hills that huddled Charmouth and Bridport, and further out, like an island in mist, the high reach of Portland Bill. . . .

In this corner of the Common, they spent the last day of Ninian's leave. Behind them was a great stretch of gorse in bloom, and brown bracken, mingled with new green fronds, from which larks sprang up, singing and soaring. They had eaten sandwiches on the Common, and in the afternoon, had climbed down the steep side of the combe to a farm to tea, and, then they had climbed up the combe again, and had sat in their corner, watching the Boveyhayne trawlers blowing home; and as they sat there, they became very quiet. In this solitude and peace, the outrage of war seemed to have no meaning. . . .

Ninian stirred slightly. He raised himself on his elbow and looked about him. . . .

"Let's go home," he said quickly, getting up as he spoke. He went to his mother and helped her to rise, and when she was standing up, he took her arm and drew it through his, and led her towards the village; and when they had gone up the grassy path through the bracken, and were well on the way home, Mary and Henry followed after them.

"Ninian feels things more than he admits," Henry whispered to her.

9

They made poor attempts at gaiety that night, and Ninian tried to make oratory about Engineers. He divided his discourse into two parts: one insisting that the war would be won by engineering feats; the other insisting that it might be lost because of the contempt of most of the military men for Engineers, which, Ninian said, was another word for Brains. "They don't think we're gentlemen," he said. "I met a 'dug-out' last week, and he was snorting about the Engineers . . . hadn't a happorth of brains in his skull, the ass . . . and I asked him why it was that he thought so little of them. Do you know what he said? 'Oh,' says he, 'they're always readin' books an' . . . an' inventin' things!' That's the kind of chap we've got to endure! Isn't he priceless? I very nearly told him he ought to be embalmed . . . only I thought to myself he'd think that was the sort of remark an engineer would make. Plucky old devil, of course, but nothing in his head. If you shook it, it wouldn't rattle! . . . He seemed to think he'd only got to say, 'Now, then, boys, give 'em hell!' and the Germans 'ud just melt away. As I said afterwards, it's all very well, to say 'Give 'em hell,' but you can't give it to 'em, if you don't know what it's like! . . ."

But the oratory failed, and the gaiety fizzled out, and after a while Mrs. Graham, finding the silence and her thoughts insupportable, left them and went to bed.

"Come and say 'Good-night' to me," she said to Ninian as she left the room.

"All right, mother!" he answered.

He tried to take up the theme of engineering again.

"It's no good trying to chivy Germans in the way you chivy foxes. You've got to think, and think hard. That's where we come in! . . ." But it was a poor effort, and he abandoned it quickly.

"I think," he said, "I'll go up and say 'Good-night' to mother. You two'll see to things! . . ."

"Righto, Ninian," Henry answered.

Mary came and sat beside him when Ninian had gone.

"I'm trying to feel proud," she said, "but. . . ."

"Don't you feel proud?" he asked, fondling her.

"No. I'm anxious. It would hurt mother terribly if anything were to happen to Ninian," she answered.

"Nothing will happen to him. . . ."

One said that just because it was comforting.

"Quinny," she said, drawing herself up to him and leaning her elbows on his knees, "do you love me really and truly? . . ."

He put his arms quickly about her, and drew her close to him, and kissed her passionately.

"But you haven't loved only me," she said, freeing herself.

He did not answer.

"I've never loved any one but you," she went on. "I haven't been able to love any one but you. I've tried to love some one else . . . tried very hard!"

"Who was it?" he asked.

"No one you knew. It was after I'd seen you with Lady Cecily Jayne. I was jealous, Quinny! . . ."

"My dear," he said, flattered by the oneness of her love for him.

"But I couldn't. I just couldn't. I suppose I'm rather limited!" She made a wry smile as she spoke. "'I felt stupid beside her. She talked so easily, and I couldn't think of anything to say. You must have thought I was a fool, Quinny!"

"No, Mary! . . ."

"Oh, but I was. I got stupider and stupider, and the

more I thought of how stupid I was, the stupider I got. I could have cried with vexation. Do you remember Gilbert's party . . . I mean when it was over and we were going home?"

"Yes."

"I *prayed* that you'd come with mother and me. I thought Ninian would go with mother, and you'd go with me . . . but you didn't!"

"I remember," he answered. "I wanted to go with you. . . ."

"Why didn't you?"

"Some one came up . . . I've forgotten . . . something happened, and so I didn't. I wanted to, Mary!"

"I thought then that you and I would never! . . . Why did you ask me to marry you, Quinny?"

"Because I love you, Mary. . . ."

"But . . . did you mean to marry me or did you just . . . sort of . . . not thinking, I mean! . . . Oh, it's awf'lly hard to say what's in my mind, but I want to know whether you love me really and truly, Quinny, or only just asked me to marry you impulsively . . . when you weren't thinking?"

"I came here loving you, Mary. I didn't mean to tell you about it so soon as I did . . . that was impulse . . . I couldn't help it . . . the moment I saw you as the train came into the station, I felt that I must ask you at once. It would have been rather awkward if you'd said, 'No.' I suppose I should have had to go straight back to London again! . . . But I came here loving you. I've loved you all the time . . . even when I wasn't thinking of you, but of some one else. I've come back to you always in my thoughts! . . ."

"Do you remember," she said, "the first time you asked me to marry you, Quinny?"

"Yes."

"I've meant it ever since then. You hurt me when you went to Ireland and didn't answer my letter. . . ."

"I know!" he exclaimed.

"How do you know?"

"I just know. And when I talked to you about it, that time in Bloomsbury when you and Mrs. Graham and Rachel came to dine with us. . . ."

"I made fun of it, didn't I? But I had to, Quinny. You'd been unkind, and I had to make some sort of a show, hadn't I? I had to keep my pride if I couldn't keep any-thing else."

"We've been stupid, both of us."

"You have," she retorted.

"I have," he said. "I've been frightfully stupid. That's what puzzles me. I'm clear-sighted enough about the people I make up in my books. The critics insist on my understanding of human motives, and I know that I have that understanding. I can get right inside my characters, and I know them through and through . . . but I'm as stupid as a sheep about myself and about you and . . . living people. I suppose I exhaust all my understanding on my books!"

"Well, it doesn't matter, Quinny, dear," she said. "I'll understand for the two of us! . . ."

10

In the morning, Ninian went away. They drove to Whit-combe Station with him and saw him off. They had been anxious about Mrs. Graham and dubious of her endurance at the moment of parting . . . but she had insisted on going to the station, and so they had not persisted in their per-suasions. And she had held herself proudly.

"Good-bye, my dear," she said, hugging Ninian tightly, and smiling at him. "You'll write to me . . . often!"

"Every day," he replied. "If I can!"

It had been difficult to fill in the few moments between their arrival at the station and the departure of the train.

They said little empty things . . . repeated them . . . and then were silent. . . .

Then the train began to move, and Mrs. Graham, snatching quickly at him, had kissed him as he was carried off. They stood at the end of the platform, watching the train driving quickly up the valley until it stopped at Coly. Then they heard the whistle of the engine, and saw the smoke curling up, and again the train moved on, and then they could see it no more.

"We'll walk home," Mary whispered to Henry. "She'd much better go back by herself!"

And so they left her, still smiling, though now and then, her hands trembled.

THE EIGHTH CHAPTER

1

A MONTH after Gilbert and Ninian had left England, Henry went to London for a couple of days on business connected with his books. Mrs. Graham had asked him to return to Boveyhayne instead of going to Ireland, until he was fully well again, and he had gladly accepted her invitation. He had written a few pages of a new book that pleased him, and he was anxious to complete the story before he entered the Army. Writing irked him, but he could not abstain from writing . . . some demon drove him to it, forcing him to his desk when all his desire was to be out in the lanes with Mary or sailing about the bay with Tom Yeo and Jim Rattenbury. There were times when he loathed this labour of writing which came between him and the pleasure of living, so that he sometimes saw foxgloves and bluebells and primroses and violets and wild daffodils, not as the careless beauty of a Devonshire lane, but as picturesque material for a description in one of his chapters. And his beastly creatures would not lie still in his study until he returned to attend to them, but insisted on following him wherever he went, thrusting themselves upon his notice continually, whether the time was opportune or not. He would walk with Mary, perhaps to Hangman's Stone, and suddenly he would hear her saying, "What are you thinking of, Quinny?" and he would come out of his silence with a start, and say, "Oh, my book, Mary!" and find that he had been walking by her side, unaware of her, unaware of anything but these abominable paper people who deluged his mind with their being

. . . and when they got to Hangman's Stone, he thought
always, "What a good title for a story!"

"But I can't leave it alone," he would say to himself,
and then he would compare himself to a drunkard, eager
to be quit of his drink, but unable to conquer his craving.
And he had pride in it, too. That was what distinguished
him from the drunkard and the drug-taker. They had no
pride in their drunkenness or their drugged senses, but he
had pride in his books, and constantly in his mind was
the desire that before he joined the Army, he should leave
another book behind him, that his life should be expressed
substantially in a number of novels, so that if he should die
in battle, he would have left something by which men
might remember him.

He had talked to Mary about his position, but she had
insisted that this was a decision he must make for himself.
Her view, and the view of her mother, was that a woman
ought not to take the responsibility of urging a man to
endure the horror and danger of such a war as this.
"Women can't go into the trenches themselves," Mrs. Graham said, "and they've no right to ask any one else to go!"
That was what his father had said.

"But somebody must go, and there are people who have
to be told about things," he objected.

"I think," Mrs. Graham answered, "I'd rather be killed
than be defended by a man who was white-feathered into
doing it, and I know I should never be happy again if I'd
nagged at a man until he joined the Army, and he was
killed. . . . I think that some women will have haunted
minds after this War!"

"It's the Government's job to say who shall go and who
shall stay," Mary added. "That's what they're there for,
and it's mean of them to shuffle out of their responsibility
and let a lot of flappers and old maids do their work for
them!"

Then their talk had taken a new turn, and in the end it
was settled that Mary and he were to be married when the

new book was finished, and then he would join the Army. There had been a difficulty with Mrs. Graham, but Mary over-ruled her.

"I won't let him go until he marries me," she said, shutting her lips firmly and looking very resolutely at her mother.

"Roger and I might go in together," Henry suggested. "I had a letter from him saying he thought he would join soon. Rachel's going to live in the country. . . ."

"She can come here if she likes," Mrs. Graham interjected. "You'd better tell her that when you go to town. She can stay with us until the war's over. . . ."

"There's the baby, of course!" Henry reminded her.

"I know," she answered. "I'd like to hear a baby in this house again. . . ."

2

London was strangely sensitive, easily exalted, easily depressed, listening avidly to rumours, even when they were clearly absurd. It was the least English of the cities, far, far less English than the villages and country towns. London's nerves were often jangled, but the nerves of Boveyhayne were never jangled. London jumped up and down like a Jack-in-the-box, but Boveyhayne moved steadily on. There were times when London was so un-English as to believe that England might be beaten . . . but Boveyhayne never imagined that for a moment. Boveyhayne did not think of the defeat of England, because it had never occurred to Boveyhayne that England could be beaten. Old Widger would sometimes say, "They Germans be cunning!" or "Us'll 'ave to 'it a bit 'arder avore us knocks 'un out!" but Old Widger never imagined for a moment that " 'un," as he always called the Kaiser, would not sooner or later get knocked out, and so he went on with his work, pausing now and then to say, " 'Er's a reg'lar cunnin' old varmint, 'er be!" almost with as much ad-

miration as if he were talking of a fox or an otter that had
eluded the hounds many times. But the cunningest fox
falls to the hounds in the end of some chase, and Widger
did not doubt that "Keyser" would fall, too. Boveyhayne, was very English in its reserves and its dignity.
London might squeal for reprisals, but Boveyhayne never
squealed. When the Germans torpedoed a merchant ship,
Old Widger said, "It bain't very manly, be it, sir?" and
that was all. Old Widger was not indifferent or without
imagination . . . but he had self-respect, and he could not
squeal like a frantic rabbit even when he was in pain. He
could hit, and he could hit hard, but he did not care to
claw and scratch and bite! . . .

Henry disliked London then, but he comforted himself
with the thought that it resembled all capital cities, that
its population was not a native population, but one that
shifted and changed and had no tradition. Old Widger
had lived in the same cottage all his life: his father had
lived there too; and his family, for several generations before his father, had lived and worked in Boveyhayne. They
had habits and customs so old that no one knew the meaning of them. When Widger's wife died, Widger and his
family had gone to church on the Sunday after her burial,
as all the Boveyhayne bereaved do, and had sat through
the service, taking no part in it, neither kneeling to pray
nor rising to sing nor responding to the invocations. But
Old Widger did not know why he had behaved in that
fashion, nor did any one in Boveyhayne. "Don't seem
no sense in it," he said, but nevertheless he did it, and
nothing on earth would have prevented him from doing
it. It was the custom. . . .

But there was no custom in London. There were no
habits, no traditions, nothing to hold on to in times of
crisis or distress. There was no one in London who had
been born and had spent all his life in one house, in a
house, too, in which his father had been born and had lived
and had died. People took a house for three years . . .

and then moved to another one. Locality had no meaning
for them . . . they hardly knew the names of their neighbours . . . they were not surrounded by cousins . . . the
roads and streets had no meaning or memories for them
. . . they were just thoroughfares, passages along which
one walked or drove to a railway station or a shopping
centre. . . .

And while Old Widger, if the thought had been put into
his mind, would stoutly have answered, "Us ain't never
been beat!" a Londoner would have answered, "My God,
supposing we are beaten? . . ." Victory might be long in
being won. Widger would admit that. But "us ain't never
been beat" he would maintain. The Londoner would admit that victory might never be won . . . and in making
the admission, de-nationalised himself. Widger, obstinate,
immovable, imperturbable, kindly, unvengeful and resolute, was English to the marrow . . . and when Henry
thought of England as a conquering country, he thought
of it as a nation of Widgers, not as a nation of Cockneys.

"And it *is* a nation of Widgers," he said to himself.
"The Cockneys shout more, print more, and they squeal a
lot, but the Widgers are in the majority!"

It was not until night fell that Henry's love of London
was restored. When the sky-signs were put out, and the
shop-lights were diminished, and the running flames announcing the merits of this one's whisky and that one's
tea were quenched, London became again an ancient city
that a man could love. . . .

"It's worth fighting for?" Henry murmured to himself as he stood on the terrace of Trafalgar Square, before
the National Gallery, and looked about him at the dusk-
softened outlines and the rich highways of shadows. One
would not fight for the England that squealed through the
ha'penny papers . . . one would gladly throttle that England . . . one would not fight for the England of the Stock
Broker and the Mill Owner . . . but one would fight hard,

fight until death, for the England of Old Widger and the England of this darkened, dignified and beautiful London.

3

He had attended to his business with his publishers, and was walking along the Strand towards Charing Cross, when he became aware of a thrill of emotion running through the crowd that stood on either side of the road.

"What is it?" he said to a bystander.

"The wounded!" was the answer.

He pressed forward, and stood on the edge of the pavement, and as he did so, the ambulances came out of the station. There was a moment of deep, hurting silence, and then came cheers and waving handkerchiefs and sobs. . . . There was a parson standing at Henry's elbow, and he cheered as if he were intoning . . . little sterilised hurrahs . . . and there was a woman who murmured continually, "Oh, God bless them! God bless them all!" while she cried openly, unrestrainedly. Unceasingly, the ambulances seemed to pass on to the hospitals, and the soldiers, pale from their wounds and tired after their journey by sea and train, lay back in queer disregard of the crowd that cheered them. Now and then, one moved his hand in greeting or smiled . . . but most of them were irresponsive, dazed, perhaps hearing still the sound of the smashing artillery and the cries of the maimed and dying, unable to believe that they were back again in a place where there was no fighting, where men and women walked and talked and did their work and took their pleasure in disregard of death and a bloody and abrupt end. . . . There was a private motor-car in the middle of the procession of ambulances, and inside it was a wounded officer with his wife . . . and she did not care who looked on nor what was said, she held him in her arms and kissed him and would not let him go. . . .

"Oh, my God," Henry murmured to himself, as the cars went by, "I can't bear this! . . ."

He wanted to kill Germans . . . it seemed to him then that nothing else mattered but to kill Germans . . . that one must put aside the generous beliefs, the kindly intentions, one's work, one's faith, everything . . . and kill Germans; unceasingly, without relenting . . . kill Germans; that for every wound these men bore, for every drop of blood they had lost, for every pang they had endured, for every tear that their women had shed . . . one must kill Germans.

He withdrew from the crowd. Somewhere near at hand, there was a recruiting office. He remembered to have seen a large guiding sign outside St. Martin's Church. He would go there! . . .

He had to wait until the procession of motor-ambulances had passed by, and then he crossed the street and went to find the recruiting office. "I'm excited," he said to himself. "I'm full of emotion. That's what I am. I'm over-wrought. Those soldiers! . . ."

In his mind, he could see the woman in the motor-car, hugging her wounded husband . . . and a soldier, lying on a stretcher in an ambulance, with his head swathed in bandages, near a little window . . . feebly trying to wave his hand to the crowd. . . .

"It's no good being sloppy," he told himself. "One can't win a war by . . . spilling over. One's got to keep one's head!"

He turned the corner of the Church and saw the recruiting office, covered with posters, in a narrow lane. He walked towards it, slackening his pace as he did so . . . and then he walked past it.

"I can't go in now," he thought. "I must see Roger first . . . and there's the book to finish . . . and Mary! . . ."

4

He had seen Roger and Rachel, and was now on his way
back to Boveyhayne. . . . Roger had agreed that he would
not join without Henry. "I can't go yet," he had said.
"When I've saved a little more, I'll go in. I want to leave
Rachel and Eleanor as secure as I can!"

There was another boom in recruiting just then, following on another German outrage.

"It'll take them some time to shape the crowd they're
getting now," Roger had said, "so that we won't be hin-
dering them if we hang back for a while. I should have
thought you'd want to go into an Irish regiment, Quinny!"

"It doesn't very much matter, does it, what the regiment is?" Henry had answered. "The labels are more or
less meaningless now. And I'd like to be with some one I
know!"

He had given Mrs. Graham's invitation to Rachel, and
Rachel had sent her thanks to Mrs. Graham. She would
be glad to go to Boveyhayne when everything was settled.

Things were clearer now. In a little while, Mary and he
would be married. Then he could go with Roger. He
would have to see his lawyers in Dublin . . . there would
be a marriage settlement to make and business connected
with the estate to settle . . . and that done, and his book
ready for the printers, he would be free.

"I wish the next two months were over," he said to himself.

He had to change at Salisbury, and while he was waiting for the slow train to Exeter, he met Mullally. He had
looked at him, vaguely wondering who he was and why his
face should seem familiar, until recollection had come to
him, and then, with a return of the old aversion, he had
turned away, hoping that Mullally had not seen or recognised him. But Mullally had recognised him, and, unable
as ever to understand that his acquaintance was not
wanted, he came to Henry and held out his hand.

"I thought it was you," he said. "I wasn't sure at first, but when you turned away . . . there was something about your back that was familiar . . . I knew it was you. *How are you?* I haven't seen you since you left Rumpell's, though I've heard of you, of course, and read of you, too! You've become quite well-known, haven't you?"

Henry smiled feebly, an unfriendly, unresponsive, mirthless smile, as was his wont when he was in the presence of people whom he disliked.

"I've often wondered about you," Mullally went on, unembarrassed by Henry's obvious wish to get away from him.

"Oh, yes," Henry replied, saying to himself, "I wish to God my train would come in!"

"Yes, I've often wondered about you," Mullally went on. "And about Farlow and Graham and Carey. You were great friends, you four, weren't you? I'd have called you 'The Heavenly Twins' only there were four of you, and 'quadruplets' is a difficult word for a nickname, don't you think? I mean to say 'The Heavenly Quadruplets' doesn't sound nearly so neat as 'The Heavenly Twins.' It's funnier, of course! What's become of them all? I saw somewhere that Farlow'd written a play, but I didn't see it. I've read one or two of your books, by the way. Quite good, I thought! What did you say'd become of them?"

"Carey's in London . . . at the Bar," Henry answered. "I've just been staying with him. He's married! . . ."

"Dear me! And has he any . . . little ones?"

Oh, that was like Mullally! He would be sure to say "little ones" when he meant "children."

"He has a daughter!"

"Oh, indeed! He must be very gratified. And Farlow and Graham, how are they, and what are they doing?"

"Farlow's in Gallipoli and Graham's in France! . . ."

"Oh, this dreadful war," Mullally exclaimed, wrinkling

his features. "I'm greatly opposed to it. I've been addressing meetings on the subject!"

"Have you?" Henry asked with more interest than he had previously shown.

"Yes, I'm totally opposed to it. All this secret diplomacy and race for armaments . . . that's at the bottom of it all. My dear Quinn, some members of the Cabinet have shares in armament works. It's easy enough to see why we're at war! . . ."

Henry could not prevent himself from laughing.

"Do you mean to say you think they got up the war on purpose so's to get bigger dividends on their armament shares?"

Mullally shrugged his shoulders. "I don't wish to impute motives," he said. "No, I should not care to do that. I believe in the good intentions of my fellow man, but all the same, it's very peculiar. It looks bad! . . ."

"You always were a bloody fool, Mullally, and you're a bloodier one now. Good afternoon!" said Henry, turning to look at the train which was now entering the station.

He hurried to secure a carriage, and while he was settling his bag on the rack, he heard the voice of Mullally bleating in his ear.

"I'm going to Exeter, too," he said. "I'll just get in with you. I have a third class ticket, but if they ask for the excess, I can pay it!"

"Oh, damn!" said Henry to himself.

5

"I can understand the difficulty you have in believing that people could behave so . . . so basely," Mullally said, as the train carried them out of Salisbury.

"I don't believe it at all," Henry answered, "and I think that any one who does believe it is a malicious-minded ass!"

"But they hold the shares . . . you can see the list of

shareholders at Somerset House for yourself . . . and
they'll take the profits. I'm quite willing to believe in the
goodness of the average man . . . in fact, I've denounced
the doctrine of Original Sin very forcibly before now . . .
but I must say that there's something very suspicious
about this business. Very suspicious. And you know
some of the soldiers are really rather! . . ."

"Rather what?" said Henry.

"Well, I don't like saying anything about anybody, but
some of them are not all that they should be. They should
set an example, and they don't. I've heard some very
startling things about the behaviour of the soldiers. Very
startling things. I don't want to say anything that may
sound unpleasant, but I suggest that you should read the
Report of the Registrar-General when it comes out. It
will cause some consternation, I can promise you. Young
women, Quinn, simply can't be kept away from the soldiers, and I've been told . . . well! . . ."

Again he shrugged his shoulders, and turned his palms
upwards and raised his eyebrows. A Member of Parliament had written to the *Morning Post* about it . . . a Conservative member of Parliament, not a Liberal or a Socialist, mark you, but a Conservative. . . .

"Two thousand cases expected in one town," Mullally
whispered. "Knows it for a fact. Seen the girls! . . ."

Mullally proposed a calculation. They were to work out
the number of unmarried girls who would shortly become
mothers, using the Conservative M.P.'s letter as a basis of
calculation.

"Thousands and thousands," he prophesied. "Hundreds of thousands. *All* illegitimate. I believe, of course,
that we make too much fuss about the marriage laws, Quinn,
but still . . . there are limits, don't you think? I mean,
we must make changes slowly, not in this . . . this drastic
fashion. But what are you to expect? When the very
Cabinet Ministers are proved to have shares in munition

works, is it any wonder that the common soldier runs riot? . . .''

"I get out at the next station," said Henry.

"Do you?" said Mullally. "But I thought you didn't change until you got to Whitcombe Junction?"

"I don't," said Henry, "but I get out at the next station!"

"I see," said Mullally.

"About time," Henry thought.

6

After dinner, he asked Mary to walk to the village with him.

"Isn't it late?" Mrs. Graham objected.

"Oh, no," he answered. "It's a beautiful moonlight night, and I feel I want to stretch my legs. I've been cooped up in the train best part of the day. Come along, Mary!"

"I'll just get my coat," she said.

When they were ready, he put his arm in hers, and they walked down the long lane, past the copse and through the pine trees, to the village.

"It's very quiet to-night," Mary said.

"Extraordinarily still," he answered.

There was no one in the village street and there were no lights shining from any of the windows, except from the bedroom of a cottage near the sea.

"They've all gone to bed very early, haven't they?" he said, glancing about the deserted street.

"But it isn't early, Quinny," she replied. "It's quite late. It must be nearly ten o'clock. We had dinner much later to-night because your train was so long in getting in!"

"Well, they're missing a gorgeous night, all of them," he exclaimed, holding her tightly.

They walked to the fisherman's shelter and stood against

the iron rail on top of the low cliff. The moon had made a broad path of golden light across the bay, from the shingle to the pinnacle on the nearer of the two headlands, and they could see the golden water flowing through the hole in the cliff.

"I'd love to bathe now," Mary said. "I'd love to swim all along that splash of moonlight to the caves and back again. . . ."

A belated sea-gull cried wearily overhead and then flew off to its nest in the cliffs.

"The water's awfully black looking outside the moonlight," Henry exclaimed.

"Ummm!" she answered.

They shivered a little in the cold air, and instinctively they drew closer to each other. Beneath them, lying high on the shingle, were the trawlers, lying ready for the morning when the fishermen would push them down into the sea.

"Tom Yeo and Jim Rattenbury are going to have a motor put into their trawler," Mary said. "It'll make a lot of difference to them. They'll be able to go out even when there isn't any wind."

Henry did not answer. He had a strange sense of fear that was inexplicable to him. He seemed to be outside himself, outside his own fear, looking on at it and wondering what had caused it. He felt as if something were pulling at him, trying to force him to look round . . . and he was afraid to look round. . . . He shuddered violently.

"Are you cold, Quinny?" Mary said anxiously, turning to him.

"Yes," he answered quickly, wishing to account for his sudden shivering in a way that would not alarm her. "We'd better go back! . . ."

What was the matter? Why was he so suddenly afraid and so strangely afraid? If it had been dark, very dark, and he had been alone . . . but it was bright moonlight . . . so bright that one could almost see to read . . . and Mary was with him . . . and yet he was afraid to look

round at the White Cliff. Something inside him, apart
from him, seemed to feel that if he looked up the long steep
path over the White Cliff . . . *he would see something.*

"Come on, Mary!" he said, turning to go, and turning
in such a way that he could not see. the Cliff.

They walked rapidly up the street. . . . "That'll warm
me," he explained to Mary . . . and as he walked, he was
afraid to look back.

"What the devil's the matter with me?" he kept saying
to himself until they reached the end of the lane leading
to the Manor.

"You're walking too quickly, Quinny!" Mary said, holding back.

"I'm sorry, dear," he exclaimed, slackening his pace
reluctantly.

He had never had this sensation before . . . as if a fear
had been stuck on to him, a fear that was not part of his
nature, a thing outside him trying to get inside him. . . .
He forgot that Mary had complained of the rapidity with
which he was walking, and he set off again. The pine
trees had a black, ominous look, and the sound of the wind
blowing through their needles was like continuous moaning.

"Are you trying to win a race, Quinny?" Mary said.

He laughed nervously. "No. I'm . . . I'm sorry! . . ."

As they passed the copse, he shut his eyes, and so he
stumbled over the rough ground and almost fell.

"What is it, Quinny?" Mary demanded, catching hold
of him.

"It's nothing," he said. "I'm tired, that's all. . . ."

7

He shut the door behind him quickly, and fastened the
bolts. Mary had gone into the drawing-room, and when
he had secured the door, he followed her.

"Mother's gone to bed," she said, and then, going to him and putting her hands on his shoulder, she added, "What is it, Quinny? Something's upset you. I know it has!"

He looked at her for a few moments without speaking.

"Tell me, please!" she insisted.

He put his arm about her and led her to the armchair by the fire, and when she was seated, he sat down on the floor beside her.

"I didn't want to tell you until we got home," he said. "I didn't want to frighten you. . . ."

"What was it? Was there anything there? . . ."

"I don't know what it was, Mary, but I suddenly felt frightened . . . a queer kind of fright. I was afraid to look round for fear I should see something . . . I don't know what . . . on the cliff. I felt that something wanted me to look round, and I wouldn't. I didn't dare to look round. All the way up the street, I felt that something wanted me to look round. . . . I'm not afraid now!"

"How queer," she said in a low voice.

"I've never felt anything like it before . . . half afraid and half not afraid! . . ."

He began to talk about Mullally. "He's a toad, that fellow," he said, "an . . . an enlarged toad!"

"I'm going to bed," she interrupted. "Good-night, Quinny!"

She bent her face to his.

"Good-night, my dear!" he said, kissing her fondly.

8

Three days later, when he had almost forgotten his fright on the cliffs, he went down to the village to get the morning papers.

"What's the news," he said to one of the villagers whom he met on the way.

" 'Bout the same, sir. Don't seem to be much 'appenin' at present," the man replied.

He went on to the news agency and got the papers, and then, hastily glancing at the headlines for the more obvious news, he tucked the papers under his arm and went slowly back to the Manor by another road than the one by which he had come into the village. There was a field with a hollow where one could lie in shelter and see the whole of the bay and the eastern cliffs in one direction, and the Axe Valley in another, and here he sat for a while, smoking and reading and now and then trying to follow the tortuous windings of the Axe as it came down the marsh to the sea.

"If Ninian were here," he said to himself, "he'd start making plans to straighten it out! . . ."

He glanced through the war bulletins, with their terrible iteration of trenches taken and trenches lost. People read the war news carelessly now, almost wearily, so accustomed had they become to the daily report of positions evacuated and positions retrieved, forgetting almost that at the taking or the losing of a trench, men lost their lives.

"There isn't much in the paper this morning," he said, and then he turned to a page of lesser news, and almost as he did so, his eye caught sight of Gilbert's name. His grip on the paper was so tight that he tore it. He stared at the paragraph with startling eyes, reading and re-reading it, as if he were unable to comprehend the meaning of the thing he read. . . . Then, as understanding came to him, he gaped about with vacant eyes.

"Oh, my God!" he cried, "Gilbert's been killed!"

9

He got up, half choking, and scrambled out of the field. A labourer greeted him, but he made no answer. He ran up the road, and as he ran, he cried to himself, "Gilbert's dead . . . it isn't true . . . it isn't true! . . ."

He thrust open the gate and ran swiftly up to the door.

"Mary!" he shouted. "Mary! Mary!! . . ."

She came running to him, followed by her mother.

"What is it?" she cried, and her heart was full of fear.

Mrs. Graham clutched at him. "It isn't . . . it isn't . . ."

He sank down into a chair and buried his head in his hands. "Gilbert's dead," he said. "He's been killed! . . ."

Mary knelt beside him, and drew his head on to her shoulder. She did not speak. There was nothing that could be said. She knew that Gilbert and Henry had cared for each other as men seldom care . . . and no one, not even she, could bring comfort to the one who was left. So she just held him. . . .

10

Mrs. Graham had left them alone. Her fear had been for Ninian, and when she heard Gilbert's name, her relief was such that she had hurried from the room lest Henry, stricken by the death of his friend, should see her face.

"I know now," he said when he was calmer, "what it was on the White Cliff. He wanted to tell me, Mary. He wanted to tell me . . . and I wouldn't look round. Oh, my God, I wouldn't look round!"

THE NINTH CHAPTER

1

IT was unbelievable that Gilbert was dead. In his mind, Henry could see him, careless, extravagant, always good-tempered and sometimes strangely wise and understanding . . . and he could not believe that he would never see him again, that all that youth and generosity and promise should be turned so untimely to corruption. Gilbert's friends would not even know where his grave was . . . they would not have the poor consolation of finding a place that was his, marked out from all the other places. . . . He had been seen, running forward . . . and then he was seen no more. . . .

"Perhaps," Henry said to comfort himself, "he's been taken prisoner. We shall hear later on that he's been taken prisoner! . . ."

He snatched at any hope. Men had been posted among the dead . . . and then, after a time of mourning, had come the news that they still lived. Perhaps Gilbert was lying somewhere . . . wounded . . . and after a while, news of him would come. Other men might die, but it was incredible that Gilbert should be killed. . . .

He became obsessed with the belief that Gilbert still lived. He went about expecting to see him suddenly turning a corner and shouting, "Hilloa, Quinny!" At any moment, a door might open, and Gilbert would walk in and say, "Well, coves!" There was a printed copy of "The Magic Casement" in the house, and Henry would pick it up, and turn over the pages. . . . "But he can't be dead," he would say to himself, as he fingered the book. "It's absurd! . . ." Even when hope died, there came times when the belief in Gilbert's survival thrust itself into his mind. When the *Lusitania* was torpedoed, he said to himself, "Why, we saw her just after the war began, Gilbert and I, and we cheered! . . ."

The brutality of the war smote him hard. In less than a year from the day when they had stood on the rocks at Tre'Arrdur Bay, lustily cheering as the great Atlantic liner sailed up the sea to the Mersey, Gilbert was dead and the proud ship was a wreck, sneakily destroyed. . . .

Gilbert had left the beginning of a play behind him. He had regretted that he could not finish it before going out to the peninsula . . . had believed that in it he would create something finer and deeper than he had yet done . . . and now it would never reach completion. The mind that imagined it was no more than the rubbish of the fields when the harvest is gathered. . . .

His own work became tasteless to him. He turned with disrelish from his manuscript. "What's the good of it," he said to himself, whenever he looked at it. He tried to put himself into communication with Gilbert's spirit, remembering that night below the White Cliff, when, he now believed, Gilbert had tried to tell him of his death. A month before, he would have ridiculed any one who suggested to him that he should attempt to speak to the dead. "Spookery!" he would have said. But now, in his eagerness to atone, as he said, for his failure to respond when Gilbert had tried to speak to him, he put faith in things that, before, would have seemed contemptible to him. But with all his will to believe, he could not call Gilbert to him. There was a blankness, a condemning silence. . . .

"I failed my friend," he groaned to himself once, "When he felt for me most, I . . . I failed him!"

2

He had gone up to the Common with Mary, and had lain there, talking of Gilbert . . . of what Gilbert had been doing this time a year ago . . . of something that Gilbert had said once . . . of an escapade at Rumpell's . . . and then Mary and he had gone home across the fields. As they walked up the lane to the house, they saw a telegraph messenger ahead of them. They quickened their pace. There was an anxious, strained look on Mary's face, and as the messenger, hearing them behind him, turned and stopped, she made a clutching movement with her hands. "Oh, Quinny!" she said, turning to him with frightened eyes. The boy waited until Henry went up to him, regarding them both with curiosity.

"Is it for us?" Henry asked, knowing that it was, and the boy nodded his head. "I'll take it," he went on. "It'll save you the trouble of going up to the house!"

"Thank you, sir!" the messenger said, and then he handed the telegram to Henry. "Is there any answer, sir?" he asked.

"I don't know," Henry replied. "We'll . . . we'll bring it down to the post-office, if there is!"

He knew that there would not be any answer. . . .

The boy went off, looking back at them now and then, over his shoulder.

"Shall I open it, Mary?" Henry said.

"Do you think? . . ." She did not complete her sentence for she was afraid to utter the thought that was in her mind.

"If it should be bad news," Henry said, "we'd . . .we'd better prepare her for it!"

They stood there, holding the telegram still unopened, as if they could not make a decision. . . .

"Open it, Quinny!" Mary said at last, and he opened the buff envelope and took out the form.

The Secretary for War regretted! . . .

He looked up from the telegram, and saw that Mary was standing in a strained attitude, waiting for him to speak.

"Is it . . . is it *that?*" she said, almost in a whisper.

He bowed his head. "Yes," he said.

She did not speak. She stood quite still, looking at him as if she were trying to find something, but did not know where to look for it. He moved nearer to her, and took hold of her hand and drew her close to him, and she lay quietly in his arms. . . . There was a bird singing very clearly over their heads, and suddenly, while they stood there, silently consoling each other, two wood pigeons flew out of the highest tree, making a great beating of wings as they flew off across the fields. There was a robin in the hedge, turning its head this way and that, and regarding them with curiosity. . . .

She stirred, and then withdrew herself from his arms.

"We must go home," she said, "and tell mother!"

3

Mrs. Graham was in the garden, and she came to the gate as she saw them approaching, waving her hand and smiling at them.

"Will you tell her, Quinny," Mary said, and she slackened her pace slightly and dropped behind him.

He turned to look for her. "Come with me," he said.

"I can't tell her . . . alone!"

There was a chilly fear over both of them. They felt that this blow would strike her down, that she would not survive it. Ninian was the beginning and the end of her life. If Ninian were gone, everything was gone. This house, the farm, the fields were without purpose if Ninian were not there to own them. . . . They went slowly forward, and as they approached they saw her smile vanish, and a puzzled look come in its place. She had waved her hand and smiled at them, but they had not waved back to her, they had not answered her smile . . . and then she saw the telegram in Henry's hand. She made a quick movement, opening the gate and coming rapidly to them.

"What is it?" she said, hoarsely.

He could not think of anything to say. . . .

"It's from the War Office, mother," Mary said.

He stood ready to put his arms about her and support her. . . .

"Give it to me," she said, holding out her hand for the telegram, and he passed it to her.

They stood silently before her while she read it. Then Mary went close to her. "Mother! . . ." she said.

Mrs. Graham did not make any answer to Mary. She still held the telegram in her hands, and gazed at it, reading it over and over. . . .

"Mother, dear!" Mary reached up, and put her arms about her mother's neck.

"Yes, Mary," she answered very calmly.

But Mary could not say any more. She buried her head on her mother's shoulder, and the tears that she had been holding back, would not be held back any longer, and sobs burst from her that seemed as if they would choke her.

"My dear," said Mrs. Graham, raising Mary's face to hers, "we must . . . we must be brave!"

She turned to Henry. "Take her in," she said, "and . . . and comfort her!"

He went to them, and put his arm about Mary, and led her to the house. "Won't you come in, too?" he said, turning to Mrs. Graham.

"No, Henry," she answered. "Not yet. I want to be out here. I . . . I want to be alone!"

She moved away, going slowly down the avenue of trees until she reached the orchard, and then she went into it, and was hidden by the apple trees. . . .

He led Mary into the house. "We can't do anything, Mary," he said. "We're . . . we're all caught in this thing . . . and we can't do anything. . . ."

She went to her room, and when he had seen the door close behind her, he turned to go back to the drawing-room. He would have to write to Roger. "First it was Gilbert . . . then it was Ninian . . . presently, it will be! . . ."

He shuddered, and tried to shut the thought out of his mind.

There was a servant in the hall. "Tell the others," he said in a cold, toneless voice, "that Mr. Ninian . . . has been killed in France!"

"Oh, sir! . . ." the girl cried, clasping her hands together.

He did not wait to hear, and she hurried down the passage to the kitchens.

"Two of us gone now," he said to himself.

He searched for writing materials, wandering round and round the room until he forgot what it was he wanted. "I'm looking for something," he said aloud, "I'm looking for something, but I don't know what it is! . . ."

Then he remembered.

"I mustn't let myself go," he said to himself. "I must keep a hold of myself. I've got to look after them . . . they'll want some one to . . . to lean on!"

He began the letter to Roger. *"Dear Roger,"* he wrote, and then he dropped his pen. He sat with his elbows resting on the table, staring in front of him, but seeing nothing. "First there was Gilbert," he was saying to himself, "then there was Ninian . . . and presently there will be . . . *me!"*

One could not believe it. One could not believe it. Why it was only a little while ago that Ninian was here, in this very room, telling them how clever the Engineers were. They were to win the war, these Engineers, unless stupid people, like the "dug-out," prevented them from doing so. There, in that corner there, over by the fire, that was where he had sat, and told them of the Engineers. He had lain back in his chair, carelessly throwing his leg over the arm of it. . . . And when Mrs. Graham had risen and left the room, unable to stay any longer, and had called to him to come to her room and say "Good-night!" he had looked anxiously after her, and then, after a little while of fidgetting and poor effort to talk lightly, had gone to her. . . .

How could one believe it! How could any one believe that this hideous nightmare was true! . . . that this horrible thing which devoured young men was not a creature of a fevered mind. . . . Presently the blood would cool and the eyes would see clearly . . . and Ninian's great shouting voice would roar through the house, and Gilbert would stroll in, and say "Hilloa, coves! . . ."

There was a sound of steps in the passage, and he sat up and listened. Then the door opened and Mrs. Graham came in. There was a bright look in her tearless eyes. Her lips were firmly closed, and he saw that her hands were clenched. He stood up as she entered, and looked at her as she came towards him. She came close to him and laid her hand on his.

"Poor Mary," she said, softly, "we . . . we must comfort poor Mary!"

She looked about the room. "Where is she?" she asked, turning to him again.

"Upstairs," he answered.

She went towards the door. "I must go and comfort her," she said. "She was . . . very fond of . . . of Ninian!"

He followed her to the door, afraid that she might break down, but she did not break down. She gathered her skirts about her, and went up the stairs to Mary's room, and her steps were firm and proud. He could hear the rustle of her skirt on the landing as she passed along it out of his sight, and then he heard her knocking on Mary's door.

"Can I come in, Mary?" she asked in a clear voice.

He could hear the door opening . . . and then he heard it being closed again.

He stood at the foot of the stairs, listening, but there was no need of him. He turned away, and as he did so, Widger came into the hall. The old man stood for a moment or

two without speaking. Then he made a suppliant movement with his trembling hands.

"It b'ain't true? . . ." he mumbled thickly.

"Yes, Widger," Henry answered, "it is."

The old man turned away. "I knowed 'un ever since 'e
were a baby," he said, and his lips were quivering.
"Praper li'l chap 'e were, too!

"It b'ain't right," he went on, looking helplessly about
him. Then his voice took a firmer, more definite note,
"Where's missus to?" he asked.

"She's upstairs, Widger," Henry answered. "I don't
think I'd say anything to her at present, if I were you!"

"Very well, sir!"

He moved away. The vitality seemed to have gone out
of him, and suddenly he had become old . . . senile . . .
shuffling.

"They'm wisht times, sir!" he said, as he left the hall.

4

Henry wrote to Roger, telling him of Ninian's death,
and when he had finished the letter, he went out to post it.
He could not sit still in the house . . . he felt that he must
move about until he was worn and exhausted. Mrs. Graham was still with Mary, but perhaps by the time he returned, they would be able to come downstairs again. The
pride with which Mrs. Graham had supported herself in
her grief seemed to him almost god-like. Once, in the
South of Ireland, he had seen a peasant woman bidding
good-bye to her husband. As the train steamed out of the
station, she howled like a wounded animal, spinning round
like a teetotum, and waving her hands and arms wildly.
Her hair had tumbled down her back, and her eyes seemed
to be melting, so freely did she weep . . . and then when
the train had disappeared round a bend of the track, she
dried her eyes and went home. Her grief, that had seemed
utterly inconsolable, had been no more than a summer

shower. . . . He had had difficulty in preventing himself
from laughing, and he could not restrain a feeling of contempt for her. "They write plays about that kind of silly
howling at the Abbey Theatre, and call it 'the Celtic
twilight.' No dignity, no decency! . . ."

He had heard sentimental Englishmen prating about
"the tragic soul" of Ireland because they had listened to
hired women *keening* over the dead. "But that isn't
grief," he had said to them. "They're paid to do that!"
The Irish liked to splash about in their emotions . . . they
wallowed in them. . . .

But Mrs. Graham's grief was more than a summer
shower. Henry knew instinctively that Ninian's death had
killed her. She might live for many years, but she would
be a dead woman. She would show very little, nothing, to
those who looked to see the signs of woe, but in her heart
she would hoard her desolation, keeping it to herself, ob-
truding her sorrow on no one . . . waiting patiently and
silently for her day of release, when, as her faith told her,
she and her son would come together again. . . .

"It's unfair," he told himself, "to compare the grief
of an illiterate Irishwoman with the grief of an English
lady!"

But then he had seen the grief of poor Englishwomen.
Four of the Boveyhayne men had been drowned in a naval
battle. He had gone to the memorial service in Boveyhayne Church, and had seen the friends of those men mingling their tears . . . but there had been none of this emotional savagery, this howling like women in kraals, this
medicine-man grief. . . .

5

They were both in the drawing-room when he returned.

"I've written to Roger," he said, to explain his absence.
"Perhaps," he went on, "there are other letters you'd like
me to write?"

"Yes," she said, "it would be kind of you, Henry! . . ."

There was Ninian's uncle, the Dean of Exebury, and Mr. Hare, with whom he had worked . . . they must be told at once . . . and there were other relatives, other friends. . . . He spent the evening in doing the little services that must be done when there is death, and found relief for his mind in doing them.

"I told the servants," he said, looking up from a letter he was writing. "Old Widger wanted to see you! . . ."

"Poor Widger," she said. "He and Ninian were so fond of each other!"

She got up and went to the door. "I must go and say something to him," she said. "He'll feel it so much!"

She closed the door behind her, and he sat staring at it after she had gone. The matchless pride of her, that she could forget herself so completely and think of the subordinate sorrow of her servant when she might have been absorbed by her own!

He turned to Mary who was sitting near him, and reached out and took her hand in his, but neither of them spoke.

What was there to say? Ninian was dead . . . old men had made a war, and this young man had paid for it . . . and everywhere in Europe, there were mourners for the young, slain for the folly and incompetence of the old and the worn and the impatient.

He released Mary's hand, and resumed the writing of his letter. Before he had finished it, Mrs. Graham returned to the room.

"Poor Widger," she said, "he . . . he cried!"

She came to the table where Henry was writing, and placed her hand on his shoulder, and looked concernedly at him.

"Aren't you tired, Henry?" she said.

"No, thanks!" he answered, glancing up at her and smiling.

"You mustn't tire yourself!" she bent over him and

kissed his forehead lightly. "You've been a great help, Henry," she said.

6

But in her room, where none could see her, she shed her tears. . . .

THE TENTH CHAPTER

1

He had returned to Ireland. In Dublin, he found a strange mixture of emotions. Marsh and Galway and their friends were drilling with greater determination than ever, and occasionally they were to be seen parading the streets. Some of them wore green uniforms, shaped after the pattern of the khaki uniform of the British Army, but most of them wore their ordinary clothes, with perhaps a bandolier and a belt and a slouch hat. They carried rifles of an old make, and had long, clumsy bayonets slung by their sides. It seemed to Henry as he watched a company of them marching through College Green that these men were not of the fighting breed . . . that these pale clerks and young workmen and elderly professors and hungry, emaciated labourers were unlikely to deal in the serious work of war . . . and when he met John Marsh in the evening, he sneered at him. Marsh kept his temper. He was more tolerant now than he had been in the days when he had tutored Henry at Ballymartin. He admitted that the Sinn Feiners were widely unpopular. There were many reasons why they should be. Dublin was full of men and women mourning for their sons who had died at Suvla Bay . . . and were in no mood for rebellion.

"The war's popular in the Combe," he said. "The women are better off now than they were in peace times. That's a handsome tribute to civilisation, isn't it? The country people are the worst. They're rich . . . the war's bringing them extraordinary prosperity . . . and some of our people are tactless. But we've got to go on. We've got to save Ireland's soul! . . ."

Henry made an impatient gesture. "Why do you talk that high-falutin' stuff," he said.

"It isn't high-falutin' stuff, Henry. I'm speaking what I believe to be the truth. The English have tried a new way to kill the Irish spirit, and by God they look like succeeding. They couldn't kill it by persecuting us, they couldn't kill it by ruining us, but they may kill it by making us prosperous. I feel heart-broken when I talk to the farmers. Money! That's all they think about. They rob their children of their milk and feed them on tea, so's they can make a few more pence. Oh, they're being anglicised, Henry! If we can only blow some of the greed out of them, we'll have done something worth while!"

He was more convinced now than ever that the Irish were to be betrayed by the English after the war.

"Look how they minimise our men's bravery at the front. Even the *Irish Times* is protesting! . . ."

It seemed to Henry to be ridiculous to believe that the English government was deliberately depreciating the work of the Irish soldiers, and he said so. "They hardly mention the names of any regiments," he pointed out.

But John Marsh had an answer for him. He produced a despatch written by a British admiral in which was narrated the story of the landing at Suvla Bay and the beaches about Gallipoli.

"He mentioned the name of every regiment that took part in the landing, except the two Irish regiments that did the hardest work and suffered the most deaths. I suppose that was an accident, Henry, a little oversight!"

"You don't think he left them out on purpose, do you?"

"I do. So does every man in Ireland, Unionist or Nationalist. You see, we know this man in Ireland . . . he's a well-known Unionist . . . a bigot . . . and there isn't a person in Ireland who doesn't believe that he deliberately left the names of Dublins and the Munsters out of his despatch. He forgot, when he was writing it, that he was a sailor, and remembered only that he was a politician . . . the kind that dances on dead men's graves!''

It was difficult to argue with Marsh or with any one who thought as he thought, in face of that despatch. The omission was inexplicable if one did not accept the explanation offered by Marsh. The tradition of the sea is an honourable one, and sailors do not do things like that . . . the scurvy acts of the cheaper politicians. . . .

''You make a fence about your mind, John,'' said Henry, ''and you spend all your efforts in strengthening it, so that you haven't time either to look over it and see what's beyond it, or to cultivate what's inside it. You're just building up barriers, when you should be knocking them down!''

It was useless to be angry with Marsh or to argue with him. In everything that was done, he saw the malevolent intent of a treacherous people.

''Look at this,'' he said one evening when the English papers had come in, and he pointed to a leading article in the *Morning Post* in which the writer stated that the bravery of the Irish soldiers showed that the Irish people had now no feeling or grievance against the English, and therefore Home Rule was no longer necessary. ''Already, they're plotting! They defile the dead . . . they use our dead men as . . . as political arguments!''

''But the *Morning Post* has no influence in England,'' Henry retorted angrily. ''It's only read by footmen and sluts! . . .''

''Some of our people are dubious,'' John went on. ''They're inclined to take your point of view, and trust the English. I'll read this paper to them. That'll pull them up. We'd have been content with Home Rule before, but we want absolute separation now. We don't want to be associated with a race that makes bargains on bodies! . . .''

''You're doing a damned bad work, John! . . .''

"I'm helping to keep Ireland Irish, Henry!" He paused for a few moments, and then, laughing a little self-consciously, he proceeded. "Do you know that poem of Yeats's?"

> *It's with O'Leary in the grave.*
> *Romantic Ireland's dead and gone,*

Henry nodded his head.

"Well, we're going to see whether we can't make Yeats re-write it. Good-night, Henry!"

2

He stayed in Dublin for a few weeks, gathering up old threads and working on his novel; but the book made slow progress, and so, thinking that if he were in a quieter, less social place, he could work more quickly, he went home to Ballymartin, and here, soon after he arrived, he received a letter from Roger, announcing that he intended to enter the artillery almost at once. *"I can get a commission,"* he wrote, *"and so I shall go in. You said something about wanting to join at the same time as me, but perhaps as you are going to be married to Mary shortly, you'll want to wait until afterwards. If I were you I should apply for a commission in an Irish regiment."*

He put the letter down abruptly. Ever since the death of Ninian, he had felt convinced that the four friends were to be killed in battle. Gilbert had been the first to join, and Gilbert was the first to be killed. Then Ninian joined . . . and Ninian died. Roger, too, would be killed, and so would he, when he joined. The death of Gilbert had seemed to him to be a casual thing, a tragic accident, but when Ninian had been killed, it had seemed to him that here was no fortuity, that Gilbert and Ninian had died inevitably, that Roger and he, when they went out, would be unable to escape this destiny . . . and everything that he

had done since Ninian's death had been done in that belief.
He would finish a book, he would marry Mary, he would
settle his estate as best he could . . . and then he
would make the end that Gilbert and Ninian had
made. . . .

But now, as he put Roger's letter down, he had a swift,
compelling desire to dodge his destiny, to elude death, to
alter the course of things. Why should he die? Why
should he yield himself up, his youth, his work, his love,
his hope of happiness and renown and honour . . . to this
consuming thing? He could look to years of happiness
with Mary, years of work on his books, years of enjoyment
of things won and earned . . . and he was to give up all
that promise and go to a bloody death in war? Not every
man who went was killed or even wounded . . . one knew
that . . . but *he* would be killed . . . he knew that, he
told himself, as well as he knew that he was then alive.
Sensitive-natured men, such as he, were bound to be killed
. . . they had not the phlegm of men with blunter natures
. . . they would not be able to keep still when stillness
meant safety . . . their nerves would go, and in that hideous hell of noise and battering, of men killing or being
killed, his mind might be destroyed. . . .

That seemed to him to be the worst thing of all. He
might not be killed . . . he might be made mad. . . .

"I can do other work," he said to himself. "I can work
for Ireland. I can try to make things friendlier
here! . . ."

He planned a group of Young Irishmen, as he named
them, to do for Ireland what Roger's Improved Tories had
hoped to do for England. They could study the conditions
of Irish elementary education; they could try to make a
survey of Irish wealth in the hope of discovering the inci-
dence of its distribution; they could make an enquiry into
work and wages, and try to stimulate the growth of Trades
Unionism. He could help to make opinion, to create a
social consciousness, to establish a tradition of honourable

service to the community. . . . There were a host of things
he could do, valuable things, for Ireland, things that were
not now being done by any one. He knew people in Dublin, Crews and Jordan and Saxon and men like them, who
were of his mind and would work patiently at dull things
in the hope of getting an ordered community. Railways!
One had to get the Irish railways reorganised and grouped.
If one could solve the problem of traffic, so that the East
and West and North and South of Ireland would be as
accessible to each other as the East and West and North and
South of England, one would have made a large movement
towards a better state. . . .

That was what he would do. He would help to construct
things, not to destroy them. He was not afraid to go to
the war . . . that was not the reason why he was resolving
that he would refuse to be a soldier. It was because he
could do better, finer work by living for Ireland than by
dying for England. People throughout Europe were already perturbed at the waste of potential men in war . . .
wondering whether, after all, it was a wise thing to let
rare men, men of unique gifts go to war. Was it really
wise of England to let such a man as Gilbert Farlow, with
the rare gift of comedy, be lost in that haphazard manner?
Ninian had had the potentialities of a great engineer.
Would it not have been wiser to have kept him to his
railway-building than to have let him fall, as he fell, to
the bullet of a sniper? . . . Already people were asking
such questions as these. If he were to go out, and were to
be killed, would they not say, "This man had gifts that
marked him out from other men. We ought not to have
wasted him!" Well, why should he be wasted? He was
not afraid. He insisted that he was not afraid. It needed
high courage to stand up and say, "I am a man of special
gift and I will not let that gift be wasted in war!" That,
in effect, was what he was preparing to do. People would
speak behind his back . . . speak even to his face . . . and
call him a coward! Well, let them do so. . . .

3

But in his heart, he knew that he was afraid to go. Almost he deceived himself into believing that he was behaving well in refusing to join the Army so that he might devote himself more assiduously to Ireland and his work . . . but not completely did he persuade himself. The fear of death was in him and he could not allay it. The fear of mutilation, of madness, of blindness, of shattered nerves sent him shuddering from the thought of offering himself as a soldier . . . and mixed up with this devastating fear was a queer vanity that almost conquered the fear.

"If I were to go in, I might do something . . . something distinguished!"

There were times when he gave himself up to dreams of glory, saw himself decorated with high awards for bravery. He would imagine himself performing some impossible act of courage . . . saving an Army Corps from destruction . . . showing resource in a period of crisis, and so bringing salvation where utter loss had seemed inevitable. But these times of glory were few and brief: he saw himself most often, killed ingloriously, inconspicuously, one of a crowd, blown, perhaps, to pieces or buried in bombarded earthworks; and through his dreams of glory and his plans for work in Ireland, there stubbornly thrust itself this accusation: I'm a coward! I'm a coward! I'm a coward!

In England, men were charging the queer people who called themselves Conscientious Objectors with cowardice, but the charge seemed a baseless one to Henry. He did not believe that he could endure the odium and obloquy which some of the Conscientious Objectors had borne. There was courage in the man who said, "I will fight for my country!" but that courage might be less than that of the man who said, "I will not fight for my country!" Henry was not a Conscientious Objector, nor could he understand the state of mind of the man who was. He was a coward.

Inside him, he knew that he was a coward. Inside him, he accused himself of cowardice. Everything in his life showed that he was a coward, that he shrank from physical combats, from tests of courage, that sometimes he shrank from spiritual contests. . . .

"I ought to tell Mary," he said to himself. "I can't marry her without telling her that I'm . . . a funk!"

But he temporised even in this. "I'll wait a little while longer," he said. "Perhaps later on! . . ."

Always he wanted to thrust the unpleasant thing a little further off. It was as if he had said to himself, "I won't deal with it just yet . . . and perhaps it won't need to be dealt with!"

"I'll finish my book first," he said, "and then I'll tell Mary. Perhaps the war will be over! . . ."

4

Mary wrote to him twice every week. Rachel Carey and her baby were staying at Boveyhayne Manor now, and Mary was glad of their company in the house, for the child gave Mrs. Graham pleasure. She enquired continually about his book. *"What a pity,"* she wrote once, *"that it was not finished before Roger went into the Army. Then you could both have gone in together."* And he had written, *"Yes, it is a pity the book was not done before Roger joined up . . . but it'll soon be finished. I'm getting on excellently with it. When it's finished, I'll come over to Boveyhayne, and then we'll settle just when we shall get married! . . ."*

Then came a mood of abasement, and he wrote a long, incoherent letter to her, telling her that he had resolved that he would not go into the Army. *"Because I'm a coward, Mary. I've thought the thing over from beginning to end, thought about it until I became dizzy with thinking, and this is the end of it all: I'm a coward. I haven't the pluck to go into the Army. That's the truth, Mary! I*

make excuses for myself . . . I pretend that this is Eng-
land's war, not Ireland's, and tell myself that an Irishman
who joins the British Army should be regarded in the way
that an American, who joined, would be regarded . . .
that Irish soldiers in the British Army are Foreign Legion-
aries . . . and I twist my mind about in an effort to make
excuses like that, to convince, not you or any one else, but
me. I think I could convince you that I ought not to join,
but I can't convince myself. I'm not joining, simply be-
cause I'm a damned coward, Mary. I'm not fit to be your
husband, dear. I wasn't fit to be the friend of Gilbert and
Ninian. I'm a contemptible thing that runs to its burrow
when it hears of danger. I'm glad my father is dead. He
hated the war, but he'd have hated to know that I was not
in it. He took it for granted that I would go . . . never
dreamed that I wouldn't go. If he'd thought that I
wouldn't join, he would never have talked to me about the
war in the way he did. My father was a proud man,
Mary, as proud as your mother, and I think he'd have died
of shame if he'd thought I was funking this. I don't
know what you'll think of me. I know what I think of
myself. I simply can't face it, Mary . . . that bloodiness
and groaning and stench and unending horror. That's
the truth about me. I'm a coward, and I'm not fit for you.
I'd fail you, dear, if you needed me. I fail everybody.
I fail everything. I'm rotten through and through. . . ."

5

But he did not send the letter to her. He had read it
over before putting it in the envelope. "Hysterical," he
said to himself, calmer now that he had vented his feelings.
"That's what it is!"

He was about to tear it up, but before he could do so,
his mind veered again. "I'll put it away," he said. "I'll
leave it until the morning, and read it again. Perhaps
I'll think differently then. I ought to tell Mary. I can't

go on just not joining, and letting her gradually suspect.
I ought to go to her, and tell her straight out. When my
book's done I'll go to her. . . ."

"What sort of a man am I?" he said again. "Analys-
ing myself like this . . . turning myself inside out . . .
poking and probing into my mind! . . . Fumbling over my
life, that's what I'm doing! Why don't I stand up to
things? What's the meaning of me? What am I here
for?"

If he could only strip himself to the marrow of his
mind, if he could only see inside himself and know what
was his purpose and discover the content of his being. . . .

"I'm morbid," he said. "I'm too introspective. I
ought to look out of myself. But I can't. It isn't my
fault that my eyes are turned inwards. I'm made like
that. I can't alter my make. I can destroy myself, but
I can't alter my make. . . .

"Perhaps," he thought, "if I were to take more exercise, if I were to go for long walks, I'd think less about
these things. I'd get healthier notions. If I were to enlist, go into the ranks, and endure all that the men endure,
that might make my mind healthier. All that drill and
marching. . . .

"But it's the spirit of me that's wrong," he muttered
aloud. "It's not my body . . . it's *me!*

"I must work. I must work hard, and forget all this
torturing! . . ."

He wrote furiously at his book, and gradually it came to
its end. "I'll go down to Dublin again," he said, when
it was finished "and see if I can't do something there that'll
make me forget things!"

He stayed at Ballymartin until he had corrected the
proofs of the new book, and then some business on the
estate kept him at home for nearly another month. It was
not until well in the New Year that he was able to leave
home, and almost at the last moment he decided not to go
to Dublin, but to travel from Belfast, by Liverpool, to

Boveyhayne. Mary had asked him to spend Christmas with them, but he had made an excuse: estate business and his book; because he could not yet bring himself to tell her of his cowardice. He felt that when he did so, she would end their engagement, and he wished to keep her love as long as he could. He wrote to her very frequently, more frequently than she wrote to him, telling her of Irish affairs. She had had difficulty in understanding so many things, but she was eager to know about them. He had filled a letter with bitter complaint of the corruption in Irish civic life, and she had asked why he believed in Home Rule. *"If you can't trust these people to manage a municipality, how can you trust them to manage a nation?"* And he had written a lengthy epistle on the state of Ireland.

"You see, dear," he wrote, *"it isn't reasonable to expect us to undo in a generation work which it took your country several centuries to do. Your people have steadily destroyed and corrupted my people. I know they're trying to make amends, but they mustn't expect miracles. You can't wave a wand over Ireland, and say 'Let there be light!' and instantly get light. You've got to remember that Ireland is populated largely by the dregs of Ireland . . . what was left after your countrymen had persecuted and exiled and hanged the most vigorous and most courageous men we had . . . and it'll take a generation or two, more perhaps, to get a decent level again. The most powerful man in Dublin at this minute is a haberdasher who owns almost everything there is to own: newspapers, conveyances and heaven knows what; and he has the mind of . . . well, an early nineteenth-century mill-owner! John Marsh spends a deal of time in vilifying the English as a mean-minded people, but my God, he has only got to look round the corner in Dublin, to see mean-minded men by the hundred. He wrote to me the other day, crowing because his Volunteers had prevented the application of conscription to Ireland, and that's a frame of mind I don't understand. He's an idealist, but all his ideals are being em-*

ployed to enable mean-minded and greedy men like the
farmers to go on being more mean-minded and greedier.
The principal argument seems to be that the Irishman must
stay at home and make money out of the war. That's a
long way from the days of the 'wild geese' and the order
of chivalry, isn't it?

"I'm a Home Ruler because I want to see a sense of
responsibility cultivated in these people, and you can't
have a sense of responsibility until you've got something
for which you are responsible. I don't doubt that out of
this heart-breaking population, a decent-minded population
will come. After all, the first settlers in Australia weren't
much better than the people who control the Dublin Cor-
poration, were they? If John Marsh had been about the
world more, had had to manage things, and if Mineely and
Connolly and the Dublin Labour people had not been em-
bittered beyond all sanity of judgment by that haberdasher
I mentioned earlier in this letter, they'd have been useful
in the way that I want Crews and Jordan and Saxon and
all those patient people to be useful.

"I wish you could meet Crews and Jordan and Saxon.
They're very dissimilar, but they've got something like
the unifying motive of a monastery, and they're willing to
serve and to plod and to be patient. I fight with Saxon
because he's a pacifist, but like all pacifists he's a very
pugnacious person, and he can get frightfully angry, but
it's pitiful to see him when he's been angry, because he's
so sorry afterwards. I'm not a pacifist, but I haven't a
tenth of his pluck. He'd endure anything, that man.
Crews and Jordan are younger than he, and very brainy.
Crews looks as if he were one of the Don't-Care-a-Damn
Brigade . . . Dublin's full of them . . . but he does care.
He has a curiously subtle brain, and I do not know any
one so imperturbable as he is. He never loses his temper
. . . at least I've never seen him lose it . . . except, so he
says, with stockbrokers and haberdashers and that kind of
rubbish. Jordan is one of the brainiest men in Ireland . . .

that, I suppose, is because he has got some English blood in him: a cynical-looking man, but that's all his fun. And he works, my goodness, he works!

"*It's with men like these that I want to work, because I believe that they will prepare the place for the foundation of a decent commonwealth. They aren't miracle-mongers, thank God, like John Marsh and Galway and Mineely. They aren't up in the sky to-day and down in the mud to-morrow. They keep to the level.*

"*Then there's the Plunkett House lot. You remember, I told you about Sir Horace Plunkett and the Co-operative Movement. Well, I want to get Crews and Jordan and Saxon to link themselves on to the Plunkett House people and form the nucleus of a new Irish Group. There are a few of the men at Trinity College who will come into it, but I'm afraid all the men at the National University are under the influence of Marsh and MacDonagh and the sloppy romantics.*

"*You see, dear, don't you, that this job of making a commonwealth of worth in Ireland is a long and difficult one. That's why we've got to be very patient. Everything's against us. We have a contemptible press, a cowardly crowd of corrupt politicians, a greedy people, an ignorant and bigoted priesthood (that includes the Protestant clergy) and a complete lack of social consciousness and plan of life. But then, what's life for, if it isn't to cope with difficulties like that. . . .*"

6

There was snow, thick and long-lying, on the ground when he reached Boveyhayne, and the *crunch-crunch* of it under their feet, as Mary and he walked home, gave him a feeling of pleasure, and the cold, bracing air exhilarated him so that he laughed at things which would otherwise barely have made him smile. The antics of Rachel's daughter, as related to him by Mary, seemed extraordi-

narily entertaining, and when he drew Mary's arm in his
and pressed it tightly, he felt that there was nothing in
heaven or on earth more to be desired than the love of a
woman and the love of a child. He had a sense of age,
of a passed boundary, that made him feel much older
than Mary. "Here I am, listening to her as she talks
gaily about a child's pranks, nodding my head and laughing, too . . . and in a little while I shall tell her everything . . . and then I shall go . . . and we will not laugh
again together. I'm holding her arm closely in mine, and
presently I shall kiss her lips, and she will put her arms
about me with the careless intimacy of lovers . . . and
then I shall tell her everything . . . and she will kiss me
no more . . . and our intimacy will shrivel up! . . ."

He wished to prolong his pleasure in this walk through
the snow, and so he took her back to the Manor by long
roads and roundabout ways. They did not climb up the
old path over the cliff because that was so much shorter
than the hair-pin road. . . . "I must tell her soon," he
said to himself, "but before I tell her, I must feel the most
of her love for me!"

He listened to her, not for what she was saying, but for
the sound of her voice, and made short answers to her so
that he might interrupt the flow of her speech as little as
possible. When he returned along this road, he would
come alone and for the last time, and so, that his memory
of her might be full, he would be no more than her auditor
and watcher. Just to have her by his side, her arm in his,
and hear her . . . that was sufficient.

They walked through the village and when they came
to Boveyhayne lane, he said to her, "Isn't there a longer
way, Mary?" and she laughed at him, bantering him because of his sudden desire for exercise; but she yielded to
him, and they took the longer road that led them past the
Roman quarries to the fir tree, standing in isolation where
the main roads meet.

"Mary," he said, as they came in sight of the house,

"I want to tell you something . . . something important! . . ."

"Yes, Quinny?"

"But not now, dear. To-night! Or to-morrow, perhaps!"

She pinched his cheek in a pretence at anger. "You
were always very vague, Quinny!" she said.

"I know," he answered. "It's a kind of . . . cowardice,
that, isn't it? I'm vague because I dislike . . . am afraid
. . . to be definite. I'm a frightful coward, Mary! . . ."

He might approach the subject by these devious ways,
he told himself. He had not meant to talk to her about his
failure in courage until she and he could be alone in the
evening . . . this walk together was to be the final lovers'
stroll, unmarred by any bitterness . . . but even in his
effort to postpone the time of telling, he had prepared to
tell her . . . and perhaps it was better that she should
know now. Here, indeed, in this snowy silence, they were
free from any intrusion. It might not be possible to make
his confession to her without interruption from Rachel or
Mrs. Graham . . . and some feeling for the fitness of
things made him decide that this outdoor scene was a better place for his purpose than the lamplit interior of the
Manor. Through the blown branches of the hedges he
could see the thick sheets of snow spread over the fields.
The boughs of the fruit-trees in the orchard showed very
black beneath their white covering, as if they felt cold,
and he looked away quickly to the haystacks in the farmyard that seemed so warm in spite of the snow. The dusk
was drawing in, and the grey sky was darkening for the
night. . . .

"Mary," he said, so abruptly that she looked up at him
enquiringly. "Let's walk back a little way. . . ."

"But, Quinny, it's getting late. They'll wonder what's
happened to us!"

"I want to tell you . . . now, Mary!"

He compelled her to turn, as he spoke, and they walked slowly back towards the fir tree.

"What is it, Quinny?" she asked tenderly, as if she would comfort him.

"I . . . I want to tell you something!"

"Yes?"

"I hardly know how to begin. It's very difficult, dear. . . ."

"What is it, Quinny?" she demanded, more anxiously.

But still he would not tell her . . . he must have her love a little longer.

"Mary, I love you so much, dear . . . oh, I feel like a fool when I try to tell you how much I love you!"

"I know you love me, Quinny!"

"And now . . . this very minute . . . I love you far more than I've ever loved you. Every bit of me is in love with you, Mary. You're very sweet and dear! . . ."

She had a sense of impending disaster, but she did not express it in her words. "And I love you, Quinny!" she said. "I can't love you more than I've always loved you! . . ."

"Could you love me less than you've always loved me?" he asked, turning and standing before her so that his eyes were looking into hers.

"I don't know," she answered. "I've never tried!"

He did not say any more for a few moments, but stood with his hands on her shoulders, looking steadily into her eyes, while she looked steadily into his. Then he took his hands from her shoulders and drew her into the shelter of his arms, and kissed her, letting his lips lie long on hers.

"What do you want to tell me?" she said in a whisper.

7

Then he told her.

"I wrote to you when I was at Ballymartin," he said,

"but I did not post the letter. I brought it with me. I meant to destroy it because I thought it was too emotional, and then I thought that perhaps I had better let you see it so that you might judge me, not just as I am now, talking to you quietly like this, but as I was when I wrote it!"

He took the letter from his pocket and gave it to her.

"I had to tell you, Mary. I couldn't marry you without letting you know what kind of man I am. I'm too frightened to go to the Front. At the bottom of all my excuses, that's the truth."

She did not speak, but stood with his letter in her hands, turning it over. . . .

"I've tried to persuade myself," he went on, "that I'm of special account, that I ought not to go to the war, but I know very well that in a time like this, no one is of special account. Gilbert said something like that at Tre'Arrdur Bay when I told him that his life was of greater value than the life of . . . of a clerk. I suppose, the finer a man is, the more willing he is to take his share in war, and if that's true, I'm not really a fine man. I'm simply a coward, hoarding up my life in a cupboard, like a miser hoarding up his money. I should have been the first to spend myself . . . like Gilbert and Ninian. I'm the only one of the Improved Tories who hasn't gone! . . . Oh, I couldn't offer you myself, dear. I'm too mean . . . I'm a failure in fineness. . . . I used to feel contempt for Jimphy Jayne . . . but he didn't hesitate for a moment. It never entered his head not to go. The moment the war began, Gilbert enlisted, and I suppose Ninian must have left that railway the very minute he heard the news. I was never quite . . . never quite on their level, Mary, and I don't suppose I ever shall be now!"

She moved slightly, as if she were tired of remaining in one position, and were shifting to an easier one, but still she did not speak, nor did she raise her eyes to look at him.

"I'm not fit to be your husband," he said. "I'm not fit to be any woman's husband, but much less yours. Even now, when I'm standing here talking to you in this safety, the thought of . . . of being out there makes me shiver with fear. It's the thought of . . . of dying! . . . I think and think of all those young chaps, all the fellows I knew, robbed of their right to live and love, as I love you, and work and make their end in decency and peace . . . and I can't bear it. I want to save myself from the wreckage . . . to hide myself in safety until this . . . this horror is ended!" He paused for a while, as if he were searching for words and then he went on. "There was an officer in my carriage to-day . . . going on to Whimple . . . and he told me about poison gas . . . the men died in frightful agony, he said . . . and then he talked about machine guns. . . . 'They can perforate a man like a postage stamp,' he said. . . . Isn't it vile, Mary?"

Her head was still bent, and as she did not make an answer to him, he turned to look away from her. He remembered how Sheila Morgan, in her anger at his cowardice, had struck him in the face and had furiously bidden him to leave her. . . . Mary would not strike him, but she, too, would bid him to go from her. . . .

He felt her hand on his arm.

"Quinny!" she said very softly, and he turned to find her standing nearer to him and looking up at him with no less love than she had looked at him before he had made his confession to her.

"I don't love you, Quinny, only for what's fine in you," she said, and her speech was full of hesitation as if she could not adequately express her meaning. "I love you . . . for *all* of you. I just take the bad with the good, and . . . and make the best of it, dear!"

"You still want me, Mary? . . ."

"My dear," she said, half laughing and half crying, "I've always wanted you! . . . Oh, what's the good," she went on with an impetuous rush of words, "of loving a man only when he comes up to your expectations. I want to love you even when you don't come up to my expecta-

tions, Quinny, and I do love you, dear. It hasn't anything
to do with whether you're brave or not brave, or good or
bad, or great or common. I just love you . . . don't you
see? . . . because you're *you!* . . ."

He stared at her incredulously. He had been so certain
that she would bid him leave her when she learned of his
cowardice.

"But! . . ."

"Come home," she said. "You must be very tired, and
cold!"

She put her arm in his, and drew him homewards, and
he yielded to her like a little child.

As they turned the corner of the apple-orchard, they
could see lights shining from the windows of the Manor,
making a warm splash on the snow that lay in drifts about
the garden. There was a great quietness that was broken
now and then by the twittering of birds in the hedges as
they nestled for the night, or the cries made by the screech-
owls, hooting in the copse.

8

Mrs. Graham and Rachel had left them alone for a
while, after dinner, and as he sat, with her at his feet,
fondling her hair, she spoke of her feeling for him again.

"I've wondered sometimes," she said, "about your not
joining . . . it seemed odd . . . but I thought that perhaps there was something that would explain it. I'd like
you to join, Quinny . . . I can't pretend that I wouldn't
. . . but I don't feel that I ought to ask you to do so. If
I were a man I should join, I think, but I'm not a man,
and I'm not likely to have to suffer any of the things that
a man has to suffer if he goes . . . and so I don't say anything. I don't know why I'd like you to go . . . I ought
to be glad that you haven't gone because I love you and
I don't want to lose you . . . but all the same I'd like
you to go. It isn't just because other men have gone, and

I don't feel any desire for revenge because Ninian's been killed . . . it's just because England's England, I suppose. . . .'' She laughed a little nervously. ''I can hardly expect you to feel about England as I do. You're Irish! . .''

''I've made that excuse for myself, Mary. Don't you make it for me. I know inside me that the war isn't England's war . . . it's the world's war. John Marsh admits that much. He doesn't like English rule in Ireland, but he doesn't pretend that German rule would be better . . . not seriously, anyhow. No, dear, I haven't that excuse. I know that if we lose this war, the world will be a worse place to live in than it is. I haven't any conscientious objection . . . I don't feel that we are in the wrong . . . I feel that we're in the right . . . that we never were so right as we are. I'm simply anxious to save my skin. And even if I felt that John Marsh were right in being anti-English, I don't feel that I have any right to take up that attitude. England's done no wrong to my family. . . . You see, dear, I haven't any excuse that's worth while . . . except the wish to preserve my life . . . and that's a poor excuse. When I think of being at the Front, I think of myself as dead . . . lying out there . . . without any of the decencies . . . until I'm offensive to the men who were my friends . . . until they sicken at the stench of *me!* . . .''

''Don't, dear!'' she murmured.

''Perhaps I shall conquer this . . . this meanness. I want to conquer it. I want to behave as I believe. I believe that there are things one should be glad to fight for and die for . . . and I want to feel glad to fight for them and be ready to die for them. But now I feel most that I want to be safe . . . to go on living and living and enjoying things. . . .''

''But can you enjoy things if they're not worth dying for, Quinny? If England weren't worthy dying for, would it be worth living in! That's how I feel!''

"That's how I *think*, Mary, but it isn't how I *feel*. I feel that I want to be safe no matter what happens . . . if civilisation is to go to smash and we're to be driven back to savagery, distrusting and being distrusted . . . I feel that I don't care . . . that I want to be safe, to go on living, even if I have to live in a cave and hide from everything. . . . Oh, my dear, don't you see what a poor thing I am!"

"Yes," she said simply.

"And yet you're willing to marry me?" .

"Yes. I can't help loving you, any more than I can help loving my country. I can't explain it and I don't want to explain it. If I were a man and England were in the wrong, I'd fight for England just because she's England. Everything makes me feel like that. When Ninian was killed, something went on saying, 'You're English! You mustn't cry! You're English!' And when I look at the trees outside, I feel that they're English, too, and that they're telling me I'm English . . . that somehow they're special trees, different from the trees in other countries . . . that they've got something that I've got, and that I've got something they've got . . . something that a French tree or a German tree hasn't got. . . . Oh, I know it's silly, but I can't help it . . . and when I used to walk about the lanes and fields after Ninian's death . . . I felt that the birds and the grass and the ferns and everything were saying 'You're English!' and I wanted to say back to them, 'You're English, too! . . .' I suppose people feel like that everywhere . . . those friends of yours in Ireland must feel like that about Ireland . . . and Germans, too! . . ."

He nodded his head. "It's a madness, this nationality," he said, "but you can't get a cure for it. Even I feel it!"

"Quinny!"

"Yes, Mary!"

There was a nervous note in her voice. She got up, so

that she was on her knees, and fingered the lapels of his coat.

"Quinny!" she said again, and he waited for her to proceed. "I . . . I want us to get married . . . soon! You'll probably go into the Army . . . nobody could go on feeling as you do, and not go in . . . and I'd like us to . . . to have had some time together . . . before you go. I don't want to be married to you just . . . just a day or two before you go. I . . . I want to have lived with you and to . . . to have taken care of your house . . . with you in it! . . ."

He folded her in his arms.

"You will, Quinny?" she said.

"Yes," he answered.

THE ELEVENTH CHAPTER

1

THEY were to be married as soon as Lent was over. Mrs. Graham, reluctant to lose Mary, had pleaded for delay, urging that Ballymartin was so far from Boveyhaven that she would seldom see her. "Two days' post," she protested.

"But you'll come and stay with us, mother," Mary declared, "and we'll come and stay with you!"

It would be quite easy for Henry to come to Devonshire, for he could carry his work about with him. Then Mrs. Graham had yielded to them, and it was settled that the marriage was to take place at the beginning of May. Neither Mary nor he had spoken again of the question of enlistment. She had said all that was in her mind about it, and what followed was for him to decide.

He went back to Ballymartin. There were things to be done at home in preparation for the coming of a bride. The house had not known a mistress since his mother's death, and his father had been too preoccupied with his agricultural experiments to bother greatly about the interior of his house. So long as he could find things more or less where he had left them, Mr. Quinn had been content.

"You won't overhaul it too much, Quinny?" Mary said to him, "because I'd like to do some of that!"

He had promised that he would do no more than was immediately necessary; and then he went.

"I shall have to go to Dublin," he had told her. "There'll be a lot of stuff to settle with lawyers!" Her settlement, for example. "I'll go home first, then on to

Dublin, and then back here. I shall get to Boveyhayne
just after Easter!''

2

Mr. Quinn had not greatly bothered about the interior
of the house, but Hannah had, and although there were
things that needed to be done, there was less than he had
imagined.

''I'm going to be married, Hannah!'' he said to her soon
after he had arrived home.

''Are you, now?'' she exclaimed.

''Yes. You remember Mr. Graham? . . .''

''Ay, poor sowl, I mind him . . . the nice-spoken, well-
behaved lad he was! . . .''

''Well, I'm going to marry his sister!''

''It'll be quaren nice to think o' this house havin' a
mistress in it again, an' wee weans, mebbe. I was here,
a young girl, when your father brought your mother home
. . . I mind it well . . . she was a quiet woman, an' she
stud in the hall there as nervous as a child 'til I went forrit
to her, an' said, 'Ye're right an' welcome, ma'am!', an'
then she plucked up her heart, an' she give me a wee bit
of a smile, an' said 'Thank ye, Hannah!' for your father
told her who I was. An' she used to come an' talk to me
afore you were born . . . she was terrible frightened, poor
woman. Ay, she was terrible frightened of havin' you!
Your father couldn't make her out at all. It was a quare
pity!''

He let her ramble on, for he wanted now to hear about
his mother, of whom he knew so little. There was a portrait of her in the house, a fair, slight, timid-looking
woman who seemed to be shrinking out of the frame. It
was odd to think that she was his mother, this frightened
woman of whom he had no memory whatever, for whom he
had no tender feeling. He had loved his father deeply,
but he had no love for his mother. How could he feel love

for her? He had never known her!... But now he wanted to know all that Hannah knew about her, for Hannah perhaps had known more about her than any one. Hannah had cared for her, pitied her....

"Yes, Hannah!" he said, so that she might proceed.

"She was sure she was goin' to die, an' I had the quare work to keep her quiet. An' she was terrible feard of dyin'!"

He listened to her with a strange feeling of pain. All that he had endured at the thought of fighting had been endured by his mother at the thought of giving him birth. He felt that now, at last, he knew his mother and could sympathise with her and love her.

"But sure what was the sense of bein' afeard of that," Hannah went on. "God wouldn't be hard on the like of her, the poor, innocent woman. I toul' lies til her, God forgive me, an' let on to her that people made out that it was worse nor it was to have a child ... but she had a despert bad time of it, for she was a weak woman, with no body in her at all, an' a poor will to suffer things. She never was the better of you!" She smiled at him sadly. "Never! An' she took no interest in nothin' after that ... she could hardly bear to look at you ... an' you her own wee son. She didn't live long after you come, an' mebbe it was as well, for God never made her to contend with anything. I was quaren fond of her. Ye had to like her, she was that helpless. She couldn't thole any one next or near her but myself ... and so I got fond of her, for a body has to like people that depends on them. Will your wife be a fair lady or a dark lady, Master Henry?"

He realised that she wished him to describe Mary to her.

"She's dark," he said. "Not at all like her brother!"

"Ay, he was the big, fair man that was a credit to a woman to have!"

"I have her photograph upstairs," Henry went on, "I'll go and get it. You'd like to see it, wouldn't you?"

"Deed an' I would," she answered.

He got the photograph and gave it to her, and she took it in her hands and looked at it very steadily.

"She's a comely-lookin' girl," she said, handing it to him again. "She has sweet eyes an' a proud way of holdin' her head. She shud be a good wife to you. I'll be glad to see her here, for dear knows, it's lonesome sittin' in the house with no one to look after. I miss your da sore, Master Henry, an' it's seldom you're here now!"

"I'll be here much more in future, Hannah!"

"Well, thank God for that! I like well to see the quality in their houses, an' them not to be runnin' here an' runnin' there, an' not thinkin' of their own place an' their own people. An' I pray to God you'll have fine childher, an' I'll be well-spared to see them growin' up to be a credit to you!"

The old woman's patient service and love seemed very noble to him, and he went to her and took her hand. "You're the only mother I've ever known, Hannah!" he said. "You've always been very good to me!"

"An' why wouldn't I be good to you?" she exclaimed, raising her fine blue eyes to his. "Aren't you the only child I ever had to rear? Dear bless you, son, what else would I be but good to you?"

And suddenly she put her arms about him and kissed him passionately, and as she kissed him, she cried:

"God only knows what I'm girnin' for!" she exclaimed, releasing him and drying her eyes.

3

He wandered about the house, touching a chair or fingering a curtain or looking at a portrait, and wondered how Mary would like her new home. It was not an old house, nor had the Quinns lived in it from the time it was built, and so Henry could not feel about it what Ninian must have felt about Boveyhayne Manor, in which his ancestors had

lived for four centuries. But it was his home, in which he
had been born, in which his mother and father had died, and
it seemed to him to be as full of memories and tradition
as Mary's home. The war had broken the line of Grahams,
broken a tradition that had survived the dangers of four
hundred years. That seemed to Henry to be a pity. Perhaps, he thought, this worship of Family is a foolish thing.
There was a danger in being rooted to one place, in letting
your blood become too closely mingled, and a tradition
might very well become a substitute for life; but when all
that was said and admitted, there was a pride in one's
breeding that made life seem like a sacrament, and the
years but the rungs of a long ladder. Once, in the days of
the Bloomsbury house, they had talked of tradition, and
some one had related the old story of the American tourist
who was shown the sacred light, and told that it had not
been out for hundreds of years. "Well, I guess it's out
now!" the American replied, blowing the light out. They
had made a mock of the horrified priest and had protested
that his service to the flame was a waste of life and energy
and time. And when they had said all that they had to
say, Ninian, speaking more quietly than was his wont, had
interjected, "But don't you think the American was rather
a cad?"

They had argued fiercely then, some of them protesting
that the American's disregard of a worn convention was
splendid, virile, youthful, god-like. Roger, Henry remembered, had sided with Ninian so far as to admit that the
American's behaviour had been too inconsiderate. "He
might have discussed the matter with the priest . . . tried
to persuade him to blow it out himself!" but that was as
far as he would go with Ninian.

"I admit," Ninian had retorted, "that it was a foolish
tradition . . . but don't you think the American was
rather a cad. It was better, wasn't it, to have that tradition than to have none at all?"

Now, standing here, in this house that had been his

father's, and now was his, and would, in due time, be his
son's, if ever he should have a son, it seemed to him that
Ninian had been right in his contention. And just as
Mary, moving through the Devonshire lanes, had felt that
everything proclaimed its Englishness and hers, making
them and her part of each other, so he, looking out of the
window across the fields, felt something inside him insisting, "You're Irish. You must be proud! You're Irish!
You must be proud! . . ."

He remembered very vividly how his father had led him
to this very window once and, pointing towards the fields,
had said, "That's land, Henry! *My* land! . . ."

And because he had been proud of his land, had been
part of it, as it had been part of him, he had been willing
to spend himself on it. There seemed to Henry to be in
that, all that there was in patriotism. Irrationally, impulsively, unaccountably one loved one's country. The air
of it and the earth of it, the winds that blew over it and
the seas that encircled it, all these had been mingled to
make men, so that when there was danger and threat to a
man's country, some native thing in him stirred and compelled him to say, "This is my body! This is my blood!"
and sent him out, irrationally, impulsively, unaccountably,
to die in its defence. There was here no question of birth
or possessions: the slum-man felt this stirring in his nature
as strongly as the landlord. In that sudden, swift rising
of young men when war was declared, each man instinctively hurrying to the place of enlistment, there were men
from slums and men from mansions, all of them, in an instant, made corporate, given unity, brought to communion,
partaking of a sacrament, becoming at that moment a sacrament themselves. . . .

4

But if this stirring in one's nature made a man both a
sacrament and a partaker of a sacrament, was there not yet

something horrible in this spilling of blood, this breaking
of bodies? Was this sacrament only to be consummated
by the butcher? Was there no healing sacrament which,
when a man partook of it, gave him life and more life?
Was there not an honourable rivalry among nations, each
to be better than the other, to replace this brawling about
boundaries, this pettifogging with frontiers? Was there
to be no end to this killing and preparing for killing?
Would men, from now on, set themselves to the devisal of
murderous and more murderous weapons of war until at
last an indignant, disgusted God, sick of the smell of
blood, threw the earth from Him, caring nothing what happened to it, so that it was out of His consciousness? . . .

While he looked out of the window, the dusk settled
down, and he could see the mists rising from the fields.
He drew the curtains, and went and sat down by the fire.
There was a faint odour of burning turf in the room, and
as he watched the blue spirals of smoke curling up the
chimney, he remembered how he had trudged across Dartmoor once, and, suddenly, unexpectedly had turned a corner of the road, and looked down on a village in a hollow,
and for a moment or two had imagined he was in Ireland
because of the smell of burning turf that came from the
cottage chimneys.

"We and they are one," he murmured to himself. "Our
differences are but two aspects of the same thing. Our
blood and their blood, our earth and their earth, mingled
and made sacramental, shall be to the glory of God!"

The door opened, and Hannah came in, carrying a lighted
lamp.

"I just thought I'd bring it myself," she said. "I'd
be afeard of my life to let Minnie handle it. Dear knows,
but she'd set herself on fire, or mebbe the house, an' that'd
be a nice thing, an' a new mistress comin' to it. Will I
put it down here by your elbow?"

"Anywhere, Hannah!" he answered.

"I'll just rest it here then, where it'll not be too strong

for your eyes. You ought to have the electric light put
in the house. Major Cairnduff has it in his house, an' it's
not half the size of this one. . . . Will I get you something?"

"No, thank you, Hannah!"

"A taste of somethin' to ate, mebbe, or a sup to drink?"

"Nothing, thank you!"

She went over to the fire. "Dear bless us," she said,
"that's no sort of a fire at all. What come over you, to let
it get that low!"

"I didn't notice it, Hannah!"

" 'Deed an' I don't suppose you did . . . moidherin'
your mind about one thing an' another! There'll be a different story to tell when the mistress comes home. Mark
my words, there will! Dear, oh, dear, oh, dear! . . ."

5

"I'm going to Belfast to-night, Hannah," he said when
he had been at home a few weeks. "I want to catch an
early train to Dublin to-morrow."

"Yes," she said.

"When I come back, I shall bring my wife with me!"

"God bless us and save us," she exclaimed, "it'll be
quare to think of you with a wife, an' it on'y the other day
since you were a child, an' me skelpin' you for provokin'
me. Well, I'll have the house ready for yous both when
you come!"

"Will you tell Matier to harness the horse. . . ."

"I'll tell him this minute. That man's near demented
mad at the thought of you marryin'. 'Be the hokey O!'
he says whenever I go anear him, an' then he starts laughin'
an' tellin' me it's the great news altogether. 'I wish,' says
he, 'the oul' lad was alive. He'd be makin' hell's blazes
for joy!' Och, he's cracked, that fella. I tell him many's
the time it's in the asylum he should be, but sure, you
might as well talk to the potstick as talk to him. He'll

drive you to the station with a heart an' a han', and the capers of him when you both come back'll be like nothin' on God's earth!''

''So long as he doesn't capsize us both into the ditch! . . .''

''Him capsize you! I'd warm his lug for him if he dar'd to do such a thing! . . .''

THE TWELFTH CHAPTER

1

HE had been to the offices of Messrs. Kilworth and Kilworth in Kildare Street, and had seen Sir John Kilworth and settled as much of his business as could then be done. Now, wondering just what he should do next, he made his way to Stephen's Green and entered the Park, and while he was standing on the bridge over the lake, looking at the dark fish in the water, he felt a hand on his shoulder, and turning round, saw John Marsh.

"I didn't know you were in Dublin," John said, holding out his hand.

"I haven't been here very long," Henry answered, "and I'm going away again after Easter. I'm going to be married."

"Married!"

"Yes . . . to Ninian Graham's sister. I've often talked of you to her. You must come and stay with us when we get back to Ballymartin."

"Yes. Yes, I should like to! I hope you'll be happy, Henry!" He spoke in a nervous, agitated way that was not habitual with him, and Henry, looking more closely at him, saw that he was tired and ill-looking.

"Aren't you well, John?" he asked.

"Oh, yes. Yes, I'm quite well. I'm rather tired, that's all. I've been working very hard!"

"Still drilling?"

"Yes . . . still drilling!"

"What are you doing at Easter, John?" Henry asked.

Marsh looked at him quickly, almost in a startled fashion.

"At Easter!" he repeated. "Oh . . . nothing! Why?"

"You and I might go for a long walk through the mountains," Henry answered. "We could walk to Glendalough and back again. It would just fill up the Easter holidays. Let's start to-morrow morning. I'm staying at the Club. You can meet me there!"

"No, I'm sorry, Henry, I can't go with you! . . ."

"Why not? You said you'd nothing particular to do!"

"I'm going to Mass in the morning. . . ."

"Well, that doesn't matter. We can start after you've been. Come along, John. You look washed-out, and the tramp'll do you good! . . ."

Marsh shook his head. "I can't go, Henry," he said. "It isn't only to-morrow morning that I want to go to Mass . . . I want to go the day after . . . and I want to go with all . . . all my people on Easter Sunday!"

"You've grown very religious, John. Do you go to Mass every morning?"

"I've been every morning now for a month. You see, one doesn't know . . . well, perhaps I am growing more religious. I won't keep you now. Perhaps I shall see you again! . . ."

"Why, of course, you'll see me again. Heaven and earth, man, anybody'd think you were going to die, the way you talk!"

Marsh did not speak. He smiled when Henry spoke of dying, and then looked away. They were still standing on the bridge, and he leant on the parapet and looked down on the lake.

"Queer things, fish!" he said.

"Not nearly so queer as you are," Henry answered. "Why won't you come with me? You won't want to be cooped up in Dublin all Easter, do you?"

"Cooped up!"

"Yes. Two or three days of mountain air 'ud do you a world of good. You'd better come with me!"

"No, I can't," he answered so abruptly that Henry did

not press the matter again. "When are you going to be married, Henry?" he asked, speaking in his old, kindly tone again.

"At the beginning of May . . . less than a fortnight now!"

Marsh turned away from the water, and stood with his back to the parapet. "Why don't you spend Easter with your fiancée?" he said.

"That isn't quite possible, John. I should only be in the way, if I were there now!"

"Or at Ballymartin. It would be rather nice to spend Easter at Ballymartin!"

"Well, I will, if you'll come with me. . . ."

"I can't do that. I don't think I should stay in Dublin at Easter if I were you. . . ."

"Why?"

"Oh, it'll be dull for you. People go away. There's not much to do. I should go to the North or over to England or somewhere if I were you!"

Henry felt resentful. "You seem damned anxious to get rid of me, John," he said. "You won't come into the mountains with me, and you keep on telling me to clear out of Dublin!"

Marsh turned to him quickly, and put his hand on his arm.

"My dear Henry," he said, very gently, "you know that I don't feel like that. I thought you'd be . . . I thought you'd have a happier Easter out of Dublin, that was all. That place in Wales, where you went with poor Farlow. . . ."

"Tre'Arrdur Bay?"

"Yes. Why don't you go there? It really isn't much further than Glendalough."

"You can't walk to it, John, and you can walk to Glendalough!"

"Oh, well, if you won't go . . . you won't go, and there's an end of it. Good-bye!"

"Wait a bit. Come and dine with me to-night!"

"I can't, Henry!" Henry made an angry gesture. "Don't be hurt," Marsh went on quickly. "I have things to attend to. You see, I didn't know you were here. I'm on my way now to a . . . a committee meeting. I'll come and see you to-morrow, if I can manage it. I'll lunch with you somewhere!"

"All right. I'll meet you here at one, and we'll lunch at the Shelbourne. By the way, John, aren't there some races on Monday?"

"Yes . . . at Fairyhouse!"

"Well, couldn't we go to them? I've never seen a horse-race in my life! . . ."

"I don't think I can manage that, Henry! . . ."

"Oh, damn you, you can't manage anything. Well, all right, I'll see you to-morrow!"

"Good-bye, then! . . ."

He went off, leaving Henry on the bridge staring after him, and as he went towards the Grafton Street gate, there was something slightly incongruous about his look.

"I know what it is," Henry said to himself. "His coat's too big for him. He always did wear things that didn't fit him!"

2

Marsh did not keep the appointment. Soon after one o'clock, a boy came to Henry, and asked him if he were Mr. Quinn, and when Henry had assured him that he was, he said, "Mr. Marsh bid me to tell you, sir, that he's not able to come. He says he's very sorry, but he can't help it!"

The lad repeated the message almost as if he had learned it by heart. "Oh, very well!" Henry said, offering money to him."

"Ah, sure, that's all right, sir!" the lad said, and then he went away.

"I suppose," Henry said to himself angrily, "he's at his damned drilling again!"

He lunched alone, and then took the tram to Kingstown, and walked from there to Bray along the coast. He felt dispirited and lonely. Jordan and Saxon were out of Dublin . . . Jordan was in Sligo, he had heard, and Saxon was staying with his uncle near the mountains. He knew that Crews lived in Bray, but he had forgotten the address. "Perhaps," he thought, "I shall see him in the street. . . ."

"Lordy God!" he exclaimed, "I'd give the world for some one to talk to. John Marsh might have tried to meet me. Fooling about with his . . . penny-farthing volunteers!"

"In a little while," he said to himself, as he descended into Killiney and walked along the road by the railway station, "I shall be married to Mary, and then! . . ."

He remembered what she had said to him at Boveyhayne, "I'd like you to go, Quinny . . . I can't pretend that I wouldn't. . . ."

He stood for a while, leaning against the wall and looking out over the crumpled sea. "I don't know," he said to himself, "I don't know!"

3

He climbed to the top of Bray Head, and while he stood there, his mind was full of thoughts that beat backwards and forwards. In olden times, the histories said, Ireland had sent a stream of scholars over the waste places of Europe to fertilise them and make them fruitful. "Now," he thought bitterly, "we send 'bosses' to Tammany Hall. . . ."

He tried to envisage the means whereby Ireland would be brought to the measure and the stature of a dignified and honourable nation . . . "not this brawling, whining, cadging, snivelling, Oh-Jesus-have-mercy-on-us disorder!"

and he saw only a long, tedious, painful process of self-re-
generation. "We must rise on our own wings!"

"But first we must be free, free from the bondage of
history, free from the bondage of romance, free from the
bondage of politics, free from the bondage of religion, and
free from the bondage of our bellies!"

"There are four Irishmen to be conquered and controlled:
the Publican, the Priest, the Politician and the Poet. . . ."

"We cannot be friendly with England until we are equal
with England . . . but England cannot make us equal with
her . . . we can only do that ourselves!"

"England is our sister . . . not our mother! . . ."

"Catholicism is Death . . . and Intolerance is Death.
Wherever there is Catholicism there is Decay that will not
be stopped until the people protest. Wherever there is Intolerance there is a waste of life, a perversion of energy.
When the Protestant ceases, and the Catholic begins, to
shout 'To Hell with the Pope,' there will be glory and life
in Ireland. . . ."

He tried to plan a means of making a change of mind in
Ireland. "We must make opinions and active brains!"
and so he saw himself urging his friends to abandon par-
liaments to the middle-aged and the second-rate, while they
bent their minds to the conquest of the schools. "Let the
old men make their speeches," he said aloud as if he were
addressing a conference. "We'll mould the minds of the
children!"

They must exult in service. "I believe in Work . . .
in the Job Well Done . . . in giving oneself without ceasing . . . in the holy communion of men labouring together
for something which is greater than themselves . . . in
spending oneself with no reward but to know that one is
spent well! . . ."

They would enlist the young men of generous mind.
They would open their minds to the knowledge of the wide
world, and would pity the man who was content only to be
an islander; and they would give the harvest of their minds

to their juniors, so that they, when they grew to manhood, might find greater ease in working for the common good. They would demand, not privileges, but responsibilities. "If we cannot make decisions, even when we decide wrongly, then we are not men!"

"We must kill the Publican, we must subdue the Priest, we must humiliate the Politician, and chasten the Poet. . . ."

"In all our ways, O God, let us guide ourselves! . . ."

It seemed to him that God was not a Being who miraculously made the world, but a Being who laboured at it, suffered and failed, and rose again and achieved. . . . He could hear God, stumbling through the Universe, full of the agony of desire, calling continually, "Let there be Light! Let there be Light! . . ."

4

He looked about him. Behind him, lay the long broken line of the Wicklow mountains, with the Sugar Loaf thrusting its pointed head into the heavens. There in front of him, heaving and tumbling, was the sea: a miracle of healing and cleansing. It would be good, he thought, to spend one's life in the sound of the sea, taking no care for the lives of other men, content that oneself was fed and comfortable. "But that would not be enough. There must be Light and More Light!"

"God," he said, "has many forms. In that place, he is a Quietness . . . in this place, a Discontent . . . in a third place, a Quest."

"But here, God is a Demand. 'Let there be Light! Let there be more Light!'"

5

He went home and wrote to Mary. "*My impulse is to tell you no more than this, that I love you. I wrote to you*

*this morning, and I have nothing to add that is news.   But
I feel an overpowering desire to insist on my love for you
. . . to do nothing for ever but love you and love you. . . .
You see the mood I'm in!   I went out of Dublin to-day,
sulking and depressed because John Marsh had failed me
and I was lonely, but now I'm extraordinarily happy.   I
feel that I have only to stretch out my hand and touch you
. . . and then I shall be depressed no more.   This is not a
letter.   It has no beginning and it will have no end.   It's
an outpouring.   To-night is very beautiful.   I went up to
my bedroom a few moments ago, and sat at the window
looking over Stephen's Green.   There was a blue mist
hanging over the trees, and the sky was full of light and
colour.   I do not believe there is any place in the world
where one sees so much of the sky as in Dublin.   It reaches
up and up until you feel that if a bird were to pierce the
clouds with its beak, it would tear a hole in the heavens and
let the universe in.   And while I was sitting there, I felt
very near to you, dearest.   In ten days we shall be married, and then you will come with me and see these places,
too.   I shall become Irish over again when I show you my
home, and I shall watch Ireland taking hold of you and
absorbing you and making you as Irish as I am.   You'll
go on thinking that you're English until some one speaks
disparagingly of Ireland, and then you'll flare up, and
you'll be Irish, not only in nature, but in knowledge.   Ireland does that to people, so you cannot hope to escape.
Good-night, my very dear!"*

6

On Sunday, he went into the mountains, and in the evening he returned to Dublin.   There was an extraordinary
quietness in the streets, though they were crowded with
people . . . the quietness that comes when people are tired
and happy.   As he crossed O'Connell Bridge, he stood for a
few moments to look up the Liffey.   The sunset had trans-

muted the river to the look of a sheet of crinkled gold, and
the sunlight made the houses on the quays look warm and
lovely, even though they were old and worn and discol-
oured. "In her heart," he thought, "Dublin is still a
proud lady, although her dress be draggled!"

He turned to look at a company of Volunteers who were
marching towards Liberty Hall. There were little girls in
Gaelic dress at the head of them, accompanied by a pale,
tired-looking woman, with tightened lips, who stumped
heavily by the side of them; and following them, came
young men and boys and a shuffling group of hungry labourers, misshapen by heavy toil and privation . . . and
as the company passed by, girls stood on the pavement and
jeered at them. They pointed to the woman with tightened lips, and mocked at her uniform and her tossed
hair. . . .

"They're fools," Henry thought, looking at them as they
went wearily on, "but, by God, they're finer than the people who jeer at them. They . . . they are serving something . . . and these Don't-Care-a-Damners aren't serving
anything! . . ."

There was a man at his elbow who turned to him and
said, "Them lads 'ud run like hell if you were to point a
penny pop-gun at them! If a peeler was to take their
names, they'd be shiverin' with fright. They'd fall out of
their trousers with the terror'd be on them!"

Henry did not answer. Indeed, it seemed incredible that
there was any fight in them . . . if he had been asked for
his opinion, he might have said something similar to what
this stranger had said to him . . . but he hated to hear
the man's disparagement, and so he did not make any
answer to him.

"I'd rather have them on my side than have him," he
thought as he moved away, "with the stink of porter on
him!"

It sickened him to see the generosity and the youth walking in the company of the hopelessness of Ireland, training

themselves in the means of killing. "If they'd put all that energy and enthusiasm into something that will preserve life and make it deeper and finer, nothing could prevail against them. If only John had more intellect and less emotion . . . if Mineely and Connolly were less bitter!"

He walked along Grafton Street, turning phrases over in his mind, angry phrases, bitter things that he would say to John Marsh when he met him.

"What have young lads and girls to do with Hate and Death?" he said to himself, as if he were talking to Marsh. "You're perverting them from their purpose! You're robbing God of His due . . . of the hope that fills His Heart with each generation!"

"But it's no good talking to him . . . he's too fond of spilling over. If he were like Yeats, content to love Ireland at a distance . . . to 'arise and go now' no further than the Euston Road . . . he might achieve something, and at all events, he'd be harmless!"

He turned out of Grafton Street into Stephen's Green.

"To-morrow," he said to himself, "I'll go to Fairy-house!"

And then he went to his Club. He was tired and sleepy, and soon after supper, he went to bed.

7

It was late when he awoke and so, feeling lazy after his day's climbing, he resolved that he would not go to the races. "I'll loaf about," he said, "and to-night I'll go to a theatre." There was a letter from Mary and one from Roger. *"Gerald Luke was killed in France last week, and so was Clifford Dartrey. Goeffrey Grant has been wounded badly. The Improved Tories have suffered heavily in the War. . . ."* Roger wrote.

When he had breakfasted, he left the Club and walked towards Sackville Street. He would go to the Abbey The-

atre, he thought, and book a seat for the evening performance.

There was an odd, bewildered look about the people who
stood in groups in Sackville Street.

"What's up?" Henry said to a bystander.

"Begod," said the man, "I think there's a rebellion on.
That's what this woman says anyway!"

"A what?"

"A rebellion or something of the sort. You can ask her
yourself! Begod, it's a quare day to have it. The people'll not enjoy themselves at all. . . ."

Henry turned to the woman who was standing in the centre of the group, endlessly relating her experience.

"I went to the Gener'l," she said, "an' I said to the man
behin' the counter, 'Gimme two ha'penny postcards an' a
penny stamp an' change for a shillin', if you please!' and
I hadn't the words out of my mouth 'til a man in a green
uniform . . . one of them Sinn Feiners . . . come up to
me, an' pointed a gun at me, an' toul' me to go home.
'Go home yourself!' says I, an' I give his oul' gun a push
with my hand, 'an' who are you to be orderin' a person
about?' 'If you don't go on when I tell you,' says he,
'I'll shoot you!' an' I declare to my God he looked as if
he'd blow the head off you. 'Well, wait till I get my
change anyway,' says I. 'Ye'll get no change here,'
says he. 'I will so,' I said, and I turned to the man behind
the counter, but, sure, God bless you, he wasn't there.
'Well, this bates all,' says I to the Sinn Feiner, 'an if the
peelers catches a houldt of you, you'll get into bother
over the head of this!' I picked up my shillin', an' I
went out. The place was full of them. They were orderin' everybody out, except a couple or three soldiers
that they made prisoners. An' if you were to go down
there now, you'd see them, young fellas that I could bate
with my one hand, cocked up behin' the windas with guns
in their hands, an' telling people to move on out of
that. . . ."

Some one came into the group, and said "What's that?" and she turned to him and began again. "I went in to the Gener'l," she said, "an' I said to the man behin' the counter, 'Gimme two ha'penny postcards. . . .'"

Henry made his way out of the group of listeners, and walked down the street towards the General Post Office.

"It's absurd," he said. "Ridiculous! A rebellion!"

But something was toward. On the roof of the Post Office there were two flags, a green flag with a motto on it, and a tri-colour, orange, white and green. There was hardly any wind, and the flags hung limply from their staffs, but as Henry approached the Post Office, the wind stirred, and the green flag fluttered enough for him to read what was printed on it. It bore the legend IRISH REPUBLIC.

"It's a poor sort of performance, this!" he said as he came up to the building.

All the windows on the ground floor were broken, and many of those on the upper floors, and in each window, on sacks laid on piled furniture, were one or two young volunteers, each with a rifle cocked. . . .

8

There was a holiday mood on the people. They had come out to enjoy themselves, and here was an entertainment beyond their dreams of pleasure. . . . It was a dangerous kind of joke to play . . . one of them oul' guns might go off, and who knows who might get killed dead . . . and it was a serious thing to seize possession of the Post Office . . . if the peelers was to come an' catch them at it an' bring them before the magistrates, they'd be damn near transported . . . but it was the great joke all the same. Whoever thought there would be the like of that to see, and not a penny to pay for it. . . . The minute the peelers came up . . . where in hell were the peelers?

It was then that they began to believe that there was more than a joke in this rebellion. There were no policemen to be seen anywhere. "That's strange now! There ought to be a peeler or two about! . . ."

Then some one, pale and startled, came by. "They've killed a policeman!" he said. "The unfortunate man! I was coming past the Castle, and I saw a Sinn Feiner go up to him and blow his brains out. Not a word of warning! The poor man put up his hand to bid them go back . . . they were trying to get into the Castle . . . and the Sinn Feiner lifted his rifle and shot him dead! . . ."

"Begod, it's in earnest they are! . . ."

"But what can they do? They can't hold out against the British Army. . . ."

"They might do a lot, now! They're mad, the whole of them! What in hell do they want to start a rebellion for? . . ."

Henry moved away. He went from group to group, listening to one for a while, and then moving on to another. There were many rumours already flying through the crowd. The Germans had landed in the West, and were marching to Dublin. A "mysterious stranger" had been captured on the coast of Kerry a few days before. "It was Casement!" The German Navy had made a raid on England, and the British Fleet had been badly beaten. . . .

A youth, holding a rifle with a fixed bayonet, stood on sentry-go in the middle of the street. He was very pale and tired and nervous-looking, but looked as resolute as he looked tired. He did not speak to any one, nor did any one speak to him. He stood there, staring fixedly in front of him, watching and watching. . . .

There was a sound of rumbling carts, and the noise of people cheering, and presently a procession of wagons, loaded with cauliflower, and guarded by armed Volunteers, came out of a side street, and drove up to the Post Office.

"The Commissariat!" some one said. "Begod they'll be

tired of cauliflower before they're through with that lot!''

It was comical to see those loads of cauliflower being driven past. Ireland was to fight for freedom with her stomach full of cauliflower. . . .

There was a Proclamation of the Republic on a wall near by, and he hurried to read it.

"What's the thing at the head of it?" a woman asked, gazing at the Gaelic inscription on top of the Proclamation.

"That's Irish," the man beside her replied.

"I know that. What does it mean?"

"Begod, I don't know. . . ."

Henry read the Proclamation through, and then re-read the finely-phrased end of it!

We place the Irish Republic under the protection of the Most High God, Whose Blessing we invoke on our arms, and we pray that no one who serves that cause will dishonour it. In this supreme hour the Irish nation must by its valour and discipline, and by the readiness of its children to sacrifice themselves for the common good, prove itself worthy of the august destiny to which it is called.

"That's John," he said to himself, "or MacDonagh! And they began the thing by killing an unarmed man! Their fine phrases won't cover that mean deed! . . ."

9

He went back to his Club, and on the way, found that the rebels were in possession of Stephen's Green. The gates were closed, and at each gate were armed guards. He looked through the railings, and saw some boys lying on the turf, with their rifles beside them. They did not move nor look up, but lay very still and quiet, with a strange, preoccupied expression on their faces. A little further on, other lads were digging up the earth.

"What are you doing?" he said to one of them, and the lad straightened himself and wiped the sweat from his brow.

"I don't know, sir!" he said, smiling nervously. "I'm supposed to be diggin' a trench, but I think I'm diggin' my grave! . . ."

A trench! When he looked at the poor scraping of earth and sod, he felt a fierce anger against Marsh and his friends swelling in his heart. "They haven't the gumption to know that this is the worst place they could have chosen to entrench themselves, even if they knew how to make trenches!" On all sides of the Green were high houses, from which it would be easy to pick off every man that lay in the trenches. . . .

There were carts and motor-cars drawn across the street to make a barricade, and most of the gates of the Green had garden-seats and planks lying against them. There were even branches, torn from the trees and shrubs, thrust through the railings. . . .

He went into his Club to lunch. "They're in the College of Surgeons, sir!" a servant said. "They say Madame's in the Green! . . ."

"Madame?" he said vaguely.

"Yes. Madame Markiewicz. They killed a policeman. . . ."

"Do you mean the man at the Castle?"

"No, sir. I didn't hear of him. They killed this one on the other side of the Green. There's cold lamb and cold chicken, sir!"

"I'll have lamb! . . ."

He hurried over his meal. He had little appetite for eating, and when he had finished, he went to the smoking-room and wrote to Mary. *"Don't be alarmed if you see anything about an Irish Rebellion in the newspapers,"* he wrote. *"It will probably be over by to-morrow. I'm quite all right. You're not to worry! . . ."* And when he had finished it he went out and posted it. "Good Lord!"

he said aloud, as the letter fell into the box, "I forgot that they've got hold of the General. I don't suppose there'll be a collection!"

He returned to the Club, but he could not keep still. There was no one, except the servants and himself, in the house, and the emptiness of it made him feel restless. Looking out of the window, he saw little girls, like those he had seen on Sunday night, running about the Green, busy on errands. . . .

"The Kids' Rebellion!" he said to himself. . . .

He left the club, and walked round the Green again, and as he passed the College of Surgeons, two men appeared on the roof, and proceeded to unfold the Republican tri-colour. They were clumsy, and they fumbled with it, entangling the cords . . . but at last they got it free, and then they hauled it to the top of the flagstaff. The people on the pavement below watched it as it fluttered in the light breeze, but none of them spoke or cheered. The rebels in the Green made no sound either. The Republican flag was hauled to its place in silence.

"They don't seem very grateful for their deliverance," Henry thought, glancing at the bystanders as he moved up the street. There was a crowd of people on the edge of the pavement, and he thrust himself into it, and glanced over the shoulder of a woman at the ground. There was a mess of thick, congealing blood splashed on the road and the kerb.

"That's where the peeler was killed!" the woman said to him. . . .

He edged out of the crowd as quickly as he could, feeling sick with horror, and again he felt a bitter anger against John Marsh.

"He was going to Mass every morning, damn him, to make sure of his own soul, but he didn't give the policeman time to make any preparation. All his high motives and his idealism tumble down to that . . . that mess on the pavement! . . ."

10

"But what's the Government doing?" he wondered.

There were no police, no soldiers, no authority anywhere. It seemed unbelievable that a number of armed youths and men could seize a capital city without opposition of any kind. He wondered whether there was any truth in the rumours that had been floating about the city all day. Could it possibly be that the Germans had effected a landing in Ireland and were marching on the city? Could it be true that the British Fleet had been destroyed by the German Fleet? Had the Government thrown up the sponge? . . .

He met O'Dowd, an official whom he had seen several times at the Club. "Where's the Government?" he asked. . . .

"Well, to tell you the truth, Quinn, I don't know. I believe there's an election going on at Trinity College. It's a damned comic affair, this!"

"Comic!"

"Well, I mean to say, it's a bit rum, isn't it?"

11

He went back to the Club in the evening. There were no lights in the streets, and as the dusk settled down, the crowds of holiday-makers began to move homewards. There were no trams running and few cars to be seen, and the tired crowd that had been standing or walking about all day, dragged itself home listlessly and heavily. There was a sense of foreboding over the people, and some of them glanced apprehensively about them. The thing had been funny in the daylight, but it was getting dark now . . . and who knew what might be lurking in the shadows? It was strange that there were no police to be seen anywhere, and stranger still that the soldiers had not appeared. . . .

There was a Sinn Feiner on guard at the gate near

Henry's Club, and sitting at the open window, Henry could see him very distinctly: a little, red-haired, angry man, who chewed his moustache and gaped about him with bloodshot eyes. There were other Sinn Feiners with him, but he was the most distinctive. He could not stay still: he moved about continually, going into the Park and coming out again, challenging passers-by, sloping his rifle and ordering it, and then sloping it again. "The thing's getting on his nerves," Henry thought, as he watched him; and while he watched, an elderly man came past the Shelbourne Hotel in the uniform of a naval officer. The Sinn Feiners saw him, and the red-haired man ordered his subordinates to arrest him. They ran across the street and attempted to seize him, but he resisted, and raised his walking stick to defend himself. A rebel caught hold of the stick, and the two men stood there, against a gateway, struggling to wrest the stick from each other. The up-and-down movement of their arms was like the quick, jerky movement of figures in a film, and for a moment or two, Henry wanted to laugh . . . but the desire died when he saw the red-haired man raising his rifle and aiming at the old man's heart. . . .

"Oh, my God, he's going to shoot him!" he shouted out, jumping up from his seat and leaning out of the window. "Don't shoot him . . . don't shoot him!" he cried. It seemed to him that he was yelling at the top of his voice, but that could not have been so, for no one turned to look . . . and yet he could hear the red-haired man distinctly.

"I have ye covered," he was saying, "an' I'll shoot ye if ye don't give in! . . ."

The old man held on to the stick for a moment or two, and then, straightening himself, he surrendered; and the rebels led him into the Park. Through the trees, Henry could see him being conducted before a rebel officer who saluted him and began to interrogate him. Then the procession moved off into the centre of the Park, and the little angry, red-haired man returned to the gate.

"In the morning," Henry exclaimed to himself, "in the morning, that little swine will sing another song!"

12

A horse-drawn cab came down the street, and as it approached, the guard at the gate turned out, and challenged the driver. "Halt!" they shouted.

"Ah, g'long with you!" the driver replied, whipping up his horse.

"Halt!" they called again, and a third time "Halt!" but the driver did not heed them, and then they fired at him. . . . There was a clatter of hooves on the street, and the horse fell to the ground, striking sparks from the stones as it struggled to rise again. The driver did not pause: he jumped from his box with amazing celerity and disappeared so swiftly that the rebels could not catch him. And while the horse lay struggling on the street, a motor-car came by, and again the rebels sent out their challenge, and again the challenge was ignored. "Halt! Halt! Halt! . . ." The chauffeur drove on, and the rebels fired on the occupants of the car. There was a swift application of brakes, and the car slithered up against the pavement . . . and as it slithered, a man stood up beside the driver, holding his hand to his side, and yelled, "Oh, I'm dead! I'm dead! . . ."

The chauffeur hurried away. . . .

The rebels gathered round the shrieking man. "Why didn't you stop when we challenged you!" they demanded.

"Aw! Aw! Aw!" he answered. . . .

"Like a stuck pig!" thought Henry. "Squealing like a stuck pig!"

His head was rolling, but he was able to walk. "He's not much hurt," Henry murmured to himself, "but he's damned frightened."

"Aw, what did ye do it for? Aw! Aw! Aw! . . ."

"Take him to the hospital! . . ."

They led him a little way towards the hospital of St. Vincent de Paul, and then, for some reason, changed their minds, and took him into the Park. It was difficult now to see what was happening. There was a derelict tram near the club, and beyond that, still pawing at the ground, was the wounded horse. . . .

"Why don't they shoot the poor beast!" Henry exclaimed.

But it would not enter their minds to put the animal out of pain. They were Catholics, and Catholic peoples, the world over, are cruel to beasts. Too intent on pitying their own souls, to have pity on animals. . . .

13

He closed the shutters and turned on the light. "I wonder where John is?" he thought as he did so. *"This* is why he couldn't come to Glendalough with me. What the hell does he think he's going to gain by it?" He glanced about the room. "It's damned odd," he said aloud, "but I don't feel frightened. I should have thought I'd feel scared. . . . Of course, as there was going to be a rebellion, I'm rather glad I'm here to see it!"

He went to his bedroom and got a pack of patience cards.

"There'll be no theatre to-night!" he said. "I think I'll play 'Miss Milligan.' . . ."

14

The silence of the house made him feel restless.

"I'll go to bed," he exclaimed. "I may as well get all the sleep I can."

He went to his room, and stumbled towards the windows.

"I'll close the shutters while I'm undressing," he went on. "I don't want to be 'potted' needlessly!"

He tried to see into the Park, but the great masses of trees that undulated like a rough sea, prevented him from ωωíng anything. There were figures at the gate . . . on guard!

"I wonder if that little red-haired man's still there," he thought. "Poor devils! Some of them must feel damned queer to-night! . . ."

He closed the shutters, and switched the light on, and then, when he had undressed he darkened the room again. "I must have some air," he said, opening the shutters.

He climbed into bed. Now and then a rifle-shot was fired, and sometimes there was a succession of shots. . . .

"In the morning," he said, as he turned on his side and closed his eyes, "they'll be cleared out of that! . . ."

THE THIRTEENTH CHAPTER

1

HE awoke suddenly, and sat up in bed. "Good Lord!" he exclaimed, "I've been asleep!" It was still dark, but less dark than it was when he came to bed. He could just see the time by holding his watch close to his eyes. "Four," he murmured. It was strange that he should have slept at all, for there had been spasmodic firing all night. He got out of bed, and went across his room to the window, and looked out, and as he looked, the wounded horse struggled to rise, pawing the ground feebly, and then fell over on its side. "It isn't dead! . . ." When he had looked at it last, it had been lying very still, and he had thought it was dead.

He looked across the road to the Park gates, but could not see any one standing there. "Perhaps they've gone!" There was a shapeless thing lying on the ground, outside the gates, but he could not make out what it was. In the dim light, it looked like a great piece of paper . . . the debris of a windy day.

There was no movement anywhere . . . the horse was still now . . . but now and then a single shot rang out, and then came a volley. "You'd think they were just trying to make a noise! I wonder what's been happening all night," he said, as he went back to bed.

2

He fell asleep again, and when he awoke, wakened by a heavier sound of shooting, it was almost six o'clock, and it was light. "That must be the soldiers," he thought,

550

listening to the heavier rifle fire. He sat up in bed, and glanced about the room. "I *was* an ass not to keep the shutters closed," he said aloud. "A stray bullet might have come in here . . . I wonder whether the shutters would stop a bullet. After all, Bibles do! . . ."

He could just see the Republican flag floating from the flagstaff on the roof of the College of Surgeons. "They're still there, then!" And while he sat looking at it, he heard the sound of some one, wearing heavy boots, coming down the streets, making loud clattering echoes in the silence. "That's funny!" he said. "People are going about already. Perhaps it's over . . . practically over! . . ."

He got out of bed, and as he did so, he heard the sharp rattle of rifles, and when the echo of it had ceased, he could not hear the noise of heavy treading any more. He stood still in the centre of the room, listening, and presently he heard a groan. He ran to the window and looked out. In the roadway, beneath him, an old man was lying on his back, groaning very faintly.

"They've killed him!" Henry murmured, glancing across the road at the hotel, from which the sound of firing had come. "They didn't challenge him . . . they just shot him!"

Four times, the old man groaned, and then he died. He was lying in the attitude of a young child asleep. One leg was outstretched and the other was lightly raised. His right arm was lying straight out from his body, and the hand was turned up and hollowed. Very easy and natural was his attitude, lying there in the morning light. He looked like a labourer. "Going to his work," I suppose. "Thinking little of the rebellion. Just stumping along to his job . . . and then! . . ."

There was a bundle lying by his side, a red handkerchief that seemed to be holding food . . . and flowing towards it, trickling, so slowly did it move, from his body was a little red dribble. . . .

Henry looked at him with a feeling of curiosity and pity.

He had never seen a man killed before. He had never seen any dead person, not even Mrs. Clutters, until his father died. He had purposely avoided seeing Mrs. Clutters' body . . . something in the thought of death repelled him and made him reluctant to look at a corpse, and so, when he had been asked if he would like to see Mrs. Clutters, he had made some evasive reply. It had been different when his father died. He had looked on him, not as a dead man, but as his father, still, even in death, his father, able to love and be loved. When he thought of death, he thought, not of Mr. Quinn, but of Mrs. Clutters, and always it seemed to him that the dead were frightful. . . . But this old man, a few moments ago intent on getting to his work in time, and now, cognisant, perhaps of all the mysteries of this world, had nothing frightful about him. There was beauty in the way he was lying in the roadway . . . in that careless, graceful attitude . . . as if he were gratefully resting after much labour. . . .

He looked across the roadway, and now it was plain that the shapeless thing that had looked in the dim light like paper blown to a corner by the wind, was a dead man. He, too, was lying on his back, with his legs stretched straight out and slightly parted . . . and while Henry looked at him, it seemed to him that the man was familiar to him. The brown dust-coat he was wearing! . . . And then he remembered. It was the red-haired, angry-looking, nervous man, who had chewed his moustache and gaped about him with bloodshot eyes. . . .

He dressed, and went downstairs. The servants were up, and moving about the house, and one of them came to him.

"Will you have your breakfast now, sir?" she asked, and when he had answered that he would, she said, "There's no milk, sir. The milkman didn't come this morning!"

"It doesn't matter," he replied. "I'll have it without!"

He went to the front of the house, while his breakfast

was being prepared, and looked out of the window. In the bushes on the other side of the road, he could see a youth, crawling on his stomach, and dragging a rifle after him. He raised himself on to his knees, and glanced up at the hotel, where there were some soldiers who had been brought in during the night, and when he had raised himself, the soldiers in the upper windows saw him, and fired on him. He got up and ran across the path towards the shelter of the trees, and as he ran, the bullets spattered about him. Then he staggered . . . and Henry could not see him again.

3

An ambulance came and the bodies of the rebel and the labourer were put into it and taken away. The horse had been hauled to the pavement, and it lay in a great congealed mess of blood that had poured from a gash in its throat. . . .

4

Later in the morning, the people began to move about, and after a while the streets were full of sightseers. It was possible now to learn something of what happened on the previous day and during the night. There had been fierce fighting in places. Soldiers were hurrying from the Curragh, from the North of Ireland, from England. The thing was serious . . . the rebels had seized various strategic points, and were determined to fight hardly. During the night, realising that Stephen's Green was a dangerous place to be in, they had left it for the shelter of the College of Surgeons. Some of them were still there, sniping from safe points.

Henry went out and wandered about the streets. If there were soldiers in Dublin, there were very few, and the rebels still had possession of the city. He listened to the comments of the people who passed him, and as he listened, he realised that there was resentment everywhere against the

Sinn Feiners. Behind one of the gates of the Park, a Sinn
Feiner was lying face downwards in the hole he had made
to be a trench, and the crowd climbed up the railings to
gape at him. A youth thrust his way through the people
and peered at the dead man, and then he turned to the
crowd and said to them, "Let's get the poor chap out and
bury him!" A girl looked at him resentfully, and hurried to a towsled woman standing on the kerb, and told
her what the youth had said, and instantly the woman
rushed at him and hit him about the head and back. "No,
ye'll not get him out," she yelled at him. "Let him lie
there an' rot like the poor soldiers!"

"They forgot, the Sinn Feiners, that these women's husbands and sons are at the Front!" Henry thought.

What madness was it that possessed them to rise? A
little group of men and boys had set itself against a Power
in the interests of people who did not desire their services.
They could not hope to win the fight . . . they had not
the gratitude or the good wishes of the people for whom
they were fighting. What were they going to do next?
They had taken the Post Office and the College of Surgeons
and other places because there was no one to prevent them
from taking them . . . but what were they going to do
next? They could not, even the wildest of them, believe
that this immunity from attack would last forever. Was
there one among them with an idea of the future of Ireland, of the complexities of government? . . .

He wanted to get hold of a leader of them and ask him
just what he proposed to do with Ireland? . . .

5

The rumours this day were wilder than they were on
Monday. A man assured Henry that the Pope had
arrived in Ireland on an aeroplane and that Dr. Walsh,
the Catholic Archbishop of Dublin had committed suicide
the minute he heard of the outbreak of the Rebellion. Then

the rumour changed, and it was said that the Pope had thrown himself from the roof of the Vatican. Lord Wimborne, the Viceroy, had been taken a prisoner, and was now interned in Liberty Hall. . . . The Orangemen, sick of England, were marching to the support of the Sinn Feiners, under the leadership of Mr. Joseph Devlin! Ireland was entirely surrounded by German submarines in order to prevent British transports from landing troops. . . .

6

There was looting in Sackville Street. Henry had made his way towards the General Post Office, for he had heard that John Marsh was there, and while he stood about, hoping that he might see him, the looting began. Half-starved people swarmed up from the slums, like locusts, and seized all they could find. They destroyed things in sheer wantonness. . . .

"Well, if a city is content to keep such slums as Dublin has, it must put up with the consequences!" Henry thought. And while he watched, he saw John Marsh going to a shop which was being looted. He hauled a hulking lad out of the broken window and flung him back into the crowd.

"Damn you," he shouted, "are you trying to disgrace your country?" He pointed his rifle at the crowd. "I'll shoot the first one of you that touches a thing!"

But it was impossible for them to control the looters, and while John guarded one shop, the crowd passed on to another.

"John!" said Henry, going up to him and touching his arm.

He started and turned round. His face was drawn and haggard and very pale.

"Henry!" he said, smiling. "I wondered who it was. I wish you'd gone away when I asked you to go. It wasn't because I wanted to get rid of you, Henry. I wanted you

to be out of this . . . so that you could go and get married in peace!"

"You can't win, John. You know you can't win! . . ."

"I know we can't win a military success! . . ." He
drew his hand across his eyes. "My God, I'm tired,
Henry!" he said. "I'm worn out. I haven't slept since
Saturday night. . . ."

"John!"

"Yes, Henry, what is it?"

"Come away with me. You know you can't win . . .
you can't possibly win. We'll go over to England together. . . ."

"I'm fighting England, Henry, not visiting it!"

"You can hide there for a while . . . until you can get
away to France or America!"

"Go away and leave them now, Henry?"

"Yes. The longer you hold out, the worse it'll be for
everybody. The people are against you . . . I've heard
things to-day that I never expected to hear in Dublin. . . ."

"I know they're against us. We thought there would
be more on our side, but that's all the more reason why
we should fight. The people are getting too English in
their ways, Henry . . . they think too much of money.
All those women in the Combe . . . do you know why
they're against us? . . . because they can't get their separation allowances! We won't win a military success . . .
we all know that . . . McDonagh and Pearse and Connolly
and Mineely and all of us . . . we know that . . . but
we'll win a spiritual success!"

"A spiritual success?"

"Yes. We'll remind the people that Ireland is not yet
a nation and that there are Irishmen who are still willing
to die for their country. They've become very English,
but they're not altogether English, Henry. They've still
some of the old Irish spirit in them, and we may quicken
that!"

"Nothing will ever convince you, I suppose, that the English aren't a robber race? . . ."

"Nothing. I daresay the mass of the people are decent enough, but I don't know and I don't care. All that matters to me is that my countrymen shall not become like them! . . ."

"You're ruining the work of thirty years, John. Blowing it up in a childish rage! . . ."

"You always thought I was a fool, Henry, but I don't think as you think. We won the Home Rule Act by fair and constitutional means . . . and they've done us out of it. The Ulster men had only to yell at them, and they gave in. Do you think they'll keep their word after the War?"

"Yes."

"Well, I don't. They'll use that damned Amending Act to cheat us as they've cheated us before. No, Henry, this is a poor hope, but it is a hope. You see, when we're beaten and those of us who are left alive, surrender, the English will be sure to do the right thing . . . from our point of view! That's one of the things we count on. They'll put us down with great firmness. They'll make an example of us. They'll shoot us, Henry . . . and when they do that, we'll win. We're not popular now . . . oh, I don't need you to tell me that . . . but we'll be popular then. The English will make us popular!"

"Isn't it a little mean, John, to hit them when they aren't looking?"

"Mean! They've hit us often enough, haven't they? They got us on the ground when we were sick and kicked us. Why shouldn't we take advantage of them?"

"The Germans! . . ."

"Why shouldn't we go to the Germans, or to any one who is willing to help us? Wolfe Tone went to the French! . . ."

"You won't come away with me?"

"No. I came here to die, Henry, not to be safe!"

They stood for a few moments in silence, looking at each other, and then John put out his hand to Henry who took it in his.

"I must get back now," John said. "Good-bye, Henry. I don't suppose I shall ever see you again. If we lose, you and your friends can come and try your way. I've always wanted to die for Ireland ever since I was able to understand anything about my country, and I shall get my wish soon. Good-bye, Henry!"

"Good-bye, John!"

"I hope you and your wife will be very happy!" He made a wry smile, as he went on. "I'm afraid you won't be able to get to England just as soon as you wished. If you'd gone when I asked you to go! . . ."

"I must get back now," he said again.

"Yes, John!"

"I'm glad I saw you. I wondered last night where you were. . . ."

"And I wondered where you were."

"I was here. I've been here since Monday morning!"

He moved a few steps away, and then turned back.

"I've always liked you, Henry," he said, taking Henry's hand in his, "even when you made me angry. I wish you were on our side. . . ."

"I see no sense in this sort of thing, John!"

"I know you don't. And perhaps there isn't any sense in it, but that may not matter. It's something, isn't it, to find men still willing to die for their ideals, even when they know they haven't a chance of success? The Post Office is full of young boys, who want nothing better than to die for Ireland. Well, that's something, isn't it, in these times when most of our people aren't willing to do anything but make money? Good-bye again!"

He went back to the Post Office, very erect and very proud and very resolute.

"By God," said Henry to himself, "I wish I had the heart to feel what he feels!"

7

He was sitting in the smoking-room of the Club, trying to write. He had written to Mary earlier in the evening, assuring her of his welfare, and Driffield, a Treasury official, who had come into the Club for a few moments, had offered to try and get it put into the special mail "pouch" which was sent from the Castle every day to London. "You mustn't say anything about the Rebellion," he said. "Just say you're all right. I can't promise that it'll go off, but I'll do my best!" The restless, excited feeling which had possessed him since the beginning of the rebellion still held him, and he was unable to continue at anything for long. All day he had wandered about the city, learning more of its backways than he had ever known before. He had penetrated more deeply into the slums than he had done when he had explored them with Gilbert Farlow, and it seemed to him that there was nothing to be done with them or with the people in them. They were decaying together, and the sooner they decayed, the better would it be for Ireland. All his counsels that day were counsels of despair. What was the good of working and building when this was the material out of which a nation must be made? What was the good of trying to make sure foundations when impatient, undisciplined people like John Marsh came and threw one's work to the ground? Was it not better that every Irishman of alert and vigorous mind should leave Ireland to rot, and choose another country where men had stability of mind and purpose? . . .

"But one must go on trying. If the house be pulled down, we must build it up again. One must go on trying. . . ."

He would get his friends together, and they would plan to save what they could from the wreckage. "And then we'll begin again! Whatever happens, we must begin again!"

He was tired of playing Patience, tired of reading, and

tired of sitting still. Perhaps, he thought, he could write. It would be odd afterwards to think that he had written a story during a rebellion. There was a great German . . . who was it? . . . Heine or Goethe? . . . Oh, why couldn't he remember names! . . . who had gone on writing steadily, though there was battle all about him. . . . He settled himself to write, though he had no plan in his mind, and as he wrote, he felt that the story, whatever it might grow to be, must be comic. "I feel like a clown making jokes in the circus while his wife is dying," he said to himself. . . .

But his restlessness persisted, and after a while he put his manuscript aside, and took up a book which he had found in the bookcase: William James's *Pragmatism:* and began to read it. He remembered a discussion of Pragmatism by the Improved Tories, when Gilbert had described a pragmatist as an unfrocked Jesuit. . . .

And while he was burrowing into the first chapter, thinking more of James's graceful style than of his matter, there was a great rattle, an incessant hammer-and-rasp noise in the street.

"Good God!" he exclaimed, jumping up and dropping the book, "what's that?"

Then it ceased, and there was a horrible quietness for a few moments, followed by the crack-crack of rifles, and then again the ra-ra-ra-rat-rat-rat-rattle-rattle. . . .

"Machine guns!" he exclaimed. He knew instinctively that they were machine guns. "It . . . it startles you, that noise!"

It went on, rattling, with little pauses now and then as if the gun were taking breath, for an hour or more: a paralysing sound, as if some giant were drawing a great stick swiftly along iron railings.

"I think I'd better put the light out," he said, going across the room to where the switch was, and as he went there was a cracking sound in the window, and a bullet flew across the room and lodged in the wall. . . .

He switched the light off, and stood for a while in the dark. Then he opened the door and went out and stood on the landing. The servants were sitting huddled together on the staircase, nervous looking, indeed, but not frightened. It seemed to him to be remarkable that these girls should have kept their nerve as finely as they had. He smiled at them, as he closed the door behind him.

"They're making a lot of noise, aren't they?" he said.

"Isn't it awful, sir?" one of them answered.

He did not speak of the bullet which had come into the room. "It must have been a stray," he thought, "and there's no sense in upsetting them!"

"The soldiers are firing across the Green," he said aloud, "at the College of Surgeons. I think we're safe enough here, but I'd keep away from the windows! . . ."

"Yes, sir, we are!"

He went to his room, and sat at the window. At this height it was unlikely that any stray bullet would come near him. But he could not see any one. He could hear the wild-fowl crying in the Park . . . distinctly, in the pause of the firing, he could hear a duck's quack-quack. . . .

8

He went to bed, and tried to sleep, but could not. The firing from the machine-guns was intermittent now, but it still went on, and there was a continuous crackling of rifle-fire. Several times he got up and looked out . . . he had a curious and persistent desire to see whatever was going on . . . to be in it . . . extraordinarily he was anxious not to miss anything. *He was neither afraid nor aware of the fact that he was not afraid.* He had simply the sensation that exciting things were happening, that he wanted to see as much of them as possible, that he was excited, that his blood was flowing rapidly through his veins, that there was something hitting the inside of his head, thumping it. Then when he was tired of straining to see into the darkness, he went back to bed again, and closed his eyes and tried to sleep. And sometimes he succeeded in sleeping for a while . . . but always the noise of the machine-guns woke him. . . .

He went to the window when the dawn broke, and looked across the Green to the College of Surgeons.

"It's still flying," he muttered as he watched the tri-colour flowing in the wind.

9

And now the Rebellion began to bore him. He could not work, and the walks he could take were circumscribed. He walked down to Trinity College and stood there, watching the soldiers on the roof of the College as they fired up Dame Street to where some Sinn Feiners were in occupation of a newspaper office, or along Westmoreland Street towards the Post Office. Wherever he went, there was the sound of bullets being fired . . . but after a while, the sound ceased to affect him. There were snipers on many roofs . . . and people had been killed by stray bullets . . . but, although the sudden crack of a rifle overhead made him jump, the boredom grew and increased. He wanted to get on with his work. . . .

The soldiers were pouring into Dublin now . . . more and more of them.

"It'll be over soon," he said to himself.

It seemed to him then that the thing he would remember always was the dead horse which still lay on the pavement, becoming more and more offensive. Wherever he went, he met people who said to him, "Have you seen the dead horse?" Impossible to forget the corrupting beast, impossible to refrain from saying too, "Have you seen the dead horse?" Magnify that immensely, increase enormously the noise, and one had the War! Noise and stench and dead men and boredom! . . .

He wandered about the streets, seeing the same people,

listening to the same statements, making the same remarks, wondering vaguely about food. He had seen high officials carrying loaves under their arms, and little jugs of milk. . . .

"I wish to God it was over," he exclaimed. "I'm sick of this . . . idleness!"

He spoke to a soldier in Merrion Square. "Do you like Dublin?" he said.

"Oh, fine!" he answered. "We've been treated champion. I 'aven't seen much of it yet, of course," he went on. "I've been 'ere ever since I landed!" He pointed to the pavement. "But I know this bit damn well. You know," he went on, "we thought we was in France when we arrived 'ere. Couldn't make it out when we saw all the signs in English. I says to a chap, as we was walking along, ' 'I,'' I says, 'is this Boolone?' 'Naow,' 'e says, 'it's Ireland.' "

"And what did you say?" said Henry.

"I said 'Blimey!' " He moved to the kerb as the soldier further along the street called "Pass these men along" and when he had called the warning to the next soldier, he returned to Henry. "I say," he said, "wot are these Sinn Feiners? I mean to say 'oo are they? Are they Irish, too?"

Henry tried to explain who the Sinn Feiners were.

"But wot they want to do? Wot's the point of all this . . . this 'umbuggin' about? We don't want to fight Irish people . . . we want to fight Germans! . . ." He looked about for a moment, and then added, as if to clinch his statement, "I mean to say, I *know* an Irish chap . . . 'e's a friend of mine . . . but I don't know no bloody Germans, an' wot's more I wouldn't know them neither . . . dirty lot, I calls 'em!"

"You know," he went on, "this is about the 'ottest bit of work a chap could 'ave to do. These snipers, you know, they get on your nerves. I mean to say, 'ere you are, standin' 'ere, you might say, in the dark an' suddenly a

bullet damn near 'its you . . . or mebbe it does 'it you
. . . one of our chaps was killed in front of that 'ouse last
night . . . they been swillin' the blood away, see! . . .''
Henry looked across the road to where a man was vigorously brooming the wet pavement. The soldier proceeded:
"Well, you don't know where it's comin' from. 'E's up
on one of these 'ere roofs, 'idin', an' you're down 'ere . . .
exposed. 'E kneels be'ind the parapet, an' 'as a shot at
you, an' then 'e 'ops along the roof to another place, an'
'as another shot at you. . . . You don't 'alf begin to feel a
bit jiggery when that's 'appening'. . . .''

10

There was no malice in that soldier. He was puzzled,
as puzzled as he would have been if his brother had suddenly seized a rifle and lain in wait for him. He looked
upon the Irish as his comrades, not his enemies. "I mean
to say, we're all the same, I mean to say! . . .'' He had
been in camp at Watford. "We was in a picture-palace,
me an' my pal . . . a whole lot of us was there . . . and
then a message was put on the screen: 'All the Dashes
report at once!' I never thought nothink of it you know.
Of course, I went all right. But I thought it was just one
of these bloomin' spoof entrainments. They done that to
us before . . . two or three times . . . just to see 'ow
quick they could do it . . . an' I was gettin' 'a bit fed-up
with it. I'd said 'Good-bye' to a girl three times . . .
an' it was gettin' a bit monotonous. 'At it again,' I says to
my pal, as we hooked back to the camp, but when we was in
the train, an' it didn't stop an' go back again, I says to
'im, ' 'Illoa,' I says, 'we're off!' An' I 'adn't said 'Good-
bye' to 'er this time. I thought to myself, 'I won't make
a bloomin' ass of myself this time!' An' there we was . . .
off at last! 'This is a nice-old-'ow-d'ye-do!' I says. I
didn't want the girl to think I was 'oppin' it like that
. . . sayin' nothink or anythink. . . . When we got to

Kingstown an' 'eard we was in Ireland . . . well, I mean to say, it *surprised* me, I tell you. . . . Wot I can't make out is, wot's it all about? I mean to say, wot do these chaps want?''

"They want to be free! . . .''

"But ain't they free? I mean to say, ain't they as free as me?''

"They don't think so.''

"Well, wot can I do that they can't do?''

Henry did not know. "You ast me anythink,'' the soldier went on, "they're a lot freer'n wot we are. I mean to say, we got conscription in our country, but they ain't got it 'ere. . . .''

There was another interruption, to enable a motor-cyclist to pass along. When he returned to Henry, he said, "You know, when we got 'ere, an' all the people come out their 'ouses an' treated us like their long-lost brother, we couldn't make it out at all, an' when we 'eard about the Sinn Feiners, we didn't know wot to think. I mean to say, we didn't know 'oo they was. One of our chaps thought they was black . . . you know . . . niggers . . . but I told 'im not to be a bloody fool. 'They don't 'ave niggers in Ireland,' I says, 'They're the same as us,' I says. 'I mean to say . . . they're *white!* . . .' ''

12

He wrote to Mary again, hoping that he would be able to get it into the Castle "pouch,'' and then he went to seek for Driffield who had promised to try and send his previous letter to England by the same means, and Driffield, very dubious, took the letter and said he would do what he could. She would be full of alarm . . . he did not know whether she had received his messages, and, of course, he had received none from her. It was Thursday now, and still the rebellion was not suppressed. The city was full of dead and wounded men and women, and there was diffi-

culty about burial. He thought of people in the first grief
for their dead, unwilling that the hour of interment should
come . . . and then, when it came, and there could not be
interment, suddenly finding their grief turned to consternation, and what had been the object of mourning love, become abhorrent, so that there was an unquenchable desire,
a craving that it might be taken away. . . .

It was dangerous to be out of doors after seven o'clock,
and so, since no one came to the Club, and it was impossible to read or write, he spent most of the evening in
brooding. . . . If the rebellion were not speedily suppressed, it might be impossible for him to get to Boveyhayne in time for his marriage . . . but the rebellion could
not last very long now, and at worst his marriage would
only be postponed a little while. His mind moved from
thought to thought, from Mary to Gilbert and Ninian, then
to John Marsh and his father and to the boy in Stephen's
Green who had been told to dig a trench, but thought that
he was digging his grave . . . and then, inconsequently,
he saw in his imagination the ridiculous figure of a looter
whom he had seen in Sackville Street, swaggering up and
down, clothed in evening dress, and carrying a lady's sun-
shade. He had a panama hat on his head, and was wearing very thick-soled brown boots . . . and loosely tied
about his waist were a pair of corsets. . . .

He laughed at the remembrance, and as he laughed, he
looked towards the window, and saw a great red glare in
the sky. From the centre of the city, flames were reaching
up, vast and red and terrible. . . .

"Good God!" he exclaimed, "the place is on fire!"

13

The fire continued during the whole of the next day. It
was impossible to get near the burning buildings, and so,
though people knew of the fire, they did not know of its
extent. The south side of the city, separated from the

north, where the fire was, by the river, knew nothing of
what was happening across the Liffey. It seemed now,
this horror following on the horror of the fighting, that
Dublin must be destroyed, that nothing could save it from
the flames. . . . Then, by what efforts no one can ever
realise, the fire was controlled, and the reddened sky became dark, and frightened citizens went to their beds to
such sleep as they could obtain.

14

The next day, the Rebellion collapsed. Henry had walked
out of Dublin, for it was easier now to move about, and
coming back in the afternoon, suddenly felt that the Rebellion was over. A man came cycling past at a great pace,
and as he went by, he shouted to Henry, ''They've surrendered!'' and then was gone. There was a cooler feel
in the air. It seemed to him that a great tension had been
relaxed . . . that, after a day of intolerable heat, there had
come an evening of cool winds. As he approached the city,
he could see groups of people standing about in the road,
and he went to one of them, and asked if the news were
true.

''Some of them's surrendered,'' he was told, ''but there's
a lot of snipers still about!''

They could hear desultory firing as they spoke.

''Ah, they'll give in quick enough now,'' a man said.
''Sure, they can't hold out any longer!''

He hurried back to the city, and when he reached the
Club, he saw that the tri-colour was no longer flying over
the College of Surgeons.

THE FOURTEENTH CHAPTER

1

On Sunday morning, he met Lander, who had a military pass, and together they went to Sackville Street. . . . There were some who had said that this was the proudest street in the world. It had little pride now. Where there had been shops and hotels, there were now heaps of rubble and calcined bricks. The street was covered with grey ash that was still hot, and one had to walk warily lest one's feet should be burnt. The Post Office still stood, but the roof was gone and the inside of it was empty: a hulk, a disembowelled carcase. . . .

"MacDonagh and Pearse and Connolly have been taken," said Lander. "They say Connolly's badly wounded. . . ."

"Have you heard anything of . . . of John Marsh?"

"Yes. He's dead. They say he was killed soon after the fighting began . . . in the street! . . ."

Henry did not speak. He glanced about him at the ruin and wreck of a city which, though it had many times filled him with anger, yet filled him also with love; and for a while he could not see clearly. . . . Somewhere in this street, John Marsh had been killed. He had died, as he had desired, for Ireland, and a man can do no more than give his life for his country . . . but what was the good of his dying? It was not enough that a man should die . . . he must also die well and to purpose. Oh, indeed, John had believed that such a death as this would be a good death, to much purpose, but it is not the dead who can judge of that . . . it is the living to whom now and forever is the task of judging what the dead have done.

"It's a pity," said Lander, "that the slums weren't destroyed, too! . . ."

"Perhaps," Henry answered, "we can build a finer city after this!"

"Perhaps," said Lander dubiously, for Lander knew the ways of men and had small faith in them.

2

They walked along the quays until they reached the Four Courts, and while they were standing there, a sickly woman, with a fretful, whining voice, plucked at Henry's arm.

"Is it over, mister?" she said, and when he nodded his head, she turned away, exclaiming fervently, "Oh, thanks be to the Holy Mother of God!"

"The Holy Mother of God had damned little to do with it," Henry said to Lander. "It was machine guns. . . ."

3

Lander had obtained a permit for him, so that he could go to England, and in a little while, he would leave the Club and go to Westland Row to catch the train to Kingstown. There was a strange quietness in his heart. He had lived through a terror and had not been afraid. He had seen men immolating themselves gladly because they had believed that by so doing they would make their country a finer one to live in.

"It was the wrong way," he said to himself, "but in the end, nothing matters but that a man shall offer his life for his belief!"

Gilbert Farlow and Ninian Graham had not sought, as he had sought, to escape from destiny or to elude death. It was fore-ordained that old men would make wars and that young men would pay the price of them . . . and it is of no use to try to save oneself. John Marsh, too, had

had to pay for the incompetence and folly of old men who had wrangled and made bitterness. . . . And now, in his turn, he must pay the price, too. One must die . . . in that there is no choice . . . but one may die finely or one may die meanly . . . and in that there is choice. Gilbert and Ninian and John, each in his way, had died finely. It might have been that he would have died meanly in Dublin, casually killed, for no purpose, for no cause. . . . Well, he had not been killed meanly. There was still time for him to live on the level of his friends. If youth has had committed to it the task of redeeming the world from the follies of the Old, Youth must not shrink from the labour, even though it may feel that the Old should redeem themselves. . . .

He would go to Boveyhayne and marry Mary, and then he would take her to his home . . . he must do that . . . and when he had given his house to her, he would enlist as a soldier. "Life isn't worth while, if one is afraid to lose it . . . a year or two more, what do they matter if a job be shirked?" "It isn't the time one lives that matters," he went on, "it's what one does in the time!"

4

As the mail-boat steamed out of the harbour, he climbed to the top deck and stood there gazing back at the shore. Exquisitely beautiful, Ireland looked in the evening glow. Up the river, in an opal mist, he could see Dublin, still sore from her latest wounds, and here close at hand, he saw the waves of mountains reaching far inland, each mountain shining in the light with a great mingling of colours. Beautiful, but more than beautiful! Other lands had beauty, too, more beauty, perhaps, than Ireland, but if he were leaving them as he was now leaving Ireland, he should not feel the grief that he now felt. This was his land . . . his own country . . . and the elements which had been mingled to make it, had been mingled also to make him, and he and it were one. It was strange that he should carry so heavy a heart to Boveyhayne, when he should have gone there gladly . . . but it was not of Mary or his marriage that he was then thinking. It was of the farewell he was making to this old city which had known much grief and many troubles. When he returned to Ireland he would go straight to Ballymartin, by Belfast, from England. He would not see Dublin again. Firmly fixed in his mind, was that belief. He would serve . . . and he would die. Foolish, he told himself, to think like that, but, even while he was rebuking himself, the thought thrust itself into his mind again. . . .

5

The boat was almost out of sight of land. He had stood at the end of the deck, gazing back at Ireland until only the clouded head of a mountain could be seen, and then that too had been hidden. He turned and looked forward, and as he did so, he saw in the distance, low in the sea, the hulls of three ships of war. The mail-boat slowed down, as they approached, to let them pass. Naked and lithe, they looked, as they thrust their bodies through the sea, sending the water up from their bows in shining arches. He could see the men standing about the decks, looking steadily ahead . . . and then the war-ships passed on to their work, and the mail-boat gathered up speed and plunged on towards Wales. Over there, he thought, somewhere in that haze, is England, and beyond England, France and Flanders and the fields of blood and pain. . . .